IO SONO AUGUSTUS
I AM AUGUSTUS

Augustus Louis Petti

Order this book online at www.trafford.com
or email orders@trafford.com

Most Trafford titles are also available at major online book retailers.

Printed in Victoria, BC, Canada.

ISBN: 978-1-4269-1985-5 (sc)
ISBN: 978-1-4269-1986-2 (dj)

Library of Congress Control Number: 2009912444

Our mission is to efficiently provide the world's finest, most comprehensive book publishing service, enabling every author to experience success. To find out how to publish your book, your way, and have it available worldwide, visit us online at www.trafford.com

Trafford rev. 3/19/2010

www.trafford.com

North America & international
toll-free: 1 888 232 4444 (USA & Canada)
phone: 250 383 6864 • fax: 812 355 4082

This book is dedicated to the love of my life Ann, my wife of 54 years, and to my children whom I love dearly; Lucille, Susan, Christine, Joseph (whom we lost), and Michele.

May this book answer all your questions . . .

Also, this is the prayer that has guided me through my days, especially when I became a father:

THE PRAYER OF ST. FRANCIS OF ASSISI

Lord make me an instrument of your peace,
Where there is hatred, let me sow love,
where there is injury, pardon,
where there is doubt, faith,
where there is despair, hope,
where there is darkness, light,
where there is sadness, joy.
O Divine Master,
grant that I may not
so much seek to be consoled as to console,
to be understood,
as to understand,
to be loved,
as to love,
For it is in giving that we receive,
and in pardoning that we are pardoned,
and in dying that we are born to eternal life.

AMEN…

Table of Contents

Page

CHAPTER 1 . . . THE BIRTH

WHO'S WHO in this Chapter

My Mother.................................. LUCIA MARIA (BUCCO) PETTI
My Father .... JOSEPH PETTI
My Brother .... MICHAEL PETTI
My Grandmother............................JOSEPINA (COLUCCI) PETTI
My Grandfather ....MICHELE (MICHELINO) PETTI
My Grandmother.................. CONCETTA (LACCONE) BUCCO
My Grandfather .... TOMASSO BUCCO
My Great-grandfather... GIUSEPPE PETTI
My Great-grandmother .... (Over 6' tall)...LICCIA PETTI
My Great-grandmother ....MARIA (D'AMICO) BUCCO
My Great-grandfather....................................... LORENZO BUCCO

1930

This is the story my mother tells. Some of the circumstances that were being explained to me sometimes appeared slightly exaggerated or possibly lightly fantasized (it was so unbelievable), or so I thought, as I sat listening intently, hanging on every word she spoke. Because it was about me, she had me as a captive listener and I absorbed everything she said.

The situations leading up to my birth need to be explained, so that the happening can be better understood. Only through the grace of God have the following experiences been possible. To begin with, common sense tells us that any woman ready to give birth should not be cruising on a ship, especially at the moment of childbirth, but my mom's circumstances dictated just such behavior. She will explain. According to my mother's description of the occurrences, here's what happened:

TO THE SHIP! The date was September 1930. My mother was nine months pregnant (with me). My father had a visa application (permission to leave the country) delivered to and in government hands. King Emanuel III was the ruler of Italy at the time. His son, Umberto, (who also would be the next king of Italy) was getting married that year. According to Italian custom, on happy occasions such as this, the monarch grants many wishes to the people who have petitioned him. One of the grants that the king signed was my father's visa request. My mother (who was a natural American citizen, since she was born in America in December of 1906) and father were free to leave Italy. That meant they could also now emigrate to the U.S.A. As soon as they were informed of the visa approval, booking the ship's passage had to be accomplished next. From the time they acquired tickets to embark, till the time of departure, they realized there were only five days. At that moment, the undertaking appeared impossible because they lived in Celenza Valfortore, in the province of Foggia, about 221 Kilometers (approximately 356 miles) from Naples, directly across the central part of Italy to the east. These were days of horse and carriage and this was the most prevalent method of transportation in Italy. In their town, there were no cars or buses or trains (nor planes for that matter), and it would take over four days to travel that distance by horse and carriage. But my father and mother were determined; that ship had to be reached! So my grandfather hitched his team of horses to the wagon (he did not own a covered carriage), loaded my mother, father and brother (my mother had given birth to my brother Michael in 1929). There was very little space for luggage, so my mother was denied the privilege of carrying all of their possessions, the bulk of which was their wedding dowry (which all married people treasured in Italy). At this point, while she was telling the story, my mother's eyes would begin welling up and tears would be coming down her face, as she described every article in her dowry that she had to leave behind. In a handmade wooden chest, she had porcelain chinaware, crystal, silverware, blankets and sheets (all handmade), cooking utensils and paintings of loved ones. All this had to be left because there was no room in the wagon. She was devastated, but the important thing was to bundle up my brother, collect essentials and begin her voyage. This she did. But what about the pregnant child in her womb? All of them prayed to the Lord that He would protect them and guide them through the journey and provide comfort and safety along the way. Onto the wagon they went, my grandfather at the reins. The trip began.

S.S. AUGUSTUS

Four days on very bumpy roads, most of them plain dirt, ensued. The group stopped at night at various inns to lodge. They were all tired and thoroughly exhausted when arriving at the Port of Naples where the ship was docked and being loaded. It was the SS AUGUSTUS, a dual stacker ship (two smoke stacks). One of the newest navel vessels launched, it was built in 1927. The ship was so large that during World War II it was converted to an aircraft carrier, serving the Italian Navy for a short time, scuttled by the Germans as a blockade at Genoa to ward off enemy submarines. So was the destiny of my birthplace, aboard the SS AUGUSTUS. But back to the story: the ship sailed the next day, with my mother, father and brother on board. My grandfather returned to Celenza Valfortore in his little horse and wagon, a little sad and very tired, but did not stop during his trip (he carried bread and cheese).

The ship's next port of call was at a dock in Portugal to pick up additional passengers. My mother was in the ship's hospital, in labor. At about 100 nautical miles, after departing from the port in Portugal, I was born. The hour was early in the morning (5 AM to be exact) of September 15th, 1930 and a Monday. My father says I was born on the 16th so there has always been a controversy concerning my birth date. Unfortunately, a certificate of birth was never issued (it would have been nice to at least have the exact longitude and latitude of my birth).

All I have is this letter, written and signed by the captain of the ship, stating that I was born and baptized aboard the ship, dated September 16, 1930 (this is the date I chose to be the official date I was born-it was the only date on the letter that could be understood by all). As soon as I was born, the attending nurse (the only medically trained person aboard) notified my mother that I was born with a physical mark on the surface of my skin, what Italians call la marca del vino, translated to mean the mark of wine, but more commonly referred to as a beauty mark. It was a dime-sized, dark wine colored growth on my right hip, about two inches below my waist. The beauty mark is gone now since doctors in the 60's considered it a cancer potential and surgically removed it during another procedure I was undergoing.

As soon as I was born, the ship's captain approached my father to discuss baptism. According to Italian custom (whereby in the absence of a priest, anyone can baptize a child), an infant must be baptized immediately (those were customs at that time but now I understand have changed). There was no priest on board and my mother and father did not know anyone aboard to select as a godmother or godfather. The attending nurse and the captain volunteered. I was baptized by the captain of the ship (who became my godfather) and my godmother was the nurse. The name given me at the baptism is described below. Try to remember this event, because in a future chapter, another baptism will take place. Because this was a conditional baptism, it had to be repeated in my 13th year, so in effect, I was baptized twice. I'll tell you all about that later. Unbelievable as it sounds, the following rendition of my birth letter was just recently translated, both in Italian and English. After 77 years! It took this long to read and completely translate my birth letter because of this book. If I wasn't so intent on learning the content of the letter we would still not know what it read. I must give credit to Mom and Michele (Our youngest daughter) who on March 11, 2007 were able to decipher both the handwriting (which is almost impossible to understand) and the meaning of the words in the letter. Here it is finally, the translated document. Now we all know what it said

My Only Evidence of Birth

My Original Birth Letter

Contents of Letter

9/16/30
The letter reads: Dichiaro io sottoscritto di avere battezzato oggi, 16 Settembre 1930, il bambino, cui o' dato il nome di Augusto, figlio di Petti Giuseppe di Michele e di Bucco Maria Lucia, fu Tommaso, nato ieri alle cinque del mattina, a bordo della motonave Augustus, della N.G.I. (Navigazione Generale Italiano) in rotta per New York.

In fede.

Tac. Cominelli Alessandro
Tappellano

English translation: I the undersigned declare that I have baptized today, the 16th of September 1930, this child, that was named Augusto, son of Petti Joseph of Michele (my grandfather Petti) and of Bucco Maria Lucia, of Tommaso (my grandfather Bucco), born yesterday at five in the morning, on board the ship Augustus, owned by N.G.I. en route to New York.

In good faith,

Capt. Alessandro Tappellano

Notation added in 1943 (lower right hand side): Baptized again unconditionally Oct. 2nd , 1943 – at St. Francis of Paola Church, Brooklyn, N.Y. by the Rev. Domenic Passaniti (This notation shows that I was baptized a second time in accordance with Roman Catholic Law, when I received my Confirmation. The letter then served as my Baptismal Certificate also.)

This explains my birth, and the circumstances that led to my unusual place of birth. What about my name! My mother and father, as Italians, have a custom of naming all the children after their grandparents (especially if they were deceased) as an honor and respect for their part in fostering the family. My name was chosen to be Tomasso, after my grandfather Tomasso Bucco (which was my mother's father's name, who was deceased). When my father was discussing the name chosen for me, the captain politely informed him that according to Italian naval tradition, since I was the first born aboard the SS AUGUSTUS, I should be named Augustus after the ship. He also advised my father that this was not compulsory, only a tradition, and that my mother and father had the liberty to choose whatever name they deemed appropriate. The turning event that led them to name me Augustus came when the captain informed them that one of the benefits I would enjoy was being able to travel on the SS AUGUSTUS without cost, as long as the ship was afloat. So, it was decided (for my benefit I guess), I would henceforth be called AUGUSTUS, not Tomasso. To this day, I don't know how they explained this to my grandmother and great-grandparents, which monitored the maintenance of customs to the point of compulsory compliance. This was a very sore subject when I would mention it. And so, this is why I was born aboard a ship at sea, and why I was named Augustus.

NOT REGISTERED AT ELLIS ISLAND. The next thing my mother explained is that because she was in the ship's hospital, and so was my father and brother (it was Italian custom to have the husband lodge with the wife in a hospital) both were not required to be processed at Ellis Island (they were already examined and found to be healthy to remain in the hospital) and therefore were landed directly to the New York port, bypassing Ellis Island. This is the reason there is no record at Ellis Island of their arrival. It only exists at the New York port recording immigration libraries.

ARRIVAL IN NEW YORK. When my mother and father arrived in New York, the first letter they received was from my grandfather Michelino who described the trip back to Celenza over the next three days. It was harrowing. He encountered road thieves that tried to rob him; it's a good thing he carried a rifle gun. He was proficient in small arms and carried a long rifle for hunting at home, a veritable discouragement to robbers of any kind. He also wrote in the letters that the women of the two houses (the Pettis and the Buccos) were assembling all of the belongings that were left behind, especially the dowry that meant so much to my mother. They intended to package all of the articles and send them by mail to them. As soon as my parents received these letters, they immediately wrote back to not do that. It would have cost a fortune (in 1930 no one there had much money) to send those items. It would not have been worth it, even though they had a great deal of sentimental value. So the decision was to leave all those beautiful gifts there in Italy and in a gesture of selfless generosity, my mother told the matriarchs to distribute all of the articles between the two families evenly. That is what was done. My mother cried, but was in peace now. My father was sad for a while but then perked up and got over it. But they still loved to tell this story of the tremendous sacrifice they made so they could come to America!

HISTORY PRIOR TO MY BIRTH. To bring you up-to-date concerning facts about my mother and father, at this point in their life, it is necessary to go back to the year 1928 and in Italy. In October of 1928, my mother and father were married in the town of Celenza Valfortore. They enjoyed a youthful courtship during their teens and decided to marry then. My father was 24 years old and my mother was 22. My father had finished preliminary school and continued in a vocational technical school studying basic metallurgy, a fancy way of saying he became a blacksmith. Shoeing horses is what he did primarily and did it so well that people in town asked him to fabricate iron railings for them, and iron fences, etc. He would tell me that, because God gave him artistic talents, he was able to create attractive works using iron as the base. He was also an accomplished horseback rider. Because his father had a stable of fine horses, it was almost natural for him to take advantage of this opportunity. But it became apparent to me, as he told me the stories; the intent was really to be able to travel. It gave him a sense of freedom to be able to move from this location to that, which gave him the intense desire to improve his horse riding abilities.

My Father in the Militarv-1926

MY FATHER'S MILITARY DAYS. Going back in time, when my father reached his 20th year, in those days Italy imposed a military conscription of two years for every male citizen to serve in the Armed Services. It was a type of National Guard that Mussolini felt the country needed. I'm not sure why he was drafted into the Cavalry (It couldn't have been due to his horse riding abilities because all of the photos we have of him while in the Italian Army were of him assigned to riding a motorcycle!), but it was an interesting coincidence. him on a motorcycle. In fact, this is where he became infatuated with vehicles. He also drove automobiles for commanding officers (he remembers driving an Alpha Romeo and a Maserati, which he fell in love with), but mostly his duties were primarily centered on handling motorcycles. He used to tell different stories about his experiences in the Army. One of them was rather bizarre. I have not been able to verify the accuracy of this story, but here are the particulars according to my father. Part of his military training consisted of survival skills in Italy. Since, in their travels, they would encounter stagnant and contaminated water along the way (Italy has all through history struggled with acquiring safe, fresh water, hence the Roman aqueducts), the method they were taught to sterilize the water was to add a bottle of Iodine (about 1 fl oz to 1 liter) to it before drinking. To develop a resistance to the toxicity of the Iodine they were given a drop of Iodine every day for a week, then increased to two drops the following week, then increased to three drops the third week and so on until they could tolerate drinking a full bottle of Iodine at one time. That took care of the drink, now he spoke of methods concerning food preservation. In his knapsack he was taught to carry dry food articles such as soppresatta (a dry salami type of meat) and stale bread (very hard, dry bread-if kept dry, could last over a month!). It's interesting how experiences of the past affect your habits of today. He now loved soppresatta and extra hard, dry bread. After serving his two years in the Italian Cavalry Armed Services, he was honorably discharged and returned home to continue his life as a civilian. But here is the thing; he claims to be able to drink a full bottle of Iodine any time he wants! Very strange… We didn't want to test this presumptuous capability of his at any time, for fear he may have lost the tolerance he developed then.

MY FATHER'S EARLY YEARS.

Back at home in Italy, my father was also a troubadour by his own account. He was musically gifted. He could play the mandolin and could sing all the local Neapolitan romantic songs, of which there are hundreds I am told! He knew them all. During the day he would labor in the Blacksmith shop shoeing horses, building iron railings and then at night, as a way of earning additional income, he was hired

Dad Troubadour – 1928

to play the mandolin and sing beneath someone's girlfriend's balcony, to bring the message of love to her in a special way from her boyfriend through my father's talents. So were the customs at those times. Very different than what we experience here and now. At this moment in the storytelling, my father would draw close to my ear and whisper these words, "What I wanted more than anything else was to go to the United States of America and own a CAR!" This was his life's goal! There wasn't a thing more important than this in terms of material yearnings. He told me that he felt this could not be achieved in the immediate environment. In his mind, his only hope was to go to New York and buy an automobile... This was his dream. This was his destiny. He worked and directed his life toward this one goal, to own an automobile. This was my father's life before meeting my mother and the beginning of their courtship days. My father tells me he fell in love with my mother the moment they spoke to each other. He had seen her in the neighborhood as a young girl growing up, because it was a very small town, but never had the opportunity to speak to her. When he returned from the service, this opportunity presented itself. It appears that a relative of my father was marrying a relative of her family so they were both guests at the same wedding. My father tells me that not only did they talk, but they also danced together for the first time. Love was in the air... My father fell head over heels in love with her (his description). My mother says in her Italian dialect that he was a great catch! If you knew my mother and her dedication to tradition, what she meant by catch was not only did she fall in love with him, but he also had the potential of being a good provider. These were two qualities that were treasured in her family and were part of their traditional intrinsic values. It was the best of both worlds. My mother was very happy. My father was also very happy because (in his own mind) she was a catch too!

MY MOTHER'S EARLY YEARS. Insofar as my mother's childhood is concerned, she also finished preliminary school in Italy, but was destined to maintain a farmer's way of life. She lost her father shortly after she was born. She had an older brother, Lorenzo, who assumed the father role and protected the family. But she, her brother and her mother had to move in with her mother's parents who owned a very large farm (Masseria di Bucco) in the town of Celenza Valfortore, Italy. My mother therefore was raised on a farm and learned all the skills akin to farming. She had to milk the cows, feed the chickens and take care of the goats and the pigs, just to mention a few. The men on the farm made all the cheeses from the milk such as the ricotta, mozzarellas, provolone, locatelli and others. Most of all, she became proficient in dressmaking, the sewing of articles of clothing including the designing and cutting of cloth. She also learned knitting and crocheting, though her most useful acquired skill was cooking. During the planting and harvesting seasons at her grandfather's farm in Celenza, over 20 employees would arrive who were necessary to accomplish the field work. They had to be fed. My mother, her mother (my grandmother) and my mother's grandmother all pitched in to help feed the hungry workers when returning from the fields. It was through the laborious trials of feeding these large groups that my mother honed her ability to prepare large and tasty meals. Her cooking ability to this day is celebrated with countless recipes that she left to our family. We now treasure those recipes. They are printed on pages and bound in booklets titled: Grandma Petti's Recipes (written mostly for the children). We will never forget you Mom/Grandma.

My Mother with Zia Luccia-1930

My mother especially enjoyed telling a few of the stories of her courtship with my father. It wasn't easy dating in Celenza in 1926 and 1927. First of all, a chaperone had to be present every minute they were together. The location of the date had to be in a house. The parents of the intended had to be officially introduced. The honorable intentions of the boyfriend (before dating begins) had to be stated to the girl's parents, in front of witnesses! It appears now, in retrospect, to resemble a legal transaction, but it was not lightly taken then. It was serious business. Then there were the difficult emotional moments that my mother would describe, when they would meet on a date at my grandmother's house while in front of a burning fireplace. Lively conversation would fill the air, but beneath the surface were the feelings of love and desire, which drive a couple to want to kiss and embrace. But they could not because the grandmother stood between them, preventing them of expressing themselves. My mother told me the enterprising way they got around this terrible impediment. Knowing my father's ingenuity, they set up a scheme between themselves to act quickly but decisively as soon as my grandmother bent over to stoke the fire logs. They would come close, embrace and kiss, while my grandmother attended the fire, then quickly return to their places before my grandmother reached her chair. As far as my grandmother knew, all was well. It was an ingenious plan and it worked. My mother would chuckle when she told this part of her life. It was a happy time. In 1927 they were engaged and in October of 1928 they were married.

MY PARENT'S WEDDING. Here is where my mother's face would begin to sparkle, when she would describe the wedding and all the events that proceeded. They were married in the nearby Church of Santa Madre in Celenza Valfortore, Italy, on a Saturday, October 2, 1928. My mother wore a white satin gown that her mother had made for her. My father wore his best suit with tie (tuxedos were not in use there at the time).

Church Mom-Dad Married

Then, this part always got to me while my mother explained; they would actually conduct a procession, arm-in-arm, walking from my mother's house to the church (just a few blocks) with the bridal party. All along the way, relative's friends and neighbors would add gifts to the dowry chest that was carried by two wedding guests until they reached the doors of the church. It was a beautiful time for them; there was great joy in the air and both were married inside the church, with the blessing of God, in front of the Holy Sacrament.

EARLY MARRIED DAYS IN ITALY. They rented an apartment in the town of Celenza Valfortore, close to their parents. They lived on the top floor. It wasn't long before my mother became pregnant with my brother. He was born in June, 1929, in the town of Celenza Valfortore and was given the name Michele (in honor of my Grandfather Michele Petti). My father continued working in town fabricating railings and iron fences, using my grandfather's blacksmith shop located in the horse stable.

Mamma and Papa"s First Appartment, Italy

My father was doing well in Italy, but he still had the dream of owning an automobile. This relenting desire would not leave him. How could this dream become a reality now, he wondered? There was only one answer: go to the United States, where cars are plentiful. It was an emerging nation and Henry Ford had revolutionized the mass production of the automobile, which could be owned by anyone, not just the wealthy. Besides, my mother was an American citizen by birth and could travel to the USA at any time. The only problem was his status. A petition to the king of Italy, if approved, would solve this impediment. The petition was submitted. Now the wait begins. Meanwhile, in January of 1930 my mother becomes pregnant with me. Actually, the beginning of this chapter describes what happened next and since you have already read it, you know what occurred after my mother became pregnant with me and how and where I was born. So ends my birth story.

There is one note to add here. It was a terrible time in the annals of history, a very distressed and devastating economic moment of the twentieth century. The Stock Market Crash of 1929 was just being felt in every town, village and sector in the United States. There were no jobs, very little food, no clothing and shelter was at a premium. This is what the Petti family was heading into when they disembarked from the ship...

CHAPTER 2 . . . CHILD

NEW persons in this Chapter

My Mother's Aunt............. ZIA LUCCIA (RAFFAELLA) D'AMICO
My Mother's Aunt's Son and 1st Cousin................JOHN D'AMICO
My Mother's Aunt, Zia Luccia's Cousin..........MASTA MAGNIFICO
My Father's Uncle in Waterbury, Connecticut...ZIO DAN COLUCCI
My Father's Aunt through marriage.......... ZIA NORINA COLUCCI
My Father's Uncle .... ZIO VINZENZO CARUSILLO
My Father's Aunt .... ZIA NINA (CIOCIA) CARUSILLO
Our "Paisanos"-My Guardians............... THE JACARUSSO FAMILY

MY CHILDHOOD BEGINS. The memories of my childhood that I recall are somewhat few and unfortunately far between. From now on I will not be presenting my mother's or father's descriptions (except when necessary) and explanations that were recounted to me. Henceforth, all of the stories will be written from my own memory. I am hoping to fill in this part of my life from my own recollections, to contribute to the history. Although many of the events are fixed in my mind, some I had to research and in the end revert to asking others concerning some of the details. All in all, I tried to create as accurate a picture of the scenes and places so that some semblance of connectivity may be reached. Hope I succeed.

The year was 1930. It was the DEPRESSION in the United States. The Stock Market had crashed the year before. There was little or no employment anywhere. When I reviewed some of the facts concerning the year of 1930, I was amazed by the disclosures: the average income was $1,973.00 a year, a brand new car cost $610.00 (which made my father very happy), a new house cost $7,146.00, a gallon of gasoline cost $ .10, a loaf of bread cost $ .09, a gallon of milk cost $ .56, unbelievable! Mr. Herbert Hoover was the President. Life expectancy was 59.7 years. Of course these numbers were all averages.

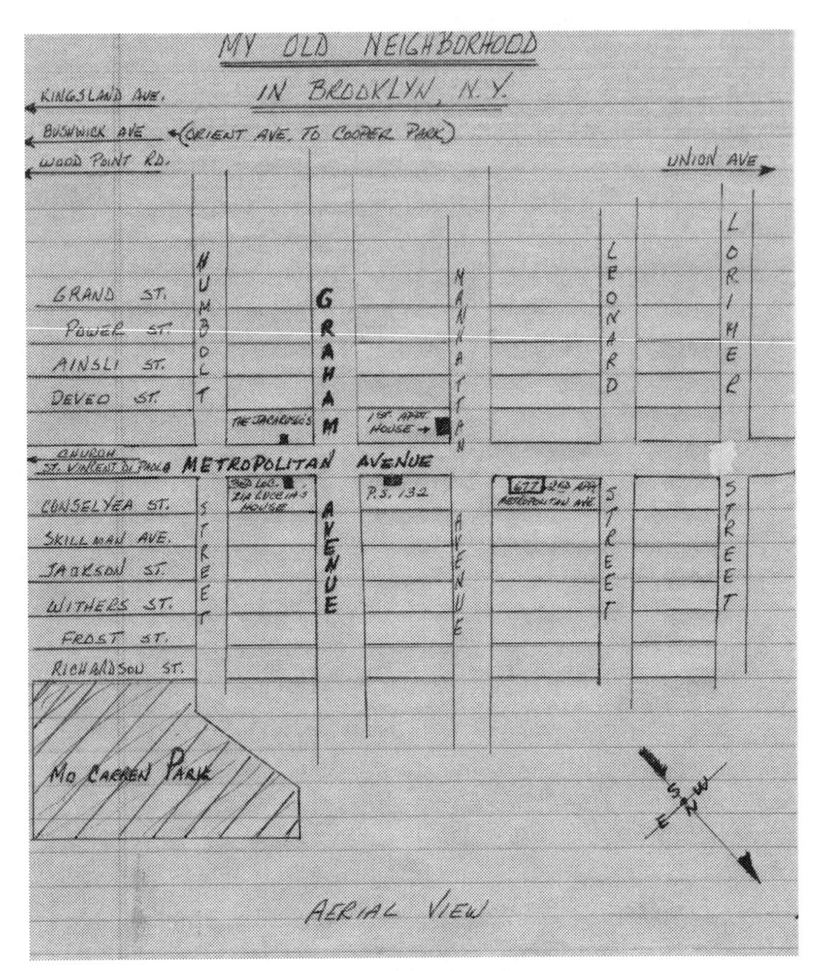

My Old Neighborhood – Map

MY FATHER'S FIRST JOB. The first thing my mother and father were concerned with is getting a job. We were living in our first apartment house on Manhattan Avenue (see homemade street map above). My mother had to stay home caring for my brother and me. After some of the paisanos (I want to define this word because it comes up often in this story-it means anyone who is from or related to; a person that lived in the same town that you are from in Italy, is a paisano-and becomes almost a family member when in a foreign country), told my father about possible relatives of his who can help with employment in New York, he began calling them or even visiting them, asking for work. In his quest for work, my father looked up a cousin who owned a small construction company in Manhattan. He was the son of his uncle, on his mother's side.

Mr. Ciocia was good enough to give my father employment. This made my mother very happy, because now they could afford to pay the rent, buy the food and purchase clothing. Even though it wasn't much, it was a steady salary and to get work during this time of the Depression was equivalent to a miracle.

As circumstance would have it, while working for his cousin, my father learned how to arc-weld in his cousin's metal shop. With my father's knowledge of basic metallurgy that he acquired in Italy, it didn't take long, nor was it difficult for my father to acquire the skills needed to weld. Unknowing to my father, this was a decisive point in his future life here in the United States. Actually, his whole working career was established by this one act in America. Obviously, this is a great example of destiny in progress. He became such an excellent welder, that in another part of this book, you will be told of the many awards and achievements he received as a result of this skill. Meanwhile, he was earning a living, and things were going well at the apartment. My brother and I were being cared for very well.

MEALS IN THE 1930'S. Food was not a big problem for the Pettis in the "30's even though it was the depression. My mother was nursing me and my brother with la mammella (Italian for breast feeding) so we were receiving all the nourishment we needed. No special formula milk had to be purchased for us. It was the natural way. All the nourishment my brother and I needed was provided in this simple and uncomplicated way. The only other type of food required, was for my mother and father. After breakfast, all my father needed was to carry a lunch bag to work and that would be it until he returned in the evening. Since my mother was at home, she was able to not only care for my brother and me but also prepare dinner for the both of them at night. My father did the food shopping when he returned home from work. The stores were very close by, most of them only one block away and most of them stayed open till 7 PM. There was "Mike Scala's Fresh Produce Store around the corner. "Mary a' Sturaiolla" an Italian Grocery Store across the street. Then there was the "Graham Ave. Bakery Shop, one block away in another direction. Between the three shops, almost all their needs were met as far as food was concerned. Since my father was raised in a restaurant environment (remember his father and mother owned a wine tavern), he also knew something about the preparation of food. I remember him in later years, preparing his own breakfast, usually of scrambled eggs and hard Italian bread. He loved eggs. He used to drink eggs too when he was young (yes, just like Sylvester Stalone in "Rocky"), with only one exception, he liked to add Marsala wine to the eggs, and then drink them down. As I was growing up, I began benefiting from this concoction too. I can't tell you how many times in my growing years that I consumed this very (Marsala in raw eggs) nourishing drink. I wonder how many "Americans" even think of swallowing whole raw eggs today for breakfast, or in place of any other meal for that matter. Breakfast for my mother and father at that time was an unusual meal here in the USA since they had just come from Italy, where the customs are so different. For example; my father enjoyed what is called; vino cotta…a recipe that can only be appetizing there in Italy. It consists of a half cup of red wine in a sauce pan, heat just till boiling, then poured over very hard Italian bread in a dish. This was breakfast for my father. Off to work he would go, with rosy cheeks and in high spirits (a play on words), whistling all the way. Quit different from our start in the morning. My mother's breakfast was a little more conservative. They both drank espresso since that is the only coffee they ever tasted in their life. In time, they weaned themselves from this to regular "brown" roasted American coffee. But at that point in time, their coffee was dark, black, demitasse coffee in the morning.

My mother was by no means a raw egg person! She liked all her foods cooked. In fact my mother leaned toward burning her food. For some reason, she had great difficulty with the gas burners on top of the stove here in America. In Italy, all her cooking was done in a fireplace setting. She had no stove. In the fireplace were steel rods, with hooks on top (to hold pots with handles), anchored in the stones at the base of the fireplace. These rods would be swung to and fro so that the pots could be positioned close or far from the burning logs. Because of this gadgetry, she began to develop skills to accommodate the log burning process and the cooking of food in that fashion. Very different now.

She was in America cooking. Here she is faced with a much more accurate and controlled fire, the burning of natural gas on top of a stove. She had to make many adjustments to become skilled in this new process. Every now and then she would revert to her old ways and you guessed it, another meal burned! But she was diligent most of the time and her recipes were always tasty. My father was so accustomed to her delicious cooking, that he rarely complained (in fact I don't remember him ever complaining). Yes, I can attest to that.

MY BROTHER MICHAEL DIES. It was during our first year in Brooklyn, New York (that's where we lived), that a catastrophe occurred in our family. The year was 1931. My brother Michael became extremely ill. I was almost 1 year old, he was two. He was taken to the hospital in an emergency. My mother went with my father to visit (I was brought to my Zia Luccia to be taken care of). He developed pneumonia. My mother pleaded with the doctors to help him. Remember my mother only spoke Italian and the doctors did not understand her. Only from the diagnosis and some crude translation from anyone nearby trying to explain to my mother, could his condition be known to her. Communication was almost at a stand still. The doctors did everything they could for my brother, but could not save him. My brother Michael died... My mother screamed. My father burst into uncontrollable crying. By this time some of the paisanos who learned of the situation began arriving to offer their assistance. When hearing the news, they began to cry while trying to explain to my parents the reason why this had to happen. They were able to speak English so they inquired concerning the events that led up to this devastation, the loss of a first-born son. Then they translated their findings to my sobbing mother and crying father. They came home from the hospital to retrieve me, all crying. When my Zia Luccia heard them coming up the stairway from her second floor flat, all crying, she immediately threw her hands to her head and loudly began praying to the Lord for peace love and understanding and to send the Angels to help; "Caro Dio, darci la forza di sopertara questa disgrazia, mandeci le tui Angeli audarechi a continuare in questa vita, in nomine Dio ed Figlio e Spiritu. Sante, Amen." Then she began crying too.

It was a very sad moment for everyone. My mother and father went into deep bereavement. Yet funeral arrangements had to be made. When my father told me what happened next, I began to understand how poor we were at the time. My mother and father did not have enough money to buy a coffin for my brother. After telling my Zia Luccia that they did not know what to do, they had no money, she said don't worry I will lend you whatever you need for baby Michael. So my parents went to the Church and spoke to the Pastor (thank God he spoke Italian) to find out what the American burial customs are for an infant here in America. They were told the baby would need a white casket (to be purchased from a Funeral Home) and that the casket would hold baby Michael. The coffin would then be brought to the Church where it would be blessed and receive The Last Rites (a Sacrament and the last), with the Priest dressed in White vestments (White vestments are a sign of jubilation), since baby Michael had received Baptism and therefore was sinless, his soul would go right to Heaven. I know it's rarely mentioned, but we have always had a special Angel guiding us along our ways, baby Michael, our little angel. One other thing had to be done before Michael could be buried and that is to purchase a burial plot in a local Cemetery (our closest cemetery was St. John) down Metropolitan Ave., in Maspeth, Brooklyn. With limited funds, my father had told Zia Luccia that he was going to purchase a single plot, but my Aunt wouldn't hear of it, she insisted that he purchase a family plot. Her very wise advice proved its value in time because now that same plot holds not only my brother, but my father and my mother as well. My father had to quickly go to St. John's Cemetery and buy the plot, he purchased a family plot for 4 places (following the advice of Zia Luccia). After the plot was purchased and the necessary time had passed (it took a day to dig for the casket), the Funeral was held, my mother dressed all in black sobbing, my father in his best clothes with a black tie holding back the tears, my Aunt dressed all in black and crying along with the many paisanos (remember most of our family was in Italy) that came to pay their respect, prayed that baby Michael would see the Redeemer and be at peace with God, his Holy Father...May he rest in peace Amen According to my mother, I was not at the funeral for fear that I might disrupt the solemnity of the holy service and also that she was so distraught, one of the paisanos took care of me at their home. But as soon as the Funeral was over I was with my mother and father and at the apartment. We were grieving... Life went on...

It wasn't long after my brother died that my father was laid-off at work because of the scarcity of new construction due to the depression and my father's cousin was on the brink of bankruptcy. My father pleaded with John to keep him on, he would even take a reduction in pay, but he needed to have some money to bring food to the table. John was compassionate but he could not keep him on as an employee, so in his generosity, he gave him some extra money to carry him over for a few months, but that's all he could do. There was no work, he could not have him just stand around. There was no alternative but to let him go. My father was very upset. How was he going to tell my mother? What about my son, he worried? He didn't want anything to happen to me. He stopped at Church on his way home and in front of the Blessed Sacrament prayed that God would give him the strength to endure through these difficult times.

1932

LINDBERGH BABY KIDNAPPING. During my second year in Brooklyn (1932), aside from the many historical events that were unfolding in the world, one of them affected me directly. It was the kidnapping of the Lindbergh baby. On March 1, 1932 at around 10PM in Hopewell, New Jersey someone had abducted baby Charles A. Lindbergh III, a 20 month old infant. The distressing news was on the headline of every newspaper in the USA and being broadcasted on the radio almost every hour all during the day. Because Charles Lindbergh was famous for his 1927 nonstop airplane flight across the Atlantic Ocean, this terrible crime was absolutely sensational! All Americans were implored to help find the perpetrator or perpetrators that committed this heinous act. The whole Nation was in arms. Anyone even resembling any person involved became suspect. The country was in a sort of "private detective" frenzy.

My mother and father, not having a radio were unaware of the occurrence. Here is my mother innocently bundling me and placing me in the baby carriage. She was preparing to go shopping to the butcher store, one block away. Off we go and we make it to the store without incidence. When my mother arrives at the butcher shop, she parks the baby carriage with me playing in it and typically goes in to buy the meat. The shop has a great big window that allows her to keep an eye on me while she's shopping. All of a sudden, a middle aged woman comes very close to the carriage and begins studying me. Then without hesitation she reaches into the carriage and lifts me out. By this time my mother, after seeing her do this, bolts out the door and grabs the woman by the arm, along with yells and screams. Remember my mother does not speak English, but even in Italian she became a formidable adversary. The other woman not releasing me was yelling: "Lindbergh's baby, Lindbergh's baby"! My mother did not know what she was talking about. My mother screamed. "Lascio il mio figlio" (let my son go), my mother, with great force, pulled me out of the woman's arms. The woman continued to point at me, yelling, "That's Lindbergh's kidnapped baby". Meanwhile people passing by began to gather, wondering what was happening. A Policeman was summoned. The crowd would not let my mother move from that spot. There she stood, holding me tight and shivering, not understanding the things that were being said by the woman that was making the accusation, nor the comments made by the crowd. Here comes the Policeman. "Ok, Ok, what's going on here, he asked?" The accuser spoke first. "That baby is Charles Lindbergh that was kidnapped yesterday!" Is that true he asked my mother. She said she does not speak English. The Policeman now addresses the crowd and asks if anyone can speak Italian and English. A gentleman steps up and volunteers to do the translation. Ask her what is the baby's name. He does. "Augustus, my mother answers." "You see, I told you that is Lindbergh's son", said the woman that was accusing my mother, Charles' middle name was Augustus! The Policeman was in a quandary. Could it be true? Is this the kidnapped baby? The Policeman had to ask more questions. (At this point I want to direct you to the "Wanted" poster shown below, especially the description of the baby.)

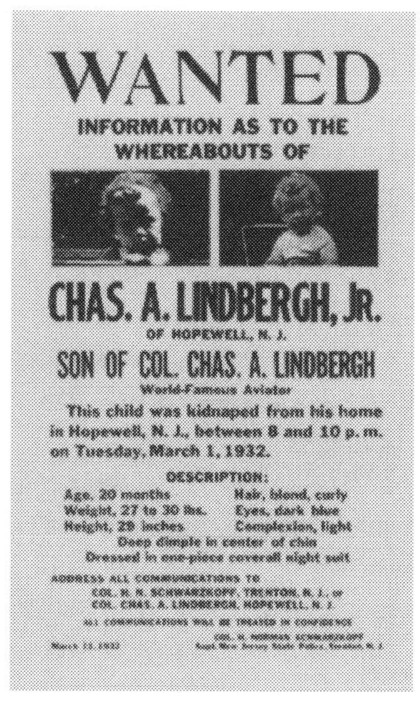

Lindbergh Baby Poster-1932

The strangest fact about this whole incident is that I was, in appearance, almost identical to the kidnapped baby. I had the same name, blond hair, blue eyes, weighed close to 30 pounds and I was about 20 months old. As the Policeman was talking to the man who was doing the translation, our cousin who was a Barber across the street from the butcher shop (this was Zia Luccia's son John), saw the commotion through his store window and came to investigate. When he saw my mother clutching me and crying, he immediately assured the Policeman (who happened to be a customer of his, whom he knew very well), that I was not the Lindbergh baby, but that I actually was a distant cousin of his. The Policeman immediately relented. Obviously a case of mistaken identity. My mother was released. We were allowed to go home. My mother hurried home. Wow, did she have a story to tell my father when he came home from work that night!

WORKING ON THE WPA. The year was 1933; President Franklin Delano Roosevelt along with Congress had instituted the WPA (Works Progress Administration) to address the widespread unemployment situation affecting the nation... My father's prayer was answered! He got a job immediately after applying, mostly due to his blacksmith skills (he still did not speak English). He managed to understand his assignments with the help of other workers who spoke both Italian and English and translated for him. One of his projects was the fabrication of a 6 foot tall iron fence around the Bronx Zoo. That was his first WPA job. He drove me to the sections he built when I was nine or ten years old to show me it and proudly pointed to the tall bars of iron he had erected. It was a special moment. I will never forget it. It isn't often that a father can point to an object that he fabricated ten years prior and show it to his son. I was very proud of him.

CUSTOMS, TRADITIONS, ETC. Insofar as the many Italian Customs and Traditions that my mother and father religiously held on to and brought to America, listing all of them would occupy this whole book. I remember my mother preparing for weeks prior to various times of the year when a celebration was called for and special foods had to be prepared for those family gatherings.

This is very important; although you will see emphasis given to certain days and almost no mention of other very important days of the year, this should not be construed to mean the others were not recognized or venerated or celebrated. For example, there is great tradition and reverence that my mother and father had for Holy Thursday, Good Friday and Holy Saturday. All of the important Holy Days were venerated such as The Presentation of Our Lord, The Ascension of The Lord, The Assumption of The Blessed Virgin Mary, All Saints Day and the Feast of The Immaculate Conception of The Virgin Mary. I remember us going to Mass on these days, but I don't recall any special customs or traditions associated to them. I can only relate what I remember. The important thing is they are "NOT" excluded as times when our family would celebrate their meaning, but that I don't remember the customs that went along with them. While I'm writing, if I remember, I will make a note of it then.

New Years Day. The first Holiday of the year (January 1st), which, in the Christian Calendar, is the celebration of Mary, Mother of God. It is also the Octave Day of Christmas and a Holy Day of Obligation. We all went to celebrate Mass that day. The remainder of the day was spent preparing a special meal, somewhat lighter than the Christmas Dinner, but still substantial. These were the customs brought back from Celenza, Italy, by my parents. Our meal was basically Antipasto (left-over from Christmas), Veal Cutlets (indurido e fritto), dipped in egg, crumbs and fried. Roasted Stuffed Capon Chicken, Peas roasted with Onions, Oven Roasted Potatoes with Oregano, Nuts, Fruit, and Italian Punch Wine to drink, then Dessert, all the leftovers from Christmas like the Angelette Cookies, the Strufoli (honey balls), the Scarolla, deep fried spiral cookies and Panetone (sweet bread with dried fruits). Did I say "Lighter"? After listing the things we ate that day, it didn't seem light at all, but my father used to caution my mother the week after Christmas to make the next meal lighter, in his words, he would say; "Piu Leggio" which means a "Little Lighter" please! And so it went. This is typical of all the First Days of the Year we celebrated with very few exceptions. That's what I liked about Customs, there were no surprises. If you remembered what you had the year before on a certain Holiday, you knew you were going to get the same thing this year, and next year, and so on. The Custom provided a rock solid foundation that you could depend on, it gave you a feeling of security and stability. It provided immeasurable happiness, insofar as celebrations are concerned. And than there were the toys, so the rest of the day, and days to come there were the toys from Christmas Day. It was fun.

St. Joseph's Day. The second Feast day of the year is St. Joseph's, March 19th. On St. Joseph's Day, the traditional custom is the preparation of small loaves of bread that are handed out to anyone asking for them, especially children. Although we did not participate in this custom in this manner, there was a family in the neighborhood that did. They were the Ferrucci's. A little history, the father started as an "Ice Man" when he immigrated to the United States, but then began selling Kerosene, and finally became the "Oil Man". He ended up with a fleet of oil trucks delivering heating oil to a large part of Brooklyn. A wealthy family, but very respectful and very religious. Mrs. Ferrucci would bake hundreds of little loaves of bread on that day and distribute them to the neighborhood children that would knock on her door during St. Joseph's Day. It was a wonderful gesture of generosity and carried with it a sentiment that filled that day with gratitude, namely that St. Joseph was a wonderful Father to Jesus, and was adopted by all Christians as Father to us all. Then there are the wonderful pastries that emerged during this holiday. There are the Sfingi or Zeppoli di San Giuseppe. Which is simply fried dough, but so delicious it boggles the taste buds. It must be eaten hot, right from the boiling oil, otherwise it loses much of its flavor, a lot like bread right from the oven as apposed to room temperature fresh bread, you know what I mean. Currently that custom has evolved to the preparation of special pastries that although start out with fried dough, end up being large pastries filled with ricotta cream or custard cream with all kinds of decorative icings on top. Quite a long way from the simple sfingi di San Giuseppe that was created in Italy and was a tradition a long time ago, to celebrate St. Joseph (I guess because he was the "bread" winner in the family).

Carnival. Let's see, the third feast day of the year was Carnevale (Carnival) which is the Tuesday before Ash Wednesday. To be honest with you, it is not a feast day of any kind but a reason to indulge in all kinds of foods because the next day begins Lent (Ash Wednesday). This is when days of fasting and abstinence begin for the religious observance of the 40 days Jesus spent in the desert, fasting, abstaining and praying for all of mankind. This day became through the ages a time to "feast before the famine" and so it was an evolutionary type of celebration. Everyone is familiar with the now famous parades they have in New Orleans and other places in the world that want to get in the act, but in Celenza Valfortore, Italy, there were no displays in the streets, where my mother and father lived. Basically it was a food thing. In my mother's town, Celenza Valfortore, some of the most exotic foods would be prepared and served at Carnevale. So my mother carried on the traditions here in Brooklyn, NY, by searching out as close as she could, duplicates of the foods and recipes she prepared in Italy. Since the following days into Lent, fish would be required in place of meat; carnevale had to be meat only. Curiously, the word Carnival comes from the root words "carnem levare", to remove meat; through time it came to mean the period of feasting and revelry just before Lent; a reveling; festivity; merrymaking. It was like our last harrah for the year. So meat it was. My mother had lots of choices because the holiday did not mandate certain kinds of meat that often customarily happens at other feasts. Whatever meat she chose, had to be elegant and very different from the daily fare type. I remember her preparing Vitello Ripeine Inforno, which is my favorite to this day (sadly no one makes it). It is Veal Ribs, Stuffed and Roasted. My mother made this "incredible stuffing" that not only wafted through the air with an aroma of pure joy, but then followed that with the most delicious accompaniment, the incredible stuffing, then to the sweet, tender, succulent veal imaginable. It was pure heaven. My mother made this almost every Carnevale. She knew it was my favorite and of course my father's too! (Alas, please don't ask me for the recipe. I don't have it…sorry). Another favorite meat preparation my mother made on Carnevale was called; Bistecca Alla Pizzaiolla, which means, Steak in Tomato Sauce with Cheese. To make this you have to buy a 2" thick, large (about 2 lbs.) Chuck Steak (no substitutes), oil a saucepan (this is cooked on top of the stove), place the steak in the saucepan, add salt and fresh pepper, add chopped garlic (lots), add peeled, crushed tomatoes to cover the meat, add a handful of grated parmesan cheese sprinkled on top, add fresh chopped parsley. Cook with the cover on to steam it, for about two hours (careful not to burn the bottom). Heat should not exceed 300 degrees. We would have these meats with Italian Potato Salad, with cooked spinach or cooked escarole on the side. My father always made Italian Wine Punch at Holidays and my mother would make her world famous (my opinion) Italian Sponge Cake with custard filling, topped with powdered sugar. Demitasse of course followed with Anisette liquor. I forgot to mention the Fruit and Nuts. It was all there. Her Customs were delicious! Thank you Mamma…

Lent. After Carnevale, we remained in fasting and abstinence for the duration of Lent (for 40 days). But, this is interesting, at that time, the Catholic Calendar required Abstinence (no meat) on Wednesdays and Fridays (with Friday also requiring fasting). This meant that we would eat fish at least two days a week during Lent. My mother (she was a Godsend!) was so experienced at cooking fish (she lived close to the Adriatic Sea in Italy-where all kinds of fish were abundant), my father and I was presented every Wednesday and Friday with a gourmet helping of all types of fish. One of her specialties was Stuffed Calamari Inforno, that's the body only of squid, stuffed with a heavenly stuffing. Delicious! She also fried all varieties of fish; one of my favorites was a very small, silver fish that was fried completely with head and fins (I believe they were baby herrings) and tasted so goooood! That's when I fell in love with eel. My father would make this one (he was a pretty proficient cook also) He would flour segments of eel, place them on an oiled baking pan, place them in the oven and baste them with a mixture of olive oil, wine vinegar, oregano with salt and pepper. His brush was twigs of Parsley which he used to splash the mixture on. The eel was so delicious; my mother had to stop me from eating it all. Thank you Papa'.

Although Lent was not a holiday but a time of fasting and abstinence and since fish was allowed as a substitute for meat during this period, many Lenten Recipe's developed and became Customs. For instance, one of the favorite antipastos in restaurants today is Fried Calamari, fried squid. Well, my mother was making this for us in the 1930's, along with many other fish meals (of course I didn't eat it as child because I didn't like it, but it was served) that my mother and father enjoyed. During Lent, the many Bean recipes Italian's prepare today developed. Such as Pasta e Fasullo, white Cannellini beans with small tubular pasta in aglia e olio sauce. Also, Lentil soup, the bean is actually named for Lent, and was a must during Lent. There were also many recipes with Chic Peas served; they were a favorite in many regions of Italy. Since it was the beginning of Spring, many baby greens were mixed into salads, such as arugula, baby spinach, dandelion (I know we treat it as a weed but Italians love it in a salad), romaine lettuce and vegetables of all kinds, like onions, carrots, radishes, tomatoes, peppers, etc. As you can see, we did not starve during this fasting season; we just ate different kinds of foods.

I could go on and on with the many special recipes my mother prepared so I feel it's best if I just mention them by name along with the feast day associated with them. At this juncture, as an after thought, I just feel that maybe this could be a subject for another writing which could be called the "Recipes of Grandma" and I'll try to recall the preparations within those pages. Another, what I call miraculous talent my mother brought to this country was her pasta making skill. She used to make homemade cavatelli (a three finger drawn shell macaroni), ravioli (ricotta filled pillows) and tagliatelli (a close resemblance to spaghetti, but shorter and made with eggs). She could whip-up homemade macaronis in a matter of minutes, when she was in the mood. Nothing could stop her. She made every Holiday special. Her cooking was superb. She baked too. She was an excellent baker as can be attested by my father and me (we gobbled up everything she baked and always clamored for more)!

When American holidays would roll around my mother would ask around with a solitary question; "Che si fa?" [what is done], meaning what is the tradition for this holiday in your country and the answer was invariably "nothing". This was very puzzling to my mother because in Italy there are very specific things to do for each Feast Day. To give an example of her frustration, for instance, Lincoln's Birthday, George Washington's Birthday. She wanted to know what we did on these Holidays. No answer. Then there is Memorial Day, the answer was "Barbecue" but she needed to know what to barbecue. No answer (or too many answers). I believe this is the reason the Petti family did not celebrate American Holiday's in any special way all during my growing years. Since my mother was so oriented to specific customs brought over from Italy, these other American Holiday's were so alien to her ways that they remained obscure. It wasn't her fault; it was the way she was brought up. Therefore, the only Holiday's we celebrated with great feelings and in special ways were the ones she remembered from her days.

Palm Sunday. The next Feast Day of the year was Palm Sunday, when my mother would make homemade Pasta, Ragu (homemade), with all kinds of meats. It was at least a five course dinner; we usually celebrated around 3:00 PM in the afternoon. After Palm Sunday Mass, we would go to the Cemetery to visit my brother Michael. At the cemetery there would be florist shops selling Palm Crosses to be placed on graves. We always placed a palm cross on his grave every Palm Sunday. At home my mother would then prepare a regular Sunday meal, with an antipasto, Macaroni entrée, ragu meat, a salad, fruit, nuts, Demitasse with Anisette and a dessert from her vast repertoire. Just something simple…

Easter Sunday. The Holiday following Palm Sunday was Easter Sunday. On Easter Sunday all the plugs were pulled. It had to be at least an eight course marathon fest! We started with sliced Fresh Ricotta in a basket, accompanied by Fresh Mozzarella sliced, with oozing cream. In another plate would contain sliced Prosciutto and Mortadelli along with spicy hot Cappacolla with vinegar hot and sweet peppers pilled in the center. This was only the first course! After the first course came the homemade ravioli. Then the ragu meat. After this, my mother served roasted Leg of Lamb smothered in garlic with crusty baked potatoes on the side. Meanwhile we are consuming fresh Italian bread all during every entrée. After the Lamb, we had salad (our custom was to have salad after dinner), my mother liked to add escarole (the white center only), including lettuce with arugula, cucumber sliced, with radishes included. We were not through yet, then came the nuts, not shelled, the whole nut, with toasted walnuts, almonds, filberts and my favorite brazil nuts. We had a feast cracking shells all the way to desert time, our favorite part of the meal. For Easter, my mother baked special pastry that is only prepared on that feast day. She baked, Torta di Ricotta, Italian Cheese Cake, Pizza di Grano the oldest Italian pastry, dating back to the Romans, Pizza Rustica, a double crusted Italian type of quiche (with sausage, three cheeses and eggs and lots of ground pepper), and then the piece de resistance, she would bring out everyone's favorite; Cacialebre, Easter Sweet Bread! Just spread a pat of butter on a slice of Cacialebre and you are in another world, just ask anyone that's tasted it. All these pastries made you quite full. But we are not finished yet, now comes the Demitasse coffee, dark roasted Italian coffee poured steaming into small cups, add sugar and at least an ounce of Anisette Liquor and you are on your way to "fairy land"!

St. John the Baptist. After Easter, the next Holiday we celebrated was the feast of St. John the Baptist, June 24th. This was a very important feast day on the Petti calendar. The reason, St. John the Baptist was the Patron Saint of Celenza Valfortore, my parent's home town in Italy. All during their growing years they celebrated this feast day in a big way. First there was a Holy Missa Cantata, (a High Mass), and the next thing I'm going to explain was the "highlight" of the day and the event the whole town waited for, it took place during Mass, as soon a Communion was Distributed, a signal was sent outside the Church where the Fugiste is waiting, who then begins lighting the fuses of Fireworks of an extraordinary kind! Not only are the explosions ear shattering, but the shells are so loud, the vibrations shake the very walls of the Church and the people inside just sit, shuddering all during the firings. Although it's scary, it's very exciting and tells the world that they are celebrating the birth of St. John the Baptist! Then begins the Procession throughout the whole town. First in the front of the procession were the acolytes, bearing the cross of Jesus, then those holding candles, then the Priests (there were three). Then behind the Priests, they would mount this very heavy statue of a bust of St. John on beams, with a group of strong men slowly lifting the beams to their shoulders until the statue was well balanced and in the air, then they would commence marching, with banners of all the different Societies of St. John the Baptist that existed in that town, then all the people would follow. My mother said it was very moving to watch. The remainder of the day was spent; you guessed it, preparing and consuming all different kinds of special foods.

HOLY DAYS DURING THE YEAR. All the Holy days (days of obligation) were celebrated by going to Mass and receiving Communion along with some special food my mother would prepare that was customary for that holiday. We also celebrated other days of Saints that had some special significance to my parents. For instance, along with those stated above, we had a special veneration to St. Anthony of Padua and to St. Francis of Assisi, Our Lady of Mt. Carmel and of course St. Lucy (my mother's name day) Then there is the Feast of San Genaro (who can forget that holiday with the wonderful way the "Neapolitans" (it's the Patron Saint of Naples) celebrate that Feast on Mulberry Street in Downtown New York, with all the decorations and street vendors, the Italian music and the crowds, and the great smells of typical Italian food cooking all day long. Nope...you can't forget that Feast!

CHRISTMAS. At the beginning of December begins the most anticipated holiday of all, Advent. When the Priest announces the First Sunday in Advent before reading the Gospel, the Christmas fever begins. Every action, every sound, every feeling is directed toward the coming of the Birth of Jesus...CHRISTMAS! All the children are talking about, wondering about, dreaming about, is Christmas and what Santa Clause is going to bring. But in the Petti family, in the beginning years, it was a little different than it is now. First of all, in Italy, (and remember that's where my parent's traditions came from), Christmas was a High Holy Day. It did not include presents(presents were not given to children until the Feast of Three Kings arrived) as oddly as it seems. It was a solemn day of veneration to the Baby Jesus. The veneration begins on the day before Christmas, (The Christmas Eve). On this day, my parents would prepare seven different recipes of fish only meals. It was a day of strict abstinence, no meat was allowed. It was to pay homage to Our Lord and Savior Jesus. But you know Italians, even though they are asked to suffer a little, they will go about suffering with all the food they can enjoy. So it starts, my mother would have their favorite Calamari Ripieno Inforno), Roasted Eel (my father's style), fried Baby Herrings, Steamed Clams, Baked Mussels with Tomato Sauce, Fried Shrimp Marinaro, and Linguini in Tomato Sauce (notice no Lobster-we couldn't afford them). Even though it was a day of abstinence, I never saw so much food! It really was a Feast. The fact that in one more day, the Infant Jesus would be born, the joy of such a happening filled everyone's heart. I couldn't fault them from feasting on that Eve. The next day was Christmas!!! What a joyous holiday. Everyone is happy. My mother has been preparing for this holiday all week long. When she came home from work (yes, my mother worked all the years I was growing up), she would begin her baking. She would bake into the early hours of the morning, every night. She would make Biscoti con peppe, Chic peas calzone, Ricotta Cheese calzone, Scarolla fritti, Strufoli con miele, Biscoti con zucchero (we call them Anginetti) and she made a candy called; Mandorlo di Terra, she also made a special pudding called Sanguinache (please don't ask me for the ingredients that goes into this one!). These were the traditional foods that were made in her home town of Celenza Valfortore in Italy. Of course they were embedded in her mind, she did not know any other, and therefore we were blessed with her memories. The cookies were delicious. To be honest with you, I don't know which I looked forward to the most, the cookies or the toys. It's the cookies all the way! They only came once a year…the toys, well they were with me for a long time…not the cookies.

NEW YEAR'S EVE. The last holiday of the year was New Year's Eve. Remember in Italy, this day is the Eve of a Holy Day, The Holy Family of Jesus, Mary and Joseph, a holy day of obligation. See New Year's Day above for the customs followed on that day. On the Eve, it is a day of abstinence, another fish day. Actually, we basically repeat the Christmas Eve preparation of fishes, only on this day it was not required to serve seven recipes for this meal. These are my memories of the holidays as we celebrated then. Boy have they changed! Compared to what we do today, some of them seem alien. Oh, well, they call that progress or is it? I wonder…

IN 1935 SCHOOL BEGINS. My parents felt that I should attend Nursery School (Pre-School) first before sending me to Kindergarten especially because I only spoke Italian. Of course I must have been picking-up some English from my neighborhood friends, but it just wasn't enough to start school with. The school was right around the block, so I didn't even have to cross a street to go. It was great, we played all morning then after lunch (this is where I came to love jelly sandwiches) we would take a nap. The rest of the day was reading and arithmetic, which really wasn't long and then its home again by 3:00 PM. Since my mother and father were both working, my guardianship fell either on Zia Luccia or our paisanos the Jacarussos. The Jacarussos lived across the street from Zia Luccia so I could choose where to go. If my Zia Luccia was not home when I got there I could go across the street to the Jacarussos, they were "always" home since one of their daughters was born mongoloid, couldn't speak and barely walked, and was in her twenties (her name was Maria Domenica). She was so special, her eyes would light up every time she saw me and she would try to talk to me, but all that came out was mumbling. The only critical thing about her care was that almost every day she would have an epileptic fit (going into uncontrollable spasms; with no cure), at which time we would have to hold her arms and legs down, to keep her from harming herself, and we would have to hold her tongue extended so she wouldn't swallow it (usually with a spoon compressed on her tongue). It was a difficult procedure especially for the loved ones, to have to witness this type of bodily transformation right before your eyes. But we loved her so much, there wasn't anything we wouldn't do for her. In fact, that was my first experience with a medical condition in our family. Since it occurred almost every day, I became proficient with the process. As an aside; many years later, while I was managing a banking operation, one of my employees all of a sudden went into a convulsion and people were screaming for help, I quickly went to her aid, by keeping her from swallowing her tongue, while getting other employees to hold down her legs and arms. I did this in total amazement of all that witnessed the scene who later came to congratulate me for my immediate and capable assistance, not knowing that I had performed the same exact thing hundreds of times before (this is why I believe God many times puts us through grueling experiences to prepare us for some future event where that experience is put to good use and may even save a life). What I liked about the Jacarussos was the number of members in the family. First and foremost, there was the mother Antionette, then the father John (Giuanno), then Concettinna (the oldest who was married, but visited often), then Eva, Natalie, Guilda, Maria Domenica, a son Salvatore, and Yolanda (my age). Seven children in all. A house full. There was always something going on there so I went there a lot. Then, of course, Yolanda and I were close friends until she died in 1942 of 'consumption" (a term for cancer or any other unknown disease at that time) we became very good friends while we were growing up (she was about 12 years old when she died). I don't think I ever got over her loss, to this day...we were such very good friends. Rest In Peace Yolanda...

1935

FIRST LOCATION CHANGE.

677 Metropolitan Ave., 2nd Floor Apt._1935

By now we had moved from our apartment on Manhattan Avenue. to the 6 story apartment house at 677 Metropolitan Avenue (shown here). Of course we had to move to the "6th" floor (this was the initiation requirement-all new dwellers were given the top floor apartment) and although it was great looking out the window to view the city landscape, with all those tall buildings, it wasn't that great when I had to take the garbage down six flights (that's about 60 steps-one way) to throw a garbage bag into the main barrels and then climb up the same six flights to get back to the radio to hear my programs. In time, we were able to move into a 2nd floor apartment.

THE RADIO. Yes, that's all we had in 1935 in terms of communication was the radio. The radio had great programs for us kids, like The Adventures of the Sea Hound, Jack Armstrong the All American Boy, Dick Tracy and The Adventures of the Green Hornet with Kato his dependable assistant. There was also The Lone Ranger and his sidekick Tonto and his horse Silver. All of these programs started at 3:00PM and went on to 5:00PM. They were so exciting, full of action and mystery. I was able to do my homework and listen to the series simultaneously until dinner time. After dinner the radio broadcasted wonderful family entertainment including the news. We had programs like The Whistler Knows and behind a loud creaking door we listened to "Inner Sanctum. For fun, we heard the antics of Fiber McGee and Molly, with all the contents of their closet come crashing down when he opened it, it was hilarious to say the least. Radio relied a lot on sound effects, since you couldn't see the scene, the technicians would create marvelous sound effects to fill-in the quiet and to conjure up an easily imagined scene. Those days are gone forever, but in retrospect they were wonderful.

1936 SCHOOL REALLY BEGINS In 1936 I entered Kindergarten. It's interesting that my memories during this period of my life are so vivid. I can not explain it but not only do I remember my Teacher, Miss Beer, but I also remember the class room and some of the activities that were conducted. After reading my teachers name, you begin to understand why I can't forget it. In fact there are only four teachers names I can remember in all the years I attended school. They are; Miss Beer, Mrs. Kiofsky, Miss Champagne and Mr. Ryan or Dr. Ryan (he was the only teacher I had that was awarded a PhD. which at that time was a degree higher than the Principle's Master degree). That does not mean I don't remember my other educators, it's their names I don't recall. In fact memories of many of my teachers are very clear and unforgettable.

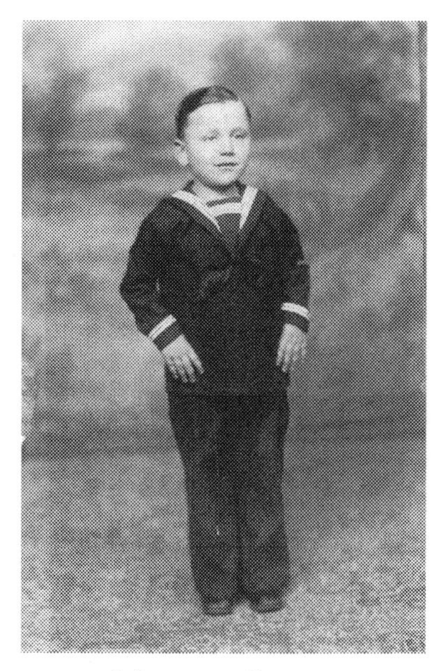

Me at age 5 or so

In Kindergarten we performed a lot of paper crafts and we sang many songs. Miss Beer played the piano which was in our room and enjoyed singing to us then having us join in. I enjoyed Kindergarten immensely. I was learning to speak English, Miss. Beer helped me all the way. Now I was able to communicate with my friends more readily. This also allowed me to play more outdoor games. I was learning and understood the rules better. Due to my physical size (tall and muscular-from carrying bags of garbage down six flights), I became a frequent choice when kids were organizing a team. So my popularity was pretty natural. In fact as the years went on, I became an athlete of sorts (wish I had chosen baseball or basketball, instead I chose running). I'll tell you more about my running career later, when I discuss my high school days. Kindergarten was a very important start in my life. I am so grateful, in retrospect, to Miss. Beer. This was one of the most important persons in my life aside from my family members. A very grateful thank you, Miss Beer!

In 1937 I began 1st Grade in Public School. The school I attended was P.S. 23. (see map on page 29.)

FOOD LINES-SOCIAL RELIEF. I'm not sure exactly what year (my guess is between 1934 and 1936) that, because my father was not working steadily, we were eligible to receive what was then called Food Relief (today it's Food Stamps). In order to avail yourself of this social benefit, you had to go to the Agriculture Department Depot, get on line and wait until they handed you food to survive. As I recall, what they distributed was milk in gallons (you received an amount related to the size of the family-the honor system was followed), they distributed butter in 1lb packages, they gave us loaves of Wonder Bread (stale of course), cheese in blocks and cans of boiled beef in unlabeled cans (except for the codes). The number of starving people gathering there at the depot was hard to imagine. Sometimes my father and I would wait a half day to receive our quota. Then we had to rush home to place the milk and butter in the ice box (that's right, there were NO refrigerators then-they hadn't been invented yet).

THE ICE BOX. Let me explain the ice box; it was a wooden cabinet with one large door on the top with two smaller doors below. The top compartment was devoted to holding a large block of ice (about a cubic foot in size) that was delivered by the ice man (you had to see this sight, up the stairs walks the ice man, with burlap folded and thrown over his shoulder, the ice block sitting on his shoulder, holding the block with ice tongs, a tool like a large scissors with hooks at the end, holding the ice in place) about twice a week (that's the approximate length of time it took to melt), of course it melted faster in the summer time, when we would buy two blocks of ice to tide us over. You're wondering what happens to the water that drains down a tube from the ice compartment to the floor where a deep pan is placed to catch the flowing water. Well, that basin or container has to be emptied as soon as the water reaches the top of the pan. If you don't empty it on time, water begins to seep onto the floor and eventually covers the whole kitchen floor (don't think that didn't happen to us) it's just impossible to predict the amount of water it takes to fill the container. I'm sure some mathematicians have computed the probability and failed because the outside temperature is a prime factor and you and I know it's impossible to predict precisely. And guess what? Who do you think had the responsibility of emptying the full pan of water under the ice box? Me, of course! It was up to me to make sure it didn't overflow. A formidable task that I took seriously. In fact, by the time we were able to purchase our own refrigerator, I believe I had solved the full pan phenomenon. At the time, I had the water running from one pan to another and then to another, (giving me enough time to empty them all, without spilling onto the floor) which was all the space allowed under the ice box.

The most interesting fact about the ice box is that it did the job, keeping most of the food on the lower shelves at around 40 degrees Fahrenheit. It really depended on how often the doors were opened and the indoor temperature. Also, the efficiency of the insulation used to surround the inside of the cabinet was an important factor. We were not allowed to dilly-dally after opening the door, before you heard my mother yelling; "You're melting the ice, close the door!" By now, you must be asking yourself where the ice came from. It came from ice plants that actually manufactured it. Scientists knew in the 1930's that ice formed in a brine solution that could be brought to 32 degrees Fahrenheit. In a factory, this could be accomplished. These ice-making factories began emerging, producing large blocks of ice, approximately 3 feet by 1 foot by 3 feet. This was the manageable size that ice men could handle on their trucks. If you could see an ice truck departing from an ice producing factory in those days, it was quite a sight. Each truck carrying about 30 blocks that would probably bring in $13.75 for the day was then a thriving business. Remember, gasoline was only 5 cents a gallon and people were working for about 40 cents a day. Well, that was life in the 1930's, ice boxes in every house (that could afford them, that is), NO TV, NO A/C, NO PC, NO CELL PHONES etc., etc. I don't know how we survived, but we did.

I divert. Getting back to the food lines, I have to tell you this. I learned to love the boiled beef that came out of the can that was given to us. I don't know who manufactured it, but it was delicious! The cans did not have labels on them, just Federal Agriculture Department stamps with codes that were not decipherable by us. I guess they contained the date canned, the place, and who canned it, but only the Agriculture Dept. could decipher it. Nonetheless it was the most sought after handout given to us. I used it for everything, talk about having steak for breakfast, well I had boiled beef and thought I was having an elite breakfast. I'm pretty convinced, that is where they got the idea for SPAM. That food that was generously given to us really made a difference. It got us through some very bad times and was literally a life saver. A lot of people would complain that they weren't given enough, or that they had to wait on very long lines, or that the pick-up depot was too far away…every conceivable complaint known to man would be spoken (my father called this "disprezzando" which means "ungrateful"). We were very pleased and that food carried us through until my father could get work. It's a part of my life that I will never forget, especially since it gave me an opportunity to get close to my father; we would have so many laughs as we waited. I loved my father very much. He was never negative about anything, even though he had good reason to hate the world at that time, but he didn't. Life was very cruel to us, but with his outlook, we pushed on and we made it. Thank you Papa'! You were a wonderful father…

MY FATHER BECOMES A US CITIZEN. My father decided at this moment in his life to become an American Citizen. He went to the local public school and registered. The course was twofold; it was a combination of language and history. To become a citizen you had to be able to speak English. You also had to have a cursory knowledge of the country's history. They taught him English and they taught him the successions of Presidents, the Declaration of Independence and the Constitution, along with all the important history that relates to the forming of the United States of America. It was very exciting for him. He was so eager to learn, I guess that is why it didn't take him long before he was able to speak a little English and to pass the citizenship test that was given. In 1935, my father had become an American Citizen. He was presented with American Naturalization Papers containing his photo embossed by an impression of the Judicial Seal of the United States of America. He was not an immigrant anymore! He was a valuable constituent of the fabric that constitutes "the people of this Nation", an American Citizen! Congratulations Papa'! I was around five or six years old at the time and almost understood what was going on. My mother was very proud of his accomplishment, it wasn't easy. He had to work, help with the house chores, take care of me when my mother went out shopping, go to school at night, study the English language and study history, including all the other incidentals that require attention in a day's activity. It was an amazing accomplishment, I thought. I wondered if I could do that today.

FATHER WORKING ON CARS. I hope you didn't forget about my father's quest to own a car. Up to now, circumstances didn't even allow my father to think of it! With his fervent goal in mind, he would frequent locations in Manhattan that specialized in repairing automobiles of all types. As he observed the many mechanics along the avenues (most of the repairs were done along the curbs in the street) fixing damaged cars, he quickly began learning how the repairs were accomplished. Because of his knowledge in handling metal it appeared easy to him, so one day he applied to a Help Wanted ad that was on the street. He went inside, spoke to the owner and was asked to show his ability by repairing a damaged fender on a 1934 automobile. He had to use the owner's tools, but he straightened out the fender to the satisfaction of the employer. Even if I say so myself, he was a "master" at his work. He knew how to handle the acetylene torch that was there, to provide the heat needed to bend the metal easily and to the correct shape. He knew how to handle any type of hammer and dolly (a heavy, hand held shaped piece of steel-used as a mobile anvil) to move metal in any direction. His test proved successful. He got the job! He went home jubilant to tell my mother the good news. This began his career as a Body-and-Fender Repairman, as the term went in the 30's. Today the skill, I believe, is called generally: Auto Body Repairman. As he developed his skill, he became proficient not only in repairing the metal parts of an automobile like the body and fenders but also the painting (which was a separate skill) and upholstery (which had to be outsourced for repair). He was able to save the owner a substantial amount of money when all the work was done in that one shop. The owner liked that. My father became a desired asset at this shop. Over the years, realizing the value he was to the owner and how easy it was for any person in the city to open up their own business offering this service to the public, my father began investigating that possibility.

MY FIRST COMMUNION. Although I don't actually remember my First Communion, since I found a photo of me in Communion dress I know I received the Sacrament because of the photo. I just don't know what happened to the certificate. When it was time for me to receive Confirmation, the Pastor of our church asked my parents for my Baptismal certificate and they could not find it. The Pastor told them without the certificate he must receive the Baptismal Sacrament again.

My First Holy Communion

MY FIRST DOG. As soon as my father could afford a dog he purchased one. Since we were living in an apartment house, he sought a small dog. He did not discuss getting a dog to my mother nor with me (he liked to surprise everyone.) One day he arrives home from work with a little bulge in his jacket and looking a little guilty. He has a big wide smile on and seems to be holding onto the bulge. Then we hear a small whelp coming from his jacket. "What do you have in there?," my mother asks. "Nothing," my father says with his smile getting wider. She begins moving toward him with her hand extended to fold back the jacket so she could see what he was hiding. He moves away, but he folds over his jacket's flap and there she was, a minute little dog in his inside pocket, looking out with a wondering look in her eyes. He takes out this very small creature and says to us, "I got us a little dog. It's a Pomeranian." We did not know what kind of breed that was until he explained it later. She was so cute! He gave it to me to hold. She was so small. About the size of a mouse best explains her appearance. She was only 4 or 5 months old. We asked if she had a name. He said yes, her name is Queenie. He said we could change it if we wanted. He had breeding papers that named the dog. We liked the name, so we kept it. Queenie it was. She was so loveable, so small. The best part was that no one had to take her out to do her duties. All we had to do is have a clean newspaper under the stove in the kitchen ready at all times. As soon as it got dirty, into the garbage it went and a clean piece of newspaper replaced it. The year was around 1934 when my father brought her home. Queenie became our most treasured pet. She followed us everywhere, into the living room, into the bedroom, into the kitchen. She loved to travel in the car. She was a great watch dog. When anyone would come near the outside door to the apartment, she would begin barking, she had a high pitched bark I guess because she was so small. She would jump up on the living room chairs and sit there or lay there. She was so small; my mother did not mind her being anywhere in the house. She had long, gold-colored hair that appeared to increase the size of the dog twofold. She became my companion until I reached 13 years old. That's when my sister was born and because of the dog's barking we had to give her away. My Uncle Dan Colucci in Connecticut took her and cared for her until the end.

When we asked my father what kind of breed this was, he began explaining some of the history concerning this type of dog. The breeder he purchased the dog from gave him the explanation. Originally, the breed was developed in China as a companion to the Emperors and their Empresses. The royalty dictated the specifications to the local dog breeders. The breeders searched all the lands for the smallest dogs they could find, with long hair and gold in color. The Pomeranian was the result. It took hundreds of years to develop. They are very popular, even today. It's because of their small size.

I loved Queenie; we were inseparable.

FATHER OWNS FIRST BUSINESS. Looking at the For Sale ads in the newspapers, he spotted a body-and-fender shop for sale in East New York, off of Atlantic Ave. Not only the contents of the shop (mostly tools), but also the lease for the building was for sale. It was an excellent opportunity for my father. All that was needed were the funds! Ah yes, the money. It just so happened that my mother and father were saving for various other things and so they had a little nest egg in the bank. Of course, he found out later that it wasn't enough. He needed more money. He had to borrow. Where would he go to borrow, the banks were very tight with lending, the Depression was still affecting all economic decisions within the commercial enterprises. The banks said "no". My father then went to those paisanos that he knew were pretty well off and could afford to advance him a few thousand dollars. He was able to scrape up enough money to make the deal. My father was now an owner of a business! The year was 1938 and my father needed me a lot. He had to get a new sign for the shop, which was "J. P.'s Auto Body Shop". It was located on Liberty Ave. in East New York. He was an immediate success. I became his weekend helper. I was 8 years old and very strong. He said he needed my strength to do the sanding (electric sanding machines had not been invented yet) and all the finishing tasks. So I began learning the auto body and fender work early on in my life. There was one process that I never did quite understand and that was the use of gasoline as the solvent for sanding patches. Although I questioned my father about the safety of this solvent, he assured me that it was the best way of sanding lead patches on the body of automobiles. Maybe by explaining the procedure, it is easier to understand the tools used at that time. First of all, a dent in a fender, although straightened out with the use of heat from an acetylene torch, does not result in a very smooth surface. The heat only brings the metal to within a relative state of the original shape, sometimes with wrinkles. More work and effort must take place to bring it to a smooth surface. The next process was the smelting lead filling. Again with the acetylene torch heating the dented surface, one would apply soldering acid to cover the whole bare metal area, then applying heat to a bar of lead until it begins to melt, with a special fireproof spatula, spreading the molten lead over the irregular spot until a relatively smooth surface has been achieved.

Believe it or not, this only brings the shape to nearly smooth. It's not ready to paint yet. Now is when I come in. That leaded spot has to be sanded. The sanding material I used was very fine Emory cloth and it had to be dipped in gasoline to allow the emery cloth to glide across the surface with ease. The gasoline also aided the cutting quality of the sanding material grit to cut into the lead better than any other liquid available. Again, I questioned this to myself (I felt there had to be a safer way) then personally experimented with water, alcohol and other types of liquids to no avail. Gasoline was without a doubt the best. In spite of the safety hazards it causes, it was the only solvent to do the job. Of course many precautions had to be taken while in use. The tray holding the solvent had to remain covered at all times when stored. No Smoking inside the shop was a must! Nowhere in the shop could there be any ignitable material. It's a good thing my father did not smoke. It was easier to maintain the no smoking requirement this way. But we had to be on the constant lookout for customers entering the shop. You cannot believe how many persons I had to warn and ask them to either put out their cigarette or go outside because the shop was filled with a flammable liquid, especially when I was sanding with the gasoline. It would evaporate quickly and fill the whole shop with gasoline vapor which is even more volatile than the liquid. Any spark or flame source would ignite the whole volume of filled air, creating an explosion. There would go the shop, all its contents and me and my Dad! It was pretty scary, but those were the conditions we had to deal with. Diligence, yes, diligence is what was needed to get us through the day. Everything was going well. Business was up. My father had his CAR! (He was able to get a total wreck free, then repaired it; voila, a new car at no cost!) What more could one want.

THE GANGSTERS. These short lived good times were going to come to an end. Just when everything was going so well, my father received a visit from two gangster type men who told him he had to move. When he asked why, they politely told him he was infringing on one of their relative's auto body shop about five blocks away. They also gave him a deadline of one week. Everything had to go, the contents, the damaged cars in for repair on the lot and the sign. The premise had to be cleaned out. Those were times of Mafia boldness. No one was safe. You did not argue with them either because that bulge under the jacket was a prominent indicator of a life or death situation. He came home and told my mother of the terrible threat. My mother said what are you going to do? He said what can I do? Hearing no answer, he began making plans to remove the contents and call all the customers who brought in their cars and asked them to take them back, he was closing. With his own car he began bringing home most of the tools, all during the week. He tried to sell some of the larger tools like the air compressor and the acetylene welding equipment but there were no buyers. Besides, one week is not enough time to sell things in those days. He did his best to empty the shop but could not do it completely. On the first day of the second week, his shop was burglarized. Everything was stolen, the sign was gone, the air compressor, the acetylene equipment, his desk, chair and every solitary object in the shop. The shop was definitely clean now! But it was sad. My father was devastated. I felt angry (being only 8 years old, what could I do), I was helpless. It took a while before my father recovered this loss. This shop meant so many things to him. It meant success in a new country, it meant a means of providing material things for the family, it meant honor and pride in the community, it was his whole life…and now it was taken away from him by gangsters. At this moment he was ready to go to the police, but my mother intervened and pleaded that he find some other way of resolving the problem. She knew that reporting the shenanigans to the police would only endanger not only himself, but the rest of the family too. It was a time when prayer was the only alternative, and pray we did.

There wasn't enough money to start another business so my father began searching the Want Ads in the newspapers looking for a job. While searching, he couldn't help taking a peek at the For Sale ads. For some reason, he became very interested in a strange deal offered there on the page. The ad explained that a Partnership was for sale in an existing body and fender shop in New York City (Manhattan). The shop was on 10th Avenue and 50th Street, on the second floor (the building had an automobile elevator to bring the vehicles up.) My father went to the address to investigate. When he arrived, he learned that the person entering the ad needed a partner to replace the one that left (due to illness). No money was needed to clinch the deal; all that was required was that the intended partner had to be a body-and-fender mechanic (which my father was). The partner was an automobile painter. The answer to their prayers! They immediately shook hands and my father was in business again. My father's partner's name was Jose'. Another "Joe". Now there were two Joes; it used to get confusing at times but often they would pronounce the other one as Jose' which differentiated them. They were great partners. They had respect for each other. They worked well together and did great financially. Everything was fine until the war broke out.

WORLD WAR II BEGINS. In Europe, Germany was beginning to threaten their neighboring countries with aggression. I was 9 years old then. Germany frightened the world by continuing its forceful occupation of Austria and the Rhineland with the invasions of Czechoslovakia followed by the invasion of Poland. This began the Second World War (WWII). The date was September 1, 1939. England and France declared war on Germany for taking Poland (who was an ally of France and England). Hitler had signed a pact with Italy, Russia and Japan early in 1936. It had built its military establishment to such a level that it could now threaten the rest of the world. The war began, and one of the first acts of Germany in the United States was to remove its German Building from the World's Fair in New York. It was dismantled and shipped back to Germany, piece by piece, the same as it was built. Only a large space remained on the World's Fair grounds. When visitors would arrive after the building was removed, they would ask, "Why is there a big empty space here-what's missing?" Then the explanation commences. "Well, you see," my father would explain, "Germany had a building there, but since the war, it was removed. They took it back to Germany." Wow...the people would say, and then they walked on. It was a strange situation. Once the building was there and now it's not. Very strange. But the World's Fair went on until 1940. The war seemed remote to attendees at the Fair.

WORLD'S FAIR-1939. That World's Fair made such an impression on me, to this day I believe I can remember most of the sites that I visited with my mother and father. Now my father owned a car so we were able to visit the World's Fair almost every weekend.

Every Saturday and Sunday we would be at the Fair, so we not only visited every building on the fair, but also we were able to enter many buildings more than once.

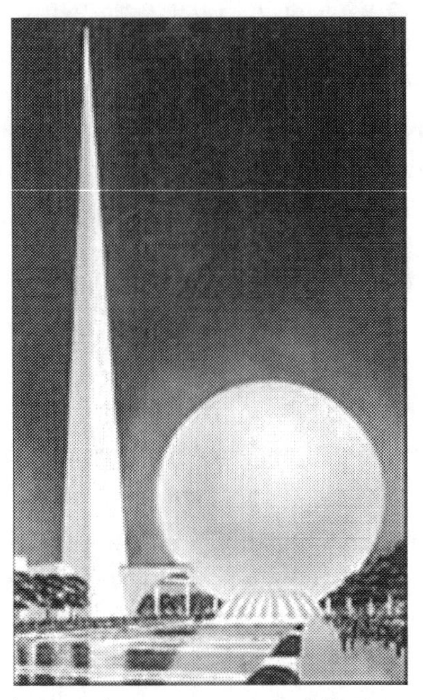

Trylon and Perisphere-1939, World's Fair, New York

I became very familiar with the exhibits to the point that I have some of them memorized. I remember the GM Building as if I were there yesterday. The little transport cars that were on a conveyance belt, holding two people, with plush upholstery and a speaker by your ears, moving slowly along the platform where you stepped into the car, into a dark short tunnel and now into blazing light with the "World of Tomorrow" gleaming below and behind glass. It was amazing, little artificial cars were moving in all directions along the highways that make-believe artists had devised. People did not move, just cars moved. They had futuristic shapes, almost round bodies, zipping along. GM had predicted that by the year 2000, most cars would be round shaped. Close, but not quite. In the center of the Fair were two structures that dominated the whole grounds, the Trylon and Perisphere. The Trylon was a tall triangular pointed structure reaching 600 feet into the air connected to a 200 foot diameter round structure that contained another miniature "World of Tomorrow" inside, that was viewed on a circular moving platform. It was spectacular! IBM, AT&T, GE, Westinghouse and NCR were the main commercial exhibitors. Westinghouse displayed the first automatic Clothes Washing Machine and Dryer on a stage. It also exhibited the first human fashioned Robot to be viewed by the public. His name was "Electro" (yes, it was a male, I think?) GM had on display a 1940 Plymouth that talked, opened its doors and hood in response to cues from the MC talking into a microphone. The car almost acted human, especially when the MC would solicit an emotion, the Plymouth's windshield wiper would swish back and forth and a hot flash would overtake the machine. The car whistled when a skimpily dressed girl passed by. The most amazing thing revealed to the audience was that there were no wires attached to the car. This was proven at the conclusion of the show when the MC walked off the stage after saying goodbye and the car followed him off the stage also saying goodbye with its doors swinging and hood going up and down and the windshield wipers going back and forth and there were no wires left behind, the stage was bare...the applause was tumultuous! What a show! I can never forget it. I must have seen it five times!

In the food sector of the fair, the dominant building was the Heinz Building. What made this company special were the giveaways. If you walked through their exhibit, a long hallway with photos of their factories and food processing systems, you learned that only humans can fill a jar of pickles. Because pickles come in various shapes and sizes, they were not able to automate this function. So, there in the photos you see women, with protective gloves, filling the jars with pickles, all day long. Although you learned a lot from the photos, the best part of visiting the Heinz building was to get a free pickle pin, a plastic green pickle with the word Heinz embossed on top, about 1 ½ inches long, with a safety pin fastener behind, and the other was that you got a free real pickle to eat. It was great! All that free stuff made you very happy. So we would frequent the Heinz building every time we visited the Fair. It was our way of saying "Thanks"...

It's at the 1939 World's Fair that I got used to waiting on line. Today, in 2007, the word online has an entirely different meaning (of course

I mean accessing the Internet), but then it meant waiting, and waiting and waiting. The lines were unmercifully l..o..n..g! (This problem was almost solved in the 1964 World's Fair by employing moving sidewalks in most of the buildings.) Before we decided to wait on a line, my father would scout around to quickly access all the buildings we planned to visit to determine which line was shorter, then selected that one out of all the others. It was a fun game, but it avoided waiting eternally for the opportunities to enter an exhibit. My father and mother also became the unofficial tour guides for all the relatives and paisanos that came to visit us with one intention, to visit the World's Fair. We would take them there on weekends and give them a royal tour of the grounds. By now, my parents knew the fair that well. At one time I remember having 7 people sleeping on the floor in our apartment, in the living room, in the kitchen. Whenever you wanted to go to the bathroom, you had to be very careful not to step on anyone. That was before sleeping bags were available and forget about air beds, they were not invented yet. All we could give them were blankets, we didn't even have enough sheets for them, nor pillows. They had to rough it and they didn't complain. As long as you gave them a cup of coffee in the morning and some jelly doughnuts, they were ready to go. I remember my Uncle Dan and Aunt Norina visiting from Waterbury, Connecticut to see the fair, along with their children Patsy, Joey and Luisa, too. My Uncle Dan would not travel without his sister Aunt Nina and her husband Uncle Pat, all sleeping on the floor. Even though my father and mother offered their bed to the elders, Aunt Nina and Uncle Pat, they wouldn't hear of it, on the floor they would go. We only had two beds in the apartment, my mother and father's double bed and mine, a twin sized bed. They refused to inconvenience us no matter how much we insisted. The Fair was the important thing, nothing else mattered. We would take them to the World's Fair and we had so much fun with them. My Uncle Dan liked to play practical jokes and my Aunt Nina liked to say funny things. Between the both of them, they had us in stitches all day. Those were good times.

MASTA MAGNIFICO. Those were only some of the incidents when relatives would come to visit to see the World's Fair, but there were many more relatives that traveled all the way to New York to see this amazing spectacle of architecture, future designs, accomplished science and technology, where predictions for tomorrow were being exhibited for any one to witness. One time I will never forget, my Aunt Luccia's first cousin, traveling all the way from Argentina, came to see the fair. An absolutely amazing feat, due not only to the distance (Argentina is about 5,303? miles away from NY) but also the fact that he drove a car all the way and it was a convertible, a Pierce Arrow, with a canvas top when it was up. He was eccentric in many ways. For instance, he was wealthy and owned a fabric weaving mill in Argentina. He had so many unusual habits, I don't know if I remember them all. This I do remember though, he would only drink mountain spring water, which he personally collected along the way, stored in a wooden barrel (kept like wine). He cooked and ate all his own food. It had to be fresh, nothing in a can or bottle. He never cooked anything in metal pots. He carried his own pots; all of them were glass glazed clay, very fragile, each one carefully wrapped in a blanket or heavy cloth. His nickname was also that of an eccentric person, he called himself Masta Magnifico (which means the Master of Magnificence). He was a very interesting person. My Aunt Luccia was so proud of him even though he was so weird. His accomplishments were unbelievable. Besides everything else, he also spoke Italian so we were able to communicate easily with him. I remember asking him a million questions, for instance, 'How did you drive through those foreign countries with some of them not having pavement to drive on?' He said it wasn't easy; he got stuck in the mud about four times and needed to pay locals to help pull him out. He carried a heavy rope for this eventuality and it was a great help then. He also spoke Portuguese aside from Argentinean, due to his business, so when he drove through Brazil, he didn't have any problem speaking to them. He was an amazing man. He wouldn't touch any meal my Aunt Luccia offered him. He only consumed food he personally prepared and only drank his own spring water. I found out later, just before he left, that he had a smaller wooden barrel of wine, stashed away in a secret place in the trunk that helped keep him going. He had so many stories to tell, I believe I forgot most of them. What I didn't forget was his name, his unusual health habits, his enormous strength, his unrelenting spirit and his car! What an admirable example. He placed an indelible mark on my mind. I never met anyone like him…and he was real! He actually did these things I described. He was without a doubt the most Unforgettable Person I have ever met! He arrived safely home after leaving in 1940.

CHILDHOOD GAMES. The games children played in Brooklyn were so varied, its going to be difficult to describe them all. Keep in mind, Brooklyn, NY was such a diverse ethnic place, games from the total globe came here to be tried and tested. The game I remember most, when I was growing up, was marbles. Marbles could be played both on a sand lot, a piece of open ground with nary a shoot of vegetation growing on it, but marbles could also be played on the street, usually along the curb. What you needed to play was a cloth bag with a drawstring full of marbles of every color combination imaginable. Everyone knows what the word "marble" means, normally a piece of limestone with striated color markings that the Greeks discovered was easily transformed to statuary. But the developer's of the "marbles" we played with, were round clear glass balls, about the diameter of a dime or nickel, with striated colors interspersed throughout the clear glass mass. Some of them were actually beautiful in their own right. There was one other key thing you needed to qualify in a game. It's called the "pee wee" or "sharp shooter". This was your single favorite small accurate shooting marble. Now it had to be treated. What you had to do was take the marble you selected under your shoe and onto a hard concrete surface and with a rolling motion, sort of grind the marble until it became opaque, very rough and voila!, it is now your sharp shooter. With this the pee wee, called that because the grinding process diminishes its size, becomes your smallest marble. Now you're ready for competition. "Who wants to play?" you would be asking friends. If you were on a sand lot, you would carve a semi hole in the ground with the heel of your shoe and then smooth it out with your hands. This hemispherical hole in the ground was called "home". Basically the object was to win the opponent's marbles by hitting them with your sharp shooter out of the playing range. Now the rules get a little involved so I'm not going to outline them, but I can't imagine how many hours I played this game. It was so much fun and required some skill to be considered a marble player. It was important to establish yourself with a reputation of being a good marble player otherwise nobody would play with you. Competition was being learned both in practice and in philosophy.

We also played numerous other games like "Kick-n-The Can," a hide-and-seek game where the one that's "It" has to retrieve a tin can that was kicked by the opponent and put the can back in its original place, meanwhile all the participants go and hide. The object of the game is for the one who is "It" to find everyone who is hiding, tapping the can three times every time at every find. This game was so full of laughs, sometimes the laughs were so intense you would lose your balance and actually fall down on the ground, laughing so hard. We had so much fun with this game, it was very popular especially since you play this with two kids, or ten or even 15 kids, it didn't matter.

Another game we played was "Simon Says". We played this right on the sidewalk with a leader who was selected using the one-potato-two-potato selection technique, you know the one. The others stood in file in front of the leader and began following his instructions, performing all the gestures commanded, of course prefaced by the phrase "Simon Says" otherwise you were out (you must leave the game). We had loads of fun with this one.

One of our other popular games was called "Mummy". As long as there are two or more participants, you can play this game. Anyone can call out the word "Mummy" at which point everyone playing must "freeze" into a motionless position. Anyone who moves is out and looses.

We also played "Stoop Ball". This is a simple game of throwing a soft rubber ball at the steps of a house or building, whatever, with the object of the game centering on the ability to aim and hit the corner of the step which for some reason or other is called a "killer ball". I guess because the ball comes back at you with increased speed so you must be very alert to catch it otherwise it will kill you, meaning if you don't catch it and it hits you, it's going to hurt (almost "killing" you- in Brooklyn's dialect). This game you play alone, so it was a frequent choice when nobody was around. When playing it with others, you would keep track of the number of "killer" balls caught. The one with the most wins.

As you can see, most of our games were played outdoors. Very few games were played indoors. In fact I can't remember any indoor game except card playing. So these were some of the games we played when I was growing up, with the games becoming more strenuous as I got older and more difficult to execute, therefore more challenging. It occupied so much of our time and was so much fun, in retrospect, it was a great childhood. The period of time that describes this phase of my growing up is between four years old to eleven years old. These were the games that I remember, of course there were others.

CHAPTER 3 . . . THE BOY

New People mentioned in this Chapter

My Grandfather ....Michele (Michelino) Petti
My father's Partner in business ....Jose' Rodrigez
My English Teacher-High School ....Mrs. Champagne
My Economics Teacher-High School.................................. Dr. Ryan
My School Friend...Philip Bonomo
My School Friend.......................................Alfonso (Sonny) Nunziata
Ann's Young Friends ....Minnie, Rosie, Carroll
Gus' Young Friends ....Mickey, Nicky, Tony

1941

BOYHOOD BEGINS. The year was 1941, when I believe my boyhood started. I was eleven years old. My boyhood was normal instead of being exceptional. I grew up in a Brooklyn neighborhood like every other boy (thank God). Many historical occurrences (which I will give details about later) around me could be considered extraordinary, but since I was so young they didn't affect me that much. I attended school at P.S. 23 with regular results. I was not a genius as my parents had hoped, but I was not a borderline student either. My grades were in the A to C average and I never remember failing a subject. My favorites were Arithmetic and Science, with English and Geography a close second. I had difficulty with History (couldn't relate the dates in my brain) and home room (thought it was a waste of time).

My Father-Shipbuilding

WORLD WAR II BEGINS.

This is one of those historical events I alluded to above. There is no doubt in my mind that my boyhood started around 1941 because events were beginning to make an impact on me. In this year, the Second World War exploded into full bloom! Up to now, it was only Germany that was at war, occupying one country after another in Europe with the rest of the world looking on. At eleven years old I was beginning to see things in a different way. I believe I even understood some grown-up things by now. Although the U.S. did not have shortages yet, some things were becoming scarce. For instance, clothing was increasing in price at an escalating pace. Selections in the clothing area were diminishing. Fashions had almost come to a full stop. Things were starting to get tough. Remember, on December 7, 1941, Japan had attacked Pearl Harbor in Hawaii (the islands were a U.S. Territory at the time and under our protection-Hawaii had not become a state yet) and almost annihilated the U.S. Naval Fleet. War was declared on December 8, 1941 by our president, Franklin Delano Roosevelt, between the United States of America and the Empire of Japan (Japan was under the rule of Emperor Hirohito). Britain, an ally of the U.S. (represented by Winston Churchill) also declared war on Japan at the same time. Then on December 11, 1941, Germany declared war on the United States, and since Italy was their ally, we were at war against Italy, too. This last round of declarations placed almost all nations at war with Germany, Italy and Japan. The Russians appeared to be fighting for survival or gain; I'm not sure which. Stalin was the Premier of Russia and led a Communist Government, an ideology that did not sit too well with other nations, so the Russians seemed to be on their own in this world war. It was a terrible war; more casualties occurred during this war than all other wars put together.

This war included oceans, the Atlantic and the Pacific. It was common knowledge that Germany was busy developing weapons back in 1939 to the present. In 1942, the newspapers got word that Germany was developing rockets with jet engines. Can you imagine that? They were inventing unbelievable weapons that the world only dreamed about. No country knew anything about jet engines at the time or rockets for that matter. Developing actual working models would catapult Germany into the lead in this war and they could possibly become a terrible threat to the world! Things were very scary at the time. Every country in the world had begun some type of a counter strategy to stop Hitler in his world-domineering scheme. He wanted to conquer the world. Somebody had to STOP him at all costs. This appeared to be the basic theme in 1942.

WAR EFFORT INVENTIONS. As I recall, the beginning of 1942 started all the shortages. Almost all the rationed foods and products were a result of the Armed Forces needs, as they were fighting the war. The rationing of sugar started. This is the one food that hurt me the most. Of course, gasoline was rationed, as was alcohol (the type used for booze - that hurt every alcoholic person in the USA!) and for once in our history, every American was sober! (just kidding) Also, nylon stockings for women were nonexistent. All the nylon produced had to go into parachute production for the GI's. We had to work hard to help our servicemen fight the war. My father quit his job in the body-and-fender business and found work at the Port Newark Navy Ship Yard, building ships for the Navy. He was proud of being a new American citizen and wanted to be part of the effort in winning the war. Since he had a good knowledge of metal, he was asked to manually fabricate some metal parts that could not be machined or produced in an automated way. But it didn't take him long to find a way of forming the parts he had to form by hand, on a machine and automatically. He invented two processes for not only producing the parts automatically, but allowed them to increase production of the parts significantly. He was awarded two certificates commending his contributions (he donated the patents to the Navy Yard).

He finally ended up in a department where the parts had to be made by hand and there were no two ways about it. But he enjoyed his work, and I remember a story that should be told about his experiences there. My mother would prepare his lunch every day and, since my father loved eggs, he requested all of his sandwiches be made with some sort of recipe including eggs. So, my mother proceeded on this premise; she made him countless frittatas, with asparagus, peppers, onions, potatoes, you name it she made it and with eggs. When she didn't have time to make a frittata, she would just scramble-up some eggs and put them on the bread. Meanwhile, at the plant, my father's co-workers were observing the endless stream of egg sandwiches my father was eating until one day one of them walked up to my father and said, "You know Joe, your face is getting a little yellowish and wrinkly, are you feeling all right?" My father replied, "Yes, I'm all right," then went home and mentioned it to my mother. She looked at his face, studying it closely and said, "I don't see any yellowing or wrinkly ness, I don't know what they're talking about. Tell them they are seeing things." So he went back to work the next day and said to the person that made the comment, "My wife thinks you are seeing things." But the co-worker insisted that my father's face was getting even deeper yellow as they were talking. Then he said, "Joe, maybe you're eating too many eggs, your face is starting to look like scrambled eggs!" They both started laughing so hard a foreman had to step in and insist they return to work. But the laughter went on even while they were working. When my father returned home, he implored my mother to stop making the egg lunches, for a while at least. My father had a great sense of humor.

In 1942 my mother became pregnant again. She was 36 years old. I'm not sure what the reason for the occurrence was, but I remember my father saying something about "wouldn't it be nice if we had a girl?" If he had asked me that question at the time, I would have said "No" (just kidding). But I wasn't asked and so we trudged on. I say "trudged on" because at that time there were many unusual changes in the Petti environment taking place. For instance, at the time my father and mother began another small business.

DRY GOODS SHOP. They opened up what was called at the time a "Dry Goods" store. This was their second try at opening up a small business. Since my mother was so knowledgeable about clothing, she felt selling a limited line of clothing and other dry goods would prove to be a lucrative endeavor. My father found a small storefront located on Metropolitan Avenue, two houses away from my Aunt Luccia's house. My father rented it. I helped him install the fixtures and furniture, the shelves and the lights. It was a cheerful little store, we used light color paint to cover the walls. The large sign arrived, it read; Petti's Dry Goods. On the second line it read; Women's Underwear, Stockings and Table Linens. Finally in the fall of 1941 my father and mother opened the shop. We had a gala opening. All the nearby paisanos visited the store to wish us well and Zia Luccia and the family sent a beautiful potted, large rubber plant, with a big red ribbon that read "Success".

We were very happy, we were in business again! My father was so motivated to own a business, it seemed to be the only thing he would talk about. My mother felt the same way. There was no stopping them, not the war, not the lack of money, not the pregnancy, nothing stood in the way! And guess who was going to be the main store attendant in this whole plan? As it turned out, it was me. Because the store had to be manned from morning to night, we had to have all our meals in the back of the shop. There were two rooms behind the front of the store, one was set up as a kitchen and the other, behind it, was a storage room. There was also a toilet adjacent to the storage room. We were very comfortable except that my mother had to cook all the meals there. After school, I was needed to attend to the customers. I couldn't go out and play too often. Boy, did I learn the Dry Goods business. My most embarrassing moments were when a customer came in and asked to see the braziers. "Mom, you got to come out here," I would cry in desperation. Then I had to go inside the kitchen to tend to whatever meal she was preparing. Now I'm the cook; there's no end to the chores I had. It was very interesting. I learned a lot. For instance, I learned that there is such a large size for women's bloomers, (that's what they were called then-they're called panties now) as size 6X !!! I don't know how many inches around they are, but they are so big that even folded in half, I was not able to hold them stretched out for the customer to view them. It was a lot of fun too. We were doing very well especially in the stocking department. Nylon stockings, which women preferred, were nowhere to be found. They just could not be supplied. But my father found a supplier in New York City, where they purchased their wholesale merchandise, who had an endless inventory of silk stockings, a close second to nylon but in great demand. It seemed like we were supplying the whole neighborhood with silk stockings. We were doing very well.

JOANN IS BORN. My only sister! The year was 1943, I was going to be 13 years old. The month was June and the day was the 19th, when she was born. She was named Josephine Anna (we called her Joann), after our Grandmother Petti. We were all happy about her birth and all looking forward to her coming home.

My Favorite Picture of Joann-1945

The time was set; it was a Sunday, when the store was closed. My father and I went to the hospital to bring them home. My mother was ready and we bundled up Joann at the hospital and carefully brought them to the car. Joann was very quiet, cooing and gaggling all the way. This was great, I thought, no crying! When we got home, some neighbors were standing on the stairway, all asking about the baby as we climbed up to the door of the building. Finally, we got to the apartment on the second floor. My father had the crib ready; my mother placed Joann in it, removed the blankets and just stood there with me and my father, enjoying the beautiful baby lying there. She was so beautiful and she didn't cry (not yet anyway). We then went into the kitchen and my father began reading the mail that arrived the day before. He opened a telegram that was written in Italian. It read: "We are sorry to inform you that your mother and sister were killed in an accidental bombing of a hospital in Naples on (then it gives the time and date.)" My father gives out a shrilling scream, "No! It cannot be!" he cried out. "Not my mother!" "Not my sister!" "Oh God, tell me this did not happen!" My mother almost pulled the paper from his hand to ensure that he read it correctly, at which time she looked at my father and began to cry; "Pippinello mi dispiace, O Dio aiuto ci!", my dearest Joseph, I'm so sorry, Lord help us! Then they both began sobbing as the reality sunk in. There I was, standing in the kitchen, watching this very sad scene. I didn't know what to do. I never met my grandmother who just died; neither had I ever met my father's sister, who was killed. All I knew was that my father was crying and my mother was crying, so I began to cry, too. My mother was also hugging my father who was standing, so I went over and hugged both of them, as we all cried.

It was a very sad moment for my father and mother, to lose two loved ones at the same time. The reason the telegram called that catastrophe an "accident" is that Allied Bomber Planes were to avoid bombing hospitals at all costs. Unfortunately, this time there was an error and as a result, many innocent people were killed. My father told me later, the reason my grandmother was in the hospital was due to her diabetes, which was in an advanced stage. My father's sister was visiting at the time. It was destiny. That is life,,,meanwhile in the bedroom is little baby Joann, but this time she is crying. Not because of the sadness, but because of hunger. By now, the baby needed to be fed. She was breastfed so there was nothing to prepare. All my mother had to do was lift her from the crib and the crying diminished to a low whimper.

As soon as my mother offered her breast, she was quietly filling up with her meal, happy and content.

It was beautiful again, having a little baby sister and the family together, even though some sadness had entered our lives. We would survive and things would be well again. Not only that, but the next day, Monday, we had to open the store and we had to be ready with dealing with customers. We also had to provide accommodations for my baby sister at the store, which my father already took care of. We had another crib at the shop where Joann was very comfortable. You couldn't blame me for pampering her all the time. My mother used to get annoyed at times; "Why are you bothering your sister all the time, she needs to sleep…leave her alone". That would take me away awhile, but not for long. Everything was going swell until one day I asked my mother for permission to go out to be with my friends and she said "no", she needed me to watch my sister, while she takes care of the customers in the store. Whoa… didn't see that coming. "But Mamma", I said; "That's not fair". "Now I'm not able to go with my friends anymore?" I said. My mother asked me to sit down. She could see that I was very upset. She was talking in Italian. I'm going to use English to quote her; "You know Augusto (she called me Augusto), your father has to go to work every day, I have to take care of Joann, the store and the cooking every day. I know it's difficult for you to be denied being with your friends at times. You see the sacrifice your father and I are making; now we have to ask you to make a small sacrifice too. Soon, we will be able to hire someone to take care of the store so your sacrifice will end. All I ask is that you be patient just for a little while". I understood and was able to accept it. Time went on. Soon it was 1944, Joann was walking and talking. Then my father became ill.

PAPA HAS AN ULCER. First, my father asked our cousin, Dr. Iamele, what could be making him so sick in the stomach. Dr. Iamele recommended him to Dr. Kessler, a gastro specialist. After visiting Dr. Kessler, my father's worst fears were realized. The diagnosis was "peptic ulcer". My father asked if it meant surgery. Dr. Kessler said; "In your case it's borderline; with proper diet and diligent care, you may be able to correct the condition." My father asked what the regime would entail, then after hearing the instructions and the diet required, he immediately realized he could not continue to run the business and the store had to be closed. After my mother learned of the situation, she agreed that the shop had to be closed, my father's health was more important than the business, she said.

We ran a two week going out of business sale and practically sold everything in the shop. The Dry Goods store was closed. It was very disappointing to turn your back on a successful business but the decision had to be made. Although it was unfortunate, my mother who was the driving force behind the business took it very well. Her attention became focused on my father's health. My father had to make intense changes in his diet, substituting many alien foods to the regular Italian foods my mother used to prepare. For instance, the drink of choice now was milk, not wine. All acid causing foods, such as orange juice, lemon juice, etc. were taboo. Alkaline foods were the preference from now on. Slowly, my father's condition eased up. He was feeling better everyday and seemed stronger as time progressed. They were good signs.

My mother was encouraged to continue with this new direction of meal preparation. She didn't mind so much, to abandon some of her old ways concerning customary Italian foods in place of curative selections of food for my father's well being. My father was getting better, but it took time and a great deal of effort. We were there for him and he appreciated our concern and efforts. He would tell us often how much he loved us for being understanding (he knew how much we missed the Italian foods). The important thing is he was on his way to recovery. That was the objective. Meanwhile, World War II was in its most intense phase. Germany had waged war on Russia too. The whole world was at war. The United States was conducting a major war effort in Europe and another major war effort in the Pacific Ocean against the Japanese. Every aspect of living was influenced one way or another by the war.

STREET VENDORS. Between the ages of 11 and 14, the world began to change for me. I now was able to see and understand many things that, although I saw before, did not quite appreciate the significance of their existence. One focus of interest was the many and varied "street vendors" that roamed the streets of New York at that time. They were a phenomenon that has passed. Their presence is sorely missed. They used to be everywhere; one of my friends would say they were coming out of the woodwork. There they were, on the streets, selling every conceivable article imaginable. Hot Dogs and Sauerkraut, Ice Cream Cones and Ice Pops, Knishes, Jelly Apples, Popcorn, Hot Tamales, in the winter Hot Chestnuts and Charlotte Rouses. Some of these I'm going to describe because you may never have encountered them.

Everyone knows what hot dogs from a pushcart are, but did you know that some vendors were such great chefs that they also offered "Greek onions" (a delicious combination of sautéed onions in paprika and other delicate spices) that they would smother the hot dog with, instead of sauerkraut? Not that sauerkraut wasn't offered and wasn't very good too, it's that some offered something else. Then there were vendors who made delicious beans that they poured over the hot dog. I don't know some sort of chili beans without the meat, I suspect. Some pushcarts had four compartments the guy would open and close. The first move he made was to grab a fresh roll from a glass compartment on top of the stand. Then with great dexterity he would open the roll to make room for the hot dog. Then with some sort of a grabber in his other hand, he would open compartment number one, that's were the hot dogs swam in hot water (not boiling), withdraw the hot dog and place it on the roll, close compartment number one, then quickly open compartment number two or three or four depending on what you answered when he asked, sauerkraut, onions or beans. Very skillful execution of rendering a pushcart hot dog and it only cost five cents! Of course he also carried Coca Cola, and any other drink you could think of at the time. All these items were all sold from Pushcarts manned by vendors going from street to street, all along the curbs of the city, ringing bells or singing a jingle they made up or just yelling the names of their wares as loud as they can. People were mostly in their apartments or in their homes and sometimes keenly sensed the presence of these vendors outside, tuning in their ears for the sounds they made, then running outside to meet them. This was another one of those phenomena that the city developed among its people. It was almost "uncanny", how they would know when one of these pushcarts were on the street close to their residence.

My theory is that it's all got to do with supply and demand. When a city dweller wants something, there will be someone ready and willing to provide it. The pushcarts in the 1930's and 1940's prospered because of this economic principle. And this is hard to believe, but their products (if it was food) were absolutely delicious. Everyone wondered how they could produce such fine products and then deliver them to your actual door, hot and steaming, or ice cold and freezing. The answer was their ingenuity! The pushcarts that carried hot foods were fueled with burning charcoal that was stoked by the attendant all day long, adding charcoal as needed for the whole trip (the charcoal was neatly stored in a forward compartment of the pushcart). Those that carried cold or frozen items used what was called hot ice which was carbon dioxide, compressed until it became a solid, reaching a very low temperature and slowly reverting back to harmless carbon dioxide as it melted over the period of a day. The perfect coolant for this purpose. Some mail-order companies still use it today to keep the product they're sending frozen. Also, knishes deserve an explanation. Vendors would transport this wonderful potato product right to you, on the street. This is my favorite potato recipe in the whole world. It is made with mashed potatoes, with a hint of onion, salt and pepper, wrapped in delicate dough, cut into approximately three inch squares and baked. Pure heaven! I loved them (can't find the same quality they had)! The other foods you're familiar with, so I will lastly explain hot tamales. Although this is a Mexican food, it was so delicious and popular; pushcarts had it in those days. It is basically a corn meal mixed with herbs and spices, inside of corn husks and tied. It looks like a small corn cob when it's placed in a paper server and it's delicious too. In this manner, they were able to deliver a hot and delicious food right to where you were standing or living. Is there anything like that today? I'm afraid not. In the 1950's, after World War II, pushcarts were banned from the streets as free agents. Starting then, you had to apply to the City Commerce department and apply for a license before you could sell on the street. That one move by the city eliminated more than two thirds of all the pushcarts that existed. The fee was so large that most of them couldn't afford it, therefore abandoned the enterprise altogether. No more pushcarts, only a hot dog stand now and then (manned by someone who could justify the large fee charged by the government). Those that did not gain a license to peddle the streets, if caught by a policeman, would be heavily fined, and that would be the end of him or her (there were some, but very few women pushing carts-it was a very hard job). This is how pushcarts were usually retired: they would bring their pushcarts to the junkyard, add it to the pile and go out and get a legitimate job. It was kind of sad because it ended an era that served an important and enjoyable service to New Yorkers. Oh well, it was great while it lasted. I'm fortunate to have that experience in my life.

Those were just the food vendors, but the city was full of other types of vendors that roamed the streets, mostly using horses to pull their wagons, loaded with all sorts of things. There were clothing wagons, pots and pans wagons, vegetable wagons, fruit wagons, there were fish wagons (believe it or not, they would bring fresh fish to your door) and last, but not least, there were junk wagons.

I should include the house delivery vendors in my review of door services available to city dwellers. There were Milkmen who delivered all kinds of milk products (right to the door and placed the bottles and articles in an insulated metal box that sat outside the door) like butter and eggs. Then there was the Bread-man, (my best friend's father was a Bread-man-the Nunziata's) who delivered Italian bread and related products like bread crumbs, Italian rolls, biscotti con peppe, etc., who came right to the door, knocked on the door and had a basket of bread products for you to choose from. Wasn't that neat! In fact, a large American company became famous because of home delivery. It was "Dugan's" and the deliverer was called the "Dugan Man", who was in command of hundreds of cakes, muffins, pies and pastry of all kinds that you could choose to purchase. I mean it was a different world. He would come to your door, knock and ask if you wanted any of their products, then the question and answer routine would begin; "What kind of pies do you have", asked the resident; "Well lets see, I have Blueberry, Apple, Lemon and Banana Cream", answered the Dugan Man; "Do you have any Rhubarb pie asked the customer; "I'm sorry, not today", he would say and the dialogue could go on and on because they made so many products (very much like Entenmanns today-except Dugan's delivered to your door).

There probably were more than those I mentioned, but these are the ones I remember. In fact, I believe it was possible for a Brooklyn resident never to have to leave their apartment or home to survive. It was an amazing time. I'm glad I witnessed this. I hope I have described it well enough to at least convey the scene aspect. Many of these institutions no longer exist...

We also received services from other vendors as I recall. Their wares were less in demand, but they would visit (I suspect they had us scheduled, although they would never admit it) periodically and usually at the exact time they were needed, uncanny don't' you think? One of them called himself the Neighborhood Jeweler. He was Jewish and proud of it. A sentence wouldn't be spoken without adding "you know I'm Jewish", "Yes we know", we would say. Oh, this is going to floor you...and he spoke perfect Italian! My mother would buy anything from him because they could talk to each other in Italian. It was a tremendous advantage over other salesmen. He had the Italian neighborhood locked in. As I remember, he was in such demand, I remember him actually telling customers that they would have to wait to place orders, the demand was so heavy. What a world that was... later on, my mother told me that the neiborhood jeweler had retired wealthy. No surprise. The other vendors that I cannot forget were the Fuller Brush Man and the Vacuum Cleaner Man. The Fuller Brush Man would somehow magically appear about every two months, just when you're out of the cleaners he sold and possibly a new mop, or brush of any kind. It was like clockwork. They also did very well in terms of sales. And then there was the vacuum man, even though you didn't need a new vacuum every time he came, because he new he sold you one last year, but he knew you needed more bags for the vacuum. And of course you would buy more bags. He had you on that schedule and sure enough, he came just in the nick of time. Oh, sure....give me a break. In spite of their chicanery, as far as Brooklynites were concerned, they were a needed group; they made living a little easier and were really essential to the activities of the day.

Worth mentioning are the other vendors that provided things that have disappeared today. Some brought the product to you in a vehicle and some provided the necessity in a store front that you had to walk to. One of those moving vendors I'm sure you will remember was the Good Humor Man. First you would hear the ringing of loud bells, ringing and ringing, then you would look in the direction of the ringing and sure as day, there is the Good Humor man. Quick, run to Mom and get some money (you didn't need much because the ice cream at the time was only five cents). I believe the Good Humor truck was the last to go in the subject of has beens. If I'm not mistaken, it was with us in large numbers till the seventies. And believe it or not, sometimes I still see a Good Humor truck around (hope it's not my imagination). At the beginning, in the forties, refrigerated trucks were not invented yet. The way they kept the ice cream frozen was with the same compressed carbon dioxide solids used by the street vendors. The back of the truck was like a gigantic icebox. It worked very well keeping the ice cream frozen and it brought us a lot of pleasure (ice cream being the highest ranking comfort food in the world.)

The next two neighborhood favorites were Mellow Rolls and Egg Cream. You could only buy Mellow Rolls in a store that sold ice cream and other frozen products. Mellow Rolls was the most delicious ice cream invented by man! (My opinion) The shape was that of a small tin can (like the tomato paste can size). I believe the flavors were limited. I think you could have either vanilla or chocolate. The interesting part about the Mellow Roll was the cone that held the ice cream. It was a sugar wafer, shaped like a half barrel, with a holding part underneath, quit similar to a regular square bottom cone we have today. It was neat. When the attendant took the ice cream cylinder out of the freezer, it came wrapped in a heavy paper cover that had two tabs, one tab protruding on each side. He would place the cone on the counter; hold onto each of the two tabs and pull. The ice cream would, unravel and easily fall into the half barrel shaped part of the cone. It's ready, all you have to do to it is eat it; and we did. I don't know how many of those I downed as a boy! We all did. It was the most popular ice cream ever and it had to be, because it was Sooooooo Meloooow and delicious! It, unfortunately, has disappeared too.

You will not believe some of the facts that relate to the Egg Cream. First of all, there is no egg in the drink. Second, there is no cream in the drink either. I don't know who named it, but whoever it was missed its contents completely. Let me explain. It's a soda fountain drink and very delicious when made properly. I worked at my best friend's father's Casper's Soda Fountain Shop often, helping when there were crowds, so I can speak with some authority. You begin with a soda glass (the shape the Coca-Cola Company made famous), and then you pump chocolate syrup into the empty glass (about two tablespoons full). Next, you add about four ounces of part frozen whole milk to the glass and lastly, you squirt with high pressure, plain seltzer water into the mix until you achieve a frothy, creamlike chocolate soda. And there you have it, an Egg Cream. Go figure...but absolutely delicious! I believe this has disappeared from our society also. Oh, and if you want to have lots of laughs, read the book called "Egg Cream", by Mel Brooks (it's very small-reads quickly). I guarantee it, you will die laughing!

Finally we have reached Italian Lemon Ice. This is a summer delicacy only known to the Italians in Italy until Italian-American Immigration began and the Italians brought their treasured secret lemon ice recipes to the U.S. Every Italian Lemon Ice vendor not only made their own lemon ice, but mixed it according to a secret recipe given to them by their father, who received it from his father and so on. Needless to say, each recipe was unique and had its own characteristics to the point where discriminate tasters would go out of their way to savor someone's Italian Lemon Ice (and there was no other flavor - only lemon ice - no choices in those days) as soon as they heard about a new one. Then the tasters would have them all in categories, The Smoothest, The One Without Pits, The Sweetest, The Most Bitter, The Best, The Worst, they would catalogue the Italian Lemon Ice establishments in Brooklyn, using every adjective in the English language to describe its taste. For me, The Best was Casper's Soda Fountain Shop Lemon Ice on Graham Avenue, near Jackson Street. The Italian Lemon Ice he made was ambrosia of the gods (and that's not because his son was my best friend either). You had to be there when Casper would make his ice. I witnessed the scene so many times, I can never forget it. Talk about eccentricities, you will not believe this description and it's all true. The first thing I learned about the process is that Mr. Casper would NOT give the recipe to his children or anyone else for that matter under any circumstance! He was very ill once, in the hospital. The shop was being run by his two mature sons. They said to him, "Poppa, we need to make the lemon ice, people are coming and want it, you have to give us the recipe." "Never," he would reply. "Let them go to Louie's until I get home." This is how it went concerning this one family secret. I don't know if he ever gave it to them. The other strange behavior was when Casper would begin the process of making his famous lemon ice. Everything was done in apparent secrecy (except his son and I were so crafty, we saw everything he did except mix it).

From spying on him all those years, we managed to write down all the ingredients, so we knew what went into it. But because he would close, lock and bar the door, after dragging in all the ingredients, we never learned the process of the actual mix. We did a lot of speculating. For instance, we were almost positive he boiled water and the sugar. We deduced this when, occasionally, he would forget something and come out of the room he was mixing the ingredients in. When he opened the door, large bellows of steam would come out behind him. I would say; "Duke, (my friend's nickname) did you see all that steam coming out?" Duke responded, "He's cooking something. What could it be - he dragged in lemons in a wooden case, a sack of sugar and lots of big pots?" "Could he be boiling the lemons?" I asked. "Naw, he's probably making a syrup with the sugar and water." "I think you're right," I would add. What we were not able to determine was how or when he introduced the lemon juice that was squeezed out of the fruit into the syrup. It may seem trivial, but the method used to mix the lemon juice into the syrup could make the difference that delineates Casper's Italian Lemon Ice from Louie's Italian Lemon Ice, so we must not trivialize that. The frustration for us was that we could not find out how he did it. That he kept a secre" forever; we could only guess. But there is no doubt that in the summer time, in Brooklyn, in our neighborhood, Italian Lemon Ice was the only thirst quencher one needed and it was Cooool and Sooooo Gooooood!

STREET GAMES. As I was getting older, I was able to participate in more and more street games that were the mode at the time. I don't know where to begin. There were so many. Ok, here's the first one. It was called Stick Ball. Two teams were setup. A long thin stick (the handle cut from a wooden broom, used for sweeping), was used as a bat. A secluded side street was chosen. The ball was soft rubber, filled with air. Three bases were outlined in chalk along the street curbs and center. The game begins. A coin is flipped. Heads you're up, tails you're up. The losing team assumes the base positions. A pitcher lobs the first ball to the batter. A Hit. The batter runs toward first base. The ball is caught by the opposing player. A throw to first base. Not in time. Player is safe at first. And so on. It is identical to baseball with some small differences in rules to fit in with the environment such as, if a car is coming, the inning does not count and is played again, when the car is through. It was a lot of fun. We played this a lot. To attest to the difficulty, someday if you have an old broom handle as a bat, secure a soft, small rubber ball and see if you can hit it. It's not that easy, I guarantee you...

We also played a lot of basketball. There were two schoolyards where quite a number of poles and hoops existed and we were allowed to use them when school was out. I don't know how many hours I spent playing basketball. As soon as two or more guys would show up at the schoolyard (of course, one would bring a basketball), basketball was the choice game to play. My mother could tell you how many times I went home with torn pants from playing basketball. "Te straccadi il calzone un altra volta?" 'You tore your pants again,' she would say as I entered the apartment. It would get her so upset. I didn't see the problem (maybe it's because I didn't have to repair it.) This happened so many times that it became a part of my life. Later, I will tell you a story about my torn pants that could have cost me from becoming your mother's boyfriend! That will come later. But basketball was one of my favorite games at this age. Since I was tall, I had an advantage over the shorter guys. My only regret is that I never learned the official rules of the game. To this day, basketball is a mystery to me, especially when I hear terms on TV such as "foul" (there were no fouls in street basketball), or a three pointer (all basketball throws could only get one point-no matter where you were on the court), and so on. It's interesting for all the basketball I played as a boy, it should be my favorite sport today, but it isn't. Is that unusual or what?

INSIDE - HOME GAMES. Most of the games we played at home during my boyhood I believe are still enjoyed today. It's remarkable that they have endured time and change and not been affected that much. My friends and I liked to play Monopoly a lot. We were always playing Checkers. My father taught me how to play the Italian card game called Brisca (Sweep). So we played a lot of cards. I recall at the time the card game called Canasta was invented and became a sensation, everyone was playing Canasta! Then I learned to play Chess on my own, but had few friends to play the game with (not many kids played Chess). When I got older and I was attending parties with girls, "Spin The Bottle" became the game of preference. Whoever invented that game had to be a genius! All you had to do is be lucky enough to be sitting in the right place so the bottle will point to you and at the other end a pretty girl, which now gave you permission to kiss that girl (without reprimand at that)! WOW...that was some game I thought! We wanted to play it all the time when there were girls and we were indoors.

There is another game we played that I don't see has lasted and that was pitching pennies against the wall. The object of the game was to flip a penny at the wall, hitting the wall and randomly bouncing onto another penny that belonged to the opponent. You would win that penny and pick it up as a reward. You would go home with a pocket full of pennies. No wonder I used to tear my pants all the time. Pennies weigh a lot!

STREET SHOOTING INCIDENT. It must have been around 1941, I was about eleven years old, and I was traveling on the subway slowly approaching the Metropolitan Avenue station. I got up from my seat before the train came to a stop, and stood in front of the sliding doors holding onto the pole near the doors. The train stops. The doors open. I get off the train and walk along the platform toward the upward stairs to the street. I was walking up the last five steps. My head was just above the ground level and I had a view of the street and all the surrounding. All of a sudden I heard screeching tires of a car, then I hear rapid gun shots coming from a machine gun. I saw the car. With the shots, I saw people who were waiting for the trolley car on the corner falling down" I saw five people fall to the ground immediately. The shots began again and another six people fell to the ground. There were about fourteen people waiting there. The car sped away, turning the next corner, with tires screeching again and accelerating to a high speed, disappearing from the street. Meanwhile, I didn't know whether to come out of the stairwell where it was safe, or to run to the aid of those who were shot. After seeing the car speed away, I felt it was safe to surface onto the street. That's what I did. I immediately went to those who were crawling across the traffic lanes of the street, to get them out of traffic danger, but they were bleeding and were crying in pain. All I could do was to help this man who was shot get across the street by pulling his arm and dragging him to the corner ice cream parlor, then asked the owner of the shop to call the police. He said he already called them. He said he would take care of this one, to go and help the others. I ran out in the street again, but now taxicabs were stopping, running to the aid of those injured, taking those that were able to the hospital. Other bystanders began helping others that needed assistance. Some were standing over those who were killed, determining their status. It happened so fast. Because I was so young, I was sent home and away from the scene by the police who came immediately. At that moment, I did not know what was happening or why. When I told my mother and father about the incident, they immediately suspected the Cosa Nostra. That was the type of thing those gangsters would do. Sure enough, in the next day's newspaper, the Daily News Headlines read: "GANGLAND STREET SHOOTING IN BROOKLYN", with the explanation that there were five people killed and the Cosa Nostra member who was targeted was standing among that group of people waiting for transportation. Five innocent people were killed, they injured their target but did not kill him and injured six others including the one they were after. In all, eleven people were shot. New York City was in an uproar. The Commissioner of Police promised the apprehension and prosecution of these criminals explaining that extra officers were in pursuit of the perpetrators. That experience left an impression that remains with me to this day. I'm surprised at the composure I mustered that day. Little did I know, this experience would be repeated in future days, but in entirely different ways and the strength I showed during these moments would be needed again.

1944 GRADUATION. This was the year I graduated from Grammar School, PS 23. In my Brooklyn, NY locality, since the high schools were so crowded, junior high schools were built to take care of the overflow. Two years were spent in junior high and two years in an actual high school of your choice (if you qualified). This reduced the number of students in high schools by 50%.

Keep in mind that New York City (which includes all five boroughs, Manhattan, Richmond (or Staten Island), Brooklyn, Queens and the Bronx had a population of over 11 million people that year! The existing high schools could not handle the number of students reaching high school age to be admitted, so junior high schools were quickly built and began relieving the congestion that was caused due to the increase in population. The junior high school I was graduating from was PS 157, a good school, within walking distance of our apartment house. It was great. We studied algebra and geometry in those hallowed rooms and were taught by caring and dedicated teachers. I learned a lot there. Only one incident I could have done without. One day a student (Anthony Simonelli-a casual friend of mine from the block) entered his homeroom and point blank "shot" his teacher dead. What a terrible thing to have happened! And in my school. And a friend of mine. The only thought that came into my mind (when I learned of the news) was that unfortunately, and everyone knew this, he came from a bad family. His father was a gangster (don't know if he was in the Gang or a free lance criminal) and I never heard anything nice about his mother and his brothers and sister who were all in jail. It was probably not his entire fault that he was mentally deranged; he seemed like a good kid when we would be playing together on the street. He lived on the next block from our apartment house. The neighborhood was in disarray after it happened. We couldn't believe what took place. Why would this kid do this? Why, why, why. No answers. No one could have made it that terrible for him to revert to this action. Unbelievable! For weeks and months, the discussion on the streets was all about this story, trying to analyze what led up to the event, trying to determine the 'why' that mystified everyone. I don't think I ever learned why he did it, only that it was a terrible thing to do. Otherwise the two years went on with no other incident of significance. I was quietly learning my lessons. Time passed.

CONEY ISLAND. I could not pass by these years of my growing up without mentioning Coney Island. At the time, in the 1940's, Coney Island had become the Enjoyment Center of the century! It had everything that you could enjoy in one place. It had sand, it had water, the Atlantic Ocean as a matter of fact, it had amusement rides and games, it had food Oh what food it had; of course it was junk food, (but we didn't know it then) so we consumed tons of it, Hot Dogs, Knishes, Pizza, Soft Custard Ice Cream, Corn on the Cob with melted butter, Salt Water Taffy and Caramel Popcorn, the list is endless. You cannot believe the games and rides that were there. Of course, I don't remember them all but there are some I will never forget. The Steeplechase is the first one I remember. It was a series of rides that were hilariously funny and included a Gigantic Rolling Barrel that you tried to walk through, not a chance, it knocked you down and while you're sitting you begin going up the side as it's rolling, then when you manage to stand up it would knock you down again. Then in the Steeplechase there was this apparently endless Slide. You sit at the top, then they give you something to sit on (a certain type of cloth-I assume anti-friction to reduce slowing down) and because it turns, you can't see the bottom, so you begin sliding and watch out here comes a bump, oops, up you go, now down you go, sliding all the way, watch out here's another turn and another bump, try to keep your balance, you haven't even begun…when is it going to end? Not yet, here comes another bump, now down you go, no end…you're laughing all the way, and until you can't take anymore, you want it to stop, then down you go again, how do you make it stop? You want it to stop, but it doesn't, down you go some more until you are screaming in laughter, now it ends, here comes the end, watch your step here, you have to stand up now. Whoa…easy does it. You are still laughing. It was so much fun. Believe it or not, you want to do it again. Then there is the Skirt Air Lift Bridge toward the starting line of the Mechanical Horse Races. Women and girls all wore skirts in the 40's, so this stunt was a tremendous hit with the guys. Unsuspecting girls would walk along a type of gangplank which they called the bridge and a hidden operator would press this button that sent a powerful spray of forced air upward sending the skirt into the air, going above their head at times and then creating an immediate response from the girl who desperately tried pushing down on their skirts to cover themselves again. But the exposure already occurred and the guys watching are all laughing because they witnessed an embarrassing experience by the victimized girls. It seemed to be a harmless stunt and became very popular with other amusement parks installing the same stunt in their establishment.

Coney Island had the most populated Fortune Telling facilities I can think of. Wherever you turned there was a Card Reading Fortune Teller here and a Crystal Ball Fortune Teller there and an Astrology Fortune Teller here. There were also Palm Reading Fortune Tellers and of course the Tarot Card Fortune Tellers. You could spend the whole day having your fortune foretold if you wished. Of course, you wouldn't get much fresh air or see much sunlight, but you would certainly know where your life was going and what to expect in the future, if you believed what you were told.

Coney Island had the world's greatest Roller Coaster Ride. I believe it was called the Cyclone and it was the tallest, the longest, the ride with the most curves and all for five cents! It was great. It was so much fun going to Coney Island and we went there often, especially in the summers when we were off from school. I can't tell you how many times I went on that Cyclone ride. Our parents enjoyed Coney Island and we did too. When we got older and were able to travel alone, we went with our friends all the time. These were experiences one could never forget. It was so enjoyable.

HOBBIES-CARS. One of my special interests as a boy (and actually became one of my intense hobbies) was learning about and repairing automobiles. It doesn't surprise me that my interest focused on cars, wondering how the engine worked and how the other mechanical parts of a car operated. After all, my father was in the automobile business. But body and fender work did not interest me as much as the power of the engine, and how that power reached the wheels to move it. So I began repairing cars. Specifically, their engines, transmissions, and torque trains (that's the transaxle and all its related parts)... What made it possible was the fact that my friend Mike's father owned about five one-car garages behind his house on Jackson Street. He rented four of them, couldn't rent the fifth one. Mike and I had just purchase a jalopy (that's what we called an old car in disrepair) that needed a lot of work. Mike asked his father if we could use the vacant garage and he said yes. Mike's father didn't know it, but it soon became Mike & Gus' Auto Shop. I actually painted a sign and we nailed it to the peak of the roof. We towed our jalopy into the garage and began working on it. To get parts, we had to go to the Junk Yard and rummage through hundreds of wrecked cars until we found our make and model, praying the part we needed was not damaged. Mike was an excellent mechanic. I learned everything from him. He said I wasn't bad either. It's hard to explain, but it was in our blood! In no time, we had that 1938 Ford running like a clock. It was a Tudor but had a rumble seat. That's a seat mounted in what we now call the trunk. Instead of a trunk, you gripped this protruding handle in an up and downward motion. It opened like an inverted trunk door, revealing an upholstered bench seat the width of the car. The swinging door portion was also upholstered and became the back of the seat. In fact, many called it the back seat instead of rumble seat. We could hold three guys back there, a little tight but they would suffer any pain to get transportation or to be with us. Of course Mike and I sat in the front. We were 'The Mechanics' after all. No one challenged us either. Not only did we repair our cars, but the word got out that we were very good mechanics and neighborhood guys wanted us to repair their cars. It wasn't long before we had a number of autos sitting in the yard near the garage waiting to be repaired. One day Mike said to me, "You know Gus, we are spending an awful lot of time here repairing cars. We're making a few bucks, but we can't go out and spend it. Do you think it's worth it?" I didn't know what to say. The money was important. Enjoying life is important. Now which is more important than the other? The answer was easy. We had the money. What we didn't have was the "fun. That's what I told him. He laughed and then he said, with a twinkle in his eye, he liked my philosophy! We immediately reduced our workweek to only two days a week (of course this was in the summertime only). The other five days was devoted to outdoor living. We went to the beach, to movies, to shows, to parties and we traveled to different places because we had a car of our own. Remember, I was about sixteen years old at this time.

SUMMER JOBS. There were about four or five years I was able to gain employment at various odd jobs during the summer months. I may not remember them all, but here are those I do. The first job I remember getting was when I was about 14 or 15 years old at Mc Carren Park on Lorimer Street in Greenpoint, Brooklyn. The park had a public swimming pool and I was an avid swimmer. My friends and I sort of developed an act appropriate in front of an audience at the pool. We were all swimmers and we were all comedians (of sorts) so I guess this was a natural outcome of these qualities. We created a Water Clown routine. The Park, after reviewing our act employed us to perform twice a day at the pool. There were grandstands adjacent to the pool for the public to sit on and the show went on every day at 6 p.m. and 7 p.m. during the summer. We all dressed as clowns (my friends were Mike, Anthony and Nicholas) and came out running to our positions, with appropriate music piped in and the audience applauding and yelling (I believe I would hear a "boo" sometimes -"there's a lot of jealous kids out there," Nick would say.) My act was to be pushed from the high board, face forward so that I would land on my stomach (called a belly flop). If I wasn't wearing extra clothing in front, that stunt would be a little stinging, to say the least, but it got a lot of laughs and that was worth it. We did a whole variety of gags that are apropos around water and seemed to entertain the audience very nicely. The management liked it anyway. We stayed the whole summer. I've got to tell you what management had us do between performances; we had to serve hot dogs and drinks in a concession adjacent to the pool between acts. It was fun. I know we were slave labor, but we were young and had so much energy, it didn't matter. All for the game, was our motto.

Another job I got the next year was at Confortti's Florist. I worked two months arranging flowers for weddings, funerals and any other occasions requiring flowers. I definitely learned what a rose is, and a gardenia and a daisy, etc., etc. And boy do I know what a gladiola is! After that experience, I could spot a gladiola from 20 feet away. We placed gladiolas in every conceivable arrangement known to man! It was the most popular flower used by florists, even though many people did not know what they were. Florists knew though. It was the hardies" cut plant on the planet and it was beautiful! No wonder every florist I knew (in future years, I worked at other florists) used it, sometime in excess. But you couldn't blame them. I found myself at times placing too many gladiolas in an arrangement until the florist would pass by and say, "Augie, too many 'glads'." Then I would have to adjust (they used to call me Augie at that age). Of course, I also learned the different types of fern or border greens. I was also learning the horticultural names of the species of flowers and plants common in florist shops. When the summer ended, I had to quit. But in subsequent jobs I had at florists, I continued my knowledge of flowers until I became a qualified florist. As destiny would have it, that was not to be my career occupation. Although I loved it. Just think, surrounded by fragrant and beautiful objects blazing with color everywhere you looked or went. It was like a little bit of heaven…I thought. But it didn't last.

The third year I gained employment in the local butcher shop. "Tony's Butcher Shop" was its name and my mother got me this job. I don't recall the specifics, but I remember my mother coming home from the butcher, with the announcement; "Tony, the butcher, can use some help this summer and he asked for you. Are you interested?" I was around 17 years old by now. I said, "OK." (hey, a bird in the hand is better than none.) When summer started, I reported to Tony and he quickly put me to work. He gave me a clean white apron and showed me the equipment that I was going to use (especially the Meat Grinder in the refrigerator room). You cannot image how many people were purchasing ground meat. I was in the refrigerator almost all day long - had to come out occasionally to warm up. Tony would say, "Whatsa matta, tooa colda?" He spoke with an accent. I would say, "Can't we lower the cold in there, Tony?" He would laugh hysterically. I didn't think my request was that funny? Of course, I knew there wasn't anything that could be done. A meat grinder I was. You might say an expert meat grinder at that. After two months of grinding meat, anyone would be an expert, let's face it. Tony did teach me some of the different cuts of meat and the different types of meat. I still am able to cut a veal cutlet (which requires a skill) and to be able to slice braciola. I didn't forget those skills. I just don't have the knives, I keep telling everyone today who asks me to do it.

The fourth year I worked in a photo shop during the summer. My job was unrolling exposed film in a dark room, fastening it to a rod, and then lowering it into a four foot deep vat of film developer made by Kodak. Then we (I worked with another guy) timed the process and when the time was up, we removed the films and placed them in the drying room, where there were fans blowing on the films to increase the speed of evaporation. Next, we had to cut the frames from the film, stack them, and then begin the printing process. We took each frame of film called a negative; placed it in a projector, with photographic paper placed on the easel base, then snapped a switch which projected intense light through the negative to expose all the detail from the film to the photo sensitive paper to produce the print. The exposed paper was immediately inserted in a tray that contained liquid developer and the magic happens. The pure white paper begins to change. First you see faint grays appearing (they hadn't invented color yet in the late forties). The grays become darker and darker until you see black and white, with some grays interspersed to create the image of the photograph that was taken. I enjoyed this job very much. There are so many stories I remember while performing this task that I don't think this book could hold them. Because the photos were of everything in this world imaginable, the images we saw many times were beyond belief. When you give a human the freedom to capture any image possible, that's exactly what your result would be, you would get everything!

3RD BUSINESS OPENED. After the war was over in 1945, my father was laid-off from the shipyard where he was working on the military production of ships. He was jobless again. He began reading the want ads in the newspapers and happened to see an ad describing a business opportunity. The person placing the ad was searching for someone to go into a Partnership with him, concerning an Auto Body Shop, located in New York City. The ad further asks that the person responding to the ad be a body and fender repairman since he was only an auto painter. All the conditions were absolutely favorable. My father immediately called the number. A person answered with a heavy accent (who was the owner looking for a partner) talking to my father who also had a heavy accent, discussing some of the particulars. A meeting was scheduled, my father attended and they immediately hit it off. The only way my father could accept this deal concerned the money requirement. My father did not have much money at the time. After the meeting, although one thousand dollars was needed to enter the partnership, it could be paid in installments from the business. The owner was of Spanish descent, his name was Jose Rodrigez (another Joseph) and of course, my father told him he was of Italian descent with the same name of Joseph. They formed a Partnership and began working together as soon as it could be arranged. The Body Shop was on 52nd Street, between 10th and 11th Avenues. The shop was on the second floor and there was no driveway for cars to be brought into the shop area except by elevator. There was this gigantic elevator that you drove the car onto (I drove many a car onto this elevator), then got out of the car, pressed the second floor button and up you went. On the second floor, you drove the car off into the assigned car stall. Many times the autos were so damaged they had to be towed to the building and pushed onto the elevator. When the auto reached the second floor my father tied a winch's cable and hook onto the bumper or somewhere else that would hold and pull it off the elevator. It sounds complicated but they did this so many times that it became routine. Jose' was an excellent auto painter and my father was an excellent auto body repairman, so both had a successful business going. My father used to ask me to help at the shop (like he did when he had the shop in East New York), which I did. There I was again, sanding the repairs my father made, only this time we were not using gasoline as a lubricant. Laws were passed by then that outlawed the use of gasoline in shops for this purpose. Boy, was that a relief. We had to use water to do the sanding now. My father was doing very well at this shop. He was able to save quite a bit of money. He wanted to buy a house. He always dreamed of owning his own home. Now he could afford it. So we all set out seeing homes for sale. None that we saw appealed to them. The search continued for years, as I recall. Meanwhile, my father's partner Jose had a drinking problem that was getting worse. It reached the point in 1948, where Jose was hospitalized for jaundice (I believe that's a disease of the liver usually brought about by alcohol abuse). My father was in a quandary. Jose could not work. My father bought out his half of the business (there goes the house money) and put an ad in the newspapers for a good auto painter. No replies. My father had to sell the business. He sold the business and made a nominal profit. At least he was able to secure the savings that he laboriously accumulated. What would he do now? As destiny would have it, in the newspapers he spotted an ad looking for a Body Shop Foreman in an auto dealership. The dealership was a Ford, Lincoln, and Mercury brand, located in Queens. My father applied and was hired immediately. Since he had his own business, it made him a prime applicant. My father became the Auto Body Foreman of "Sol Shieldkraut's" dealership on Liberty Avenue in Queens. This would be his second to last place of employment.

HIGH SCHOOL. Just before graduation from Junior High School, I decided to pursue an academic course in life and chose to attend Boy's High School. It was 1947. To enter this school, a student had to qualify by taking very difficult tests and satisfying the school with an exhibition of dedication and determination toward a successful completion. This I did, but not without the help of my friends, Philip Bonomo and Alfonso Nunziata. Hearing all the things my friends cited about academics vs. a trade convinced me to go academic. The last I heard, my friend Philip was an Aircraft Engineer in the US Air Force and my best friend Alfonso (we called him Sonny) is an Optometrist and has an office on Metropolitan Avenue and Graham Avenue in Brooklyn, NY. I can't begin to tell you how much they helped me. I will never forget that! In fact, it was listening to them every day on our way to school that I was convinced to take the academic path in education rather than go to a trade school. Those were the choices in those days. I'm glad I followed their lead.

The two most important teachers I had in high school were Mrs. Champagne and Mr. or Dr. Ryan. Mrs. Champagne was my English teacher, who I will never forget. The very first day of class is usually spent kibitzing around, chatting with the students who were strangers in the class, in an effort to become more familiar with the group. You know the type of anxiety that fills the room, wondering who the teacher is, and how am I going to like the course. You know the feelings, trying desperately to answer all the questions that come up in your mind when you're starting a new class.

At my Junior High School graduation-1946

Well, it was nothing like that in this class! Instead, the teacher stood firmly in front of the class and just looked (without saying a thing) at each and every one of us until we stopped talking and stopped kidding around and until our complete attention was on her, at which time total silence had filled the room. Then she spoke these words; "In the beginning was the Word, and the Word was with God, and the Word was God." WOW…What an opening in an "English" class! The introduction was mind-boggling for so many reasons, to this day I am still considering the many meanings that could be extrapolated from the quotation (later we were told that it came from the Bible, John,1,1 …and this was public school!). My first impression was, Oh, my gosh, I never thought of the "WORD" in that way. My next impression was, I never realized how important the WORD can be. Then an avalanche of thoughts just cascaded in my mind of the many times the WORD changed the face of the earth and in the secular world to boot. For instance; "Give me liberty or give me death" (Patrick Henry). All of these types of quotations came into my head. It was an experience that has never left me. From that moment on, I respected the WORD in a special way that endures to this day. And because my first language was Italian, my concentration on English became more intense because of that focus and became a "high priority" in my life. Thank you Mrs. Champagne, you helped me concentrate on an important subject in my life that has been with me ever since.

The next experience that made life-altering changes to my future was the course I took in Economics, being taught by Dr. Ryan. Dr. Ryan was Irish, and he wouldn't let you forget that for one minute. He was so proud of his heritage (I'm sure he made me aware of mine, too, and to hold it in great esteem) that he actually greeted us in class speaking Gaelic. He taught me what "Erin Go Brae" means (Ireland For Ever), along with other words that escape me now (after all I haven't thought of it for over 60 years). He was so instrumental in shaping my life, I can only stand in amazement at that accomplishment. Dr. Ryan's lessons had the ability to remain with me like a super glue. In fact, one of his lessons was the source of much trepidation when I was in the Air Force (I will cite that incident in Chapter 4 - his teachings received the big test in my life and he was right). In retrospect, I feel that he was instrumental in directing my course in the working or career aspect of my future. I didn't realize it at the time, but now I feel his words were directing me when I had to make certain decisions that led me from one job to another. An example was around 1958. I was working at Republic Aviation Corp. as an Aircraft Inspector. President Eisenhower convinced Congress to "cut government spending" by canceling every non-essential government contract in the US. Our contract was cut and I was laid-off. No job. Millions of Americans looking for a job. There were no mechanical jobs to be had. I was desperate. I applied to "every" want ad in the newspapers. Well, a bank ad responded and was interested in me. A bank! I never worked, or knew anyone who ever worked in a bank! What did I know about banking? But then, Dr. Ryan's lessons entered my brain. "Economics"; that's what banking is. You can do it! He prepared me for it. Take it! I did. Well, history shows that for the next 9 years, banking occupied my entire life. Thanks to Dr. Ryan, this endeavor was very successful and I seemed to know what I was doing…it had to be those lessons!

There were many other teachers that influenced my life and, although I can't remember their names, I remember their faces and their teachings. My Geometry teacher was very special. He immediately recognized my enthusiasm for the subject. He called me aside at the beginning of the class term and told me that I had great potential. It must have been the spark that ignited my love for the subject. For some reason I had no difficulty memorizing all the idioms or theorems required. Geometry was a natural for me. I would get a 100 on every test until the Teacher asked me to (instead of taking the tests) help him score the other students' tests. I enjoyed this class immensely. Geometry has always been a favorite subject of mine since.

In high school, I became more extroverted and joined more activities. I joined a Debate Club, and a Drama Acting Club, and a Journal Arts Club , etc. Since one of my friends was very popular in the school, he asked me to be his Campaign Manager for the election of President. And, although we put up a good fight, our opponent won. My friend and I learned later that they used unorthodox methods in their quest, so it was heartening to realize that we probably would have won if things were square! Then there was a long list of subjects one could choose from in terms of courses to study. I remember taking English Literature, Advanced Geometry, Basic Physics, Chemistry, and Spanish. And I believe I joined every club and extra curricular activity listed. I was determined to learn all I could about the world and life that this school was offering. The challenge begins.

I took the Boy's High entrance tests and passed, placing me in the highest level. I was accepted. It's off to High School I go. Life was very different in High School. Even though Junior High School is supposed to prepare you for High School, the environment was too different. It was a new world for me. Very exciting and very challenging. I plunged into the school work completely. I would assume that by now you deduced this school contained only male students. I cannot imagine why boys should be separated from girls in the 1940's (and I feel scholars were wondering why also at the time); anyway, I got heavily involved in the Track Team. I immediately joined and began running for the school. There was one important draw back; we did not have a Gym! No track existed at the school. We got instructions from the coach but had to find a local track to practice on. Of course, I had Mc Carren Park, where there was an excellent track, so I spent a lot of time there running. It was fun.

I should mention the composition of Boy's High School in 1948 and 1949. The school was located in the Bedford Stuyvesant section of Brooklyn. This was a predominantly black neighborhood. The school population was approximately 60% Black and 40% White. The reason I'm explaining the population mix is because even though it existed, there were "no" racial incidents during my tenure. While I was going to school (this may sound naïve but true) I didn't even know what "racial incidents" meant. We all got along together, and not with much effort, it was just a natural human environment. We were all there to learn. The school subjects were the important thing. Graduation was the goal. College was next. The school was good to us. Thank you "Boy's High School"!

HIGH SCHOOL SPORTS. Sport class was super because now I was getting serious about organized sports. Running had my attention at that time (why didn't someone aim me towards basketball- after all I was almost six feet tall at the time?) I guess my interest in running was prompted by the fact that it is basically a "solitary" sport. Nobody shouting out "orders" to you while you are performing. It's either "a good job" as exclaimed by the coach or "you have to do better the next time"; a definite lament. I could live with that, so Running it was. I began training in the neighborhood fields that existed in Mc Carren Park (see street map for location).

My running career is vague to me and I recall very little of it. I'm trying to analyze why; probably because, although I was a competitor, I never won any First Place or Second Place or Third Place awards. But I did represent the school and I was a member of the team and I did pretty well as a participant. I was satisfied. So, I pursued this sport all through high school, where the competition became a little intense. The coach there did not want to hear any words from the loud speakers except; "Boy's High Track Team Wins!" again. Can you believe the pressure! Oh well, I endured.

STREET ACTIVITIES. During these years, you cannot imagine how many street activities emerged and became almost passions in certain respects. They included street types of sports, or street projects, or street crafts.

All types of activities occurred and I would like to describe those I remember. What comes to mind first are the "Soap Box" racing cars we built. They are not the type you see now, with four wheels and sleek design. Oh, no…our soap boxes were just that, wooden boxes nailed onto a three foot long, two-by-four that had "metal skates" nailed to the bottom two ends. It had two handles nailed to the top of the box, for steering and balance. It was quite an interesting contraption. I don't know when it started, but it was so much fun. It wasn't hard to build either. Here is my "artist's conception" drawing of it as I remember:

Soap Box Racer-Home Built

After we built it, we would go racing down the streets and onto the sidewalk. It could go anywhere. We would gravitate to those streets that had smooth surfaces (no pot holes) and a downward incline, this way we wouldn't have to pump that much with our feet. Now going uphill was very different. To propel the soap box on a steep incline, you had to push (we called that pumping) against the ground in a very forceful manner in order to move your car upward. It was so much fun that when I was ten or eleven years old, it had become the rage at that time. Almost every boy (and I saw a lot of girls) had one. Some people used to call them "scooters" but they were not motor driven, they had to be pushed manually. Every kid who built one would give it a name. Although it sounds foolish, it did have the purpose of establishing ownership. Mine was called "The Cyclone" (naturally referring to wind speed and the Coney Island ride), even though it didn't move that fast. I don't see them anymore.

While I was describing the wheels for the above soap box I mentioned metal skates. Almost every Christmas after reaching age 8, every one of us would ask Santa to bring us Roller Skates. I guess in 1938 and on, roller skates were invented and immediately acquired widespread use with children and some adults too. They were comprised of four metal wheels for each foot, mounted on roller bearing axels and all made out of metal. They contained a cam in the back that kept your shoe from sliding off and a set of shoe grippers in the front that could be adjusted with a "Key". It's the first key I had to keep track of. It got lost all the time. When we were on skates, I can recall, the only conversation between us was; "Can I borrow your key?" (they were interchangeable). The skates had to be adjusted constantly, especially if you were wearing sneakers. The front clamps didn't grip the rubber soles that well and, with the twisting and turning you do while skating, they would loosen and come off. Leather shoes were the best if you were going roller skating. In the city, you were allowed to roller skate not only in the street but on the sidewalk as well. Can you imagine, you were standing on 8 wheels, how could anyone fall? But fall we did, they would roll right under your shoe and down you would go, until you learned to balance on them well. They were a lot of fun, except for the black and blue's inflicted. Later, when the skates wore out (the wheels would get smaller with the grinding action and they would rust too), we would reconstitute them by using them for locomotion on our "Soap Box Racers", so not much got wasted. They were great!

Another street activity that emerged while I was nine years old was not only dangerous but inflicted a great deal of injury when executed improperly. It was called "The Rubber Band Gun". Believe it or not, it was considered a Toy by the kids and by the adults too and many parents actually made the guns for their kids. I made my own (and many more for my friends-I was the handy one in the group). It was made from wood. It had an "L" shape. The key element was the trigger portion. First you must fabricate a tongue and grove joint where the barrel and handle of the wooden gun is joined. Then you must cut the groove part of the corner joint on a diagonal, on both sides so that when you're finished, only the tongue part is left. That's the trigger of the gun. Now you have to staple a heavy duty rubber band to the underside of the barrel part, so that you can stretch the rubber band over the front barrel and to the back, hooking it onto the tongue of the wooden gun. Now it's ready for the ammunition which is a three quarter inch square piece of cardboard. It is inserted between the two rubber band strands, stretched across the barrel length. Now you're loaded and ready to fire. Take aim and push up on the rubber band hooked around the tongue, and whsst, away the cardboard square goes flying. No matter what, it should never be aimed at anyone's eye! That was the number one rule we had to follow. It, unfortunately", was a lot of fun, too. What made it fun, really, wasn't in the shooting of it, but in making the ammunition. Cardboard had to be cut in ¾" squares by the hundreds. Groups of us would get together with loads of cardboard and scissors, joking all the time and laughing for hours. I remember spending more time cutting the cardboard squares than shooting the gun. The most prevalent thing we did with the gun is to have neighborhood fights using the guns, but not before building a barricade or fort (we would call it) which was made out of cardboard too. In those days cardboard was everywhere. Historically, it was a major industry at the time.

Everything seemed to be packaged in cardboard. I remember three of our paisanos worked in a cardboard factory.

Wooden Play Gun

I'm talking about plain, flat, 1/16" cardboard, not corrugated board (which is about ¼ " thick with corrugations in the center). You know, the type shoe boxes are made out of. In fact, that was the premium type of cardboard we searched for to make our little squares. Those were the "Rubber Band Gun" days. I'm glad they are gone now (a little too dangerous, I think), although I never had a bad incident playing with that toy.

SOCIAL CLUBS. In the neighborhood, there emerged what were called "Social and Athletic Clubs" that seemed to be everywhere. These clubs were usually set up in store fronts that could not be rented to any other enterprise because of overabundances. Nobody wanted them. So, groups of guys would get together with each handing in a dollar or two a month, to take care of the rent. If you had ten guys, at $2 each, the $20 a month rent would easily be paid. These guys were mostly discharged Veterans that were in World War II and needed a place to congregate without "Loitering" on the street, which was a crime. I was not allowed to join; too young. But a lot of my friends had brothers that belonged to these clubs so we learned a lot about them. Besides, we were often called by them to run to the store to get those things they needed. For a nickel we would be asked to run over to a coffee shop and get them some coffee. Or they would ask us to go to a grocery store for a sandwich, a Yankee Doodle or Twinkie, or something. It didn't matter, we felt honored to run errands for them. After all, most of them were Veterans and we were proud of them. They would spend the time playing Poker and sometimes Crap. Although gambling was not allowed, for some reason there wasn't that much policing going on at these places. I suspect it was because of their veteran status. Many of them did play chess and checkers, though. You may ask; "Why were they able to spend so much time there?" The answer is "unemployment". There were no jobs to be had. Remember, the country was in a Military Industrial mode until the war ended in 1945 - now it was back to Civilian Industry. The changeover took time. The United States had to undo most of its factory priorities from military production to civilian needs. While the re-tooling was taking place, unemployment was at its peak from the end of the war to 1950, when another industrial surge was mounting. What took place from the 1950's to the present is mind-boggling. What I remember most is television, color photography, Xerox copies, radar to guide airplanes and the electronic boom! Of course, there were many others which all combined to create that revolution.

Another type of club that proliferated in the neighborhood was the Athletic Club. They appeared identical to the Social Clubs except they were primarily involved in some sort of sport, be it baseball, basketball, tennis, usually forming teams to compete with other clubs in the same sport. The members would go out to open fields and practice, practice, practice. On weekends, they would be scheduled to play games against each other and actually formed tournaments vying for awards (you know, trophies-some of which were monstrous in size). There was one club that had its main wall completely covered with shelves, from the ground up, displaying their "trophies" proudly. Wow…what a wall! We had to walk about a mile down Metropolitan Avenue to see that one.

My main reason for focusing on these clubs, which may sound insignificant, was to show their important function to preserve "peace" in the neighborhood. Instead of allowing these proud veterans to roam the streets endlessly, the clubs offered an outlet allowing them to congregate and expend their energies in a non-destructive manner. I'm convinced that these Clubs avoided the formation of violent Gangs and thereby afforded a sense of peace and tranquility to our streets. No one, to my knowledge, ever criticized the existence of these clubs, I imagine because they saw the value of their presence. That's another by-gone institution that was present in the neighborhood helping everyone pursue their endeavors in peace. They will be missed.

BOWLING AID INVENTION. In 1944, my father, who was an avid bowler at the local Church Society (The Society of St. John the Baptist who was the Patron Saint of Celenza Valfortore), began wondering about the subject of bowling ball control improvement. He began considering the possibility of inventing an aid that would allow bowlers to improve their score significantly. He noticed that there was a space created when holding a bowling ball, between the ball and your palm, which in turn does not allow good control of the release of the bowling ball. If a device could be invented to "bridge" this gap, then possibly more control over the release of the ball could be achieved. That was the initial premise. So the concept began. First drawings had to be designed, which in turn, would determine the direction of the execution toward the final prototype. The drawing turned out to be more difficult than expected. Although he had the complete image in his mind, as soon as it was put on paper many faults began to appear. He and I had to work out all the impediments. For instance; although we had solved the problem of occupying the space from the bowling ball to the palm, its result was not acceptable because, we found out later, that practically every hand has a variable distance that required an adjustable device. We hadn't thought of that. We designed it to fit our hand and felt that was sufficient. Not so. We had to go back to the drawing board when this hurdle was encountered. Now that we were aware of the need for an adjustment type of mechanism, what type would work best for the contraption? Our brains were tested. First, we tried this idea, then we tried another. We came up with about five different types. We were not happy with any of them. It took us additional time to come up with a satisfactory adjustment design. But we did this. It's important to note, this actually took us years to accomplish. I'm talking about not only the design, but also the hand made final prototype that could actually be tested in the real environment. We worked on the model intensely until we were happy with the outcome. It was ready for the test. My father tested it and it improved his score 15 to 20 %. It was a success as far as we were concerned. We decided to Patent this new idea. There wasn't anything like it on the market at the time. After my father fabricated the device in metal (actually steel) and tested it successfully, we decided that the production method should be towards plastic production instead of metal. My father suggested we produce one in plastic and test it. But the patent process was started and since we had a relative in Washington, D.C., (a distant cousin.) who was also a patent attorney, it would not cost him the usual fee. Eventually we acquired the third patent my father applied for. It meant that the idea would be protected for 17 years from the date of issue and that it was definitely an improvement in the U.S., deserving an American patent. When we received the patent in print, we were ready to offer the device to leading manufacturers of bowling merchandise. The first company we wrote to was a very large bowling ball manufacturer (Brunsick) who wrote back to us saying that although the idea had a lot of potential, they wouldn't be interested because it may violate "Bowling League" rules. They did not want to go through the expense of investigating if it would go contrary to bowling regulations. That was rejection No. 1. Then there was rejection number two, then number three and so on. All rejections. My father and I were very disappointed. We really thought this was the "one"! Oh well, there are other ideas to work on. In fact my father and I were interested in an exciting new "Navel Hull" design that could revolutionize sailing ships forever! We were building a model to test first. So, we were much occupied and didn't have time to become depressed over this marketing failure. We had so much work to do, designing, fabricating testing, etc. More about this new invention later.

MUSIC IN THE 40's. There was an emergence of Super Singers that became so popular in the 1940's that it is difficult to explain. As soon as I begin listing to these superstars in the field of music, you will begin to envision the intense impact they had on the young people of the day. They seemed to stir emotions in us we didn't even know we had. We were all teenagers at the time. When I give you the name Frank Sinatra, I don't know, you sorta get goose bumps or something. It is very hard to describe, but I'm sure, if you were a teenager in those years, you know what I mean. Up to the 1940's, the music on the radio (that's all we had then, but it was a very popular pastime, just listening) mostly consisted of pleasant singers that can carry a tune and tempo who were doing their thing on the airways. Nothing spectacular. Then came the forties, and on the "air" we heard someone called Frank Sinatra singing "That Old Black Magic". WOW…this was something else. He actually got a reaction out of you. I don't care what you were doing, as soon as he began singing, you had to stop, listen, get emotional, enjoy the lyrics, then the goose bumps would come and you would remain in some sort of a mild ecstasy for a few seconds, then it would subside. It was absolutely phenomenal! And Frank Sinatra wasn't the only singer to affect you this way. There also was Perry Como, Bing Crosby, The Andrew Sisters, Dinah Shore, The Ink Spots, Nat King Cole and Vaughn Monroe. These are the ones that come up in my mind, but there were many more. I did not mention the famous Band Leaders that emerged, with their heavenly renditions, not only of the old favorites but the new songs as well. There was Glen Miller, Artie Shaw, Woody Herman, Tommy Dorsey, Kay Kaiser and who could forget the whimsical Spike Jones & His City Slickers? It was a wonderful era for music. Radio was at its peak, the Disc Jockey was invented. Only those disc's were only for the Victrola Record Player, (a portable case that turned the record around with a pick-up needle and was driven by a spring devise that you hand cranked to wind-all mechanical) the discs or records were made of a Bakelite compound with a durable hard wax surface, then they were stamped to engrave the sound tracks and revolved on the player at 78 revolutions per minute. And they were about 10 inches in diameter. Pretty big, wouldn't you say? Yet it was one of the first successful memory storage media developed in the world in history. The technology was beginning. We have seen, in the last 50 years, a change from these crude 78 rpm, 10" Disc. records (which only held about 3 minutes of music each) to the CD's (which hold from 18 to 22 songs each) and more recently the MP3 Players that can hold more than 2,000 songs (that's about 6,000 min. or 100 hours of sound and they can be the size of your palm)!! That's progress! In one of my science magazines, they are talking about developing what is called "nano" technology, which will bring devices that perform these functions to the "atomic and molecular" size! Boy, are MP3's going to get lost then. Imagine having a player the size of a pinhead! Anyway, during the 1940's the music scene was like a gigantic wave, flowing over the masses. We were all affected in one way or another. Teenagers would do anything to go see Frank Sinatra performing at the Paramount Theatre in New York and more than once, a kid would skip school to attend this mind-boggling experience of listening to the Crooner, as he was called. You can't imagine the affect this had on our society at the time. This not only affected the student (who lost a day's lessons), but the parents (who usually found out what their kid did), to the Truant Officer, to public transportation (increase in kids traveling), to the Police who had to contain the crowds, to the Newspapers (reporters who had to cover the stories). The list goes on and on. Obviously the affects were extraordinary, it was a time of extreme change, and no one had ever witnessed this kind of behavior among the young, ever. All brought about by very talented and passionate singers and performers. I should mention something about the clothing style at the time because it was an integral part of the movement. Almost everyone wore shoes called Loafers with a shiny penny pressed into the front flap of the shoe and Bobby Socks. Everyone wore Bobby Socks (by the way when I say everyone and all, always allow for an exception or so – I'm trying to say the majority, which is too long to write I guess so I opt for all or everyone-glad I got that out of the way). So the Bobby Sock generation was created. I believe it lasted to about till the 60's, when teenagers were introduced to Television. That's when everything changed! I'm going to give you some of my experiences about this age (the 60' and on) later in the book. I just want to give some of my favorite songs and singers in my teenage years (the 1940's), here they are; "I'll Be with You in Apple Blossom Time", The Andrew Sisters; "Racing with the Moon", Vaughn Monroe and "You Made Me Love You", Frank Sinatra (the songs are in quotation marks). These are the ones I remember the most but there were many others that I would be singing to myself all the time. It was a wonderful age for me.

MY GRANDFATHER COMES TO AMERICA. I'm not really certain of the year, my Grandfather Petti, who lived in Italy all during the years I was growing up, decided to come to America. I believe it was 1947 or 1948. He came here to find a job and work for five years, then go back to Italy with a Social Security Pension. And that is exactly what he did. Since he traveled by ship, we had to go to meet him at the docks in New York City. I would be meeting him for the first time in my life. I couldn't believe it. All the years we communicated with him through letters and photographs and now, I was actually going to meet him. It was very exciting for me. We also had Joann with us, who was four years old or five. My mother was there and, of course, my father was there and so happy to be able to see his father again. There he was, a jovial cheerful aging man, but he was young at heart. He hugged us all and gave us the Italian kiss on each cheek. He laughed and chuckled a lot. He was so happy. It's a good thing we all understood Italian because that's the only language he spoke. We were all asking him how the trip was. He said fine and began asking us how we were and the chatter began. He was such an interesting grandfather. He played the piano (self-taught) and sang many songs I never heard before. When I was growing up and much younger, I recall listening to the radio and tuned to a local Italian station (there was such a large contingency of Italians in New York that a radio station was broadcasting in Italian exclusively) and I listened to artists such as Bengiamino Giglio and Carlo Butti, who were world famous Italian singers and rendered all the beautiful Neapolitan songs all day long. I learned the lyrics of all those songs by just listening. But my Grandfather did not sing any of those songs. He sang what I called ditties. They were something like our Nursery Rhymes, but put to music. Here is one he taught me that I will never forget:

Lu vi, lu vi, mo sine ve,
Cha cigarette a' mocha, va
Faciendo u' sceme.

Chorus

Ma come bella la prim'amore,
Chi 'nitene sine po scordare!

Translation: "Look at him, look at him, here he comes, with a cigarette in his mouth, he goes being a clown. Chorus: Oh, how beautiful is the first love, whoever has it should forget about it!" (Obviously advice from a buffoon - this was a very funny song.) There are more stanzas to this ditty but they are a little bawdy...you should have seen my grandfather laugh when he would sing to you and watch you when you heard the bawdy words and were shocked. You couldn't believe those meanings coming from him, but they were the songs of the day that were sung in the little towns of Italy, especially in Celenza Valfortore, Foggia, Italy. They meant no harm.

My grandfather's main goal was to find a job and work for all the years here in America that he could. My father got him a job at Sol Schieldkraut, at the dealership as a night watchman. He did this for five years, until 1952 and then went back to Italy in accordance to his plan. There he lived as a "Gallant 'U'omo". It means "Man of Means". My aunts would send us letters describing his new status and how he paraded in his white suit, strolling across the town square almost every day. He also enjoyed smoking those Italian cigars called Stogies that women can't stand the smell of. He was living the life he dreamed of and was very happy. He would write to us sometimes and thank us all for making it possible and how he didn't know what he would have done without us. It was very moving. He was a poet also. Very talented.

Anyway, I just have to tell you this story that unfolded when I came home on furlough before going to my next assignment. I was in the Air Force and just finished Basic Training. When I got home, my grandfather and I began talking about the military and he asked me where I was stationed. I was puzzled with this question because I thought, "What does he know about Texas?" So, I divertingly said, "Oh, Grandpa, even if I told you where, you wouldn't know what I'm talking about!" He pressed on, "No, tell me where you're stationed in Texas?" So, I obediently told him, "I'm stationed in San Antonio, OK!" He immediately said, "I was there!" I could not believe my ears. "How could you have been there Grandpa?!" He said, "It's a long story, but here it is shortened, "Many years ago in the 20's, there was a lot of "immigration illegitimacy" going on between countries especially in Italy. Italians would do anything to come to America. Well, I was one of those foolish enough to attempt entering the U.S. with illegal papers. When I entered New York, I was warned by intelligent paisanos to flee the city because Federal Immigration enforcement officers were collecting all those here illegally and sending them back to Italy. So, I began traveling to elude the government officers. I reached Texas and was in the town of San Antonio when they caught me and deported me back to Italy. So, you see, I know San Antonio!" I was flabbergasted! I didn't know if he made it up or if it really happened! Why would he make up such an amazing story like that? I just had to ask him to verify the details solemnly. He said, "Augusto, so help me God that is the truth!" I had to believe him. And I never forgot! Can you imagine that! He traveled across the whole United States to keep ahead of the "G" Men", as they were called at the time. This story really took me a long time to digest…I had so many questions then that he answered, one at a time until I began understanding the whole picture, all the whys, all the when's all the how's and all the what's. Above is a really short version, but it did happen and it happened to my Grandfather. What a "small" world!

EMPIRE STATE BLDG-PLANE CRASH. On July 28, 1945 a twin engine military airplane crashed into the Empire State building. It was traveling about 200 miles per hour and struck the building on the 79th floor. The fuel ignited upon impact affecting some of the floors above and below. Many deaths occurred as a result. The impact also caused injuries on the 80th and 81st floors. Some elevator cables were severed causing the cars to come crashing down, injuring and killing people that were on other floors too. It was a national catastrophe due to the ramifications. Many cities had buildings that contained at least 80 floors, this left them vulnerable too. Why did this happen? Wasn't the pilot aware of his direction? It was early afternoon when it happened but very cloudy, and it was a little "misty" and some humidity was in the air – just enough to hamper visibility. What happened? The FAA began an intense investigation into the occurrence.

I'm citing this catastrophe because it coincides with a significant course of events that would have directly affected a family member. Zia Luccia, whom I introduced to you in Chapter 2, had a daughter Mary, who was married to Dr. Louis Iamele (my godfather). This event is about Dr. Iamele's father, who was a Master Carpenter and worked for a company contracted out for the Empire State Building construction and renovations. On the day of that crash, early in the morning, Mr. Iamele Sr. awoke with an upset stomach. His wife, Dr. Iamele's mother, took his temperature. It was a little high. She looked at him and said; "I don't think you should go to work today." He said, "I must go into work today, they are delivering the cabinets we ordered weeks ago and they must be installed immediately." "But you are not well," she said. "I cannot be out today," he retorted. He began getting dressed. As he was dressing, he felt a little weak and began fainting. When he experienced these symptoms, he instantly sat down, looked at his wife and said, "Call our son." Dr. Iamele was in surgery and could not respond at that time. Mrs. Iamele convinced him to stay home, at least until their son could come and diagnose the problem. Well, (thank God) the operation in surgery took him till 1:00 p.m. By the time he arrived to see his father it was 2:00 p.m. After examining his father, he said, "Pa, you're not going anywhere, you're coming down with something. We'll have to take some tests to find out what you have." The doctor took a blood sample and left to bring it to the laboratory for analysis. Meanwhile, 3:00 p.m. rolled around and the news on the radio was ear piercing! Plane crashed into Empire State Building. People Killed. People Injured. Will give you details as soon as they come in. These were the main news reports. All the Stations were reporting the same news. When the doctor heard the news, he immediately called his mother and father and thanked God for the "medical condition" that forced his dad to avoid being at that location. Everyone that learned of this incident came to one conclusion, that it was "divine intervention" that determined this destiny. Everyone was so grateful that God spared this soul. No one was happier than Mrs. Iamele and all her loved ones.

I told this story because it paralleled so closely to our recent "9/11" terrorist catastrophe. Why it's significant to this book is because I was personally in the midst of the Empire State Building event and directly affected as a result of the accident, therefore am deeply sympathetic to those victims and loved ones that suffered so much after the Twin Tower disaster. It was a "major" event in my life and I will never forget it.

MET ANN-1946. I wasn't aware of it at the time, but this next experience was an earth changing event for me. The occasion was the meeting of young "Anna Teresa Passero" who later became my girlfriend, then my fiancée, then my wife, then your mother and finally your grandmother and great-grandmother. She was fifteen years old and I was sixteen.

First Photo of us-Ages 16 &15

I'm sure you would like to know how we met, well here it is! According to my recollection, we met at a movie theatre called the Greenpoint Theatre, naturally, located in the Greenpoint section of Brooklyn. It's difficult to remember every single detail, but some of the things that I saw or heard or sensed, I can "never" forget. For instance, our first interaction (keep in mind, we were very young then) was what I called the "The Popcorn Incident"! Ann and three of her girlfriends were sitting in the balcony of the theatre, right behind the railing up front. That's also where we were, in the balcony except we were about three rows behind them. I was with three of my friends also. Her friends' names were Rosie, Carroll and Minnie. My friends' names were Mike, Nicholas and Anthony. We had purchased a bag of popcorn before going to our seats. While the movie was showing, we began tossing the popcorn into the air, sending single pieces of popcorn in the girls' direction, trying to reach them. Specifically, Ann had a helmet type of hat on her lap, facing up - so it became a container. It caused a little game to start, so we were trying to get the popcorn into the hat. We were missing at times, accidentally bouncing off their shoulders or arms, causing them to turn around and saying, unconvincingly, to "stop it". So we did not stop. We kept on throwing the popcorn which now intensified the game, causing them and us to laugh whenever popcorn was thrown. It became a hilarious situation. I know we had a lot of fun, joking around like that. It was a very pleasant game and it was also a type of flirting that did not become tense or unpleasant at all. It just flowed into a very enjoyable encounter and was the basis of our first introductions. After the movie was over, we uncannily met outside the theatre with the dialogue centering on the throwing of the popcorn, especially how many times we missed the hat. We were laughing all the time. I seemed to be attracted to this one beautiful girl with the dark eyes and dark hair. I wish I knew her name, I thought. My friend Nick (Nicholas, he was the oldest) suggested we give each other our names. Of course, only first names were given. That's when I heard her name for the first time. "ANN", she said! This name, unpredictably, would be with me for the rest of my life. I didn't know it then, but the impact of that meeting would affect the both of us, forever… I'm glad I finally wrote it down here in the book. I'm glad I met you Ann. Your coming into my life made me very happy, it made me whole, it made me a complete person! With humble gratitude and love, I say "THANK YOU, ANN"; you are the light of my life! And would you believe it, she saw something in me that attracted her, too! Isn't that great! But the story is not over yet. Because we were so young, we obviously were not aware of the significance of this encounter. It was just a casual meeting and after it passed, the presence seemed to have disappeared, but the experience of the encounter itself would never be erased from our subconscious. We did not see each other for quite a while. I don't remember how long. There were many forces pulling us in different directions at that age. We had to continue school, where my curriculum was quite intensive. My track team needed me; I was embedded deeply in sports. And I was taking care of my sister who was about three years old. I had a lot of responsibilities that did not dovetail with Ann's, so we were not together too often. This part is incredible, but since we had to take public transportation to go and come from school, we would meet occasionally on the subway train. It was then I was told by her that she made a Novena every Monday evening (that's nine Mondays of prayer for a special intention) at our local church. Every now and then, I would plan to attend the Novena also. After I entered the church, I would immediately look for her and when I spotted her, I would find a pew a few rows behind her. Don't ask me why I did that (not many things a teenager does can be rationalized). It was just nice to watch her during the prayer service, I guess. Anyway, it was after the service that I was anxious because that's when we would see each other, smile to each other and begin talking. You know, in every relationship there are impediments. Here is the one that had to be hurdled: This was the time Ann was put to the test by none other than her own friend Rosie. One day, Rosie said to Ann, "What do you see in that guy Gus? He walks around with torn pants all the time," she added. "I'm sure you could do better than that." Obviously, Rosie did not like me. But Ann defended me and told her, in spite of those things, she still liked me. Ironically, Rosie was the Maid of Honor at our wedding! The more I learned about Ann, the more I liked. It was wonderful. Looking back now, it's also evident that it was meant to be. It was ordained (my recollection tells me) that we would fall in love…

In 1946 many changes were taking place. The war was over, Germany and Italy had surrendered and Japan surrendered, too, the year before. All the things that were rationed were becoming available again, especially the sugar. Boy, did I miss that! But now the bakeries and pastry shops were flourishing. You could buy a dozen buns for twenty five cents. Could you imagine that?! My father would send me to our neighborhood bakery with a single dollar and I would come back with a whole pie and two dozen buns! We had a feast. Of course, what we didn't know is what that sugar was doing to our body (with the genetic weakness the Pettis had for diabetes I'm talking about) and in looking back conclude that it wasn't that smart. But science had not informed us at that time of the danger, so we had one feast after another until the sugar hunger was quenched. That took a long time, though.

The next three years were filled with many dates with Ann until a point was reached that could be defined as going out steady. We were girlfriend and boyfriend at this juncture, and it was getting close to the year 1949. It was my high school graduation year. Many important decisions had to be made. I had to decide on choosing a career that would determine what College to go to. My mother wanted me to be a lawyer and my father wanted me to become a doctor. They would not relent. I told them I didn't want to be either, so they countered by withholding any funds needed to go to college. I had no money.

Scholarships were so scarce that you had to have a 160+ IQ or "ace" a scholarship test to qualify. I couldn't do any of these. I was in a quandary. I remember it got so emotional between my mother and my father that I began threatening them with some very outlandish alternatives. I'd rather not reveal them here since, in major parts, they were the ranting of an angry and immature boy...let's face it. After I was able to collect myself and try to make some sense out of the situation, a number of options began to appear. The first thing I remember doing was trying to find a way out of this dilemma . I remember one of my friends, Mike, had decided to join the Army. He went down to the Army Recruitment Center for his physical examination and would you believe he failed it! He was too short. He measured four feet eleven and a half inches tall. He was one half inch too short. You had to be at least five feet tall to be accepted by the Army at that time (I think they changed that now). He even put layers of cardboard in his shoes, to get taller, in an effort to make the height requirement. "Obviously it wasn't enough cardboard"; he said, then we gave him the scientific explanation, he probably compressed the cardboard on his way to the examination! Anyway it occurred to me, that this could be a way out of my dilemma. I was nineteen years old and I could join any military service, without telling my mother or father. I went to an Air Force Recruitment Center and volunteered into the Military Service. I was accepted immediately. It was November1949 when I told my mother and father I had enlisted (who took it rather calmly, as I recall – I guess it really was a relief for them, not having to pay for my schooling). The real tough notification was to my girlfriend Ann. How am I going to tell her I'm going away. What reason would I give her for enlisting in the Air Force? No answers came to me. I didn't have a clue. But I knew how I felt. I knew I loved her. I know, I'll propose marriage, I thought. We have time. There's a whole month ahead of us. I was scheduled to sign the induction papers on December 7th, after which I would be shipped out. OK. That's the plan. First I have to set up a date with her. During the date I will propose (but I don't have a ring, oh well, I'll deal with that another time). It was a beautiful night as I recall, I took her to a favorite restaurant of ours called Aunt Jemima, something like our KFC but with Southern elegance and with waiters that served you at plush chairs, with linen covered tables, but the food was similar (famous southern fried chicken). We even had a Champagne Cocktail together (our first cocktail together and no we weren't checked for age - it wasn't that critical in those days). After dinner, on our way home, we parked the car (my father loaned me his car) by the park. I proposed for the first time...and was somewhat "rejected"! I didn't understand why? Although her explanation seemed to answer the "why" question, I had difficulty understanding it. She said it was because she loved me, that she said no. She was pursuing an unselfish road and wanted me to have the freedom to go in whatever direction I wanted, while away from home. After she heard that I planned to leave for two years, her thoughts were only of me, but she promised to be there when I returned, if I still wanted her (what a foolish question, but I didn't tell her). It was a very sad departure. We both loved each other and usually people in love plan to be near each other and here I am planning to be away for two years. Little did I know that the Korean War would break out during my enlistment and increase the duty time to 3 ½ years. So this is how I departed in December of '49.... surrounded by all this anxiety and absolute mystery of what was to come. The Big Question was, "What Did The Future Have In Store For Me?" Let me tell you what happened next...

CHAPTER 4...MANHOOD AND SOLDIER

New People mentioned in this Chapter

Ann's Father (My Father-In-Law................................Erminio Passero
Ann's Mother (My Mother-In-Law.................Assunta (Testa) Passero
Bishop of Guam....................His Excellency Richard G. Baumgartner
Air Force Chaplain on Guam .... Father Leonard Burke,Capt.
My Platoon Buddy..Jack Working
His Brother .... Bart Working
My Airman Friend ....Bill Lancaster
Air Force Chaplain in NM .... Father John Moegling,Capt.
Best Friend in NM .... Dan Inglese
Best Friend in NM .... Philip Sculley
Partner / "Paisano"-My Father's .... Salvatore Scrifugia

1949

WINE MAKING AT ERMINO'S. After meeting Ann's father, I learned very quickly that he made the finest wine in the world in his basement every year. Not only was he astute with the process of wine making, he was also a connoisseur of grapes, in any color or shape or taste. It was the autumn of 1949 when Ann and I were seeing each other regularly. We were so in love with one another we could not bear to spend a moment apart. Partly because of this, I was becoming involved with many activities that were conducted at the Passero home. Mr. Passero (Erminio and later, my wonderful father-in-law) was very involved with the production of homemade wine which he needed when his current supply ran out. I, of course, offered my help especially since some of his older paisanos were not able to assist this year. According to New York City law, a household was allowed to produce and store 200 gallons of wine for personal use only (it cannot be sold). Mr. Passero was very conversant with the law and would make only that much wine every year (even though he didn't think it was enough – but that's another subject). When the time came for him to go out and purchase the grapes, he would need much help in preparing for the wine making event. Wooden barrels (that were already used and now empty) had to be taken apart and scrubbed with stiff bristle brushes and clean water. Although I described the process in one sentence, the task was not at all that simple. Each barrel held about 55 gallons of wine, therefore four barrels had to be dismantled and scrubbed. Each barrel had four steel bands holding them together with 16 planks falling apart when the bands were removed, not including the 10 boards comprising the top and bottom covers of the barrel. All in all there were approximately 32 pieces to a barrel and we had four of them to clean, which meant we had to deal with a total of 128 pieces. It didn't seem that involved at the time, while we were cleaning them but I couldn't help counting them. Erminio was very cheerful. He actually enjoyed this type of work (I'm the one that was squinting and wincing at every move). Later on, as I became more familiar, I realized why he was so cheerful. My theory was because he envisioned all the wonderful moments of intoxication he would enjoy in the future and it made him very, very cheerful.

But there was another side in the making of wine. The many technical aspects of the process were very serious business. For instance, the selection of the grape was the most critical aspect of all. Aside from the type of grape (i.e., Alegante, Zinfandel, Muscatel, etc.) to choose, he also wanted to know where it was grown (what part of the US). He liked California grown grapes as opposed to Upstate New York grown. Also, the grape had to be fresh, it had to be juicy, it had to be sweet, the skin had to be thin (it had to pop out when squeezed), it had to have small or few pits, the grape had to have a certain flavor when he tasted it and above all it had to be big and plump. I never knew a single grape had all those qualities, but I was learning. When we went out to purchase grapes, we would go to the vendors and he would ask them to open a case (the grape came in wooden crates of about 28 lbs each, with wooden slat tops nailed shut) and he would begin tasting and testing against all the qualities mentioned above. He had a great sense of humor; he would hand me a grape and say' "taste it and tell me what you think." I would bite into it, swirl it around in my mouth (imitating all the actions he would perform) and then say, "This is good, very tasty." He would begin laughing and barely get out these words, "I wouldn't even give this to my 'pigs', come on let's get out of here." Obviously, I hadn't reached the height of my grape tasting skills yet. But I was trying. At the next grape stand I did a little better. I was getting more sophisticated, especially with some of my responses to his questions. He said I had potential, but had to keep working harder at it. We went to seven grape stands that day until he was satisfied with what was offered. Then we would return to the vendor that had the best of the lot and purchased about 80 cases of grape to be delivered to the house, stacked on the sidewalk close to the basement door. When the grape was delivered, I helped cart the cases into the basement which was an enormous task. I had to wait until Mr. Passero and Uncle Tony returned from work, about 5 PM and then we would start. A 2 X 10 inch by 8 foot long board was laid over the basement steps and the cases came sliding down where they had to be picked up and placed near the grape crusher. As I remember, this took about two hours of really hard work. The compensation for all that work was a delicious dinner of Macaroni prepared by my favorite other mother (Ann's of course) and an excellent glass of wine, aged to perfection. You couldn't ask for better pay than that in those days. I loved the Passero's, they were so generous and every gesture they made came from the heart (gee, I wish I was more like them, I would think). I enjoyed being with them, especially during the wine making process.

The next step that had to be taken was the crushing of the grape. We needed the women for this phase. Because of the difficulty in each process it was divided among the sexes and this is almost custom, the work assignment was a given. The women would crush the grape by turning the handle attached to the crushing wheel (a large wheel with pointed wide squared metal studs about an inch high), this process was necessary to break open every grape to allow the juice to run out. The men would carry the heavy crates to the crusher and move the crusher to each barrel to be filled. When all four barrels were filled with the crushed grape, they were left out in the open to ferment. It took seven days for the fermentation process to produce the correct amount of alcohol for the wine (or grape juice) to become stable. Now the grape juice that has turned to wine had to be squeezed and barreled (and sealed-only with a small opening for ventilation). By squeezing I mean (all the material in the barrels-grape skin, grape seeds, grape vines and leaves) going into a wine press for filtering and extraction. His had a 2 ton press I believe. When we were finished pressing out the crushed grapes, there wasn't a drop left in the press. Every bit of liquid was in the container under the press. This liquid was then funneled into the cleaned barrels waiting to be filled. It was an absolutely fascinating procedure and very rewarding. As soon as the grape juice, turned to wine, it was in the final stages and contained in the aging barrels, my father-in-law sighed with relief. Another year's supply is now in place. Time for celebration! And celebrate we did. Out came last years wine and some from the year before and some from the year before that. He poured out wine in our glasses that was eight years old! That was good! I'll never forget those days when I helped my father-in-law make his wine… Thank you "Papa' Erminio", you gave me many treasures…

ITALIAN SINGING WITH ASSUNTA. Before I begin telling you about some good times I had with Ann's mother, I must remind you that she only spoke Italian. Thank God I could speak in Italian too. This one ability added so much to the bonding that occurred between Mrs. Passero and me. Not only was I able to communicate with her about all the daily activities but also in a special way because of our commonality in the field of music. Assunta was familiar with many of the Neapolitan songs that were taught to me by my mother and father and by my Grandfather Michelino. I was going out with Ann for many months without being aware of this common interest. We both knew the same songs that they sometimes sing in the streets of Naples, but most certainly in the homes. It actually was a national pastime in Italy and of course was passed down to the children almost naturally. As I recall, it was a quiet night, when Ann and I had no place to go (it may have been raining outside), we were in the kitchen having a piece of fruit, some nuts and a glass of wine when Ann said' "You know Gus, my mother can sing that song you and your parents sing called "O Sole Mio"." That's all she had to say. I turned to Assunta and said, "Do you know that one?" She said, "Yes." And from then on, Ann's mother and I would select a song to sing every time we met! It was so much fun! After we would sing a song together, we would laugh and laugh and laugh. It was hilarious! I couldn't carry a tune but knew the words that I just blurted it out, but she had a melodious voice and sang them with emotional meaning ending up with a very interesting but very funny result. It was so much fun! I will never forget those moments. Thank you Mamma Assunta, you added so much value to my life. There was only one of you! I will never forget you either!

WINE DRINKING WITH ERMINIO. Whenever I would come knocking on the Passero door and Mr. Passero answered, I could predict the question he would always ask. "How about a glass of wine before you go?" he would say. Heaven help me if I said "No". He would immediately inquire if I wasn't feeling well. So I always said, "OK", and we would sit down and have a glass of wine while Ann got ready to go out. I have to tell you, it wasn't a terrible sacrifice, to give-in to his badgering. His wine was delicious! I enjoyed it so much Ann made a comment once and was concerned about her father's insistence, asking if it was too much. "Are you kidding" I replied. "I love it!" Not only is the wine tasty, but it also puts me in a great mood. "I think it's great". She said she was going to talk to him about forcin" me to drink and I said "Please don't do that, he means well and I enjoy it" So nothing came of it and I went on being social, having a drink with my favorite to-be father-in-law every time I came to call on Ann. I would often kid around with Ann telling her that "The reason I love you so much is because I get a glass of wine whenever we go out" I don't know why, but this remark didn't sit to well with her. All I can say in defense is that I was only 19 years old and my father never made wine! It was a new experience for me. And a nice one at that! Thanks Papa' Erminio for the glass of wine, you have always been special in my book...

JOINED THE AIR FORCE. It was December 7, 1949 when I entered the United States Air Force Processing Center in New York City. Here I expected to receive my shipping notice and make preparation for the journey, whatever it was. I had no idea what was to come. All I knew was that I wanted my record to read; "Was accepted into the US Air Force on December 7, 1949" (it was a "patriotic" gesture of mine). But that was not to happen. Many, many forms had to be filled-out there at the center and one of them asked for all the information contained on my Birth Certificate, the one document I did not have. I showed them the Letter that the Ship's Captain gave us. "Not acceptable"; the Air Force Captain said. First off, no one could read Italian there. I even volunteered to translate it for them. They said no. The only acceptable course they said they take was to contact Washington DC where copies of all incoming foreign ships Log's are stored, to ascertain my birth aboard the SS Augustus. So the search commences. I was told to go home, it wouldn't be till tomorrow before they would receive the information requested. I did that, but was disappointed that I could not join on the 7th . It was a little tough to accept this delay, but I did., I returned on the 8th and the processing continued since they received the confirmation that my birth was recorded in those Log Books. The next incident will bring you back to a reference I made in Chapter 3, concerning High School and my teacher Dr. Ryan. Although my recollections of this Processing Center experience is sketchy, I will never forget the answer I gave them when the processing officer asked me if I understood the NSLI Life Insurance offer the Air Force was making to me. If I would accept it and for how much, the maximum was $10,000.00. To their amazement, not only did I know about this government life insurance policy but was able to intelligently make the proper selection (thanks to Dr. Ryan at Boy's High who thoroughly taught this subject excellently)! I naturally chose the $10,000.00. Of course those were the days of typewriters and carbon copy paper. In 1949 there were no computers or electronic keyboards. I had to wait for the officer typing the information to complete each form and for hours just sat there until all the information concerning my records was put on paper. Then I was asked to sign all the papers and on December 8, 1949, I became a member of the United States Air Force.

I was shipped-out within the week. Said my "Good-byes" to Mamma and Papa' and little Joann (she was about 6 years old). I was sent to Lackland Air Force Base in San Antonio a Basic Training location in Texas. They gave me specific instructions on what I could bring and what I could not bring. My manhood development was starting. Here in the service, you couldn't do whatever you wanted, as you did before. Here you had to follow orders, whether you liked it or not. You learned very early on that to disobey would be followed by punishment of the type you don't even want to think of.

THE TRAIN TO SAN ANTONIO. What has always puzzled me is that I joined the United States Air Force; therefore you would assume that I would be transported via Air, but instead I have always traveled via land carriers to get from one base to the other, during my stay in the Service. So they scheduled me to leave New York City on a train direct to San Antonio, Texas. The train was called; The Silver Streak and boy did it travel fast (at least I thought so). I arrived at the station in New York (Grand Central Station) at least an hour early. There were other guys waiting there that I assumed were going to the same place, so I asked and sure enough they were going to Lackland too. We introduced each other and boarded the train when it arrived. An interesting circumstance is attached to a somewhat uneventful trip to Texas. On board, traveling on the same train, were the famous basketball players from The University of Southern Texas who had just won the National Championship and came to New York to receive it. They were on their way home now and onboard that train. So picture in your mind these six foot plus, young athletes roaming the train, sitting in the lounge car, eating in the dinning car, drinking in the bar car, everywhere. Also remember I was six foot two inches in height and weighed a mere 148 pounds also (I wasn't aware of it, but I looked just like those players). You cannot believe how many passengers stopped me to ask how it feels to win such an award. It became very difficult to try to explain that I was not on their team and that I was not even a basketball player. People would come up to me without even asking me about the championship but directly wanting to see the "Gold Basketball" (the players won) and carried in their belt loop. "I don't have one"; I would say. They would look at me in disbelief and walk away. You would think that after a number of people had mistaken you for them and told you're not one of them, the inquiries would end, but "noooo", the questions kept on coming all during the trip. It was an embarrassing situation after a while. I couldn't understand why they kept it up. Then it dawned on me. New passengers were boarding at every stop. They almost all knew that this team had won this prestigious award. The Radio was blasting the news for days. For all those sports enthusiasts out there, it was common knowledge. I didn't have a chance! Oh, well, I'll just answer their questions as calmly as I can. So I continued my trip with this attitude and it helped.

What a train experience this was for me. First of all, the Air Force provided me with First Class Pullman tickets. I and all my buddies were in the First Class section of the train. We were assigned private Pullman cabins with pull down beds for our convenience. WOW, what treatment. I couldn't believe it. Not only was it my first train ride but to travel 1st Class, only happens in the movies! The next incident (and it was pleasant) will sound like fiction but it really happened. I was in the Dinning Room waiting for the waiter to bring me the menu, just after stopping in Kansas City, Kansas, where passengers left and or boarded the train. The dinning car was crowded so the waiter was very busy. I waited quit a bit. Coming into the car I saw this elderly gentleman walking towards me followed by this very pretty young girl, both coming my way. When they reached me, the gentleman said; "Excuse me but Is this place taken?" pointing to the empty seat across from me. "May we join you this evening, kind sir"; he added with a definite southern accent. Was I in a movie or something, quickly looking around for a reality check? Nothing in sight, no cameras, no lights, no director, I guess it's the real thing. Addressing them I said; "No one is sitting there; you're welcome to join me". "Thank you"; they both said and sat down across from me. The man then extended his hand to me and announced; "I'm (don't remember his name), Senator from the state of Kansas and this is my Secretary (don't remember her name either). "We are on our way to Texas to attend a convention"; he added. I immediately responded with my introduction; "I'm Gus Petti who just joined the US Air Force and am on my way to basic training". This delighted him and he responded; "That's fine, absolutely fine", then made small talk with his escort discussing the food possibilities. It was just at this moment that the waiter came to our table, addressing the young girl first. "What will you have Miss?" then proceeded to enumerate the items from the menu. She said all she wanted was coffee. The Senator also ordered coffee. They had told me they just had dinner before boarding the train. Now the waiter asked me what I wanted. I looked at the waiter and said; "What would you suggest?" He immediately responded; "Why Kansas City steak of course. We just received a load of them.". "OK", I replied; "cooked medium rare with corn and mashed potatoes, please". The waiter thanked me and left. The Senator then looked at me in absolute amazement and said;

"Son, do you know the size of a Kansas City steak, it's monstrous?" "No", I answered; "but how big could it possibly be?" (Not knowing what was coming) He said; "You'll see". Then we made small talk. The time must have gone swiftly because here the waiter was coming holding a large tray almost above his head to clear the diners that were eating. He stops, lowers the tray and I see this gigantic steak. Oh, my gosh, is it big! (My estimate was about 14 inches in diameter!) Before the waiter moved the plate from the tray to the table, the Senator said; "Can I watch you eat that, Son?" I said; "Suit yourself; I don't consider it a great feat". And I began; bite by bite, the steak dwindled until it disappeared right before his eyes. He sat there in amazement, commenting to his secretary as I ate the steak. Really, to me it wasn't a big deal. But they were amazed. When I finished, the Senator said; he has never seen anyone finish a Kansas City steak. That was a first for him. Not knowing, that at that age, I could consume two of them. He thanked me for the privilege, I acknowledged the pleasure of the acquaintance and they left. The best part of the meal is I didn't have to pay for it; I had a coupon the Air Force provided to pay for all my meals. I was happy. The steak was delicious and hearty. Back to my cabin and get ready for another night riding the rails. It took us about three days and two nights to arrive at our destination of San Antonio. As soon as we got off the train, the first thing I had to do is go to the toilet. The Conductor pointed to the direction it was in. I left my gear with one of the guys and proceeded to the toilet. When I was standing in front of the doors, I began looking for the Men's entrance. It wasn't that easy. First of all there were two sets of bathrooms. One read BLACK, then Men and Women and another set of bathrooms that read WHITE, then Men and Women. Can you imagine four doors for two genders? I stood there in wonder. Never had I seen anything like this. But the message was very clear…I was in the land of segregation and even though I did not agree with the situation, I had to be careful, otherwise pay consequences. It was my first awakening of the conditions in the South. A whole lot of emotions filled me at that point. First of all I did not agree with this treatment. Second I was embarrassed to be part of the white sector. Third, I never saw whites go to this extent to voice their racist feelings toward one another. It was too much for me and it hit me too soon, even before I slowly learned of the condition, so that I could handle it in time. Nope, I had to deal with it now! It was very difficult for me to rationalize, to say the least. Describing this incident probably led you to understand the frustration and anger that swelled-up within me at the time. And there was no one to discuss it with. Most of the men assigned to my unit came from Alabama, Mississippi, Oregon, Texas, Kentucky, etc. I didn't have a chance. The argument had to remain with me. The rest of the time I had to tolerate whatever unpleasant issue arose of this nature. For three months I had to endure the ideology of the South to maintain peace. And so I did, but there were incidents that occurred (which I'm not going to relate here) during my stay that tested me often.

GI BASIC TRAINING. Needless to say, I completed Basic Training successfully. I didn't know it, but I seemed to have an affinity for the military.

In Western Garb at Lackland AFB, Texas-1949

I did not balk at an officer giving me a command. I apparently was used to discipline and found it easy to follow orders. Many of my platoon buddies asked me how I did it. Many of them found it very difficult adhering to a command (especially a dumb one) given by a platoon leader and ,boy, did they get punished. The main purpose of Basic Training I learned later was to prepare us for military living. First and foremost, the largest hurdle was shedding the civilian attitude. From now on, you listened to whatever order you were given and accomplished it, to the commander's satisfaction. That was hard. I don't remember how many push-ups my platoon mates had to do as punishment for either not performing a command or not performing it to the satisfaction of the officer giving the order. I would say in the "thousands" and that's not an exaggeration! Of course I had my share of the punishments too. I would falter every now and then, but most times I would try to avoid failing in this regard.

Basic training not only included military training but required intensive physical testing. Doctors examined every part of my body, yes I mean every part! We also had to have our teeth examined. Low and behold, the Dental Doctor discovered some pretty bad cavities. They were in two of my molars. The teeth had to be pulled according to the doctor. Out they came. It wasn't that bad, but I lost two of my chewing molars. It probably affected my health to a degree but I was so young, I overcame that small deficiency quickly.

Being the tallest guy in the platoon, I was designated platoon leader. My duties were to make sure lights went out at 9:00PM every night and everyone was outside the building, in formation, by 6:30AM, every morning. You can't imagine how many guys I had to literally drag out in the morning. Gee, some guys cannot wake up in the morning. They used to give me such a hard time, but they knew when it came to push, in the end I had to win, otherwise they would go on report and now answer to a higher command. Not too pleasant. I would eventually get them all out and standing at attention. Then the roll call began. Only last names were called, unless there were duplicate names, at which time the first initial was yelled out along with the last name. We had three Smith's in my platoon, which irritated the Platoon Sergeant enormously. You would hear; "L. Smith, T. Smith and B. Smith". Am I glad there was only one "Petti". Our response upon hearing our name was; "Here, Sir!" This formation happened in the morning and in the evening, after all our duties were completed. Aside from miles of marching, most of our time was spent in Classes learning all the subjects necessary to move on to other parts of the service. Naturally it was basic, all rudimentary subjects were taught. Many subjects were difficult to observe because we never were associated with these subjects before. The hardest one to take was First Aid on the battlefield. Actual films of wounded soldiers were shown (and the vomiting in the class would start). Airmen would excuse themselves, run outside and throw-up for the rest of the class. Fortunately I never got sick this way. I suspect reading all of Dr. Iamele's books on surgery that were stored in my Zia Luccia's basement helped me escape those queasy feelings. In fact nothing grotesque that was shown on military films ever affected me detrimentally. I seemed to be immune to their bold presentations.

One of the promises I made Ann before I left for San Antonio was to send her my address of every AF base I go to during my enlistment. As soon as they gave me the address, I sent it to her. Then the letters began arriving. I enjoyed those letters very much especially since my mother and father were not that experienced at writing in English so their communication with me was sparse. Of course my letter writing habit was not akin to Ann's either, in fact I don't remember writing to her at all for the three months (But you should not read anything into that fact, remember I was only 19 years old and was a little immature) but I did call her on the phone and did talk to her before my next assignment.

3 DAY PASS. We were told early that at the conclusion of our three month stint, a three day pass to be spent in San Antonio, would be granted every soldier, under the condition that you passed all the courses and requirements assigned. The guys were planning this get away for more than two months. As they reviewed their activities with one another, an interesting thing happened. As plans were unfolded in the barracks, everyone could hear the details, those who liked a certain guy's plan would confirm his participation and groups were being formed. Of course most of them were geared toward girl pursuit, of which I was not interested in. After all I had my girl in Brooklyn and did not have to go on this female safari that they were planning. And so it went. More and more groups were forming as the months elapsed. I was not part of them, nor were two others in my platoon. One was guy definitely was "unsocial" and no surprise, but I couldn't figure out why this other one was not joining a group (I did not know this but his not joining a group was to my benefit as we will see). Anyway at the conclusion of the three months, it was Thursday evening, our passes

were given to us. Those with passes went into town in uniform so they must be on their best behavior. The groups were eager to commence their military holiday and getting all spiffed-up for tomorrow. Although I chose to refuse many invitations from my buddies, I sort of felt left-out and a little blue. At that moment, this one fellow, his name was Jack Working approached me and invited me to go with him touring the town (the reason I remembered that name is due to its odd usage-I only heard the word "working" as a verb in a sentence). He was from Austin, Texas and his brother was coming tomorrow morning to pick him up and take him around San Antonio. I should mention that the other groups did not have this type of transportation. They had to use buses and other public transportation to get around. Of course I said; "Yes, a positive Yes". I couldn't believe it, one moment I'm lamenting of being left out, the next, I've got the best deal in town. Isn't life great!

Sure enough, the next day Jack's brother Bart was waiting for us in the Visitor Parking area at the base. When we got there, we began discussing the itinerary immediately. No time was lost. We just had breakfast, so we decided to visit the Alamo first. It was getting exciting. When we got there and viewed the Alamo, I was somewhat disappointed, mostly because of its size. It was much smaller than I had imagined. In the movies it appeared gigantic, but in reality it is actually the remains of a much larger Missionary Church, whose other parts, were blown away by Mexican canons, during the battle. But in many other regards it was very interesting. There was a guide who explained all of the details occurring during the battle, including all those famous Americans, who gave their lives (and many more I presume) grateful for the bravery and sacrifice that was instrumental in preserving our country's lands. It ended leaving me in a somber mood and very pensive. The down mood would soon pass because we were on our way to a special restaurant, right on the banks of the San Antonio River for Lunch. These guys knew everything about San Antonio. Although I don't remember the name of the restaurant, I cannot forget the view (overlooking the river) or the food. It was Mexican of course. I love Mexican food. I don't know what they ordered, but I started with a bowl of chili-hot. The word hot here does not stand for temperature when referring to Mexican food; you know it stands for a high level of spiciness. And HOT it was. I can almost taste it now, but it was so delicious. I have tried to duplicate that taste in some of my recent attempts at chili recipes without success. Then they ordered Enchilada's which were completely alien to me, my curiosity got the best of me so I ordered the same thing. Well I believe I fell in love with them instantly. So far, they were the most delicious Mexican food I ever tasted. They would be my favorite from now on. Viva la Enchilada!

It was getting late, so we decided to go to some special Bars that Bart knew. I never saw so many Taverns. I immediately wondered if the people in San Antonio did anything else except drink boos? But then on second thought I realized it's probably the Air Force base that's causing the existence of so many drinking places. Let me explain these bars to you. I believe they were specifically designed for military enjoyment. They contained everything a person away from home would miss. Of course there was the boos, that's the same in every bar. Equipped with beer dispensers behind the bar counter, there were the ordinary bottles of hard liquor on the many shelves behind the bartender including glasses and all the requirements needed to mix a drink. It was the interior of the establishment that got my attention. Each bar seemed to have a theme in addition to the drinks. We frequented a number of bars that night so I was able to make a comparison (until I couldn't see anymore-just kidding). I did get a little under the weather but I was able to reach the barrack when the evening was over. Let me describe some of these places. The first one was called; Western Shooting Gallery. On each table was a rifle placed at each chair position. The rifle had a wire attached to it. On the walls of the bar were targets of all types. Bears roaming, deer prancing and rabbits running here and there. All you had to do is load your rifle and shoot at any target you aimed at. If you hit your target you would get a point on the tally board listed on the side of the wall. It was all electric but relatively exciting. The scores indicated your marksmanship and also recorded your score toward a free drink when you reach 10 points. Here's a phenomenon I noticed at those games, the more you drank, the lower your score. It was a self reducing master scheme. You just could not get drunk playing this game. To get drunk, you had to buy your own drinks! We had some fun in this one. The next tavern we went to had Pin Ball machines all over the place. One could play pin ball all the time they were there at 10 cents a round, it wasn't bad. If you hit their jackpot points, you would also get a free drink. Well the incentives were there and the GI's were there in large numbers. All these joints were crowded. So we moved on. The next one we visited was like entering a room in India (I can't remember its name); the place was full of smoke that was coming from incense burning in every corner, in front of images I did not recognize. In the center was this gigantic brass coffee maker (they had a special name for it-something like Ishtar I believe). We realized this was not a boos bar but a coffee bar. So we sat down for some very weird coffee. I don't know what was in it (even though the waiter explained the content) but it was good. Then we continued to the next bar. The next one was unbelievable. It seemed like we were in an aquarium. Half the walls all around, including behind the bar, were glass panels displaying so many types of fish I couldn't count the different varieties that were swimming around. This was a tranquil place. Except for the piped in music, which was low, it was much quieter than the others. We were able to talk here a lot more than in the others. Jack and Bart were talking about their origins and encouraged me to talk about mine. They both were born and raised in Austin, Texas on a cattle farm. Then I told them I was born (I did not want to complicate things telling them I was born on a ship) and raised in Brooklyn, NY. We had so many questions to ask each other about our origins, that before you knew it, it was time to return to the base. We had a great time. What a surprise compared to the way it started. We did this for the next two days and had a ball.

During Basic Training, one of the main objectives the military had in store for us was to test our academic abilities. Aside from tests asserting one's IQ level, there were other tests determining candidacy for Pilot Training School (they were always searching for pilot candidates within the masses). It was up to the Air Force to find the pilots for tomorrow's airplanes. No High School or University for that matter tests students for possible pilot capability. It's a military thing; the responsibility therefore rests with the military to develop its own pilots. Well, I was told that I had the potential of being a pilot. I was sent to Lowry Air Force Base, Denver, Colorado for processing after completing my Basic Training. More about this later.

PARENTS BUY FIRST HOME. Before departing for Denver Colorado, I was sent home on a one week furlough. It was around Easter when I arrived home in Brooklyn, NY. My parents had an important announcement for me. They were ready to buy a home of their own! Wow, that was earth shattering news! Joann was around six years old now and my mother and father had saved up enough money to be able to afford a home of their own. Up to now we always lived in apartments, only dreaming of owning our own home. There was a house on 3 Orient Avenue that was for sale. My father asked me if I would go with him to see the house. I said yes, and we went. What an experience that was. The house was a two and a half story wooden house. It had two kitchens (it was a mother and daughter house), with three bedrooms on the top floor with a bath room. The second floor had a living room, dinning room and kitchen. I liked it and so did my father. Now all we had to do is convince my mother that it was a nice house. When she got a chance to see it, she agreed that it was nice. The structure was sound and all, but the lighting in the house was very strange. Of course we changed it as soon as we became the owner but the lighting only had 25watt bulbs in all the rooms. It was so dark inside the house you had to be careful where you were stepping. At first my father and I thought it was an eccentricity of the owner, but then we learned that he was an Electrician and it was a money saving attempt on hid part. We also noticed that all the occupants that we encountered during our visits all wore very thick eye glasses. When we returned to our apartment we all commented on the Cyclops eye glasses we witnessed worn by the residents. We also asked ourselves; "Didn't they know what they were doing to their eyes?" We could not help noticing the travesty there, but we were buying a house, not correcting an injustice. So the house was bought. My parents were now the proud owners of their own home. What an accomplishment for two (make that four) immigrants arriving in America with only a few Lire's in their pockets! It was a time for celebrating and celebrating we did. Out came the wine, then the music, then the cheers and finally the food. My mother made all of our favorite foods. My father got his homemade ravioli and roasted capon, I got my veal stuffed breast and the ravioli's that are my favorite too. We had a feast. I had to apologize for not being able to help with the move from the apartment to their new house, but I would be away when the move takes place. My parents understood. The next time I came home, they were already in the Orient Avenue house and enjoying it immensely. The house came with a very large garage where my father continued fabricating another the invention. This was the beginning of the J2-AQUATRON concept (a water craft design capable of traveling at accelerated speeds-safely). He began building it at this location. I helped him build this structure from the beginning. In fact I physically stored and worked on the craft in my garage (and for a short time in Jerry's garage) till the year 2000, when circumstances forced me to abandon it altogether and it was sold for junk. It was the end of the J2-Aquatron, an ambitious invention that I felt would have revolutionized future naval design. Although I sent the craft to salvage, the concept is burned in my mind and will never be forgotten as long as I'm alive.

SENT TO COLORADO. The train ride to Lowry Air Force base from Brooklyn, New York, was uneventful except for the upward ride that the train had to take to reach Denver (the mile high city) in the Rocky Mountain range. When I arrived, an AF (I will use the abbreviation AF to signify Air Force) Sergeant was on the platform to greet us and take us to the base from the train station. It was the beginning of May and very cold. What I noticed while we were being transported by military bus was seeing little children in their BVD's playing in Institution Playgrounds in the bitter cold. At first I thought this was cruel treatment of unfortunate children until another airman close by asked the Sergeant that question and he answered that those scenes were of Tuberculosis Institutes helping the children get some sun and the cold did not affect them at this height in the mountains (A fact that stayed with me all during my stay in Denver, that you don't feel the cold when you are so high up). What a relief. And what a revelation that was. I did not know that. From where I stood it looked like suffering and yet it was medical humane treatment. I learned not to jump to conclusions after that experience. I arrived at the base a little wiser. We were brought first to the Quartermaster for sheets, pillow and blankets. Next, we were brought to the barrack. At the barrack we were assigned sleeping cots. Next we were brought to the "Mess Hall" (name for Dinning Room). Those are two of the three essentials for survival in this world, Food and Shelter (we already had our Clothing). We were ready to start the training.

The qualifications for pilot training school were grueling. Not only was a certain level of intelligence required but also top physical health was a prerequisite to the program. I entered a whole battery of written "tests" as soon as I arrived at the base. Then began the medical physical examinations. During one of the examinations, while my teeth were being looked at, the Doctor said you have two molars missing. "I know"; I said, "They were removed by an AF Doctor while I was in basic training, in Texas." He said; "You know Son that disqualifies you for entry into the Pilot Program", (They had a habit of telling you directly, without feelings). I said; "What! How could the loss of two teeth affect my qualifications so much?" He answered quickly; "Pilot Training here is for supersonic pursuit jet planes that require resistance to at least 6-7G forces, to withstand this you must have all your teeth in your mouth." You can imagine how disappointing this news was to me? I didn't even want to go into the argument of why didn't the Doctor at Lackland AFB try to save the two molars instead of pulling them. I just felt very depressed. Now what? I thought. What are they going to do with me now? I had lots of questions and searching for answers. On the second day after I received the news, I was summoned to Headquarters to meet with the Commanding Officer. I had to dress in official uniform and arrived about 15 minutes before the hour. The Colonel was very nice and seemed to have some compassion for those receiving disappointing news even apologized for the way I was treated, with the explanation that military processes are not always fair and sometimes have a lot to be desired. I felt a little better after the meeting. At the meeting he also told me that in my tests, I scored high for Aircraft Armament and he was going to recommend me for that MOS (Main Occupational Specialty). There were several bases that had Armament Training facilities and coincidentally Lowry AF base was one of them so I didn't have to be transferred. School began the beginning of the next week after receiving the news. I began questioning myself why I ranked so high in an occupation that if I had to choose it voluntarily would never have been chosen by me especially since I am against all types of violence. At the time, I could not understand why I was being led into this path. But being in the military, I told you about the first order of the day is to obey commands without question. That's what I did. Off to school I went. Wouldn't you believe it, in class, a test was given starting with a disassembled rifle to see if you could reassemble it in a specific amount of time. I was able to reassemble the rifle in the allotted time. "Great"; said the Instructor. "Have you ever done this before?" he asked. "Nope"; I said, "Never". He then said to me; "Petti, you got it!" That remark sort of convinced me that maybe I did have the mechanical inclination toward armament and didn't know it. Of course rifles were not the only gun I studied; there were all types of pistols along with the rifles, but then there are machine guns up to 50 caliber and then canons. Believe it or not (and this is not classified information) canons! I couldn't believe it when they presented me with Handbooks describing canons mounted in airplanes. I must tell you this, that when a canon is fired in an airplane during flight, the recoil of the canon actually stops the plane in mid air. Of course the interruption is of so short a duration, it does no affect the overall movement of the craft. But they did research and found that the blast of a canon did stop the plane in its course and even measured the duration, listing it for the records. Many amazing facts came from the study of armament that I will reveal as we go along. In addition to hardware of this type, we also studied Bomb Sights, Cameras and Explosives including Bombs. My favorite subject was Bomb Sights. We studied the Bendix type (which became obsolete while I was still enlisted). It was an optical system and very interesting. Circumstances in the future had me working on aircraft cameras for most of the time I remained in the AF. The study of bombs was very enlightening since I always wondered how they worked, well now I know. Then there were the explosives. This is where you report at school and there is a military bus waiting to take you to the Firing Range. The firing range in this case is where surplus or discarded explosives are detonated with a big Explosion and it's over. But very scary while in progress. After some of my classmates went out to the field area (that's where the object is to detonate lies) and exploded some obsolete bombs, I was sent to do the same. Of course the group was safe in a Bunker with a little horizontal space serving as a window to view the happening. The Lieutenant sent me to detonate a 500 lb General purpose casing (with no fuses), just the explosive inside. My job was to prepare an ignitable fuse with a detonator, timed sufficiently to provide me with safe exit from the explosion site. OK, detonator in place, find the end of cord fuse, ignite it, walk to Bunker for safety. When I returned to the Bunker, the Lieutenant said; "Good work Petti" and BOOM went the bomb, with shrapnel everywhere crashing to the ground. I felt good. I don't know if it was due to the compliment or the explosion? Anyway my schooling went well. Still I had a lot to learn about Western living.

WESTERN LIVING IN COLORADO. I don't know if it was because I was so young or so naive but many of the adventures that I'm writing about would have been terribly frightening if I had to experience them now, but as I recall I took most of them in my stride, especially at that time. The first one was Horse Back riding. I never had ridden on a horse. I used to see them pulling wagons during my childhood, but I never rode one. Not only did I have to learn (because everyone did it in the west) horse back riding but I learned it on a mountain, with most of the paths along mountain trails at a mile high above sea level. Most people, when learning how to horse back ride, only have to look down from the mount which is about 4-5 feet above the ground, but I not only had that height to contend with but also had an added 300 to 500 feet down a cliff you're usually viewing as you walk along the mountain trails and the horse likes to walk right along the edge! How's that for "scary"! After doing it several times, you get used to it. And let me tell you, some horses are as stubborn as people sometimes! It's very difficult handling those types. But I managed and actually began enjoying it. My buddies and I would go horseback riding most weekends, weather permitting.

Another pastime was dancing. Yes, the USO at the base, conducted music and dancing for any serviceman interested, every Saturday and Sunday evening. Since I had just learned to dance, I didn't want to forget what I had learned so I attended frequently. All the women were volunteers and from a local Church, hoping that their gesture would make some serviceman happy. And that it did. Some were very good dancers. After awhile you could identify the good dancers and when they were in attendance, they were the most popular. Age wise, they were mostly on the "old" side, but were very cheerful and energetic.

One of my guy buddies became very friendly with two sisters who invited him and all his friends to their home for Banana Cream Pie and coffee. We all went and were greeted with the most delicious Banana Cream Pie I ever tasted, ever. The women were so sweet cheering us up all during our visit. May God bless them. I have been searching for a Banana Cream Pie to match that excellence ever since. It's a futile search I know, but I just can't help myself.

The pastime I could have done without is drinking alcohol. What a thirst you get when you are a mile high. We would (me and my buddies) go out every night, after duty, to all the local bars and taverns, drinking beer all night long until we were walking unsteadily home. You cannot imagine how many different bars we visited. Here are some examples; we went to the Longest Bar in the US. We were at the bar with the Woman's Face on the Floor (famous for a stain in the wooden floor assumed to be the image of a beautiful woman's face - I think they made a movie about this), then there was the Oldest Bar followed by the Tallest Bar…for some reason in Colorado every bar had to have a distinction otherwise it was not frequented. Well, it goes without saying that the gimmick worked, because we had a new goal to achieve every night. It's a good thing I was not into hard liquor at the time otherwise I don't know how my buddies would have gotten home every night. Yep, I had to carry them home most of the time.

Since we were so close to Wyoming (land of the Rodeo), we would go there to see some of the most thrilling rodeos ever performed. If you thought Bronco riding is difficult, it's nothing compared to Brahma Bull riding. I don't know how many riders were injured right there in the stall, forget about them getting into the rink. One time they had to replace four riders before the Brahma Bull came out of the stall. This one blew my mind. We watched the whole Rodeo and were ready to go back to the base, when one of my buddies said he thought he recognized one of the riders, so at the end of the show we went to the back of the rink, where the riders got ready and began searching for this guy. When my buddy saw who he was looking for; a hearty greeting took place and he introduced us to his partner. His partner reveals to me that he is from Brooklyn, NY and lived in Bushwick a short distance from where I lived. What a coincidence, not only did I encounter a guy from my neighborhood, but a rodeo rider too! "How did you get interested in Rodeos?" I asked. "It's such an unusual profession for a city guy; I added. "Yep" he said, then he explained that he answered a Cattle Rustling want ad in the newspaper when jobs were hard to find, went to Texas to work, and the rest is history. He loves being near animals and wouldn't want to do anything else. Wow, and this was a person born and bred in Brooklyn! Maybe there is hope for us that were brought up in the city, I thought.

Meanwhile, Aircraft Armament School continued. I graduated the course and was curious to know what the next assignment was.

Colorado AF Base-1950

The postings on the bulletin board answered that question readily. There was my name: Private First Class A. Petti report to Selfridge Air Force Base, St. Clare, Michigan. This is how we received every assignment. On the bulletin board, for everyone to see. No privacy, no respect (just kidding). Actually, it's very efficient. Can you imagine how many envelopes and private letters were saved by utilizing this method. Now I had to pack and ready myself for this next trip. Had to write to Ann to ask her to tell my parents about the new assignment and will send her my address as soon as I arrive. No furlough this time. I am to be ready immediately for transportation to Michigan. Of course it's by train (but no Pullman first class this time). To the train station we were brought by Air Force bus, the train arrives and we were on our way. The train ride was very similar to the one I took to Texas.

SENT TO MICHIGAN. When I arrived in Michigan, it was bitter cold. Snow had fallen and was piled up all around the buildings. I couldn't believe how cold it was. Even the vapor from my breath was freezing (I exaggerate). It was cold. After being equipped by the Quartermaster with the proper bedding and fur hat, I followed the squadron Sergeant to my barrack for orientation (this is where you receive all the information about the base and its facilities). What I noticed at first sight was that no one seemed to want to leave the barrack (I guess because of the cold). So we began playing cards passing the time until we were assigned duties. Next we had to leave the barrack to go to dinner at the Mess Hall. Now I know why they gave us Fur Hats, not only were they appreciated but we wore them all the time sometimes even indoor. It was weird, I wasn't used to that, but the necessity justified the use of such a hideous article of clothing. Of all the Air Force Mess Halls I've eaten in, this was the worst! Never had I tasted such awful food to the degree that I had to find an alternate, at least for survival sake. One of my buddies suggested the PX (Post Exchange-it's a military store that has almost everything) that every AF base had operating. He suggested the Hamburgers. So I went to the PX and ordered a hamburger to taste. It was delicious. They fixed it with lettuce and tomato, with a special sauce and a slice of pickle, but it was out of this world delicious. It may sound trivial, but to me it was a type of salvation in a way. It not only satisfied the psychological trauma I was experiencing, but it solved my hunger trauma too. I practically had all my meals at the PX after that find and hamburgers were the only food I consumed for the next four months.

My Aircraft Armament work assignment was very interesting. I learned that this was an Aircraft Training Base that not only contained Large Bombers like the B-19, which were propeller driven, but also pursuit fighter planes both propeller and jet driven. Jet planes were beginning to replace all propeller type aircraft during those years. It was an intense transition time for the Air Force and there was a need for top mechanics to handle the new technology. I really wasn't aware of the opportunities, probably due to my immaturity, but my skill and work assignments led me to one project after another.

Meanwhile I learned that in Europe, the United States was given approval by Spain to open seven Air Force bases there. The Air Force was asking all its Airmen for volunteers to man these new bases. I immediately volunteered. I could speak, read and write Spanish at the time and just think, it would only be a train ride away from Italy and all my relatives. I could visit all my relatives often. What a great assignment that would be. I checked the Bulletin Board every day, hoping to see my name listed there. I wrote to Ann telling her that I was volunteering for duty in Spain. I would be sending my address if that happened.

Meanwhile my work revolved primarily around Bomb Sights and Aircraft Gunnery Cameras. They had sufficient mechanics for the gun turrets and the guns but they were experiencing a shortage in mechanics for the more technical instruments. So I became well versed in the cameras and the sights. Just after I took a test for a promotion, the bulletin board yielded my name, but not to Spain but to the Island of Guam, in the Pacific Ocean Mariana Chain. What a disappointment! Who makes those assignments anyway, I asked myself? What made them ignore the qualifications I had for the post in Spain? I thought I was perfect for that assignment. What went wrong. Well, I did find out how this happened later. A buddy of mine that worked in Headquarters explained the process they use to make assignments in that office. It seems whomever is responsible for this task takes the two lists, one with all the volunteers for foreign duty and the other with all the needed MOS's (Military Occupational Specialty) on the other list, then just fills in names where the blank spaces occur. Destiny again! No regard to qualifications or special abilities was utilized during the process, as logic would dictate. There was my name and the assignment was "GUAM", in the Pacific Ocean. Even the name "Guam" was unknown to me at the time. I had to find a map of the world (which I did at our library) and discovered how far it really was.

I couldn't believe how close it was to the Philippines and Japan and Korea. Why, that's the other side of Planet Earth! I thought. Now that I knew where it is located, my next question was when will I be sent? That answer came very soon, the next week in fact. I would ship-out in June, but I would be given a two week furlough first. To my home I went, to see my mother, father and sister and to say goodbye. (Remember my enlistment at this point was for only 2 years and it was 1950). Of course I would be able to visit with Ann also. Her High School graduation had been planned and coincidentally would occur during my visit. Not only did I attended her graduation but I was able to escort her on "Prom" night too. On Prom night she looked beautiful! She took my breath away. I couldn't help recalling a phrase Bishop Fulton Sheen used when describing ones first love; "God sprinkles star dust on your loved one and the shine is so bright it blinds you". I'm sure Ann was sprinkled with star dust that evening, I was so blinded I couldn't see anything that evening except where the light was coming from. That's the night we danced the Mexican Hat Dance for the first time and every time after that, whenever they would play it at different affairs, we would immediately get up from our seats and get right into the dance with great enthusiasm (probably to relive those moments at the Prom). We had a wonderful time (that's my take on that special Prom date night - but Ann has a different story to tell about that evening – ask her sometime). To me it was like walking in a wonderland all the time I was with Ann. Then it was time for the goodbye. It was difficult, but there was no getting away from it. We kissed (she was in tears), we embraced and we parted. I left a little sad, but the unknown in the future seemed to dissolve the sadness as I continued my journey.

TO GUAM VIA SAN FRANCISCO. I got on a train to California this time, on my way to San Francisco, which was the port of embarkation for vessels to the Pacific Ocean. No more First Class Pullman. This train ride was very different. I had to sleep in a seat and was not privy to the first class dinning car. Those were hard times (just kidding). Being so young, none of these circumstances even fazed me. These are mostly my current thoughts that keep getting in the way. The first leg of the ride was to Chicago where we changed trains then onto

California. It was a long ride; I don't remember the duration but for some reason 5 or 6 days and nights come to mind. It was uneventful which increased my anxiety to reach San Francisco. We arrived. I got on a military bus to the AF base there; I believe it was called Anderson AFB. We stayed a few days there; then boarded a Merchant Marine Ship called the "United States" to begin our cruise to Guam. At the dock, we were greeted by the Red Cross volunteers who had set up counters with coffee and doughnuts but for a price" Each cup of coffee cost 5 cents and each doughnut cost 10 cents. At the time that was a bargain price but I thought the Red Cross was a charitable institution. Anyway it cost me close to a dollar by the time I had enough coffee and doughnuts to keep me going. It's funny; I never forgot that they "charged" us for those farewell treats!

Aboard the ship, when they showed me my quarters I knew I was going to have it rough. The sleeping portion of the bunk was just 6 feet long and I stood at 6'2"! Oh well, I'll just have to sleep with my legs folded I guess. Yes, that worked out well. We had no duties aboard ship so we played cards almost the whole voyage there which was estimated to be about 14 days. What was coming ahead could not be anticipated. We hit a terrible storm out at sea, a storm so fierce that I thought it was going to be the end. Without exaggeration, through the small round portal windows I could see the bow (front) of the ship actually submerge into the sea as the wind and the waves pounded us. The ship was moving in all directions. All around me, soldiers and merchant marine crewmen were getting sea sick, throwing-up everywhere even before they could reach a receptacle? It was all over the place. For some unknown reason I did not get sick (someone said it was because I was born at sea). So what duty do you think I was assigned? Yep, I had to clean up all the messes. But not for long because my resistance to the seasick illness attracted the Chaplain on board (a Catholic Priest) who asked me if I could assist him with his work on the ship. I immediately said yes (anything to get away form this horrid duty). For the rest of the voyage I was the unofficial Chaplain's assistant. I set up the Chapel for services and helped him distribute Communion at Mass (those were the days when Liturgical Law required a Patton to be placed under a communicant's chin to catch the Sacred Host if it fell out a person's mouth) and to servicemen who were in the Infirmary that could not attend Mass. It was pleasant work and I enjoyed it a lot. Even after the storm, I continued helping the Chaplain in his spiritual caring for the servicemen on board ship It was my first experience assisting a Chaplain.

1ST VISIT TO HAWAII. Our first port of call (port we dock at) was Hawaii. We would approach the Island of Oahu through the straights of Pearl Harbor where the Japanese had sunk most of our Navy. At the time the Battleship Oklahoma that was sunk, was just a rusty hull leaning on its side, lying in the water, protruding through the surface. We passed it on our way to the city of Honolulu which was our port of call. While we were passing the Battleship Oklahoma the ship's Captain announced over the loudspeakers that a moment of silence was asked of everyone aboard, in memory of those that perished during that attack. It was a somber moment. We stood there watching the hull of that gigantic ship pass by while we remained silent, honoring those men that gave their lives for our freedom. I will never forget it.

It wasn't long after that scene that we were approaching the port at Honolulu. Off in the distance we could hear the faint sound of Hawaiian chants. The sound attracted the attention of most of the servicemen to the starboard side (the right side of the ship when looking toward the front), where they began assembling to the degree where the ship was listing (dipping down on its side). We were getting closer and we could make out the gathering of Hawaiian women in grass skirts swaying in the wind and singing Aloha, with their arms and hands moving along with the sounds they were making. It was exciting. Remember we were pretty far away and although we could hear them and see them, they really weren't clearly in view. Our minds began filling with thoughts conjured up of Hawaiian movies most of us went to see, with Dorothy Lamoure and Bob Hope, in Hawaiian scene with her in a grass skirt singing and dancing. It was a wonderful memory. But as the ship got closer and closer the scene began to change, the apparent slim girls we thought we were seeing in the distance began appearing as very heavy, gold toothed females trying to make us happy. As soon as the singers became clearer to the servicemen and they were able to distinguish their real looks, the ship began to level-out probably due to the disinterest of the soldiers after the first apparition. Although guys can be cruel about the looks of females, the fact that these women came out to greet us was something to be appreciated. There are always a few that know their place and are able to understand generous gestures by local people. They went out to them in a cheerful manner as soon as the gangplank was fixed. The women had armfuls of beautiful flower lei's to stretch over our necks. A Hawaiian Official greeted the Captain and waved his hand to us, welcoming us to his island and wishing us a pleasant visit. We stayed at the Honolulu Hotel for all the days (don't remember how many) that was needed to replenish supplies on the ship for the next leg of the trip to Guam.

It seems the Chaplain I was assisting on board was a Horticulturist whose parents owned a large greenhouse farm in Connecticut. They grew orchids of all types. He told me he was on a discovery mission. Searching for a rare type of orchid for his parent's farm to propagate. It was called the Bull orchid (And had a Latin name I don't remember) and it could not be found in the US. If he was able to purchase one, it could be sent home where they would care for it and hopefully allow it to multiply. They would be the first to offer the species in the U.S. The Chaplain was very excited. He also had another mission, this one was for his Holy Order he was a Dominican Monk and his order had a Mission on the Island of Molokai where a Quarantined Colony of Lepers lived. He had boxes of Medicine to bring them and was warned that he could not enter the compound but should leave the boxes at the Gate and then leave, that's how contagious the disease is. For some reason, Leprosy was a very prevalent disease on these Islands. They had to Fence In those affected so that others would not come in contact with them. The Island of Molokai was only about 6 miles south of Oahu and could easily be reached by a small launch craft. The Chaplain went and delivered the boxes of medicine they so urgently needed. On his return he explained to me how strange it felt just leaving the packages at the doorstep of the Mission, without a word to anyone, then leaving, not knowing if they received the life saving medicines. Of course they later communicated their gratitude by Ham Radio to our base Operator that day, which made him happy to know that they were received. Now he was focusing on his other project. He was given a contact in the states that was a dealer in Exotic Orchids and may help him find the species he is searching for. The Chaplain left one day to reach an address given to him by this dealer and lo and behold he returns with this beautiful Bull Orchid. Naturally I did not see the beauty that he saw in this flower, to me it had no color with a weird shape, but the Chaplain was elated and tried to imagine how happy his mother and father were going to be when they received it. The Chaplain then carefully wrapped it (he knew how to protect it against impact) by stuffing cotton balls under each petal, gave it a good drink of water, sealed it and immediately brought it to the Post Office. It was on its way. When we arrived on Guam, he assured me that it arrived safely and was doing well in his parent's greenhouse. Everyone was happy and so was I.

Of course we had to tour the Island to the degree time would allow. First on our agenda was Waikiki Beach and Diamond Head. Off we went with some buddies, we took a taxi and went to those places. Believe it or not but Waikiki Beach did not impress me the way it did when I saw it in the movies. In fact, as I stood there, I thought Coney Island looked better (no offense intended). The ocean was unusually calm and I didn't see those gigantic waves that I saw in the movies. It was somewhat of a disappointment but the real fascination was the story about Diamond Head. This is a tall Rock that juts up into the sky, about 400 feet high, to the right of Waikiki Beach. The taxi cab driver told us this story. He said, back in Hawaiian history, when only native tribes existed, Kings ruled the different tribes of the Island. Some tribes even were at war with one another for some reason or another. One of the warring tribes had a Prince who fell in love with a Princess of an opposing tribe. They went before their Kings (who were their fathers) to ask permission for their hand in matrimony. They were denied. Both Kings forbad their children from seeing each other after the request. The two lovers made a pact with each other to meet at the top of Diamond Head at a certain time. There they would promise their love to each other and then take their lives by plunging down from the rock. If they could not "love" each other in peace, then they did not want to live in this world filled with hate and contempt. And so they jumped and the legend began. The legend goes on to say, after their children's death, the tribes reconciled and were at peace with each other for the rest of their history. That's the legend behind Diamond Head (I believe they made a movie in the USA about this story too). It was very interesting and moving. Next we went to a Pineapple Plantation where they described the growing of pineapples. That was a fascinating visit. The soil in Hawaii is so fertile, vegetation grows everywhere. Most of the nutrients in the soil derive from the volcanic ashes that are constantly falling from the many active volcanoes all along the Hawaiian Island Chain. Hawaiian's also told me that they grow the most delicious "potatoes" in the world! I didn't taste them but that is quit a claim. We all know they grow the most delicious macadamia nuts in the world, but potatoes; I don't know? Anyway the stay at Hawaii was great.

On to Guam now, which was our next destination. We again boarded the ship and set sail early in the morning. The sun was shinning bright and the sea was calm. It seemed like a perfect day to me and we were on our way. A few days went by when we were told that tomorrow we would be passing the one hundred and eightieth meridian. "What was that"; I asked? That is half way around the world I was told. The earth is divided into longitudes that are imaginary lines (invented by ancient mariners-using geometry) drawn from the poles. We know a circle contains 360 degrees across the diameter and so does the earth. At the 180th Meridian something happens to a human aboard a ship who passes it. Let me explain.

MEMBER OF GOLDEN DRAGON. At this meridian there exists an International RULE that must be obeyed. It is an imaginary Hierarchy called "The Order of The Golden Dragon". It comprises of a Ruler who is Neptune (naturally, we are out at sea) who is administered by many Court officials (I forget their names but I recall most had names of Greek or Roman sea gods). The next thing we were told is that tomorrow we are to wear special clothing otherwise we would experience the wrath of the King. We were told to wear fatigues with as loud a tie as possible. All this was mumbo jumbo to us. We didn't know what was going on. Everything that was being said was all a mystery to us. But we knew that we had to obey. What made it tough is that wearing a tie with fatigues is against military regulations in the AF? You could get a court martial for dishonoring your uniform that way. Most guys were in a quandary. Since the Court made such a special appeal I felt that to disobey would be a mistake. I wore my worst tie that morning. The Captain got on the loudspeaker and ordered everyone on deck to get some fresh air (Oh sure, it's all part of the gimmick-I thought). Sure 'enough, here come the Court attendants (all dressed in costumes-looked a lot like Adventures of the Caribbean, mostly pirate outfits). But there were standouts like one was dressed like a big pig and another only wore a large diaper. At this point we didn't know what to expect but the mystery didn't last long. Here they come down the deck, walking over to some, saying something to them and then taking a large scissor, they would cut their tie in half, throwing the cut part overboard into the sea. Nobody understood why they were doing this; I think that's what made it so intriguing. Of course my tie was cut also. The next thing we heard was another announcement over the loudspeakers, "All those whose ties were cut are to report at two bells (naval time-7 PM) here on deck in front of King Neptune's Court. What now; I wondered. The scuttle that was spreading was that all those whose ties were cut must undergo an initiation before the King. You wouldn't believe how some guy's imagination would come up with ridiculous possibilities. Some said they are going to "cook you in oil", some said; "You are going to walk the plank blindfolded", and you get the idea. All sorts of stories were circulating as to the possible initiation horror they are going to put us through. After hearing these invented stories, you know we were very anxious by the time we had to report. But here it was, close to 7 PM, time to go up on deck and face the music. As we cleared the open hatch, I could see the whole Court, they were sitting on what looked like grandstands with King Neptune at the top (with his long beard, crown and three pronged scepter and in robes-very impressive). Below him were the big Pig and that one in a Diaper. Below them were all those dressed in Pirate outfits, all laughing and having a ball (at our expense obviously). Ok, let's get through this quickly; I'm not enjoying it. And it begins; each person with a cut tie is brought before the King. The charges are read. The Court votes (always with their thumbs down) and the punishment is announced. "One slice of Sardine Pie!" Ewe… (that must be eaten in front of the Court) and one or two (dependent on how defiant an Airman is in front of the Court) raw eggs broken on top of ones head, dripping down your face while standing there at attention until dismissed. All in fun. They were howling with laughter. I couldn't' wait to be dismissed to run into the Latrine to wash my mouth and wash my hair and face. In the end, when you look back, it was fun! The next day, all those initiated were presented, in front of the Court, a beautiful card, depicting a Golden Dragon with the words "Member of the Order of the Golden Dragon". In smaller type; "Holder of this card has reached the 180th Meridian". Not too distinguished a certificate, but I treasure it because of the memories it allows me to recall. Also, it is a very exclusive Order since there aren't that many Members in the world today (interestingly, when you "fly" across the 180th meridian today, this ritual is not performed and no one gets a card). This process is only performed when sailing across the Meridian I am told. In a few days we passed Wake Island which was just a large bar of sand. There was nothing growing on it which seemed strange. Another interesting sight to me. Just a few more days and we began approaching some high cliffs and began seeing a number of Navy vessels including Submarines docked along the shore. Our ship now was waiting outside a narrow canal for a cruiser to guide us through the Agan'a Bay inlet. We have reached Guam, finally! Fourteen days at sea, but we have arrived. After we docked, an AF bus was waiting to bring us to the base. We were told by the officer on the bus that just two days ago a terrible Cyclone (tropical hurricane) hit Guam, destroying many buildings and injuring many people. On our trip to the base, the officer had the bus driver stop at an Airplane Hangar site to view the damage it caused. I couldn't believe my eyes, there right in front of me were mangled steel beams that were 2 inches thick, twisted like pretzels, as if they were clay. Let me tell you, the scene helped me to understand the brutal force that wind has, and created a respect for Natures forces within me. As soon as we arrived at the base, the officer brought us to the Quartermaster and you know the routine. This time our quarters were slightly different than what we were accustomed to, we were living in what are called "Quonset Huts". I don't know the origin of that name but they are not "square" shaped but more like a semi round shape for the roof allowing rain water to run off the roof quickly and efficiently (Remember we are in the Pacific where "Monsoon Rains" occur without notice and are very heavy downpours, for example: sometimes a foot of rain an hour!).

The name of the Air Force Base was "North Field Air Force Base". What I saw was a Squadron of B-19 Bombers with some F-80 Pursuit planes parked there also. This gave me an immediate picture of the type of planes I was going to be working on.

Our B-19 refitted with a lifeboat for Air Sea Rescue

Two incidents occurred at this point in my "travels". As soon as I reported to the small headquarters Office of the Land and Sea Rescue Flight, a Master Sergeant processed my records that spoke with a very heavy southern accent. "Y'all from New York?"; he asked. "Yes sir"; I responded. "Ya' mus be won 'o dose big city wise guys then?"; he added. "No sir!" I retorted. "Well, we'll see." He said. Then he proceeded to address all of us. We were five new additions to his staff. As it turned out, he put me on KP duty and Latrine duty more times than I want to remember. It's as if he had to break me of the habit of being a wise guy (which I "wasn't), I guess. He never explained why he had it in for me. We did have our differences though. I remember one time; he insisted that I sign a paper releasing my right to the NSLI Life Insurance premium payment requirement. It seems Congress back in the US passed a law providing free premiums for all US Servicemen that signed the waver. I would not sign the waver. The Sergeant was adamant, "Every other soldier in my command signed, why won't you?" I explained why, but he would not accept it (Although signing the waiver grants you free premiums, accepting this privilege denies you of all the Dividends the program earns for you and I calculated the difference is in my favor by continuing paying the premiums). He was ticked especially, since it was preventing our division from receiving a 100% subscription signing FLAG from the General of the base for total subscription. I knew he couldn't force me to sign. I didn't want to sign. We never got the FLAG! I guess the Sergeant considered that is the behavior of a city wise guy, I don't know? What I do know about him is that whenever I was close enough to him, the smell of liquor on his breath was appalling. I don't think he ever was sober. He was a career soldier. He did not know what life outside of the Military Service was. He was in his 60's when I met him. Very close to retirement he told me. Good luck Sergeant...

TRIP TO ROTA ISLAND. The first Air Sea Rescue assignment I was given was to accompany a team to search and locate downed aircraft that already crashed into the boon docks (military word for Jungle) on the Island of Rota (about 30 miles north of Guam and measuring about 3 miles long by 1 mile in width-very small). Once these airplanes are located, they must be painted with a special florescent yellow paint in special diagonal stripe formation. This was necessary so that subsequent planes flying above the old crashes were not reported as new crashes which would then commence a brand new Air Sea Rescue search, only to find out it was an old crash and does not require such action. Our task was after the craft was located; we would get out the paint and begin painting the yellow diagonal lines. Since there were about 11 crashed planes in the boon docks on the Island, we had to stay there a number of days. We sailed there aboard an Air Sear Rescue yacht. As soon as we arrived, the governor of the island came to greet us along with his entourage of Island people. They were very cordial. They ushered us to the governor's house (a military Quonset Hut that was provided by the US government) and told us we could lodge there. They spoke very little English. Keep in mind there was no electricity, no running water, and no sewage. It was pretty bare to say the least. Since I was beginning to pick up some Chamorro words, I got along very well with the governor. He told me that at night, for about an hour, he would turn on the Island's electric generator, so that the radio's in the homes (It seems everyone had a radio and the population was about 600 inhabitants) we estimated about 200 huts (they built huts on top of four palm tree trunks, about six to eight feet off the ground (this is to protect the structure during Monsoons, which can deliver six to eight feet of water a day and the rising water level would clear the hut. The hut was only one story high, with openings for two doorways to the outside and four or five window openings, but no doors and no windows. The hut is wide open at all times. This is to help reduce resist when the wind during a Cyclone hits (tropical hurricane) and the floor was bamboo strips, but not at all like our floors. These strips had a ½"space in between. They "never" had to sweep the floors. All the dirt fell right through to the ground below. It's one of the features I appreciated most. Of course this description also holds true for the huts on Guam. They were all made the same. And the roofs were corrugated galvanized tin. They purchased the roofing material from the US Government on the Islands. It was the least expensive and the most durable material available for the job. One of the advantages to other methods and materials was that during a storm, the wind would lift the different pieces of the roof and blow them away. But because of the density of the material and its aerodynamics it wouldn't go far and land close to the hut it came off of. After the storm, the owner would go retrieve the pieces and replace the roof quickly. It seemed odd to us to find all the roofs made out of corrugated metal but it was an excellent material for them, it solved so many problems that we were unaware of.

You probably are beginning to realize that these are the Mariana Islands in the Pacific Ocean (I'm talking about the Mariana Trench Islands-there are approximately about 130 of them all along that 3 mile deep trench-Guam being the largest Island of the group). They were all formed by what I call "land swells"-that were actually undersea volcanic eruptions that surfaced but did not erupt. Then over the thousands of years from their surfacing, the formation of coral added mass to the volcanic portion. Darwin was the first to discover the process and enlightened the world with this finding. The Island of Rota was another land swell that emerged from the sea. Before I was sent to this assignment, I was also trained as a scuba diver so I was able to investigate all of the beautiful coral that was growing around the Island. It was breathtaking, the colors, the formations, the existence of such creatures were unbelievable and to think they actually formed most of these Islands. The mission was a success at Rota. We found all the aircraft that had crashed and painted them all. We felt good about this task. Even the Captain in command was happy with our work. We said goodbye to the Island governor and the others and sailed back to Guam.

Top Technicians on their mission to the island of Rota – Marianna Straights (There I am on the left)

TOP SECRET REPORTS. This is another interesting story about the military that sometimes defies explanation. First I have to review my MOS with you. I was an Advanced Aircraft Armament Technician specializing in Bomb Sights and Armament Cameras. But the Air Force assigns me to an Air Sea Rescue Division of a Squadron. This Flight's airplane's have NO ARMAMENT! The airplanes I was assigned to service, have no bomb sights, have no turrets with machine guns and no military cameras. After this revelation became known to the high military officers, I was summoned to Headquarters for consultation. The Commanding Officer, a full Colonel, began talking to me with a slight smile on his face; "It seems some type of mistake is facing us", he said. "You must know by now that we have no armament to maintain"; then he said that I was welcome to learn and maintain the rescue equipment they used (which I knew nothing about) or as opportunity would have it and because I scored so well in administrative activities in my tests, he had an administrative opening in Headquarters I would qualify for. I immediately opted for the Headquarters desk job! It was Destiny again, weaving the blanket of my life. That's when I learned to type on a typewriter. He sent me to Typewriter Training School. Then after that, for about 3 months I was responsible for preparing a SECRET report that were sent to Washington, DC every night. To do this I had to have a CLASS Q Clearance, which was granted by the FBI. How all this came about I'll never know. What I do know is that the FBI performed a check on me at home by visiting all the neighborhood shops I frequented asking a lot of personal questions and writing all the answers down on paper. I'll never forget when I finally got home at the end of my tour, I went to my barber and he said; "Hey Gus, are you in some sort of trouble? FBI agents came here asking if you were into drugs or did you gamble; you know questions like that." I started to laugh and said; "No, it was just a routine check, I wasn't in any trouble." It did tell me that the Class Q clearance was very serious stuff, to go this far to verify an applicant's qualifications.

KOREAN WAR IS ANNOUNCED. In July 1950, the United States of America declared war on North Korea. Although the two countries were at war with one another from that time, little activity occurred for the next few months. Then in November, Marines were sent to establish North and South boundaries, prompting the North Communists to attack with such force that they almost removed us from the zone. The retaliation begins. Bomber planes were ordered to pound every square inch of North Korea. That responsibility fell on us at Guam; we had a squadron of B-19's that could carry quit a heavy load of bombs. All Airmen were put on alert duty, working 12 hour shifts, loading bombs or performing other necessary duties to push the North Koreans back north. Because I was trained in Rocket Installations I was assigned to load and arm rockets on all the Fighter planes. The sweep was successful. The Americans pushed from Pusan (not sure of spelling) in every direction north.

My 2 year enlistment was frozen. The Air Force told me not to expect leaving in two years. As long as the Korean War is on, it's very questionable that they will honor the original subscription. It was a little disappointing hearing this announcement. But the Country comes first. During that conflict I was keeping count of how many rockets I loaded, but later abandoned the record keeping. And of course I would write a message on almost every one in chalk (it helped keep my sanity), depending on how much time I had. Some planes would come in just for refueling and rearmament and then take off again. No time for my messages. I wasn't that creative and usually copied messages other guys were writing. Some of those messages were so descriptive I even was impressed at the time. I wrote those phrases more than once. While the Korean War was in progress, many other activities were affecting me.

In a few months, some of my buddies discovered the fact that I could paint with artistic flare and insisted that I paint an image of the Squadron's Emblem at the front end of our Quonset hut quarters. For morale boosting, I agreed to the request. The emblem was a gigantic mule with wings (depicting the B-19) with a rowboat attached to its belly (depicting the rescue craft that is dropped by us to save lives). It took me about two weekends to draw and paint the object while up on a scaffold, but they all liked it when it was finished. A lot of servicemen came to see the painting, even the Flight Commander (who later asked me to paint the sign over our Flight Hangar that identifies us) came to see and compliment me.

Me painting emblem on Quonset Hut.

This was not to be my future for long. Destiny had other plans. While I was an Administrator at Headquarters handling Secret material that was very important, I did attend Mass every Sunday at the Chapel. Consequently I became a regular member of the church there and met and became friendly with the Chaplain, Father Leonard Burke. I also became friendly with the Chaplain's Assistant Charlie who was leaving soon, since his service time was ending. During one of our discussions, he asked if I would be interested in working with the Chaplain. I never thought of actually being a permanent assistant , but it sounded like something I would enjoy doing (since I had a taste of this aboard ship) so I was considering it.

MY FATHER'S FOURTH BUSINESS. While I was overseas, my father began another business. This time it was with a "paisano" in the neighborhood. He and this friend of the family whose name was Salvatore Scrifugia came up with this idea of selling Fresh Killed Chickens. Now remember it was 1950 or 1951 and this was a viable neighborhood enterprise especially since Italians were not happy with store bought, (from local butcher shops) dressed chickens (their unhappiness came from not knowing how long the chickens were on the shelf). Salvatore had connections with some local farms that would deliver poultry for a very reasonable price. In fact the percentage of profit was so large that I questioned the transaction when my father wrote and told me about it. He said there is a 40 to 50% profit margin for these sales. It was hard to believe, but on this premise, the two of them embarked on another business venture. They had to find a special concrete floored store that could accommodate lots of running water. The running water was to wash all the feathers and other accumulated litter away from the selling area. The shop had to have space for chicken coupes, a de-feathering machine and a back room where the chickens would be prepared for the next process. They were able to find a space on Bushwick Avenue, which was not within walking distance from the house but could easily be reached there by car. The shop was set up quickly, made operational in short order, with a large number of customers already frequenting it. Keep in mind that Italians (their largest contingency) and other ethnic groups made a lot of chicken soup during the cold months and especially enjoyed roasted chicken, with many other chicken recipes in between. I believe everyone's heard of "Chicken Cacciatore" and "Chicken Paramigianno" and we shouldn't forget the Italians (who invented the "Brassiere" –which is our Barbeque) liked to roast chicken on an open flame (basting it with a little olive oil, wine vinegar and parsley). They were doing well when Salvatore got sick. He suffered from Asthma and now was in an advanced stage. My father tried to keep the business going alone but it was too much for him. They decided to sell the business, which they did. I never got to see the shop, but my father said it was a very well designed and run chicken shop. The people liked it a lot. It's too bad they couldn't continue operating it. Who knows, the shopping ads may have run today with these names in their advertising sections: Petti & Scrifugia Poultry, fresh, range fed chickens, organically grown! Who knows what the ads would have said. Anyway, it would be my father's last business attempt. After this one, he never got the urge again to start another enterprise…Oh; he would talk about starting others, but never did. Of course he was getting older and all that energy that is necessary to establish them is just not there anymore. It was special though, listening to plans he would conjure up for another great business! I enjoyed his spirit and his positive attitude when he would describe many imagined enterprises that his mind would formulate. Thank you Papa', for all those memories and for your unrelenting desire to make a difference in the world and your inimitable way of proceeding, full speed ahead!!!

BECAME A CHAPLAIN'S ASSISTANT. Back to Guam. As soon as I accepted the position of Chaplain Assistant it was like a whirlwind. Before I knew it, some Airmen came to my quarters, took all my belongings and brought them to the Chapel by order of the Chaplain. There was room at the Chapel that could accommodate not only me but another assistant and two Chaplains. Although there was only one Chaplain and only one assistant, there were two rooms vacant. I had my pick, so I chose the room with the most sunshine (which I found out later was not too swift since Guam's average daily temperature was 85 degrees F.). It was great though, especially since I became used to the heat. I figured if Guamanian's can stand it, so can I (I thought this out before afternoons reached 119 degrees F. and sometimes higher!!!). That's probably why the natives stop working in the fields in the afternoon, find a group of Palm trees providing necessary shade, sit down and take a snooze until the breeze brought in cooler ocean winds. This was practically the standard in terms of tropical survival behavior that I observed all during my stay on Guam. Natives invariably followed this routine every afternoon when they could not reach the water. The Island of Guam was approximately 6 miles wide by 8 miles long. If you were able to walk over 38 miles, you could circumnavigate the total land mass of this Atoll Island. I was told that in the late 18th century, Darwin identified Guam as an Atoll. It was the result of evolution of millions of years allowing coral to form the larger part of the Island. It originally surfaced from the sea bottom as a geophysical swelling (my term) to the height it is now (highest points are approximately 200-400 feet above sea level). The remainder of the Island is composed of Coral that has been growing around the swelling for the millions of years. In fact our Air Force North Field runways are situated on the coral growth. Normally runways need 8 feet or more of concrete to support airplanes like the B-19 (because of its weight). But because the coral base is so dense, only 3 feet of concrete on top of the coral was satisfactory. At the base we also had Helicopters (Sikorsky type I believe). One of the Helicopter Pilots was a regular church attendant that I met and while talking about the Helicopter, he asked if I would like to fly one. I said; "Are you kidding?" He said; "No, that it was easier than you think." In those days I would try anything once. We made arrangements, he gave me some basic instructions, sat me in the pilot's seat and said; "Take 'er up!" When I gained control of my trembling legs, I put my hands on the controls, pulled the throttle and up we went, and just as quickly, down I came. It was exciting, but I only went up a few feet. He felt I could fly it, but I didn't have that much confidence in myself. If I was given more instructions, I may have been able to do more, but that never happened. Nonetheless the experience was unmatched. I will never forget it.

As a Chaplain's Assistant, not only was I responsible for preparing all the Liturgical rituals but I aided the Chaplain with administering to the souls of those in need. Of course that included all those who come for help. Many Airmen came to the Chaplain's Office for all sorts of reasons. Those of minor consequences were referred by Fr. Burke to me for processing. For example, if an Airman is low on cash, I was authorized to give him an advance, which we knew he would never pay back and since I knew that this was the Chaplain's own money it was truly an act of charity. We had many Airmen coming to us with marital problems and problems at home with ill mothers and ill fathers…all sorts of problems that can affect the well being of a soldier. We tried to handle them all. The toughest ones were concerning those living in "sin". When their sinfulness became public, the Chaplain had no choice but to deny them the Holy Eucharist at Mass (this is Cannon Law) and the Chaplain gave me the responsibility to identify them at Mass for him (his eyesight was giving him problems). It was very hard for me to say to the Priest at Mass, while standing next to him, "Here comes Jack…no Communion". The Priest would then nudge him past when he arrived…it was the most difficult thing I ever had to do. For me, denying anyone the Holy Eucharist is unthinkable, yet it is the "Law" and must be obeyed! There were many other times where the duties of a Chaplain's assistant were very pleasant indeed, especially on Guam.

Father Burke had a great relationship with the Island's Bishop who was a member of the Holy Order of Saint Francis, he was a Franciscan. We were performing a lot of favors for Bishop Baumgartner. When he was short a Priest (due to illness or an emergency) at any of his Churches around the Islands, we would receive a call and drive out to the Church and celebrate Mass, which was very interesting. Although the Mass was said in Latin, the congregation recited their prayers in Chamorro, the language of the Guamanian people. My Chaplain and I did not know the language. So we were silent while they prayed…a little strange for us. We attended so many beautiful ceremonies. We were invited by the Bishop to attend the blessing of a new Convent for the Sisters of St .Clare. It was a wonderful ceremony with all the Nuns dressed in white, singing hymns and praying a good part of the day with all the people joining in, with the Bishop in his splendid robes, blessing the building and the people. It's a memory I will always have. We also would be invited to various religious ceremonies that were conducted by the various religious societies around the Island. There were by count approximately 8-9 Churches around the Island, not counting the main Cathedral of Agan'a where the Bishop resided.

Every Saturday and Sunday, after Mass, we would be invited to a different Church that was celebrating a religious activity such as First Holy Communion or Confirmation, or Baptism, or a Wedding. Then there were the religious Holy Days. Believe it or not they celebrated Christmas Day and Christmas Eve just the way we do except there are no Christmas trees (they were replaced with palm trees), they also celebrated The Immaculate Conception of the Virgin Mary and the Assumption of the Blessed Virgin Mary. They had a special adoration for "Mary" and celebrated the month of May the way we do, dedicating every day with prayer in their closest Church. They also celebrated Palm Sunday and Easter (including all their special foods), with one difference. During the Palm Sunday Mass, every person brought their own palm branches (I'm talking 2" to 3' long palms) and during the Gospel, at different times they would all wave their palms in the air. It was a very emotional sight and to me it was something I would never forget! They also celebrated the Ascension of the Lord, the Holy Trinity, and Pentecost Sunday. I should have mentioned this at the beginning but the Guamanian population was 98% Catholic. It was easy to talk to them (those that spoke English) about religion; there was never a disagreement since the Christian sentiments were practically "Island-wise".

Try to picture this Island in your minds. I will try to paint a verbal picture for you to fully understand the beauty of that island. I called it Paradise! It lies in tropical waters close to the equator. The temperature averages 80 degrees daily with afternoon highs into the 115 degree zone! It's warm to say the least. Although some other types of trees exist on the Islands, mostly imported by the Spaniard's during their occupation, the Island contains all species of Palm trees, swaying in the Ocean breeze perpetually. The Ocean beaches are very different from ours because of the palm trees. They cover practically all of the sand areas and provide shade almost up to the waters edge. It is truly a paradise when you're lying under the shade of a palm tree that is swaying in the breeze with the waves rushing on the shore. The sounds and the view and the warmth are like a symphony that is lifting your soul to the heavens (my personal impression). A true paradise on this earth... and you could enjoy this every day of your life there! No wonder the Guamanian's are so peaceful. They are so content with life, as they have it, that peacefulness is the only way to go. I should also explain that they have never had to deal with hunger since fishing is available to every inhabitant of the Island. Also, they have a species of palm tree called the Bread Fruit Palm that provides them with abundant carbohydrates. The fruit looks like a swollen pineapple that is very soft and breaks apart to produce something like dinner rolls. And they taste like dinner rolls too (similar to fresh baked bread). Sooooo delicious! Then there are coconut crabs which grow to twice the size of our lobsters but are caught on land (they burrow a hole under a palm tree and are easily trapped there) and taste just as good as lobster. There are other animals such wild boar (brought by outsiders), etc.. Suffice to say, Guamanian's have never been in want of food, ever! They are a wonderful people, I liked them very much.

Just one of the many paradise views of Guam

As you are beginning to sense, my whole world changed there. Instead of working on airplanes or preparing Secret documents for the Air Force, I was now in a Spiritual environment, tending to the spiritual needs of all the souls on the Island. And toward that end, I found myself in entirely different circumstances that amaze me to this day. The Chaplain and I visited every Hospital on Guam! Whether it was a military hospital or a civilian hospital, we visited, offering confession and communion at every locale. We went to the Navy Hospital on Agan'a Bay. We visited the Marine Hospital close by to the Navy base. We were asked to visit the Army Hospital to help the Chaplain there who could hardly keep up with his duties. Of course the Air Force Hospital was our main responsibility, we spent much time there. One hospital I will never forget is the Guamanian main Hospital at Agan'a Bay that contained hundreds of tuberculosis patients. For some reason (scientists did not know why at that time) Guamanian's contracted TB at an alarming rate. Here we saw young teen age boys and girls all suffering TB. There were young children too. Of course there were also adults who had it, but it was those young faces I cannot forget...all doomed, because there was no cure and the medicine they needed was not available. We did bring medicine when we visited and although they appreciated it, it wasn't enough. Those were very hard times for me, but the Chaplain got me through them and always with the quote of Scripture spoken by him to me.

The Chaplin and I also attended every religious affair on the Island and although that sounds like an impossible task, keep in mind that the island only had approximately 900 homes with about 3,000 inhabitants. With only 9 Churches and one Cathedral it was not a tough duty. We were able to meet every invitation that was made either by the military or by the secular population. Only certain emergencies kept us away. One of them I will never forget. The Chaplain and I were called to the North Field runway one afternoon concerning a pursuit plane crash. When we arrived, they were removing the Pilot form the burning plane. They put out the fire. We ran to attend to the pilot. When we got there we found he had been burned beyond recognition. His hands were burned off. His feet were burned off. His head was completely burned to the degree that it assumed only a round shape with no hair, ears, nose, or mouth. The Chaplain gave him Extreme

Unction (The Last Rites) immediately and they carried him away. (I described this event to try to convey the ravages of war) May he rest in peace, Amen. It was very sad. It was war…

I spent about a year and a half on the Island of Guam. It was the longest period of time I served at a single location during my enlistment of 3 years and 9 months. During that time I acquired many friends and had many acquaintances. One person that I became friends with as soon as I became a Chaplain's assistant was Bill Lancaster. During our friendship he told me he was an orphan brought up by a myriad of families. He had the most cheerful personality you would ever encounter. He had an unusual way of greeting you. He would come up to you, shake your hand and while doing so he would look you in your eyes and say; "Peace be with you!". He would say this if it was morning, afternoon or evening. Everyone knows, or should know that this quotation comes from Scripture. It is described when Jesus enters , through the wall, to the locked room where the Apostles gathered in fear. As soon as they see him he says; "Peace be with you!" to ally their fears. This quotation of Jesus' is repeated at ever Mass today. What foresight Bill had. To think, what I thought was odd, has become a religious universal greeting, hopefully to ally our fears and bring us closer to one another in an atmosphere of peace! Bill was ahead of his time.

THE ENGAGEMENT RING. Time passed so quickly on Guam. All during my assignment on this Paradise Island, I never became depressed or longed to be in another place. For some reason, it satisfied all ones needs physically. The temperature was perfect, the sun shone almost everyday (except during Monsoon season-which was only a few days) or when a Typhoon hit, but they came fast and moved out quickly. My family at home in the USA and Ann was the only thing I missed. I should note that all during this time, I wrote to Ann and was in close contact with her. In fact, one of my desires centered on making her an engagement ring (with the intent of proposing marriage). At the AF base we had many clubs to keep the Airmen occupied. One of them was a Jewelry Club. The Instructor actually taught the subject of diamonds and gold and silver craftsmanship. I joined the club and designed an engagement ring for Ann. Of course it was going to be a secret. I didn't tell her anything about it. Not only did I design the ring and fabricated it, but I also conceived of a dramatic way of presenting the jewel in an extraordinary package . The Instructor really got into it. He really liked my idea so he gave me extra help, sometime more than I wanted . Anyway, I bought the diamond (wholesale price of course), crafted the mold for the setting and executed all the necessary steps. The melting and pouring of the gold into the wax mold I designed. Then the finishing of the gold setting until it sparkled. Then I proceeded to the setting of the "stone" (diamond). Voila! A beautiful engagement ring! Even the Instructor said it was worthy of a master craftsman's piece. Now I began focusing on the presentation. It had to travel over 14,000 miles, back to Brooklyn, via Postal Services. It had to be as small as possible. It had to be strong and it had to dazzle the receiver (of course, Ann)! I designed it to satisfy all these requirements. Let me see if I can describe it; it was about 10" inches square and constructed of plywood. It could only be opened one way, which was important because it had to be facing up when it was opened. I installed a special handle on the door that compelled you to open it correctly. Inside, I upholstered it with beautiful red silk, puffy cloth, covering all the wood. At the base, I installed a small 3" Buddha (used for incense burning – with a small compartment between its legs to hold the incense). I removed the cover to the incense compartment and replaced it with a beautiful red silk pillow that had a crease in it to accommodate the ring. I placed the ring in the pillow and sewed it in, concealing the stitches. Before placing the Buddha in the box, I strung very small wire from the top of the box, just above the ring, where a strong light would be installed, to behind the Buddha where I fixed two AA batteries to provide electricity for the lamp. All of the electrical wiring was connected to the door with a sensitive switch that would turn the light on when opened. It was finished! I don't know how many times I tested it. It worked every time. I was so excited and proud! This is really going to "floor her", I hoped. She won't be able to resist this super engagement proposal; she will have to marry me after receiving such a dynamic gift! So I thought...what immaturity I displayed (my only defense is that I was "young", I'll leave it at that). I hurriedly brought the neatly wrapped engagement ring to the Post Office and mailed it, asking the clerk how long he thought it would take to arrive. I needed to know this because I planned to contact her by Ham radio, to know what her answer was when she received it. My radio message was very simple. "Will you marry me? Love Gus." The postal clerk said about 5 days (it traveled by Air). So I waited the 4 days and on the 5th I began sending my radio message. At the base, my friend, a Ham Operator sent the message to another operator about 100 miles away, then to another operator bout 100 miles away until it reached the Mainland, then it traveled faster because there are many more operators on the air waves until it arrived in Brooklyn somewhere, who was within local phone calling distance, then called her and gave her the message on the phone (not much privacy but excellent timing and free) and all this on the same day she received the ring! Everything worked out perfectly except one thing, the box arrived crushed. The door was broken during its travel and had to be pried open hence the lighting effect was missing. Next, since Ann's father had to pry open the box, he was the first to peer inside and did not understand the presence of the Buddha. Of course when he gave it to Ann, she explained it was there only to hold the ring. I'm sure Ann was impressed, but all that work and it did not affect her the way I had planned (Oh well…I was beginning to learn that Man proposes, but God disposes.). Needles to say I did not get the answer I was expecting. Although she thought it was a nice gesture, she was not ready to commit. Of course she thanked me for the ring. I told her she could have it and she kept it all these years until it was stolen in a house burglary, experienced in Morris Plains. Will give you details in Chapter 6.

NORITAKE CHINA. Even though being in a new place is exciting and there are many opportunities for adventure, I would get home sick often. My thoughts and feeling would always reflect back to my relationship with Ann. Everything I experienced would somehow be troubling, and all I could think about was Ann. She was on my mind constantly. And I sincerely believe that is what motivated me to enter this next unusual transaction. I have mentioned the PX (Post Exchange) which was a type of military department store where great deals could be found. For some reason, as I window shopped in this vast showroom, certain products caught my eye and seemed very good deals. You see, the military can buy products not only wholesale but minus any import or government tax which brought the purchase price of products very low, way less than back in the States. When I spotted the cost of the Noritake China per setting, (A famous Japanese brand of porcelain) I couldn't believe it. I went to the attending sergeant and began asking all the usual questions such as "Ok, if I buy an eight place setting will I get an additional discount? He said, "Yes." "Can I ship the merchandise home to Brooklyn and how will that be accomplished?" He said; "We crate all the fragile plates in excelsior, then pack them in a wooden box for the trip home and it's all guaranteed!" "And the cost is very reasonable because the transportation is by land". That was a deal! I purchased an eight piece setting, with four small platters and one large platter. The design was simple. All it had was two gold bands on the edge and a small band inside of each piece (it was called the "Goldlane"). Unfortunately, over the years, the set has practically disappeared due to breakage. But if you want to see it, some pieces still survived and are on the first shelf over the pantry cabinets, in the garage. Look for them, they are made of the "purest" porcelain and have gold bands (22 kt. gold) on each piece. The trademark Noritake is underneath each piece also.

The next thing I will tell you about this China is remarkable. Each place setting had eight pieces to it that means 64 porcelain fragile pieces had to be packed along with five larger pieces with the expectation of traveling 0ver 14,000 miles, from Guam to Brooklyn and not break; seemed almost a miracle. Since I made the purchase just before leaving Guam, I arrived home before the crate was delivered. When it arrived, (Ann and I unpacked it) we immediately noticed that the large platter had broken and feared the worst. But as it turned out, not a single other piece was broken. We received a refund for the broken platter but could not find a replacement for it in the local department stores (There were others, but not this "model"). First we were sad at discovering the broken piece, but then we were glad because there was no other damage. We used that set for "many, many" years. Only a few dishes remain. Remember it comes direct from Guam, by sea and land.

GORHAM STERLING SILVER. After purchasing the China, I began thinking of the rest of kitchen and table necessities in a home. Of course, we would need Silverware, I thought. Let's see what they have here in the PX. Actually they had a lot of stuff. As I was looking around I spotted this stunning design. It was the Etruscan design that I had just seen in a book I was reading about ancient history. The Etruscans were the first civilized people to migrate to Italy. They were responsible for beginning new cities in the northern regions of the country and one of their favorite designs (it is displayed on many of their earthenware discovered and made by them) which is a continuous square starting from the center to its outer boundaries. Since Ann wasn't there to help with the selection I chose it for the both of us. But she liked it when we received it. I did not tell you that the pieces I was looking at were Sterling Silver the most expensive type of flatware possible (in Silver that is, of course there is gold too). This little item was a little more expensive than the china, though. In fact I couldn't afford an eight piece setting. I could only afford a 6 piece setting. The sergeant explained that this was a very popular item in the States and we could add to it when I get home. Don't' let this get around but I only paid $131.00 for the whole set. It is probably worth almost $2,000.00 now. There are about 46 pieces to it. We keep it under our bed. It's in a special Silverware Case that is walnut in color. Take a look. We never use it. Please don't ask me "why"?

LET GO, LET GOD. I'm trying to remember all of the events that helped me grow up a little. One that comes to mind pertains to an appointment the Chaplain had with the Bishop one Sunday. I was the driver of the car, besides being his assistant. I reported to the Motor Pool (name of area where vehicles are stored for military use) to pick-up a car to transport the Chaplain from the Chapel to Agan'a where the Bishop waited. Meanwhile, the Chaplain arranged to wait for me in front of the Chapel. I began driving the car from the Motor Pool down the road, when just about five blocks away from the motor pool I began experiencing engine failure. The car finally conked out and stopped on the side of the road. I got out, opened the hood and began inspecting. Lot's of extraneous gasoline was leaking from the carburetor which is not normal. I could not repair it. Had to go back to the motor pool, so I began walking. Meanwhile, since the Chaplain was outside the Chapel, I could not communicate with him to apprise him of the situation (this is way before cell phones). Back at the motor pool after talking to the pool sergeant about the problem. He suggested taking another car and he would recover the other with a tow truck and repair it. So I took another car and began my trek to the Chapel to pick-up the Chaplain. I was about 1 mile away when I spotted a swarm of African Sea Snails (which the Japanese brought to the Island as a food source - they were gigantic snails) crawling across the road in front of me. I knew better than to proceed. I was forewarned of these happenings and was cautioned not to go over them since crushing them produces a slime that prevents steering control. So there I waited. One hour, two hours, they finally ended their migration and I could proceed. When I arrived at the Chapel, there was the Chaplain still waiting, cool as a cucumber. I was steaming mad, when I stomped out of the car, displaying my displeasure about all the circumstances, after explaining everything to him in a very upset manner, he quietly patted me on the back and said, listen Petti; in circumstances like this, just "LET GO, LET GOD", "It's as simple as that"; he said. After thinking about it awhile, I began to calm down and eventually got a grip on myself, and actually was able to shake off all of the ill feelings that were affecting me. It was similar to an adrenaline surge that acted instantly. I was all better. We drove off to see the Bishop and explained the reasons for the delay. All was well again. I would never forget that advice again; "Let Go, Let God" and it helped me from that day on. Thank you Father. Thank you Lord.

RETURN TO USA FROM GUAM. I was stationed on Guam for over a year now. The USA was making progress in Korea to the point where the war was dwindling down to just a Police Action. All those Airmen who had gone beyond their enlistment time were being considered for reassignment in the United States. I fell into that category. On the "Bulletin Board" I saw my name listed for reassignment to the States. I was being sent to Alamogordo, New Mexico, at the White Sands Proving Grounds. It was a rocket firing range, where most of the land missiles were tested for performance. It was also the site where the fist atomic bomb test took place. A very historical landmark but the assignment was puzzling because I wasn't carrying my Aircraft Armament MOS any more, my MOS was Chaplain's Assistant and that is what I was being sent there for. They needed a Chaplain's Assistant there and I guess I was the next name on the list to fill the space.

2ND VISIT TO HAWAII. My time on Guam was ending. I had to say goodbye to everyone. The hardest one to say goodbye to was the Bishop, my Chaplain Fr. Burke, my special friend and all the other friends I made on the Island. It was very difficult indeed. But with a heavy heart I said my goodbyes and left the Island as cheerfully as possible. The trip home was by ship again. This time we would be traveling in reverse direction. We made the same stops though. Even though we pass the 180th Meridian again, this time there was no Court and no King Neptune to serve initiations since we were already members of the Order of the Golden Dragon. But I neglected to explain another phenomenon that occurs at that meridian and that is, on the way East, each new calendar day starts at that point on the globe, therefore before I reached the 180th going to Guam, I lost a complete day, which means I went to sleep on Tuesday night, then went across the meridian and woke up on Thursday! Thursday? "What happened to Wednesday?" I naively asked a sailor aboard ship. He explained the rotation of the Earth (which I should have known from School but forgot) and how time zones were established from the Greenwich Time Zone (London "0" degrees) to the 180th , the International Time Zone and that it was established to catch up to the calendar . The countries lying east of the meridian were in the prior calendar day, therefore a day ahead. Because of this time change, on our return, when passing the 180th Meridian another very strange occurrence took place, and that is, the same day was experienced twice. In other words I went to sleep on Tuesday night, slept the whole night and woke up on Tuesday morning again! I thought that was very weird and I had never experienced that happening ever, but there it was and it was reality! Now we were on our way to Hawaii again. We had to dock there to take on supplies and refuel the navel vessel, it was propelled by heavy fuel oil. This time when we stopped, we didn't go touring because we thought we visited everyplace of importance (how naïve we were) so all we did was go to Luau's and ate, and ate, and ate. We also drank quit a bit. I couldn't believe how expensive beer got in just over a year, they were charging us $1.50 for a bottle, when we were there in 1950 it was $.75 a bottle. It doubled in more than one year, wow! We attended a Luau (a Hawaiian Feast including a Roasted Pig in a Pit) and all other native foods. I especially enjoyed the different preparation made with pineapple, they were delicious. Of course there is always Poi (a mashed fruit dip) served every place. No chairs, you sat on the ground with your legs crossed. The table was raised about a foot off the ground so that you could get close to the table edge. It was very comfortable (that is when I was 20 years old-I don't' know if I could do it now). To roast the pig ling (it wasn't a large pig at that) they dug a hole where the roasting was to take place then they filled up half the hole with large rocks (about 10 inches in diameter) then added kindling and wood then started a fire. When the flames died down they would remove as much of the ashes as possible, then carefully remove half the stones (all during this time, others were preparing the pig, adding pineapple marinade and wrapping it in special palm tree leaves that are very big), then they lowered the pig into the middle of the pit, then they added the hot stones that were removed in the beginning. Now the roasting starts. After a few hours, the top stones are removed again and a steaming roasted pig emerges. They place the roasted pig on the table at one end, and then they slice it and serve it to all the guests at the table. It was wonderful. I noticed that a lot of Hawaiian's enjoy eating with their hands. I guess they were not used to using silverware at the table. It didn't bother me, although it seemed to annoy some of my buddies. Oh, and the way they prepare their rice is out of this world. I don't know what they put in it, but it was so delicious. I could eat that rice for all of my meals forever! We also went to night clubs that had stage dancing, where the Hula and the Flaming Knife (I forgot the Hawaiian name that was announced) dance was very popular. The men danced this customary presentation. They came out dressed in cloth around their midsection, with large Machete like swords, waving them around awhile, then in a moment, the blades were blazing with fire still waving them to the beat of the drums. It was very exciting and very entertaining. This was a different Hawaii than we visited before.

It was more intimate and filled us with warmth and closeness that did not occur on our first visit. Thank you Hawaii!

There were no Hula (300 lb. plus) women on the docks when we left Hawaii this time. It was kind of somber and quiet while we slipped away from the dock. We were now on our way to San Francisco, California. We couldn't believe it. We are going home! Another few days and we will be sailing into San Francisco Bay, under the Golden Gate Bridge and to our dock for disembarking. Then our feet will be planted on our home earth! That was going to make us very happy. We couldn't wait.

On the bulletin board, aboard the ship, next to my name was my new assignment. I was to report to Holloman AFB, Alamogordo, New Mexico, otherwise known as White Sands Proving Grounds (that's where "Hangar 51 is located-you know where the "Aliens" are presumably kept). I was not given a furlough to visit my parents and Ann so I was a little disappointed. But that is the military. You cannot predict them. There had to be a reason, I thought.

When we docked, I want to tell you how we were greeted. We were met by the Salvation Army Volunteers that were serving coffee and doughnuts. But this time they were free. We didn't have to pay for their service the way we had to pay for our coffee and doughnuts when the Red Cross served them on our way to Guam. This was very different and I will never forget it. These selfless and very generous people were so cheerful and helped raise our morale immensely. It was so nice to see smiling faces asking us how we were and how was the trip and so on, and so on.

ASSIGNED TO NEW MEXICO. Holloman AFB was the name of the base I reported to. As soon as I arrived, I met the new Chaplain I would be assisting. His name was Father John Moegling and he was a Captain in the USAF. It was a pleasure meeting him especially when he made me feel so at home upon my arrival.

My Chaplain, Father Moegling-
White Sands Proving Grounds-1952

This time there were no quarters in the Chapel as there was on Guam so I was assigned to quarters with USO Airmen, specifically with musicians who played in the military band and orchestra. That's where I met Dan Inglese and Phil Sculley (who was Dan's friend when I arrived-but soon became my friend also). It was great, Dan was a saxophone and clarinet player and Phil was primarily a piano player but could play any percussion instrument too. It was an interesting group of friends. Here I brought Spirituality to the group, Dan brought Music and Phil brought Scholarship and music (he had a degree in philosophy too). What was even more interesting is that even though we had such varied backgrounds, we all had one goal. That goal was to get a furlough home as soon as possible. I didn't tell you but Dan was born and raised in Brooklyn, New York, and Phil was born and raised in Manhattan, New York and we wanted to visit our parents and relatives and friends so badly that we spent most of our spare time planning that event. Our first obstacle was that we could not afford to travel from New Mexico to New York by any means of transportation available. Train fare was way above our means. Air fare was out of the question, it was too expensive. Then, when we were close to desperation, our thoughts were actually contemplating hitch hiking across the US! Could you believe that? And we were going to do just that when another opportunity came our way. Phil told us that one of the officers in his division wants to sell his car for $150.00. Dan said' "If you can get him down to $100, it's a deal!" Phil went back with the counter offer and the owner said fine, but the car had some problems. Oh, oh, "what problems" I asked? The car needs a motor job! When Phil came back with the news, he asked if any of us knew anything about cars. I could see the picture that was coming; "I do", I said. Dan knew nothing about mechanics and neither did Phil, so of course the burden fell on me. They both said; "Great" we'll buy it. We all chipped in and bought the automobile (I worked so hard on that car that I blocked out the make and model in my mind - I don't' remember it at all). Now the fun begins. When we went to get the car, it was sending up so much smoke that we thought we were going to get into trouble with the MP's on the base. But luckily we got the car to the base Hobby Shop where a number of Airmen were repairing their cars. If it wasn't for this Air Force Garage and its tools and the fact that you could purchase auto parts at wholesale prices, it wouldn't have happened. First of all I had to disconnect the whole engine, then lift it out of the car for mounting onto an engine stand. Next I had to remove the compression head exposing all the valves. I also had to remove the crank shaft, which meant all the pistons had to be removed. I also removed all the valves, thank God it was only a six cylinder engine. After taking micrometer readings of all the bearing surfaces (the crank shaft and the inside cylinder walls) it became evident that they all needed resurfacing work. I had to take the crankshaft to a machine shop in town for that operation, but the cylinder surfaces I did with a honing tool. All this work took me about two weeks, working each night to 9 PM. By now you must have guessed on how we were going to get to New York. Of course we were going with this car. Well, through some miracle, I fixed the engine and installed it back into the car. The funniest thing that happened is that when I finished, I had seven bolts, with nuts and washers leftover, not knowing where they belonged. When I told Dan and Phil, the jokes began. We laughed so much, it was hysterical. Do you think we worried about it? Not on your life! We were so young, a little thing like that didn't phase us at all.

Our next concern was obtaining a furlough that would allow us all to travel at the same time. This we were able to accomplish, of course with the help of our Chaplain, who put in a good word for us. It was all arranged. We were given a 10 day furlough. We decided to drive twenty four hours a day, straight through to NY. We gathered all our gear, packed it in the car and began our journey. As I recall, our first plan was to have each one of us drive four hours each, then rest six or eight hours, then take over again for four hours of driving. Well it did sound good when we proposed it, but it was another thing to accomplish. The first shift was Dan's. After two hours of driving he said he was tired so Phil took over. Dan went to sleep in the back of the car (it was a sedan with four doors). As soon as we reached Texas on Route 40, the car began to act up. The engine was lacking gasoline at times and was coughing a lot. It was worrying Phil and Dan, but I told them it was not serious and nothing to be concerned about. At a gas station in Oklahoma, the attendant told us we were experiencing vaporization which occurs when the gasoline in the line, before reaching the carburetor due to excessive heat, begins vaporizing. It happens to a large number of people in the summer there, because it's the heat that is doing this. He suggested wrapping an old towel around the feed line to the carburetor and keeping it wet all the time. That fast fix should cool the line enough to prevent the gasoline from vaporizing.

Dan Inglese, Phil Sculley and me

He also suggested we purchase a two gallon, sweating canteen to tie on the bumper filled with water (to pour on the towel periodically). This procedure worked well, except for the time one of us forgot to wet the towel on time. We learned: after all it was our first cross country trip with a car. One funny thing that happened in Arkansas while Phil was driving was when we stopped at a diner on the road to get some breakfast. After getting back in the car, it was Phil's turn. We started out on the road (both of us fell asleep-Dan in the front and me in the back.) When we woke up about 1 ½ hours later, Dan and I noticed we were heading for the same diner that we had breakfast in. "Where are you going?" Dan asked Phil. "I don't know," Phil answered. "Well," I said "it appears we are back where we started." Phil told us there was a detour soon after he got on the road and he followed the signs which apparently led him back to where we started. In those days, everything sounded funny to us. We began laughing and laughed all the way home. All we had to say was, "Take me to your Diner," and the laughing would start again. The trip took us close to two and a half days, but we made it. When we arrived in Delaware and began seeing New York signs, both Dan and Phil began complimenting me on the mechanical work I did that allowed us to make the trip for less than $400! Smugly, I replied, "Did you have any doubts?" In those days I had a lot of confidence, which worked to everyone's benefit. I humbly accepted the compliments…

We dropped Phil off at his home in New York City, made plans for our return and left for Brooklyn. When we arrived in Brooklyn, Dan asked to be dropped off at his house and gave me the car to drive home. By now, my mother and father had purchased the house on Orient Avenue and were living there. I drove to the house, pulled up the drive way and was met by two gigantic dogs. They were Doberman Pinchers that I never met before. They were very friendly and became friendly immediately. My father was walking towards me greeting me in Italian, of course, with his arms outstretched. He gave me such a tight hug and kissed both sides of my face. I reciprocated. And now my mother was coming and the process was repeated, with enough Italian well wishes to even test my knowledge of Italian words. Of course, little Joann was with her and I greeted her too. We then went into the house and my parents and sister were so excited about the new house, they couldn't wait to show me around. It was the first time I was home since they purchased it. I don't know if I could take any more. Remember we just drove across country and I was a little tired. I politely excused myself, went to my room, dropped on the bed and went fast asleep. When I awoke, I smelled that inimitable odor of garlic and basil and only one picture came into my mind: MACARONI! Oh, yes…it was waiting for me, a beautiful dish of Ziti con Ragu…it was soooooo delicious! Thank you Mamma, you're the best! I couldn't believe how much I missed so simple a food as I did that.

I do not like admitting it, but at that age I was smoking. Everybody smoked. You just fell into the fold and before you knew it you were smoking one pack a day, then two and for some it became a serious problem. There was no talk of ill health at the time. All the tobacco companies were touting their own brand, the test was not "is it good for you" but rather is a Camel better tasting than a Lucky Strike? Can you imagine that? There was absolutely no talk of it being a health hazard. Everyone smoked, ignorant of it's affect on the body. My father also smoked (I have a theory, the reason men die sooner today than women, is because more men smoked in the 50's and 60's than women.) I just wanted to tell you that I smoked until 1964, when the Surgeon General of the United States of America announced on national television, speaking to the American people and told them that cigarette smoking can be harmful to your health. I immediately took the pack of cigarettes from my pocket and threw them down a water drain in the street, vowing to never touch a cigarette again. I have been true to that vow till today. I will never smoke anything, ever!

The next important thing I had to do was contact Ann. I wanted to know what her feelings were when she received the engagement ring I sent. I knew she received it, but I didn't know what her reactions were. Well, I soon found out. It wasn't pleasant as I recall. It started with her saying; "How dare you send me an engagement ring in the mail!" "How romantic is that?" she asked. I didn't know what to say. I on the other hand thought it was a wonderful idea! Go figure. Now I was getting the real scoop. Although she appreciated the work I did and the ingenuity I put into it, according to her, it was not appropriate. I was starting to understand. What did I know? (This was the only excuse I could come up with). But we kissed and made-up. The next few days just whizzed by. Before you know it, I had to return to New Mexico with my friends. Off I went to pick up Dan and Phil, then begin our journey back. It wasn't easy. The engine kept acting up due to the heat. I realized that I was a good at mechanics of the engine but didn't know squat about carburetors. Well, in spite of a lot of unnecessary stops, trying to get the gasoline from vaporizing and causing vapor lock as we traveled, we eventually made it back to the Air Base. Everything was the same as we left it except one thing, now we had a car. Now our planning had changed course. Instead of going by bus to Alamogordo and to Museums, we now had wings of our own that could take us to El Paso, Texas and Lands Beyond !

That meant we could now go to Ciudad Juarez, Mexico and the BULL FIGHTS! And that is what we did. The three of us became bull fight aficionados of the first class. We loved the bull fights. We went every Saturday, without fail. We were so into it that the Chaplain asked to join us one day. We were happy to take him. He enjoyed himself immensely, with only one question on his mind, "Was it humane?" Of course Phil responded to that inquiry, by reminding him that this was Mexico's national sport, not ours, and for them it does not cause any concern (especially since the bulls are donated to the poor of the city-not wasted). But our desire to go to Mexico every Saturday was not primarily due to the fights but more so about the food that was served in the many restaurants of Juarez. The Mexican food that was served was "out of this world" as Dan would say and we agreed with him. Also, the entertainment; the entertainment was everywhere, in practically every restaurant we frequented. Music was being played wherever we ate and it was Jazz, or Classical, or Mexican. Almost every type of music was played there. It was wonderful, thanks to Dan, who knew practically every musician that was performing, talking to them about the music and requesting songs we were familiar with. It was great! And the food, I became convinced that "Mexican Beef" is better than "Texan Beef", a competition that has been in existence from time immemorial. It was so delicious. No matter what cut of meat you ordered, you could cut it with a fork. How did they do it? And the taste was so good, you automatically made a comparison every time and the best would always be the Mexican beef! Now comes the best part…remember it was 1952…the price of a full dinner in Juarez was

$1.29!!! And for this price, you are offered, in addition "all you can eat"!!! I couldn't believe it either! Yes, there were times when I had a second dinner and once or twice, a third dinner (and it wasn't gluttony, it was hunger, honest!). You probably guessed by now why we were so thrilled with visiting Juarez, it had everything one could wish for in terms of off-time endeavors. I didn't get to mention the beer. Mexican beer was another special thing. It was a lot stronger than American beer and therefore had an extra kick and for less money too. You just couldn't beat the deal. Juarez was the place to go when you wanted to eat, drink and be merry. The Texans themselves crowded the Rio Grande border to get across, you should have seen the lines. When you passed the Mexican border it cost one penny to enter and two cents to return (please don't ask me why-I never found out why-sorry). We will never forget El Paso or Juarez nor the good times we had there. Our friendships became very close with Dan and Phil. Till this day I still think of Dan, who now lives in Florida with his wife and children and Phil who moved to Massachusetts to teach somewhere and lost touch with us (we have been separated for over 55 years now and no longer write to each other). It seems friends are a temporal thing…they do not last forever. But thank you Dan and Phil for being my friends during that time, I won't forget you.

The month of September in 1952 was approaching and the question of my enlistment was discussed many times with the Chaplain until one day he said to me, "I think they are going to let you go". Yahoo! That means a discharge, the Air Force was going to release me so that I could go home! Sure enough, on the bulletin board I read my name for the last time; "Petti – Discharge Pending". The next thing I knew they were summoning me to the Quartermaster to return all Air Force property that is still useable. For instance, all my parade uniforms had to be returned. I was issued firearms that had to be returned. Now I knew it was for real. There was no doubt about it. I was going to be Discharged soon. I put on a happy face and nothing could change it. The Chaplain knew why I was so happy and so did my friends. They weren't in the service as long as I was, so they understood my joy. On September 22, 1952, I received my "Honorable Discharge" from the United States Air Force and was free to leave! After signing all the forms, I said my goodbyes to Father Moegling, to Dan Inglese and to Phil Sculley (I left the car to them) and to all my other friends and acquaintances and left the base. The trip home was by train as you would have guessed. Although it took days, the elapsed time did not faze me…I was on my way home…that was the only thought on my mind. I would be going home to my mother and father and sister but especially to Ann.

When I arrived, it took a while to readjust. Now I was back home, nobody to wake me up. In fact no reason to get up at all, but my father put a stop to that. He said; "When are you going to get a job?" A job! Give me a break, Papa - I just got back from 3 ½ years in the service… don't I deserve a little time off? He replied pensively; "How are you going to afford to live?" "What about your future?" "If you have any plans, I'm sure they are going to require some sort of savings." Yipe's… that's too much thinking, especially now. I hadn't thought about any of that! I thought I would vacation a while, I told him. That didn't sit too well with him. He explained that vacations are for those who can afford them and I had nothing. He was starting to make sense, especially when I reviewed the facts that he cited. Then I asked for a little advice. "What should I do?" He suggested I search the newspaper job ads and see if I was interested in what was available. I purchased the New York Times on Sunday and began reviewing the ads. You cannot imagine how confused I was. First of all, my military training was in aircraft armament. That's the only trade I knew. Are there any job ads for that trade? No, there are not. Obstacle number one. The second subject I have experience at is being an assistant to a Chaplain or Catholic Priest. Are there any jobs needed for that task? No, there are not. Obstacle number two. Well, those are the only two subjects I'm qualified for and there are no jobs for them in the newspaper. What do I do now? I know, I'll apply to every job that's advertised and see who will take me. In other words; "Shoot Crap". And that is what I did. On the fourth interview I had, the Personnel Director seemed interested and asked me to return to meet another person in conference. I returned. They were interested. I got the job! The company was R.H. Macy's. The department was the International Department. I didn't even know what it was at this point, but I gathered up all my strength and reported for work. The department was on the fourth floor at the time. It was very large. There must have been over 100 people working there. I learned later that it was Macy's foreign merchandizing center. Here is where all of the Macy's buyers came to review the myriad of samples sent by manufacturers from all over the world. We would be receiving (during the slow season) more that 20 items a day, from Czechoslovakia, India, France, Italy, the list goes on and on. Every country that is on the map was sending a sample of their product for sale here in the US. And I was the receiver of these items. I had to log in every sample received and report it to the Foreign Sale" department, with its price tag and quantity estimate, including shipping schedules. A copy also went to our Foreign Accounting department to calculate the Importation Tax and Transportation costs. All associated dollar factors had to be determined before the item could be shown to the various Macy's buyers. After this phase of the operation, I had the responsibility of preparing a show to exhibit these new products for a gala affair, all devised to make the samples as attractive and interesting as possible. We had a large Show Room where we could hold 50-60 buyers, seated. We had to invite them from around the United States. The show room shelves had to be full. On the day of the show, I would help the Vice President in charge of sales, explain all the particulars for each sample and then they would begin ordering. They each had order cards; each item had a Product No. and of course, Totals had to be given. You would be surprised to see how many items they would purchase from these manufacturers. When a Buyer feels that something would sell, they would order thousands of items! It was amazing to witness the process. Sometimes the Manager of the Foreign Accounting department would tell me the totals that were ordered in dollars, it would come to tens of thousands (and this was in 1952!) Anyway, I was certainly pleased when he would divulge this information because I translated that to mean "I did a good job" and, of course, the products had something to do with it too. Although this was my basic job, during Christmas the whole store concentrated on "store front" sales. This meant that all department personnel spent the holiday serving customers on the floor. We were assigned to different departments in the store to help with the surging sales that occurred at Christmas time. I helped in many departments but primarily in the Small Appliance department. This was my favorite, so I asked for this duty all the time and was mostly assigned to it. But when I found out that if you sold Large Appliances you received what they called stipends (I don't know why they didn't call it "commission" because that's what it was) I began opting for the Large Appliances department to make the extra money. But I must say, although I didn't stay there long, I learned a lot about merchandizing and sales and foreign imports. R.H. Macy's was my first place of employment and they treated me very well, and I will never forget my experience there. Just for comparison, to today's personal income, I was making $55 dollars a week as basic salary. It was the average blue collar salary in the '50's.

COURTSHIP WITH ANN. While working, you must be wondering what I did after work and on weekends. I believe I can answer that with one word; Ann. We were going out steady now. A good part of the week was devoted to dating. We would go here and there and everywhere. One of my favorite dates was when we went to LaGuardia Airport and picnicked in the park area, watching the Propeller Airplanes take-off from the runways (I guess I was Air Force homesick.) But that was exciting spending time with Ann, explaining all my experiences on Guam to her. She was a great listener. She told me about her job, how she records the various types of monetary exchanges that increase or decrease daily. She worked for Deak and Co., Foreign Monetary Exchange in downtown New York. Isn't that funny, we both worked in foreign departments. She worked there all the years after school, till now. On Monday nights we would attend Novena Services at our church. During the week, we would go to the movies or plan something with the family. Time was moving fast for us. I explained about my fiascos with my marriage proposals and although they didn't fare well, they did happen so they became part of the dialogue almost every week until finally we decided on setting a wedding date. Yes, we decided to get married! I let Ann decide on the date. Let's face it, I had no clue when it comes to favorable dates. She asked if May 2nd of next year would be OK? I said fine, it sounds OK to me. So we sent out the invitations and began making all the preparations. I know I am reminding you all the time, but it's important to know our heritage and what is expected of two newly married people in the Italian tradition. There were so many rules, it was unbelievable. First, the couple are obligated to offer an Italian reception. That meant there had to be an Antipasto, then a first course pasta serving, followed by a roast of meat, followed by a salad, followed by fruit and nuts and then the wedding cake. A six course dinner was the minimum appropriate meal. And that's only the food. Then there are the drinks. There must be unlimited wine at every table, with beer and hard drinks available on request too. That was a surprise to me because, up to that time, my recollection of Italian weddings was the serving of Italian rolls! What they did was to prepare the rolls at home, filled with ham and cheese, baloney or salami, wrapped up in cellophane paper and stacked on a large tray. The wedding reception would be at a large hall where the guests would be seated on Boston cane chairs listening to a live band and dancing when it suited them. Then the rolls would be brought out by two family members and tossed to the guests as they walked by. In fact, many critics at the time began calling them "Italian Football Weddings" (because your food would be thrown to you and the roll resembled a football in the air.) It was a curious time and certainly the time for change and, well, we made a slight change. It did not go over well with our parents. "What, no macaroni?" they said, when they learned of our plans. They could not believe we would "ignore" custom. "But we were Americans," we said. How could we be shackled by Italian customs in America, we argued? We weren't winning. They were ganging up on us, until Ann spoke up with this undeniable fact. They were not paying for our wedding, we were! If they were paying for it, we would do it their way, but since we planned to pay for it ourselves, we would follow our best judgment. That seemed to settle it.

THE WEDDING PLAN. We then continued our preparations and planned an "American" wedding (in other words the food would be what is usually served here in the USA). Our reception was to take place at the Howard Johnson's Reception Ball Room on the second floor of the restaurant at 95-25 Queens Boulevard, Elmhurst, NY. It was a beautiful place. Very bright with windows all around and since we were going to be married in the morning, it would shine light everywhere. We wanted it to be bright. Howard Johnson's became famous in its restaurant for serving delicious turkey with signature gravy, with peas and mashed potatoes. It was definitely American but it was delicious and therefore appeased a lot of Italians who were our guests.

The wedding church was St. Cecilia's Roman Catholic Church on Henry Street in Brooklyn, New York. Ann chose this church because she went to Grammar School at St. Cecilia's and had very fond memories there. It was a very large, grey stone church that was well known in the neighborhood. The officiating priest we asked to perform the ceremonies was Fr. Malachy Flaherty, OFM, a Franciscan priest who we became close to during our initiation into the Third Order of Saint Francis. When I returned from Guam, I was a member of the Third Order and Ann became interested in becoming a member also. Our group was in New York directed by Father Malachy, a wonderful teacher and leader who introduced us to one of our most spiritual experiences. He was so wonderful; we decided to ask him if he would honor us with his presence at our wedding. He agreed and said he would be honored to attend our most important moment in life!

THE RINGS-ONE FOR YOU, ONE FOR ME. The wedding rings were purchased by Ann and myself; no surprises here. We wanted our rings to be special and since we couldn't afford the Tiffany types, we selected plain heavy duty types (I guess a prediction of our life to come.) They had to last our whole life! Of course, they had to be inscribed, to engrave our words onto an everlasting metal, gold. Usually Ann would ask me to compose words encapsulating our love for each other so they could be etched onto the rings, but not this time. It seems Ann has been thinking about these words for some time now and she proposed the phrases to me before we purchased them. She said she would like mine to read; "Mio primo, mio unico amore"! (With her appropriate gender grammar on her ring). Which means; "My first, my only Love". I was speechless when I heard her speak those words. They were so beautiful and in Italian too, my first language, but our language also. I guess it's a universal emotion, when you hear something that comes from the heart; it affects you in a special way that is difficult to describe. I felt that way. We loved each other so much! These words only added to the way we felt toward each other. We were so happy. The rings were purchased and the engraving was ordered. We held hands all during the transaction, looking at each other only the way lovers do.

I would like to add an aside here that absolutely mystifies Ann when I bring it up. To this day, even though 54 years have gone by, I remember exactly how much we paid for each ring! I don't know why, but that thought will not escape my mind. Psychologically I believe it's got something to do with a past desire of becoming a Jeweler or something like that, but nonetheless we paid $33 for each ring. It could also be because at the time, I held the number "33" to have some kind of significance, in a good way, for me. All during my experiences in the Air Force and my job at Macy's, the number 33 kept appearing whenever a pleasant event occurred and it made me happy. So here, it happened again, when I was with the joy of my life and I can not forget it! I'll leave it at that. (So you don't get the wrong idea, I should admit, I don't believe in lucky numbers.)

It became a little difficult in arrangements at the church. In order that we gain permission to have St. Cecilia's become the church where we would have our wedding, we had to secure a release from our local church, St. Francis di Paola, which proved to be more difficult than we thought. Within church rules, each parish must perform nuptials only within its own boundaries. Since both Ann and I were parishioners of St. Francis, we were not allowed to go to another parish for our wedding. It was a pretty big problem but Ann was able to reconcile all of the interested parties. The appointment was set with St. Cecilia's. The date was set. There would be a wedding at St. Cecilia's on May 2, 1953 where two souls will join hands and proclaim their love for one another with a vow, before all the family and friends. It's going to be wonderful.

THE WEDDING. I couldn't believe I was getting married! I went to pick up the tuxedo and checked to see if Rexie (yes, my brother-in-law was going to be the Best Man) got his. Ann informed me that all the flowers were ordered and confirmed. Everything was set. Was Rose Tosinni (she was the Maid of Honor-it was Ann's best friend) all set. Yes she was ready. I guess there is nothing to do but wait for the day and time and then go. And the day arrived. It was Saturday, May 2nd,

1953, I awoke around 5 o'clock in the morning (I couldn't sleep.) The wedding was scheduled for 10:30 AM. It would be a Missa Cantata (Sung Mass) Liturgical celebration. Everyone was getting dressed for a formal wedding in the morning, which is a little different (we were following the etiquette appropriate at that time) than a wedding at night. The clothes are different for the men. A lot of grey is used in the suits, the suit had to be tail" and ties, as I recall. In fact spats (a grey felt covering on the shoes) were called for also, but since it's optional, I did not to use them. Before I got dressed, I had a special appointment at the barber shop to get a close shave and have my hair trimmed. There I was at the barber at 6 AM knocking at the door. The barber was up and approaching the door to let me in, with a big smile. He spoke with a heavy Italian accent; "Eh, youa getta upa early today?" He greeted me as he opened the door. "Si, questa e la giornata del mio matrimonio!" (Yes, this is my wedding day!)I responded instinctively in Italian. "Ah, che bell'tempi de la vita!" (What a beautiful time of life!) he said and chuckled. He pointed to the chair and I sat down. It's interesting how the mind works, but at that moment I should have been thinking of all the ramifications of marriage and how to plan our future, you know "big thoughts", but the fact is all I could think of was him coming at me with this very sharp razor and my main concern was my face so I said naively; "Please do not cut me!" Of course, he laughed and said; "Son, do you know how many years I've been doing this?"(with an accent) I said, "I know, I know; it was a foolish request but I'm a little nervous." He said he understood and finished the shave without incident. Was I relieved when I looked at myself in the mirror, I couldn't believe the difference between my appearance from when I shave myself and after this shave. This is so much better! No wonder many men get shaved at the barber shop, but I couldn't afford it, so DIY (Do-it-yourself) shaving will continue. I rushed home to get dressed. It was getting late (there is the "nervousness" again). It was around 7 AM. My mother and father were awake now. I asked about Joann. She was still sleeping, my mother responded. I said "That's OK, she has time, let her sleep." Breakfast was first. I don't remember what I had eaten but it must have been good since my mother purchased so many special things for guests that traveled far to attend the wedding. Well I had first "dibs" on that food and am afraid I took advantage of it. It was around 8 o'clock by now and I was starting to get dressed when I heard my father call me. :"What is it?" I called back, "I need help with this collar" he said. "I'll be right there," I said and began walking into their bedroom. There was my mother all dressed up with her cocktail dress, fixing her hair. She looked beautiful. There was my father struggling with his collar, but not able to button it. I said "Here let me help," and buttoned the wing collar, then helped him tie the cravat around the collar. "There, that does it." I said. He looked in the mirror and said "Is that the way it goes?" "Yes," I said. We were not too familiar with this type of menswear, but we did it. We both got ready by 9 AM. At 9:30 AM, I would be picked-up by the limousine to take me and Rexie to the church. I asked my mother about Joann and she said she was getting dressed and had breakfast. "Good," I said. Well, everything seemed to be going according to plan. Let's see, do I have the rings? Yes, here they are in the cases. OK. I guess I have everything, I'm ready to go. My father said, "The limo is outside and the driver said he is waiting." I'm on my way, but first, as old Italian custom demands, I must first kiss my mother, then my father, then my sister and then I could leave the house. These rituals seem to get in the way at times but in retrospect I find they are really necessary even though we're blinded at time as to their value. The gesture of kissing family members brings us many of the qualities we need to go on; they especially gave us the strength to endure in whatever the event required. My parents and sister looked beautiful and were so happy for me, you could see it in their faces, and it made me feel good! I got into the limo and we drove away to pick up Rexie. When we reached the church, it was amazing to see all the flowers around the altar. The Pastor showed us to the room where we would wait until the ceremony began. So we waited; I gave Rexie the rings, then we chatted trivially until an altar boy opened the door and called us to come out to the altar. This was the "moment"; I am proceeding to become wed! I was nervous. "Stay steady" I had to tell myself. One step in front of the other...that's it. You got it, you're doing it, great, you got to your spot and you're OK. Good, hang in there, the music is beginning, the priest is there, and the bridesmaids are marching down. Wow, look at all those people! Here comes the Maid of Honor. Ann will be next. I wonder how she looks. There she is with her father, Oh my God, she is beautiful…they are playing

"Here Comes the Bride", they are marching towards us…everyone is smiling (I don't know if I'm going to make it-hang in there Gus)…here they are, Erminio lifts her veil and kisses her…he gives me her hand… Oh, JOY!!! The Heavens are pleased!…We will be joined in minutes!. I cannot believe her radiance! I cannot believe I hadn't fainted yet. Time seemed to stand still for me. I will never…ever…forget that moment!!! "I now pronounce you Husband and Wife!" the priest said.

MY NEW LIFE HAS BEGUN…

I AM A HUSBAND…

Our Wedding Picture-May 2, 1953

CHAPTER 5…THE HUSBAND

New People mentioned in this Chapter

Assunta, Mom's Mother .... Assunta Passero
Erminio, Mom's Father..Erminio Passero
Auntie Rosie Our Sister-In-Law .... Rose Passero
Uncle Tony, Mom's Brother............................Antonio (Rexie) Passero
Our Aunt Mary, Ann's Sister and Uncle Julio's Wife .... Mary Galano
Our Uncle Julio– Married to Ann's Sister ....Julius Galano
Family Photographer and a Paisano .... Michael Di Vito

1953

THE WEDDING RECEPTION. Before I begin to tell you about the reception, I must start with the announcement that I am now a HUSBAND!!! This is a Title that I treasure a great deal for many reasons. Number one, it is the first Life Title bestowed on me for merit (excuse me for not being humble here). I earned this status, by adhering to strict rules and by making many sacrifices to achieve the role. One of the major benefits is that when someone calls me a Husband that means there is a Wife and that feeling cannot be explained. It is overwhelming…in today's vernacular it's the equivalent of Awesome… The moment I became a Husband I knew that I was united in love with Ann and we were one. It was the most wonderful event of my life! (having lived past this point, I realize that there would be more.) So, in this chapter, I will be referring to Ann as my Wife (I will not be using her given name again as I have prior). OK, I can continue now, back to the reception of Mr. & Mrs. Augustus L. Petti…

The place: Howard Johnson – The Cloud Room – Second Floor. The location: Queen's Boulevard and Horace Harding Boulevard, Queens, New York City. The time: One o'clock in the afternoon. The date: Saturday, May 2nd , 1953. The weather: Cloudy with occasional rain – clearing-becoming sunny. The atmosphere: Jovial.

When my Wife and I got there, most of our guests had arrived and the band had started playing introductory music. We could hear the roar of the crowd and it made us happy, we smiled at each other, which was our way of knowing that all was going well. Then the Maitre d' ushered us to a room to wait for the ceremonies to officially begin. We spent all that time taking pictures. The photographer was our paisano Michael Di Vito (I remember his name because it's engraved on all our photos.) Besides he was a special friend of the family (and a 5th Avenue professional photographer to boot.) Not having a studio of his own, we proceeded to my parents' home and took all the portrait photos there. You can see my parent's wallpaper in all of our photos. (Just for the record, I put up that wallpaper-It's interesting that my work would be memorialized this way!) After taking these formal photos, all the other candid photos were taken at the reception ballroom. If you want to see who attended the reception, go to our wedding album, most of them are there in those photos. You will also see the wedding cake in those photos which was a pure whipped cream vanilla cake with strawberry filling which was a first at an Italian wedding in our family! (Traditionally, it was ricotta cream, doused with rum). All of the Italian eyebrows were all rising when they were presented with the food (It was American food!) "Where is the'antipasto?," one commented. "Shhh," the person next to her said. "There is no antipasto; there is a fruit cup instead." "Where is the Chianti wine?" another whispered. "There is no Chianti." was the response. There on all the tables was Virginia Dare white wine only. "Are we having macaroni?," asked another. "I don't know," came the answer. And that is how it went. Boy, was it a big surprise to everyone! It probably was one of the reasons it was such a big hit with most guests. The actual luncheon fare was a fruit cup as an appetizer followed by a salad, then we had their famous Howard Johnson's Roasted Turkey with stuffing and gravy, with mashed potatoes and peas and carrots followed by the whipped cream wedding cake and Howard Johnson's famous ice-cream. A far cry from the traditional Foot-Ball wedding that was the norm then. It was delicious; even my mother and father congratulated us on our choices of food. We had fun!

FIRST 3D PHOTOS. Another first that occurred at the wedding was the experimental taking of 3 Dimensional photographs! Mike's friend (who was also a photographer) wanted to experiment at our wedding by taking his first 3 dimensional photos, using a newly developed Stereo Lens camera. He needed our permission before he could proceed, which we cheerfully gave him. Also, the photos would be taken gratis. The final photos were given to us on film (no paper), mounted in plastic holders so they could be viewed in a special stereo viewer that was backlit, producing a multi dimensional image that is really neat. Unfortunately, the concept did not take-off as expected. Take a look at them, they are with the wedding album. They have withstood 54 years of time so far and are packaged with the viewer. You can actually see depth in the photos. My favorite is the one of us in the car (especially the Orchids).

Meanwhile at the reception, the introductions were beginning. We were brought close to the reception room doors where the guests were waiting. The Maitre d' announcing the parents, then the Best Man and the Maid of Honor and we were next! "And now, presenting for the first time as Husband and Wife, Ann and Augustus Petti"...with the music playing, we marched to the center of the ballroom floor. The band began playing the song; Let Me Call You Sweetheart and we both started dancing. It was wonderful. Everybody was applauding. We were so happy. Our parents were so happy. Everyone there (I believe) was so happy. It was a very happy day (and someone coming into the room at that moment yelled out, "The sun just came out!) That made it perfect!!! We looked at each other and Ann said, "God's blessing!" And I said "Thank you, Lord!" Not just for the sun, but the whole day, all those years of courtship, for her love and for God's blessing, it was a moment of intense thanksgiving. We were truly grateful !!

THE "BUSTA BAG" CUSTOM. That's pronounced; Boosta . One tradition that was not abandoned at our reception was the carrying of the Busta Bag. This is a special large satin bag that is traditionally carried by the Bride as she and the Groom go around greeting all the guests at their tables. While chatting during this greeting with family and friends, one of the guests graciously hands you an envelope (in Italian, an envelope is called "la busta") that the Bride gratefully accepts and places in the bag. At the end of the table visits, the busta bag is quit full and this is the traditional way that Italians present the married couple with their wedding gifts. It was the most popular way of receiving wedding gifts at the time (a custom carried over from Italy) which seemingly weathered the storm of time and continues to this day at some weddings. Our family and friends were so generous! We couldn't believe it. After opening all the envelopes and reading the congratulatory wishes of our parents, our families and our friends, we couldn't help but begin sobbing as one gift after another flowed onto the table. We were so grateful. We were so full of love, for our parents and families and for all our friends. How generous they were. We couldn't be happier! Thank you all, we loved you. You brought us so much joy!!!

After the wedding, we were driven home to Ann's house. We got there after her parents had arrived and they were all in comfortable clothes. That's what we wanted too, to get out of the formal clothing and get back to normal casual wear. We changed and now guests from the wedding were arriving. This is another Italian custom, that is to invite family members on the Bride's side to stop over at the house for some pastry and coffee (that's usually cannoli and espresso). The Groom's parents do the same thing; they invite their family and friends to stop in at their home for the same things. Meanwhile, we were describing our honeymoon plans to the family. We were to take a taxi to New York where we had a reservation at the Plaza Hotel on the edge of Central Park. Uncle Julio said, "No way, you're not taking any taxi cab today! I will take both of you to where you want to go." How could we say no, it was Uncle Julio talking. He would not take "no" for an answer. So we gathered our luggage, loaded it into his trunk and went to the hotel. He was joking all the way there. He was a treasure, we will never forget that ride. At the hotel we registered as Mr. & Mrs. for the first time! It was a little strange. It was a new life, everything was new! We didn't realize it at that moment (with the adrenaline flowing at the speed of light in our bodies), that we had a lot of adjusting to do! The bell boy took our luggage and led us to the elevator and to our room. After settling in, we got a chance to look out the window and what a beautiful sight, all of Central Park was in focus! We had to stay there overnight because our plane did not leave until the next day.

In the morning, after breakfast, we had this compulsion to seek out a church and spend some time praying before we left. As we left the hotel lobby and came onto the street, there was a little Franciscan Church where they were preparing for a mass. We immediately entered and attended as Wife and Husband, one of the most beautiful masses that we will never forget. In this solitude and spiritual surrounding, we thanked God for all his blessings and vowed to continue following His Commandments and love forever. It was a very spiritual moment for us and we were humbled as we realized we were receiving so many gifts from the hand of God! Thank you Lord, we both said quietly…Mass ended…

THE HONEYMOON. We went back to the hotel, gathered our luggage and proceeded to La Guardia Airport by taxi cab. There are so many firsts happening to us, it's difficult starting a sentence without saying, 'And this was a first!', but it's true. We were going to fly to Buffalo (since we would be spending the next week at Niagara Falls on our honeymoon.) And it would be a first plane ride for my Wife! Of course, being in the Air Force I flew many times, especially on Guam so it was old stuff for me. But my Wife was a little nervous and understandably so. Here are some interesting facts about this trip: In the 1950s, air travel was very different than it is today. Firstly, all passenger airplanes were propeller driven (even though jet engine airplanes were invented during World War II – in the 40's) and a little awkward. The planes were supported by three sets of wheels. Two landing wheels and one tail wheel which caused the airplane to drop down in the rear, so the aisle between the seats was on an incline of about 15 to 20 degrees. This meant that when you entered the plane, you had to walk uphill and sometimes pull yourself up the aisle by grabbing the top of a seat for support and leverage, and if people were already sitting in the seat you are grabbing, watch-out…I don't know how many people's shoulders were grabbed in the process when attempting to grab a seat for balance. You had to see how many innocent passengers that were disturbed this way became annoyed and would not accept an "I'm sorry" comment by the perpetrator as they walked by.

The second bit of information, that is very different from today, is that every passenger's name was recorded on a Flight Bill and called out before takeoff to verify their presence on the plane. And here is something none of you know: My Wife and I did not travel under the names of Mr. & Mrs. Augustus L. Petti. You see, Ann was responsible for securing our airplane tickets and since she was close to a travel agency at her workplace she would purchase the tickets there. It seems this travel agency could grant discounts to anyone willing to use other people's tickets who had cancelled for one reason or another. We were such people. To receive a substantial discount, my Wife purchased two tickets to Buffalo that belonged to two other people. Her name aboard the plane was Miss Beatrice Wellingsly and mine was Mr. Roger Williams. Can you imagine us replying to these names when the stewardess called them? And here is another fact, we were in different seats, three rows apart! My Wife wasn't even near me! It was kind of weird. Anyway, as soon as we sat down after the drastic uphill climb to our seats, since my Wife was in front, she had to turn around to signal to me and utter a few words across three rows. A clergyman sitting next to my Wife immediately realized we were together but sitting apart and offered to change seats for us. We did and I was very grateful to him, but he said it was nothing and he was glad to do a good thing. So we did travel next to one another, but it required God's intervention obviously. We were grateful and couldn't thank that clergyman enough. The flight didn't take long, about an hour as I recall. After we claimed our luggage we looked around and to be honest with you, I was looking for the Water Falls. All along, we were saying to one another that we were going to Niagara Falls. The name Buffalo was never spoken during our dialogue so when we arrived I thought Niagara Falls was there at the airport - how naive of me. When the reality of the moment called for us to find some sort of transportation to get to Niagara, a Limousine driver that was parked there approached and offered to take us (of course for a price). We accepted and began our 45 minute voyage to the Falls. As we were driving, we couldn't help notice the large waterway that appeared to be a river but in reality was the water coming from Niagara Falls. When we arrived at the Niagara Hotel (the same hotel in the movie with Marilyn Monroe) we could hear the roar of the falls but couldn't see it that all. We signed the registry as Mr. & Mrs. A. Petti again, now it was becoming more comfortable. The bellboy picked up our luggage, took us to the elevator and up we went to our room. The room was great, it overlooked the Niagara Rapids (rushing water) which to me looked like a river but they didn't call it that. When we opened the window, the roar of the moving water was almost deafening. We had to shut the window to cancel out the sound somewhat. In the lobby we had collected some brochures and began looking at them. We immediately learned that across the New York State part of Niagara Falls is Canada (Now don't laugh, at that age, we didn't know that!). Although we wanted to go there, we realized that I wasn't born in the US and therefore would need a valid birth certificate to enter Canada (we knew this from a past experience encountered by Auntie Mary Galano-who was detained by the Canadian's because she had a photo-copy of her birth certificate instead of the original). So we considered Canada off-limits insofar as this trip was concerned. Okay, then where should we go on the state side? Oh, there were many places, of course there are the "Falls", that's number one, but then there are the "Rapids", that's number two, then there is a Museum in town, that's number 3 and so on. It looked very exciting.

NIAGARA FALLS. The next morning, after breakfast in the hotel restaurant, we went immediately to Niagara Falls. What a spectacular view! It was breathtaking to see all this water moving rapidly over the edge of a cliff about 300 feet above the Rocks of Ages as they called them which were actually a formation of gigantic boulders that broke away from the top edge, millions of years ago, it created an image in our minds that will be hard to forget. I began taking photos of the sights and I had taken my father's movie camera that took 16 mm film (long obsolete film camera now) and was able to capture the force and the beauty of that cascading sea of water. While I was photographing the scenes, I heard a tour guide say; "Over 33,000 barrels of water fall over the edge every second!" Can you imagine that? That is a lot of water!

I was pleased with the photography that resulted. Usually many have all kinds of problems with their honeymoon photos, but all of my photos and filming was successful. Thank you, Lord! You can see the photos in our album and the films have been converted to video tapes which is on one of the Petti History VHS tapes (year 1953 section) I gave each of you. There are some shots I am especially proud of on the video; the view at the top of the Falls where you see the water going over the edge, I had to lean far over the Observation Railing to get that scene and my Wife was yelling and holding my legs at the same time so I wouldn't fall over, but I wanted to get as close as possible to show the amount of water moving over the edge. I got it, even though I took an unnecessary risk to get it! But you know I was 23 years old and most probably did not think it was too dangerous at the time (I certainly would not do it now!). Oh, well we live and learn.

Then we wanted to go to the Foot of the Fall's. There was an entrance where the falls crashed on the Rocks of Ages and visitors could put on waterproof gear and walk on a wooden pathway that was built on boulders. The rocks were not in the direct path of the cascading water but you could get very wet from the splashing and mist that occurred due to the falling water. Luckily, the pathway was closed for repairs. Thank God!...but the adjacent path along the rocky part was open so we changed into the raingear and went walking along the Foot of the Falls. It was a lot of fun! Believe it or not I took my 16 mm camera to that spot and we have movies of it (but no sound) pictures of us walking there at the Foot of Niagara Fall". Those, I believe, are monumental videos and should be viewed just for the shear adventure that they provide. We got all wet anyway, which made us laugh so much. We might as well have walked there in our street clothes for all the protection the raingear provided. It was a joke!

After we dried off, our next adventure was the Rapids and the best way to experience them is to ride across on the Cable Car that is a little down the waterway. When we saw it, for some reason it didn't look too strong to say the least. Before we got on, a tour guide explained that it was Spain's gift to the United States back in the 20s! Wow, I thought, and it's been operating this long? That's over 30 years ago. Is it safe, I wondered? Yeah, other people are getting on it; we'll be okay. It was held on by cables and operated by a large motor pulling it back and forth across the span of the gorge where the rapid water is rushing and very dangerous. In fact, the rushing water actually caused whirlpools that were looming underneath of the cable car when we got to the middle. "Look down," said the loudspeaker, "and you will see perpetual whirlpools that no boat can navigate nor can anyone swim past them." It was very interesting and very exciting to hover over them in the Spanish Cable Car!

THE WHITE HAIR'D MAN. Our next adventure was the Niagara Museum. This was one of the most interesting museums I have ever visited. First, it was very old (in terms of modern museums) so it was very musty (or should I say dusty), full of spider webs and loads of dust all over the place. Most of the articles on display were different kinds of man made containers used to go over the falls with. There were wooden barrels, metal barrels and one that looked like a miniature submarine. Even though it became illegal in the 30s to go over the falls, people still did it. There were many photos of those who succeeded and those that did not. My attention focused on a photo of a white-haired young man. I began reading the caption next to the photo. It seems, sometime in the 40s, an electric company wanted to string a high voltage line across the rapids at a point where a small rock in the center of the water existed. Using a modified whale harpoon they fired a rope toward the rock hoping to anchor it since they could not span the whole rapid at one time due to the distance. The plan was to attach a heavy rope from both shores to the rock in the center of the rapids which would allow them to install the electric wire across the whole body of water. The first rope from one side attached itself to the rock and they sent this one young man to that rock, while holding onto the rope, to assist with the attempt from the other shore. The man got to the rock safely. This was all being performed in daylight. Now the firing of the rope from the other side began and was not that successful. They tried all day without being able to secure a rope to the other side. Meanwhile the young man remained there because they lost the attachment from the other side while working. The man was stranded and night was approaching. No boat could withstand the torrents of that water. There was no alternative but to leave him there until morning when attempts would resume to save him. Then the caption makes this next fact very emphatic. He had black hair when he landed on that rock. The next day, they began sending a rope to the rock to rescue him and were successful. When he returned from spending the night on that rock his hair turned pure white, not a streak of black anywhere and the photo on the wall proves that. His associates could not believe it! They immediately called for the local newspaper photographers who recorded it for posterity. These were copies of the photographs that were taken. Although all the science I've read says this cannot happen, that intense stress cannot remove all the pigment that is contained in hair overnight, well here is positive proof that it can! I like to tell this story because it has caused another mystery for science and cannot be explained. But the best part is that the man was rescued and he lived to a ripe old age, but with pure white hair, starting in his twenties! He must have had a lot of explaining to do during his years alive. It was such an interesting story, I could never forget it. The one fact I got out of the whole incident is that stress can do more damage to your body than scientists know about. And not necessarily over time, it can do it to you instantly too! So we must be aware of stress at all costs. I hope you got the same message.

RETURN FROM HONEYMOON. It's time to go back home and resume our working life. On the plane we went from Buffalo to LaGuardia Airport, New York, only this time the manifesto listed us as Mrs. Ann Petti and Mr. Augustus Petti and we had side-by-side reserved seats. It was a new life. We were on the threshold of bright horizons together. We were very happy! As soon as we arrived home at 1 Orient Avenue, Brooklyn, New York (we decided to live with my mother, father and sister in the same house) we were greeted by my mother and father and sister, all asking about the trip since they knew nothing about Niagara Falls except that it was a place on the map. We began explaining all the sights and the places of interest.

ANN COOKS HER FIRST BREAKFAST. The reason I want to describe my Wife's first breakfast is not to embarrass her, but to point out how far she has come since then. While I'm explaining the circumstances, you must remember that Ann never cooked at home in her growing years. Her mother prepared everything, and like so many other women at the time, the preparation of food was not very high on their priority list. Anyway, what she lacked in cooking knowledge was made up in newlywed enthusiasm. On the first morning of our arrival at my parents' home, she arose before me and quietly went downstairs to our basement kitchen. There she unpacked (most of our wedding gifts were still packed in boxes); the new electric coffee pot and a brand new toaster oven (they were very large) that had a special feature called an Additional Cook Top which was comprised of a thin tray that could hold eggs and bacon to be cooked on top of the electric oven. In fact, it was so new that it still contained a photo on paper that fit into the tray, displaying two cooked eggs and four slices of cooked bacon. She carefully removed the paper and broke two eggs, placing them identical to the photo, then placing four slices of bacon in similar fashion, then closed the top. She set the dial for cooking. Next, she went to the coffee pot, rinsed it out, filled it to the proper level of cold water, fitted the stem and strainer in the pot ready for the addition of the ground coffee. After measuring out the proper amount of ground coffee, she placed the top on, plugged it into the electric outlet and proceeded cooking it. By this time I had arrived in the kitchen. We hugged and kissed, and then I smelled the coffee. "Dear," I said, "you made breakfast?" "Yes, I wanted to surprise you!" "That's wonderful!" I exclaimed, and sat down at the table anxiously awaiting my first breakfast cooked by my own loving wife. She placed the plates and coffee cups, knives, forks and spoons at the table then went to the coffee pot which I heard had just finished perking. She began pouring the coffee into my cup, but the liquid was the color of clear water! I immediately said, "Ann, did you put ground coffee in the pot?" "Yes!" she said puzzled. I instinctively opened the coffee pot and looked inside the strainer and sure enough the coffee grounds were there, but they were not wet, they were still dry. How could that be I wondered, I heard the water boiling in its perking cycle when I came in? Upon further investigation we learned that the stem was filled with coffee grounds, preventing the boiling water from coming up and into the strainer. I have never seen that happen in my whole life, but there it was! I immediately assured her that it was no problem and easily fixed but she took it to heart and felt bad. "Okay, forget about the coffee, what else did you make that I can have?" She took my plate and quickly went to the toaster oven, lifted the lid and began crying uncontrollably!!! "What is it Ann?" "The eggs and bacon did not cook! They are still raw!" she said while crying. I then went to her aid, looked at it (by now the bacon was swimming in the raw eggs and it was a mess, not a pretty sight) and said, "That's all right, Dear, nothing that a frying pan can't fix." (I actually wanted to laugh at this point, but I sensed it wasn't the right time). Well, at that moment, I tried to help her salvage the messed up breakfast. Anyway, the crying stopped and we had our breakfast in peace without any further incident that first morning. But I must admit that was the only goof my wife ever committed in the preparation of food and there has never been a duplicate incident since. Amen to that! It was a very funny event, but I don't think Ann thinks so.we had the honeymoon photos developed and during the week we were able to show the family the pictures and the movie film. They especially enjoyed the movie film I guess because of the motion; they could see the cascading water coming over the falls, the Rainbow Bridge and the huge Horseshoe Falls on the Canadian side. It was great. I believe they are the best movies I have ever taken (except when I took those of the children).

FIRST SIGN OF PREGNANCY. Meanwhile during the week, my wife became ill. She got nauseous in the morning and complained of not feeling well during the day. Being novices at this, our first course is to revert to home remedies. She began drinking hot tea which helped a little. Then she stayed away from fatty foods, which also helped a little, but it seemed stubborn and apparently was not going away. We both realized that the best course now was to see a doctor. My wife made an appointment and went to visit our family doctor. After preliminary questions were answered and after a physical examination, the doctor looked at my wife and said "You're pregnant!" "Are you sure, doctor?" came the retort. The doctor chuckled and said, "Of course I'm sure, you have the classic symptoms!" "Oh my gosh, I didn't think it was going to happen this soon!" she exclaimed. She then asked for an estimated date. He said, "Probably sometime in February or March, we will know more as you progress." What good news, and couldn't wait to get home to tell me! I was still working at R.H. Macy's and wouldn't be home till 6 p.m. When I got home, my first question was, "What did the doctor say?" She was all smiles. I should have known, but didn't know...this was the first time. She looked at me and said "I'm Pregnant!" "Oh, my God!" I said. "I'm so happy" I added. "We're going to have a baby!". It was pure "heaven" during those moments of revelation...it was the happiest moment of our life to know that we would be sharing this experience of love together. Just the thought of bringing another being into our world was an unbelievable joyous event. We were so happy...and when we told our parents and relatives they were so happy for us. So now the "nine month" wait began!

My wife was still working at Deak & Company, the international exchange business in downtown New York. They exchanged money from one country's currency to another and for that service they collected a fee. For example, if you lived in Mexico and owned Pesos but had a monetary transaction with a USA company, you needed US Dollars to pay your debt. Deak would buy your Pesos at the government rate and convert it to US Dollars to satisfy the recipient transaction. Now my wife was not feeling well enough to continue working so she stayed home. During the next nine months, a lot of dialogue was being exchanged between us. My wife was earning about $55 dollars a week and I was earning around $50 dollars a week (Yes, she earned more money than I did). At $105 dollars a week, we were able to survive, but now we had to add an infant to our survival group. The expenses would certainly increase, how would we meet the needs. We both concluded that my income wasn't enough, especially since the cost of living was rising. Also, I didn't want the mother-to-be working, so we would be losing another salary. There was no getting away from it; I had to get a better paying job after the baby was born. So I began my search. It wasn't easy, most of the jobs out there were not paying much more than I was making. My wife went to work when she was feeling better so she only worked a few weeks during the nine months, which was okay with me. I felt that was a better way of proceeding towards the final months. But I continued working at Macy's and was even promoted to Assistant Sales Rep. in the Foreign office. In fact one day while I was washing my hands in the Men's room, the Vice President I was assistant to, said to me; "He was very happy with my performance and that if all goes well, I will probably be replacing him when he retires". Then he added these ominous words; "It only took me 17 years to get where I am". Seventeen years!!! I couldn't wait seventeen years! I thought silently, I've got to get out of here. Not that I was ungrateful - R.H. Macy's was very good to me. It was the time lapse that was very disturbing (especially since I needed more money now - not 17 years down the road.) This made me more aggressive in my search for another job, but to no avail. The job market was in a slump. There were only a few jobs being advertised, jobs that I did not necessarily qualify for. Even though, now looking back, conditions seemed very bleak, but as I recall at the time we were unaware of the severity of our circumstances. We were so caught up with the prospects of becoming a mother and a father; I believe that overshadowed everything else. It didn't matter that I was only bringing home $60 dollars (remember I got a promotion) a week. It really wasn't enough, but through some magic that we weaved (or Ann weaved), it was enough for now.

WHERE WE LIVED IN BROOKLYN. I mentioned that we lived at 3 Orient Avenue, Brooklyn, New York, which was my mother and father's home. We lived with them during our first year of marriage. It was a two and a half story home that had the following configuration; three steps down from the street level was our kitchen. It was a fairly large kitchen with a refrigerator. It had a large sink with hot and cold running water (don't laugh, not all kitchens had hot water in the 50's.) Under the stairway was a small toilet. There was a furnace room behind the kitchen that produced steam for the house, it kept us very warm in the winter. On the second floor, which was about nine steps up from the street level, was the other kitchen (which was my mother and father's kitchen.) Then there was a large living room and a large dinning room on that level. There was a top floor, another nine steps up from the second floor level, where the bedrooms were. There were three bedrooms on the top floor with a full bath. The bedrooms were, one for my mother and father, one for my sister and one for us. We had adequate space in that house. It was a generous gift from my mother and father to be able to live there while we became established as husband and wife, with a little one on the way. They were very good to us. We were comfortable there.

As a bonus, the house was only two blocks away from the subway station. The subway is what I took to work on 34th Street, New York City, where Macy's was. Until Lucille was born, there is where we lived. My father was working in Queens, at Sol Schieldrkraut, Lincoln, Ford and Mercury Dealer as foreman of the Auto Body Shop. My mother was working as a seamstress on Meserole Street in a clothing factory; she was also the Union Representative and The Floor Lady (a role she enjoyed immensely.) My parents had so many interesting stories to tell us that occurred during their working hours. My sister was growing up fast and attending school. She was about 8 or 9 years old by now. Everything was going along smoothly.

BEGAN WORKING AT REPUBLIC AVIATION. In my search for a new job, a newspaper want ad caught my attention concerning aviation production. Since I was somewhat familiar with airplanes, it was worth investigating. I applied and they hired me as a final assembly technician. I believe I began work there in September of 1953. They were located in Farmingdale, Long Island, just adjacent to Republic Airport. The transportation there was not that difficult. I would go by subway to the Jamaica Terminal, the transfer to the Long Island Railroad and ride to Farmingdale. The station was within walking distance from the plant, although most of the time I drove there with my 1939 Plymouth. Republic Aviation built fighter planes. The F-14 was a jet fighter plane that was in great demand by the armed forces at the time. Even though I was a little apprehensive about the job, I threw myself into it with all my abilities. It worked! After two months, the foreman liked my work so much he promoted me to Expert repairman. I was now assigned to repair jobs that others goofed. It was a very responsible position because I had to correct (and according to specifications) other mechanics' blunders. I never lost track of the importance of this task. There were lives at risk. I even enjoyed the work to boot. In fact after three months, they asked me if I would consider going to Airplane Inspection School, then becoming a Final Assembly Line Inspector. I said, "Yes, with pleasure!" Off to school I went, which was a breeze. When I returned, I was inspecting final assembly installations before the planes were released for test flying. It was not only interesting, but it was exciting too. And I got a raise, now

I was making $90 a month. I was getting nearer earning a salary close to our combined income. But it still wasn't enough. I had to find part time jobs to supplement my income. You will not believe the different types of jobs I held as part time endeavors during this phase of my life. I would answer any want ad that had the hours I needed to work around my 7AM to 3PM job at Republic Aviation My first part time job was being a night watchman" (I don't remember where). And I held many other part time jobs that escape me now because they didn't last long.

Meanwhile we were celebrating all the holidays as they occurred. St. John the Baptist, St. Joseph, the 4th of July, all the birthdays that were coming around in the family and Thanksgiving. This was an interesting holiday and because my mother hosted it we had antipasto, lasagna and roasted capon (a large chicken) with italian salad and sponge cake with custard filling. Nothing American; no turkey, no stuffing, no cranberry or potatoes, no mushrooms, etc.,etc. It wasn't my mother's fault though; she didn't know how to prepare those recipes, so she cooked what she knew. Anyway, we got through it, but it was tough going, let me tell you! Then there was Christmas Eve and Christmas Day, we got so many gifts. Then there was New Year's Eve and New Year's Day. This holiday was always celebrated at my wife's brother's apartment on Power Street. We were not only invited for the ushering in of the New Year's Eve celebration, but also for New Year's Day where they served Roasted Lobster and all the accoutrements (and there were many!).

WAITING FOR LUCILLE'S BIRTH. And my wife was getting bigger. It was her 8th month. One more month and the baby would be born. We couldn't wait. The anxiety was getting to us. No matter what we were talking about, the subject always ended with the anticipation of the forthcoming arrival! What are we going to do? What will we name it? Here the subject was, if it's a girl it would be named after my mother and if it's a boy it would be named after my father. This is Italian tradition! So we began with the naming ritual; if it's a girl, we said to my mother, we will call her Lucia, the same as your name. "No," she said. "That's an Italian name, you should Americanize it." So we made a number of suggestions: "Lucy" we said; "No, I like Lucille better." (I Love Lucy – with Lucille Ball - was a favorite program on radio then.) Then we dealt with the boy's name. If it was a boy, it would be named to respect my father, it would be Joseph. The two names were determined, if it was a girl it would be called Lucille and if it was a boy it would be called Joseph. Middle names were optional as to whom they would be after, in those days they didn't have a way of knowing the gender of a newborn before birth. It was all a mystery. I think that's what caused the anxiety level to rise to such a tumultuous level. We were very on edge as the month of February approached. I remember saying to my wife who was carrying our child; "Ok, now please don't get too worked up about this, stay calm," about 100 times during those days (I exaggerate)!!! The time was getting near. We were patiently waiting. What was it going to be? When was it going to happen? The next Chapter tells the whole story!!! (Chapter 6)

THE "TITLE" HUSBAND REMAINS. Although this is the shortest chapter of my life, in terms of solo responsibilities, in reality it is the longest title I will hold for the remainder of my life. As my life titles change, being a husband remains. Even though in the next chapter I become a father, I am and will always be a husband too! And that is my first and primary title when it comes to my relationship with Ann! It's interesting that from now on, life begins to complicate a husband's role. Pretty soon, I will become a father along with being a husband, then a grandfather along with being a father and husband, then a great-grandfather along with the other three roles. I don't know how I did it? Obviously, without God's help (in my case) it could not be possible. One thing I must say is that I feel wonderful about the whole assignment, if it can be called that. So remember, I will be a husband from now on and will never change from this role, even when others are added on.

CHAPTER 6 ... FATHER

New persons mentioned in this Chapter

"Lucille" Our First Born .... Lucille Ann Petti
"Susan" Our Second Born .... Susan Carol Petti
"Christine" Our Third Born .... Christine Marie Petti
"Joseph" Our Fourth Born (deceased)................ Joseph Erminio Petti
"Michele" Our Fifth Born .... Michele Marie Petti
Assunta, Mom's Mother .... Assunta Passero
Erminio, Mom's Father... Erminio Passero
Auntie Rosie Our Sister-In-Law .... Rose Passero
Uncle Tony, Mom's Brother........................... Antonio (Rexie) Passero
Dr. L. Iamele (my Godfather)................................ Louis Iamele, MD
Daughter of "Zia Luccia" (Married to Dr. Iamele)........... Mary Iamele

1954

Before I continue, I must tell you that this will be the largest but the greatest Chapter of my Life. Thanks to you, my Five Children, who presented me with the Title of Father, which I will cherish forever, have brought me to this age! I also want you to know that each of you was my guiding star all during this part of my life and will be for the rest of my existence.

Also, since so many new persons will enter this chapter that I felt it would not be practical to list them all above (In the "New persons mentioned" section). So please, allow me this one exception... I'm sure you will recognize yourself when you are reading these passages (the newly introduced people, I mean). I will describe each person when first mentioned; their relation to me and the event occurring that is new in my life.

ABOUT BOO-BOO'S. Here comes an apology... There are those of you who can remember the date, the time, the place, etc.,

etc., of any event affecting your past lives. As you will find out, on the ensuing pages, I am not one of those persons. If, in this book, you find an incorrect date, or incorrect time, or incorrect place, it is because I am only human. Please make any correction deemed necessary to improve the accuracy of my writings, I won't mind. I must tell you, that I have tried, with great effort, to record information as accurately as I can. But keep in mind that a great deal of the information I cite, was mostly given to me by one of you, and of course becomes subject to all sorts of contortions during the writing process, both in copying and in typing. Hope none of my boo-boo's cause you to much pain. I also ask you to remember this page in the future, especially when raging about an error! I would appreciate it...

Note: Because we had five children and the events that I will be telling overlap, mostly due to simultaneous occurrences, I decided to codify all sections relating to one child or another. The codes I will use, preceding a section title will be to identify the relating child:

CODE FOR

L – LUCILLE ANN
S – SUSAN CAROL
C – CHRISTINE MARIE
J – JOSEPH ERMINIO
M – MICHELE MARIE

L-OUR FIRST CHILD IS BORN. The month of February, 1954 was approaching. The date of our first child's birth was getting closer. The pregnancy was in its ninth month.

In this Chapter and all subsequent Chapters, because of the changing role and new responsibilities, I will call my Wife (Ann) "MOM".

At that particular time we were living with my mother and father at 3 Orient Avenue, Brooklyn, N.Y. The house was owned by my mother and father. We occupied a second kitchen that was situated three steps below the outside sidewalk level (it was a "mother and daughter" home). We also had a large bedroom on the second floor where we had prepared a second bassinette for baby Lucille (another was set-up in our Kitchen). It was a 2 ½ story house. My mother and father occupied the first floor (up about six steps) where another kitchen existed, along with a large dining room and a parlor (we called the living room a parlor then). Their bedrooms were on the second floor too. That's were Joann's bedroom was also (my sister), she was about 11 years old.

L-CHOOSING A NAME FOR LUCILLE. There was no question about what name to choose for our first born. As I mentioned in the prior chapter, according to Italian tradition, the first born must always be named after the fathers mother (baby's grandmother) or father (baby's grandfather). Therefore, without a doubt, the baby's name will either be Lucille or Joseph, depending on gender. In our family, this tradition would be followed; mom and I both agreed (it also made life a little easy). In retrospect, because the tradition is now fading, I recall some daughters of mine wrestling with names of all sorts, checking books that list thousands of names, having thoughts of all sorts, going through stressed sessions of name trying until one is selected. Then, after a name is selected, the anxiety of wondering if it's the right name! Following our Italian tradition eliminated all of this. So in a sense, I'm extremely grateful of the Italian traditions we followed.

I'd like to take a moment with a word about my job at this time. I was working on military aircraft at Republic Aviation in Farmingdale, Long Island, NY. My first assignment was riveter, then Master Riveter, then Final Assembly Line Inspector. As a result of this experience, I was an expert on the PF-114 Attack Pursuit Airplane, but that's it! All that knowledge never helped me land any other job I ever pursued. Anyway, that was my occupation as we waited for baby Lucille to be born.

It was the night of February 26th, I still hadn't retuned home from work since my working tour was 3PM to 10PM (the night shift). I would arrive home around 11:30PM/ and mom would wait for me. Only this time, events would be a little different. Mom tells me, she had just washed her stockings (by hand) and was about to hang them on the clothes line (my father and I installed it in the furnace room), when all of a sudden she saw a very large rat walking high along the pipes, she gave out a loud scream and went running upstairs where my mother and father were sitting. My father said; "What's the matter" and she told him about the rat in the furnace room. He immediately ran down and began investigating but could not find anything (her scream must have scared it away, he thought). My father comes back and tells her it might have been a stray cat and not to worry (he probably wanted to calm her down especially in her condition) but mom says that fright must have started the birth process, because she was experiencing signs that were expected in anticipation of childbirth. By this time, I had arrived home from work. She explained all that transpired and asked what we should do. I didn't know, (after all it was my first) so she called Auntie Rosie for some guidance. Auntie Rosie suggested she call the doctor. So she did and he said to go to the hospital, they will evaluate her and report the findings to the doctor. That's what we did. We closed the small piece of luggage that was prepared (with necessities) and took it to the car. We drove to the hospital; it was St. John's Hospital in Long Island City, Brooklyn, New York. It was a Catholic Hospital with Nuns exclusively staffing all the facilities. After we arrived, I was told to wait in a certain area, then a Nurse Nun came to me and handed me a large brown bag (with mom's clothing) and told me to go home and wait until the doctor contacted me. Mom went about 21 hours that day before the doctor called me (I followed the orders to a tee). It was in the early hours morning on February 27, 1954 at 1:39 AM according to the birth certificate. I'll never forget the Doctor's words over the phone; "Mr. Petti, you are the proud father of a beautiful baby GIRL!!!" Then he gave me the statistics, "Congratulations, you can visit any time today".

L - "I AM A FATHER" "I AM A FATHER!!!" I exclaimed out loud even though it was so early in the morning. My father heard me and asked if everything was alright, I told him we had a baby girl (tell my mom) then apologized for the yell and reassured him all is well, he can go back to sleep now. I couldn't hold back the joy! Just think; I'm the Father of a Baby Girl! It was overwhelming…I couldn't believe it…A BABY GIRL!!! Thank you Lord. What a Blessing! We are going to name her Lucille Ann, after her wonderful Grandmother who was named after St. Lucy, the Patron Saint of Eyes and her beautiful and marvelous mother! And all this took place without me being present at the hospital. In those days, they did not allow the husband in the delivery room, like they do today. In fact they didn't even want any expectant father to wait in the waiting room, the way they depict in movies. I was nowhere in sight, I was home. I wasn't even there to hold mom's hand during those crucial moments. I think I miss that? I'm so glad they allow the husband to be present nowadays. But none of this took away from the happiness I felt. I couldn't wait till morning so I could go visit my new daughter and to see her new mom. The first thing I did in the morning was to gather up all the telephone numbers I was going to need. As soon as 8:00 AM rolled around, I just had to call everyone! First I called my mother-in-law, Assunta and told her and my father-in-law, Erminio the good news. They were delighted and so happy. Of course their first question was (and this is an old Italian customary inquiry that's always asked when there is a birth) "Is the baby healthy?" "Yes" was my answer; "Oh, good" they would reply. All the Italians I know seem to say the exact same thing. It is as if it is written in stone in their brain. Then they began asking for all the statistics. They wanted to know when she was born, how tall she was and her weight. After I gave them these facts, Assunta asked if she could come with me when I go and visit them. "Of course", I said; "I'll pick you up at 9:30AM". She said "OK, I'll be ready".

Actual date born......February, 27, 1954..........Lucille Ann Petti.... at 1:39 AM......

L-THE HOSPITAL VISIT. When we arrived at the hospital (me and your grandmother Assunta), I rushed to the Reception desk and asked what room mom would be in. The Attendant told me the room number and grandma Assunta and I went to the room. As soon as we entered, we immediately saw little baby Lucille being held by mom, lying there in the bed. We were just about to approach mom and the baby to kiss each of them (another old Italian custom) when a Nun entered the room yelling and screaming saying; "Get out of this room...RIGHT NOW!" We both turned and left the room almost in terror. Outside the room, the Nun apologized for the outburst, but even though we were unaware, we were countermanding their sterility code. In order for us to visit, while a new born baby is with the mother, we have to be dressed in sterile garb and we weren't! I forgave her…after the explanation…now I understood. After explaining all this to Assunta (she only spoke Italian) we both chuckled and were allowed to visit , mom, now that the baby was brought to the Nursery. There was mom, smiling and radiant. I leaned over and kissed her and whispered "I love you mom". Her mother, Assunta, also kissed her and congratulated her then asked her how she was feeling. A little chattering ensued, and then I asked mom where the Nursery was, I wanted to see my baby! When I got to the Nursery, there were so many babies there; I had trouble finding my new daughter. But there she was…how beautiful, with her little hands moving in the air, with her little hat on and her name on the bassinette tag; "Lucille Ann Petti". I was smiling all the time…it's absolutely amazing how this little bundle of joy can effect you! I was so happy and had to rush back to mom to let her know how happy I was. At that moment, I remembered my Chaplain on Guam, explaining to the parents of a newborn who were asking about Baptism, about the wonder of birth and how a baby is God's greatest gift to the married couple and how, God becomes a partner in the creation, not only of new life, but also in the creation of a new SOUL. It is a miracle that can only be wrought with God's help! Praise to you Lord Jesus Christ…Thank you for our precious baby Lucille!!!

In those days, the mother and child had to remain in the hospital for four or five days to insure there were no complications. When it was time, I went to bring mom and baby Lucille home. We had everything ready. We tucked our new daughter in her new bassinette with all those frills. She was Goo-Gooing all the time, until she got hungry, then the crying came. Her crying wasn't very loud. I think I can live with that, I thought. OK, mom "what do we do now?" Mom instinctively knew what to do. Of course my mother was close by in case we stumbled. Everything went well that first day. We enjoyed taking care of the baby. Then the visitors began coming the next day. We had to give all that information over and over again until everyone was informed. It was fun. Believe it or not things settled down and it was becoming civilized at last. Our baby care skills were improving every day, but the process was very different than it is today. For instance; the doctors (at that time did not want the mothers to breast feed the baby) but asked us to prepare milk bottles for the baby. This entailed first sterilizing (lowering the glass bottles in boiling water at least 212 degrees for 10 minutes or longer) the baby bottles right after their use for storage. When it was time to make the formula, the sterilized bottles were filled with the formula milk then placed in special racks to go through sterilization again, by lowering them in boiling water; including the nipples and bottle caps (sterilization was my job). After all the bottles with the milk were sterilized, they had to be fitted with the sterile nipples, capped, then cooled and then stored in the refrigerator until they were needed. As soon as we were down to two or three bottles in the refrigerator, mom would remind me to start making more formula. And so the beat goes on. This was the procedure we followed as baby Lucille was growing. And since the baby bottles were in the refrigerator, ice cold, they had to be warmed to body temperature, around 98 degrees, before mom could feed the baby with the milk. Oh, I almost forgot. Diapers were not made of paper as they are today. What were used were diapers of heavy white cotton cloth which had to be washed daily. This task was mom's. Please don't forget this was 1954! We did not have an automatic washing machine like today. Although we had a washing machine, it only agitated the clothes to wash them, but did "NOT" wring them out (or "spin dry" them). After rinsing the diapers manually, they had to be put through a series of rollers to squeeze out all the water. Can you imagine that?! Each diaper had to go through the rollers and we had quit a few. Then the damp diapers had to be placed on a clothes line to dry (no gas or electric dryer either!). It was hard work, but worth it. Very, very different from today!

Now the fun really starts. Just think, I was a father now and Ann was a mom. Even though these new titles were real and vital, we had not become very aware of their significance at that moment. We were so young, I was 24 years old and Mom was 23. We just returned from our Honeymoon 10 month's ago. Our marriage wasn't even one year old! Yet, here we were, starring at the little "baby" in mom's arms, loving it to pieces and trying to get a hold on life. Where were we going? What were we going to do? There were so many unanswered questions; we had to defer them to some other time, to remain sane.

The task at hand was the loving and caring of this innocent daughter of ours. And that is what we did and that is what kept us sane. And I believe philosophically, that this one focus of life, answered all the questions (without our need to go searching for answers)!

L-NEWS 1954. There is no doubt that the most important event of 1954 in the world was the emergence of Elvis Aaron Presley! He was a shy 19 year-old when he cut his first record, "I'm All Right Mama" in Memphis, Tennessee. Within two years, he was asked to appear on the famous Ed Sullivan Show which guaranteed his stardom"! Fans screamed when "The Pelvis" (as he was known) would thrust his hips on the stage. Many grownups, including myself, did not understand this reaction. As you will learn, there were many other times when I did not understand young peoples reactions to occurrences of the day. But that's just me…it's probably got something to do with my past childhood, that causes an event or series of events to effect my perception the way it does, of things today. But that's what makes us all different and becomes our nature.

Another news item that was broadcast as headlines at the time of baby Lucille's birth was the launching of the Nautilus, the world's first atomic submarine. You will recall the famous Nautilus in literature was the name given to the first submarine conceived in a grandeur fashion, in the book 20,000 Leagues Beneath the Sea, by Jules Verne (French Scientist and Fiction Writer). Not only did Jules Verne invent the concept of a total subsistence type of submarine but he also introduced the world to the possibility of Atomic Power, which was the energy source of the underwater craft in his fictional book. He had so much foresight in the scientific world. And this American submarine just launched contained much of the imaginary devices that Jules Verne concocted in the early 19th century; a metal craft that could remain submerged for years if need be, without resurfacing, and an unlimited power source that could propel it anywhere on the surface or below the high seas, forever. Truly amazing! Meanwhile another news item concerned our President, who at the time was Dwight D. Eisenhower, and who proposed to Congress lowering the voting age to 18. In June of 1954, the Soviet Union opens the world's first atomic power station that generates electricity. It seems as though it was a year for births, not only was Lucille born, but also atomic energy was the source of the other two births (namely the First Atomic Submarine and the First Nuclear electric generating plant). Very interesting.

This year, the United States Congress added words to the Pledge of Allegiance that read: Under God

In the area of trivia, Frank Sinatra won an Oscar for his supporting role in the movie, From Here to Eternity. Marilyn Monroe marries baseball legend Joe DiMaggio, the song Papa Loves Mambo makes it easy to cha-cha. RCA begins selling color TV sets for $1,000.00 each and Robert Young stars in TV's Father Knows Best (a role I would be playing as soon as baby Lucille grows up). In sports, an amazing runner broke a world barrier (a mile in less than 4 minutes), by Roger Bannister a British medical student who ran the mile in less than four minutes (exactly 3 minutes, 59.4 seconds). No one thought a human could do this! You see Lucille; records were being made the year you were born, a legacy that probably deserves some attention.

L-BABY LUCILLE'S BAPTISM. After seven or eight weeks of becoming used to the new surroundings, we had to concern ourselves with baby Lucille's Baptism. We had to discuss this with the parish priest to establish the date and time. Then we had to let the (to be) Godmother (Comare-in Italian) and Godfather (Compare-in Italian) know they were selected (who according to Italian custom should be the Maid of Honor and Best Man of the wedding). In our case it would be Rose (Tosinni) Gallo and Uncle Tony Passero. They were so happy when we asked them to be the Godparents. The time was set, the celebration began and everyone had a good time. You can see all the invited guests on the VHS tape which I had copied from the 16mm camera film that I kept for years. The Baptism took place in the Church of St. Francis di Paola in Brooklyn, N.Y. (check your Baptism Certificate for the actual date). We believe it was in April, 1954 but we are not positive. In the video you will see Uncle Tony and Rose Gallo wearing heavy coats. It was very cold that day, but baby Lucille was bundled up so much (at the insistence of both Grandmothers) that I believe you were sweating. At the church, as the ceremony progressed, baby Lucille was so calm until the Priest said, "With this water, I baptize thee, in the Name of the Father, and The Son, and The Holy Ghost, Amen." (Before the Second Ecumenical Council – we referred to the Third Person of God as The Holy Ghost – now it's The Holy Spirit) As soon as the cold water flowed over your head, the crying started (I suspect the cold water was not comfortable). I expected it, because at almost every Baptism the Chaplain and I performed in the Air Force, that's the moment almost all the babies began crying. It was a wonderful ceremony with Uncle Tony holding the lit candle while the priest recited the ancient prayers welcoming you into our Church as another member and another soul. God bless you baby Lucille, I whispered. After the ceremonies we hurried to the house where everyone was waiting (and drinking and eating) to greet the new member of Christ's Church!!! The words, "Happy Baptism" every one would say to you, were repeated over and over again. There you were in a beautiful Baptismal white dress smiling at all the guests. It was a wonderful moment and we will never forget it. Happy Baptism baby Lucille!!!

L-NO SMOKING IN HOUSE. During baby Lucille's Baptism and all future First Birthday celebrations, all of the family members learned of this unusual rule I had. There were not many absolute rules that I would impose during my fatherhood phase except this one (And all my children know the other; "no sleep-over's".) This one is "No Smoking" in the house. For some reason, (The world was not made aware of the dangers as yet.) I would not allow anyone to light up a cigarette in the house after baby Lucille's birth. Of course I thought it was offensive, and since I had difficulty breathing when someone smoked near me, I could imagine how much more a little baby's lungs would be affected by it (just common sense). Before I announced the edict to the relatives and to any visitor, I spoke to mom who agreed whole heartedly as soon as I mentioned it. So it was. I asked everyone that was about to light up a cigarette to please go outside and smoke. At first, they thought I was kidding, but they soon learned I was not! Although most of the men gave me a hard time, the one that I had the most difficulty with was with my brother-in-law Rexie (Uncle Tony). In fact, it got so bad trying to make him accept my requirement that I had to call in mom. It took mom quit a bit of dialogue to convince him that in his home he could smoke all he wanted, but not in our home! Of course our main concern was to protect our new born daughter and not to start an anarchy state. Again, remember this was 1954, almost everyone smoked (including me) and there were no cautionary reports on the Radio or in the Newspapers of the dangers of cigarette smoking. I was not a scientist and could not back my rule up with scientific proof as to its validity, but I stood firm and would not give-in. To the point where I was getting a reputation among the relatives of being a "Hard Person" and that something had to be done. Don't worry, nothing ever came of it. Just loose talk. But I must tell you that it got a little tough when there was a houseful of visitors. I couldn't be everywhere to monitor, so I had to come up with a solution. This is what I did; I painted a very large sign that read; No Smoking Inside the House, Please and posted it near the front door, this way any visitor couldn't help but see the requirement as soon as they entered. This worked very well, especially since no one had ever seen a thing like that in anyone's home! Since it was so unique, it was remembered and turned out to be very effective. From now on they referred to me as the sign painter among the relatives, but it didn't bother me, I was thinking of my child's health only. I believe there is a photograph of the sign in one of the scenes in our photo album collection. You should look in the albums dated 1954-1966 if you want to see my art work. I will talk about my other mandate rule (no sleep-over's) later when the event occurs. Otherwise I was pretty easy going as a parent. All other parental rules could be argued or arbitrated except these two (No Smoking and Sleep-over's'). After all "Father Knows Best", right? One thing for sure, I was ahead of my time. So much for No Smoking…

A NEW HOUSE FOR SALE. I know I keep reminding you, but I was working at Republic Aviation in Farmingdale at the time. and during the many locker room talk sessions I had with fellow workers, one day a fellow employee mentioned a big builder in the town of Brentwood who plans to construct over 2,000 homes at very reasonable prices. When I got home, I asked mom if she would accompany me for a visit to see the model. I was told they have model homes and they are taking deposits on new homes planned. She said, Ok, but with some reservations, like; "How can we afford a new home?" and "Isn't it very far away?" Of course two very valid objections, but they did not faze me, my youth cancelled all arguments of this nature and I felt nothing could stop us. We took the trip on a Saturday or Sunday (my mother took care of baby Lucille) and it took us around 2 hours to reach! There were the models with a great big sign displaying the selling price, (mom and I will never forget it) the sign read "$ 9,999.99"!!! My first remark to mom was; "ninety nine cents? I don't believe it!" "Yep," mom said, then adding the obvious comment; "one more penny and it becomes $ 10,000.00!!!" To us it seemed an astronomical amount! We could never afford this house, "let's go" I said. Then mom said; "Wait, since were here, I would like to see it inside." At this point there were many additional"words spoken between us but eventually ended in an agreement to go inside and peruse the place, at least. We went in and it was beautiful! Mom loved it and I liked it a lot too. We spoke to the salesman. He said if you can put a $10.00 deposit down (Can you imagine $10.00!), the house will be reserved for us until we can find a way of purchasing it or he will return the full deposit if we don't. That was fair. We gave him ten dollars, received our papers and left. All the way home, we discussed the possibility of accomplishing the purchase. We couldn't come up with the right numbers. I was making $65.00 a week that meant we couldn't afford a mortgage payment greater than $65.00 a month according to our Bank Manager whom we were talking to. The mortgage for $10,000.00 would be about $70.00 a month for a 30 year mortgage. Too much! We couldn't afford it. But wait the Bank Manager said, "If you can come up with $500.00 in cash, you can reduce your mortgage and then only need $65.00 a month to pay off the new mortgage amount!" "Where would we get $500.00?" I said to mom. "Maybe I could go to work suggested mom, there are a lot of jobs for women, then when we accumulate the $500.00 we could buy it", she further suggested. "What about the baby, who will take care of the baby?" I asked? She said; "Maybe my mother (Grandma Assunta) could take care of her, we will ask her." After getting an OK from her mother, we also had an additional plus because our sister-in-law Rosie also volunteered to help Grandma care for our baby Lucille. Mom got a job at the first place she applied. It was a New York City, Civil Engineering Corporation that built gigantic structures around the world. They needed a Secretary and mom fit the job. She worked three or four months and we were able to save the $500.00 we needed. Then she left the job, but they were informed beforehand, yet they pleaded with her to stay on. She had to go, baby Lucille needed her mother. We put the money down on the new house in Brentwood and as soon as it was built and finished we could move in! Just think, OUR OWN HOME!!! It was very exciting just thinking of it. We didn't know what to expect. Who would be our neighbors? What school would Lucille go to? What Church is close by? There were many, many questions… and no answers. It appeared to be a complete mystery. But it wouldn't be long before all those questions would be answered. After visiting the building site a number of times, we could see the house actually going up and it was comforting to see the progress (see photo below).

1955

OUR FIRST HOME. In the winter of 1955, just before our baby Lucille was one year old, we moved to Brentwood, to live in our new home. There we were, mother, father and child standing in a home that was OURS!!! It was a brand new emotion. We were so happy! Even baby Lucille was happy; all she did was smile for a long time. We looked at each other and wondered, Is it possible this little bundle of joy knows it's our Home? Our answer to each other was a resounding, YES…she knows!!!

Our New House under construction in Brentwood,L.I.

The house was small but adequate. It was a little Ranch House type, all the rooms were on one floor. We had three bedrooms, a living room, a bathroom, a kitchen and a dinning eating area extended in the kitchen. There were two entrances, one into the living room and another into the kitchen. Between the kitchen and the bathroom was an entrance to the basement. The basement was full size in proportion to the house. We certainly had enough room for things. Since it was a Ranch style house, it did not have any attic space. The design of the structure allowed one to walk in a circular fashion through the inside hallway to reach any room. That feature we really liked! The only inclusion we would have wanted was an outside entrance to the basement. This I solve later in the chapter.

Of course before we moved in, furniture had to be brought to the house and carpeting had to be installed. Baby Lucille had her own little room. All kinds of decorations for the baby's room had to be put up. She would be in a crib now, out of the bassinet, especially since her one year old birthday was coming up. In fact, baby Lucille was showing signs of wanting to walk. She was always reaching for things and it appeared that she would be willing to move her own little legs to reach the object she was reaching for. We encouraged her. Just by holding her hands, she began moving her feet one after another, step by step. It was fun. At the same time she began attempting speech by imitating us with the words "mommy" and "daddy". Every day was another accomplishment. It was marvelous! Raising the baby occupied all our time and focused all our attention on just one thing, baby Lucille growing up. It was such a blessing and we were very thankful. Thank you Lord for this JOY!

L-LUCILLE IS 1 YEAR OLD. Soon, February 27, 1955 arrived. We were living in Brentwood, Long Island, NY. All the preparations for baby Lucille's first birthday celebration were made; all the grandmothers and grandfathers were invited (even though they had a two hour long auto trip to make from Brooklyn). My father would drive the other grandparents to our home with pleasure and as many other relatives that could make it arrived. I took movies of the grand occasion so the attendees could be viewed along with the main activity of the singing of Happy Birthday to You and the Blowing-out of the candle was all recorded there for posterity. There is even a bonus there on the film, I don't remember if it was my mother or my father that smeared baby Lucille with the icing from the cake. All in the spirit of the celebration, I guess. It was a fun day. Everyone enjoyed it and they got to see our new home for the first time. They liked it, of course, but they had many suggestions like, "Why did you put the coach over there? It should go over here." Or "Why did you paint the living room beige? Green would have been better." We just listened and laughed. That's a phenomenon our Psychologists know very little about. Why do people all want something else??? Anyway I had a more urgent matter to attend to and needed help from my father and father-in-law concerning the basement. The basement only had an inside entrance (In the Kitchen was the door) and I wanted an outside entrance added. Naturally, I had to do it myself, since I couldn't afford to have it done. So I began explaining the plan to them, which to my surprise they both agreed was a good one. It meant breaking the basement wall (which was poured concrete) to provide a doorway from the back of the house. Then I would have to pour concrete steps and a wall to allow an entrance from above the ground to the lower level where the new entrance to the basement would be. In addition to help from my father and father-in-law, my uncle Julie also volunteered to help me. Now I knew I couldn't fail. With the help of these experienced men, I could build anything, I thought! So, the materials were purchased and the construction began in the early spring. They all showed up, and it wasn't long before we had dug the hole outside and tore down the wall of the basement where the new door would be installed. It was a major improvement to the house and was enthusiastically received by all our relatives and friends. It also was a great help for me, now I could enter the basement from my gardening chores without tracking mud in the house. I really didn't realize the enormity of the project until after I completed it. "I attempted that?" I questioned myself in amazement. That's a very big job! What was I thinking? I wondered. Oh, well, I did it and it's over now, so we will just enjoy it. Even mom enjoyed it. Now she could bring out the daily wash to hang outside in the sunshine, right out from the basement, where the washing machine was. Yes, we had a clothes washer but we did not have a dryer (it wasn't invented yet) so the diapers and clothes had to be hung on clothes lines" outside in the back yard and remember the wet clothes had to be rung out dry with a roller mechanism to squeeze all the water out also (there was no spin-dry cycle either). That's what 'bringing up baby' meant in those days! A lot of work...but worth it! Oh, and I'd like to describe the clothes line that Mom used. It was a clothes line strung around a tree like metal structure. It had a single metal pole center, with outstretched metal arms where the clothes lines were strung. Some called it a clothes line carousel others called it a clothes tree, anyway it wasn't clothes lines stretched out from pole to pole (although some did do that). This was the most popular way of hanging clothes out to dry then. It worked well.

Baby Lucille was growing up and was a joy. During the two years, baby Lucille was in her initial development stages, such as walking, talking, learning, we were primarily occupied with our work and maintaining life in the suburbs. It was a new life for us (remember we were city people and found it somewhat difficult slowing down our pace, but we tried).

Baby Lucille was a wonderful child. Even though we were novice parents, she actually helped us develop our parenting skills to the maximum. These were our first attempts at baby care, Just take a look at the films I took of mom bathing you baby Lucille in the kitchen sink (On VHS Tape, "The Petti's"- Year 1954). Notice the dexterity mom exhibited with the precise allocution of the gigantic bar of soap used to accomplish this feat. Masterful is the only adjective I can assign that scene! And remember, that was the first time mom ever bathed a baby! So, you were in good hands. You seemed to reflect the wonderful care you received by the gentle and loving way you developed each and every day. It was a joy for both mom and me. The next major occurrence took place after your second birthday, mom was pregnant with Susan. Time moved so fast. It only seemed like yesterday that you had just begun walking and talking, now we are expecting another baby. But that's the way it was. It really had no affect on you. Nothing changed for you. Yet, it meant many changes for us. Mom and I looked forward to the new addition. We were becoming a family" fast! That was wonderful!!!

THANKSGIVING DAY. On Thanksgiving Day, in 1955, we began celebrating this American holiday at our home in Brentwood. We came to this decision for a number of reasons. The main purpose was we wanted to keep the baby home and warm. In November it can get cold. Keeping the baby home also helped us take care of her better than when we traveled. Also, since Thanksgiving does not fit Italian tradition, there were no protests from our families. Let's face it; they did not know the American customs or American recipes so they were able to concede this duty to us. It took a little doing. For instance, in the beginning they suggested having Lasagna with Capon Roasted Chicken instead of Turkey, which we gave-in-to to avoid conflict. But slowly we would begin substituting authentic Thanksgiving fare, like one year we would drop the La Sagna and substitute Chicken Soup with egg noodles. They didn't complain! Then the following year we substituted the Capon with a real Turkey. If it wasn't for the delicious stuffing and gravy mom made, there would have been protests, but they were happy with it. The full conversion finally took place in time, but it took years to accomplish. I have to credit mom for the ease in making the transition.

Thanksgiving then became an Ann & Gus Petti tradition. All the talk about Thanksgiving centered on going to Brentwood to have a fun filled and happy Thanksgiving. The food got better every year, thanks to mom. And I would come up with different accoutrements like pumpkin pie and apple pie, to add to the festivities. Every one enjoyed it, so it continued way into the 1980"s. Close to thirty years. Thank you FAMILY for your closeness and the many compliments for the Turkey, the Stuffing and the Pies.

ITALIAN FOOD. I felt it important to explain the Italian attitude (or the Petti's attitude) concerning food. Although I do not believe I have captured the exact attitude of every Italian, all those I have met pretty much have the same feelings about food. First of all it is a very important and paramount subject on their list toward survival. Also, it must have numerous qualities, that when viewed by others, the behavior appears almost at the level of obsession. For example, when preparing raw food, it must be fresh, nothing else is acceptable. And, since many regions in the world have developed intensely tasting food, such as cheese, then only cheese from that region will do. The same for plants, such as tomatoes, they must have been grown in the San Marzo area in Italy. Then there is Balsamic Vinegar, it can only come from the Modema area in Italy. I have not mentioned the quality of olive oil, we all know that olive oil comes in extra virgin, virgin, ultra-fine, fine, etc., quality levels. I used these examples to introduce you to the complexities of foods that Italians contend with, but is not restricted to Italians only. Many other nationalities pride themselves in choosing specific ingredient for the preparation of their ethnic foods. It's only that Italians often obsess about what food to prepare. And then there is the recipe that must be followed. Not only must the food be right, but the recipe must be right also. Then there is the occasion, the time the recipe must be executed is also tantamount. It goes on and on. And in many cases, there is past wisdom in many of these requirements. For instance, never attempt to make our famous Anginette Cookies (traditionally made for Christmas) at any other time in the year, you will regret it (if you want to know why, you have to ask me in private). When you put all the experiences and all the knowledge associated with food together, I guess you can begin to understand the Italian attitude toward food. We Petti's never fought it; we just embraced the attitude and became obsessed... That's why we act the way we do about food. It is very important to us. It must be fresh, it must be the best and it must be prepared right. As long as you follow those principals you are doing well!

The main reason I devoted a full section to the subject of food, is due to the fact that in every subsequent section when I am explaining a special occasion, you will hear me talk about the food that is prepared for that feast and sometimes go on and on about it. And I suspect you will wonder why I describe the foods at great length and probably overemphasize them. This is just my way of justifying that weakness. Now you know how important that is to me and probably understand me a little more.

PALM SUNDAY CUSTOM. Every Palm Sunday we would attend church, where the anticipation of Holy Week would be described for us at Mass. The children would be asking all sorts of questions about the things that would be happening during this week. One of the customs they were intently interested in was my weaving of the palms that was taught to me when I worked in a neighborhood florist in my teenage days. Even though I could weave intricate palm shapes from the leaves of a palm, I stuck to the task of making small crosses that they could learn easily. So began a special custom of making crosses on Palm Sunday. So every Palm Sunday I would make little crosses with the Palms distributed at Mass for all the family members, which was quite an undertaking. I would spend almost the whole day fashioning the crosses. But it was beautiful seeing all those crosses in the children's rooms which made the endeavor very worth while. Now some of our grown up children make their own little crosses and the custom continues.

EASTER SUNDAY CELEBRATION. It seems, in our family, all the Holidays were celebrated at one family's home all the time. Easter belonged to Auntie Mary and Uncle Julio. The Galanos requested that we celebrate Easter Sunday at their home every year. It's interesting how certain family dynamic functions evolved. Since this perpetual invitation to celebrate this joyous Christian holiday existed and was to be held at the Galanos, my mother and father did not protest and cheerfully celebrated it with us. In Italian culture, sometimes there is a little quibbling among the elders about where a special holiday is to be celebrated, but not with us. If you wanted to host Easter Sunday, you got it. If you put in a bid for hosting at Christmas time, you got it. We personally had Thanksgiving Day reserved for hosting. If you wanted New Years Eve, you got it. The unwritten law of course was fairness. Every head of a family household should be allowed to host at least one major holiday. Our family's had no problem with that requirement. And so, every Easter Sunday celebration was held at the Galanos. When it first started in the middle 1950's we would dress up baby Lucille and then baby Susan and drive to Westbury to have a wonderful time, celebrating the Resurrection of our Lord and Savior, Jesus Christ. Auntie Mary would prepare many special Italian foods. We had lots to drink and then the extraordinary desserts would be served. Just thinking about it makes me happy.

We would laugh at the many stories that were being told. My father always had a funny story to tell. Your grandfather Erminio told some interesting stories about World War I, in which he served. Uncle Julio would make us laugh with all his different experiences, especially when he goes to stores to buy something. I believe I even remember some of them now. How we miss your Uncle Julio who brought so much joy to our celebrations. Thank you Uncle Julio... So it's settled, Easter Sunday is to be celebrated at the Galano home. We spent every Easter Sunday there as long as I can remember, way into the 1980' if I'm not mistaken. Thank you Mary and Julio for your generosity and good times, you were a wonderful part of our life. I'm sure my children will never forget those moments…

THE AUTO ACCIDENT-GUS. I believe this serious accident happened sometime in 1955. The reason for the uncertainty is that because of the severity of it, I believe I have subconsciously forgotten the actual date. The automobile accident took place on my way home from my part-time work as a night watchman at the Concrete Plant in Westbury, L.I., on a Saturday morning, in the early hours around 2:00 or 3:00 AM. I was driving on Fifth Avenue in Brentwood, traveling north, past Pilgrim State Hospital. It was very dark, I was approaching the hospital grounds intersection, which had a little hill before reaching the corner, when I looked, there was no traffic coming, but as soon as I reached the corner, all of a sudden a car appeared speeding at me from the passenger side, so fast I did not have time to maneuver around it. The inevitable happened; the car came crashing into mine with such force that I was thrown from the car, out into an open field and landed about 20 feet away from my car. When I came-to (I must have been knocked unconscious), I got up and saw both cars smoking and someone screaming, coming from the direction of the other car. I ran over and saw a girl lying on the ground; bleeding profusely (I found out later that this girl was the driver.). The screaming girl was a passenger and was pointing to the girl on the ground; "Help her, help her" she screamed hysterically (there was a young man standing with her too). I immediately bent over the injured girl to check for breathing because she was not moving. When I put my ear to her chest, I couldn't help but smell the strong odor of alcohol (Which immediately led me to believe that she was drunk when she hit my car.), but she was alive, she was breathing. I announced her being alive to all the bystanders and not having any means of communication I suggested someone go into the middle of the road and purposely stop cars coming by and ask them to stop at the next available telephone to call the police, or the hospital for an ambulance. It just so happened, the next car that was stopped out on the road contained a Doctor who immediately took the injured girl in his car to the hospital. She was spared and she recovered.

Since I was injured too, a policeman (The police eventually came about 2 hours later, they were having radio problems that night.) and because my injury did not appear life threatening, they asked me who my doctor was, called him and he asked them to bring me to him, so they brought me to Doctor Nigerian (my primary doctor) for diagnosis and treatment. My injury was above my nose (the doctor suspected I hit the rear view mirror) and although it did not appear to need stitching at the time, after the wound healed, it left a significant scar and in retrospect maybe should have been stitched at the time (my opinion). After some healing took place, I began wondering where I got the strength or the wherewithal to do all the things I did at the scene of the accident and then a thought came to me, adrenaline, it had to be the adrenaline, I assured myself. Also, while in the Air Force I did study First Aid as part of the Chaplain Assistance training. It seemed as though I was running the whole accident scene, ordering people all about (remember there was no means of communication with anyone especially the police), trying to save a life, which I did, only to have her sue me later (by a swindling Lawyer we later learned-he had to give up his license later), so the Lord took care of that! It was interesting how this circumstance played-out. I learned later after the driver of that car had healed from the wounds, I received a Subpoena, claiming that I ran into her and caused the accident, suing me for $50,000. There are many different kinds of "people" in this world, but I feel the absolute worst are licensed Lawyers called Ambulance Chasers. These so called Lawyers have alerts set up at local hospitals that inform them of any seriously injured person resulting from an auto accident. Here is the false philosophy they operate on; they know that any person suffering any extreme injury in an accident will have the sympathy of a jury and can sway any court decision their way, no matter what the actual facts are. So, without even determining who was at fault, I was accused of causing the accident (can you believe that). Luckily, I was insured by Allstate Insurance at the time and when I reported the accident, they said not to worry about a thing, they knew the Lawyer (Who was known as an Ambulance Chaser) and said we have dealt with him before, no problem. Sure enough, at the proceedings, when the damage to my car was described (of course my car was totaled); it was evident that in order for me to strike her car I would have to be traveling sideways! She lost, Allstate won, it didn't cost me a penny, but I couldn't believe how much lying and dishonesty can be contrived in instances of this nature to hide the truth. It was an important lesson in my life and mom and I never forgot it.

Naturally, I had to get another car. This time my Godfather, Dr. Iamale, came to the rescue. He had this 1952 Nash convertible that was outlandishly painted pink and cocoa brown, I believe, that he wanted to get rid of it (If you have never seen this car, I suggest going to the Internet to see it). It needed some work and knowing that I could repair it, he gave it to us. Although it was definitely not the type of car I would buy, I appreciated the generous gesture. It surely saved our transportation dilemma. Thank you Godfather! (He will be remembered as long as I live, and to make sure of that, I adopted his name at Confirmation - he is the Louis that is my middle name).

1956

S-OUR SECOND CHILD IS BORN. Actual date born.... April, 8, 1956....Susan Carol Petti...10:39 AM... I was working for Sylvania Corning Corporation as an Inspector, in Hicksville, L.I. We were expecting the baby any time now. I suggested that mom call me if I am at work and she feels she has to go to the Hospital, no matter what time it was. I had just arrived at work when my supervisor said I had a phone call. When I answered, it was mom. "It's time", she said. "I'll be right there", I responded. The company was very understanding and allowed me to leave right then and there. Into the car I went and off to the house I drove, always staying under the speed limits, this was a well patrolled zone that I was very aware of. I got home in about a half an hour, mom was ready. . We called our neighbor (Our neighbor's were Frieda and Eddy Pollack) to have them baby-sit Lucille while I took mom to the Hospital. I grabbed the suitcase and off we went. This one was really going smoothly (Thank you baby Susan). We were so happy. Got to Southside Hospital, Bay Shore, in about 15 minutes. We even had time to fill-out the entrance registration even though the nurse put mom in a wheel chair. I was asked to wait a few minutes, to take home her clothing, which I did and then the nurse asked me to go home. "The Doctor will get in touch with you when it happens." She said. As I recall, I just had gotten home, Frieda had left and it was snowing outside, with very large snow flakes falling softly on the ground, it had captured my complete attention, when the phone rang. It was the Doctor, saying, "You are the proud father of a beautiful and healthy baby Girl!" She was born at 10:30AM, (then he gave me the statistics) and mom is doing fine! I was so happy. I yelled out, "I Am a Father" again, only this time there wasn't anyone to hear me except baby Lucille so there was no response.

I was so happy! I couldn't hold back the joy! Just think; I'm the father of another baby girl! It was overwhelming...I couldn't believe it...A BABY GIRL!!! Thank you Lord. What a Blessing! We are going to name her SUSAN, after her wonderful Grandmother Assunta. And all this took place without me being there at the hospital. In those days, I have to repeat, they didn't allow the husband in the delivery room, like they do today. In fact they didn't even want any expectant father to wait in the waiting room, the way they depict the waiting scene in the movies of the day. I was nowhere in sight. I wasn't even there to hold mom's hand during those crucial moments. I think I miss that? I'm so glad they allow the husband to be present nowadays. But none of this took away from the happiness I felt. I couldn't wait to see you and mom!

I had to tell the world about our newborn child! "Where are those telephone numbers, I have to call the family and tell them the good news". Ah, here they are, I have to call mamma and Papa', then mamma Assunta (wait till she hears, we are calling the baby Susan, she will be so happy) and Papa' Erminio, they are going to be thrilled! Then I have to call Auntie Mary and Uncle Julie along with Uncle Tony and Auntie

Rose, then my Sister and Uncle Vinny, everybody has to get called! It was so funny, because the first question they all asked "Is the baby healthy?" "Yes" was my answer;" "Oh, good" they replied. All the Italians I know say the exact same thing. It is as if it is written in stone somewhere and must be repeated at this moment. Then they began asking for all the statistics. They all wanted to know what time you were born, what your height was and how much did you weigh. So I was on the phone for a couple of hours. Now that everyone got the news, it was time to go visit my baby Susan and mom at the hospital.

We were living in our own home at 157 Timberline Road in Brentwood, Long Island, NY. The year baby Susan was born to us was 1956. Baby Lucille was a little over 2 years old and she walked, she talked and boy did she have questions, especially when baby Susan was brought into the house. Thankfully, all her questions were good questions and answerable.

So, for the record, on April, 7, 1956, at 10:30AM, on a Saturday morning, at Southside Hospital, Bay Shore, Long Island, our second bundle of joy baby Susan was born!. Mom remembers the snow too, when they put her in her room, after the birth, she was placed near a very large window and saw the big snowflakes drifting down and she thought, how beautiful, God has blessed us with another beautiful daughter. "Thank You Lord for this blessing", she said to herself, as she marveled at the falling snow.

S-CHOOSING A NAME FOR BABY SUSAN. Before baby Susan was born, a name had to be selected. Again, according to our Italian tradition, the name of the Grandparents must be given to honor and respect them. But Grandma's name was "Assunta", (Lucille was already used for the other Grandma) we couldn't give an American child such an intrinsically spelled Italian name like that (And Grandma Assunta agreed - in fact she said "please don't give the baby that name it's too Italian!). What gave us another spelling of the name, as time went on, was the common English translation that they used at Grandma's Textile Shop where she worked as a seamstress. They all called her Suzie which of course was a nickname, but derived from the American name Susan. So, Susan it was! The name seemed to solve all the impediments that we encountered. It would bring honor and respect to Grandma Assunta, who deserved every bit of it, but would be acceptable in American society too. Also, in those days, it was the duty of every Italian parent to come up with, not only a female name but also a male name. Therefore Susan would be the female name and Joseph (for Grandpa Petti) would be the male name. We had no way of knowing if the newborn would be male or female (The medical sonogram had not been invented yet). Everything then about child bearing was mysterious. We could only act on possibilities, although today, it would be a seemingly peculiar approach, but at the time it was challenging and fun.

S-BABY SUSAN BAPTIZED. Baby Susan was baptized in the next two months, in June and her Godparents were Auntie Mary and Uncle Julie. They were so happy to hold the newborn and take baby Susan to the Church. The two Godparents looked so nice, all dressed up, taking little baby Susan to the Blessed Sacrament and pledging baby Susan to become a member of The Body of Christ, The Church. The ceremony went very well. Baby Susan did not cry when the Priest poured the holy water over her head. In fact there wasn't any crying at all this time. It was beautiful. I have photos of this taking place, along with a Video tape with scenes showing the action (See "The Petti's" VHS tapes, year 1956). Most of the relatives attended the festivities that were offered to celebrate the event. Baby Susan was so cute and whenever someone would be holding her on their lap, baby Lucille would come over wanting to hold her hand and looked wide-eyed at the very white long dress that baby Susan wore (another Italian custom). Those were precious scenes. I can't help remembering them and I often tried to capture those scenes in photographs or on film. I caught some of them as you can see, when viewing the photos or videos.

S-WORLD NEWS-1956. This was the year for the emergence of the Soap Opera, a TV style of story telling that has lasted till today. The two beginning soap operas were The Edge of Night and As the World Turns. The American people reelected Dwight D. Eisenhower as their President. In January, the first VCR prototype was demonstrated in Chicago, Illinois. Seven days after Susan was born, Prince Reiner

III married American Actress Grace Kelly. Over 1,200 guests attended. The Andrea Doria (an Italian Luxury Cruise liner) was supposed to be unsinkable but in spite of the engineering trappings, the ship sank in less than 12 hours after it was broadsided by a Swedish liner, The Stockholm (who was fitted with a prow designed to break ice-bergs) as they approached Nantucket on July 25th. Fifty-two people died. They were sailing in opposite directions when the collision occurred.

Aside from Proctor & Gamble's introduction of Crest the first fluoride toothpaste, the fist Pampers disposable diapers for babies was put on the market (but we continued to wash and dry the cloth type though). Charleton Heston and Yul Brenner star in the Ten Commandments movie. (This next item is for Bill Lee) New York Yankee Don Larsen pitches the first and only perfect World Series game in history.

Although many world wide events were unfolding, life continued at the Petti's in a normal and caring way. Now there were two children to love. And believe me that took all the time and effort we could muster. All other family activities also continued, as I will describe…

SUNDAY MASS. As soon as baby Lucille began walking, mom and I would take you to Mass on Sundays. It's interesting to note, this was no ordinary church we would go to celebrate the Holy Mass. It was a Drive-In Theater! Yep…we would put you in the back seat of the car along with mom (no car-seat, they were not required yet) and we would drive up Brentwood Road to the Brentwood Drive-In Theatre, park the car next to a speaker-phone and attend Mass, with the Priest and an Altar set-up under the gigantic screen, in front of the theater. To receive communion, you would exit the car and walk to the front of the Drive-in where the Priest would be distributing the Holy Eucharist and return to your car. During the Offering, Ushers would come to your car with a basket for you to drop in your contribution envelope. It was an unusual environment to say the least and of course it was a temporary substitution of the real church which was under construction at the time (the original church, St. Anne's Chapel, only held about 60-100 people). But although the settings appeared strange, it was innovative and practical for the interim.

As the children were being born and growing, we managed to attend Mass every Sunday when possible. As time went by, our babies began walking and talking and getting a kick out of dressing up every Sunday. It was very exciting for them, choosing the clothing they would be wearing, the shoes, the hat...yes each girl wanted to wear a hat and on special occasions, especially Easter Sunday, even Joseph wanted to wear a hat. This amazed me, because I am anti-hat and thought my son would be the same...but I was wrong. All the children enjoyed going to Mass on Sundays which continued even when we relocated to Williston Park, and finally to Morris Plains. Mom and I have so many wonderful memories of the children progressing through the rituals and the receiving of the Sacraments of Penance, Communion, and Confirmation. Then when they grew up to adulthood, receiving Marriage, brought the circle full-round. Those were beautiful times... Thank you Lord for allowing us to witness those moments...we will treasure them forever...

FOURTH OF JULY. The celebration of the 4th of July has always been at Uncle Tony's and Auntie Rose's in Brentwood, NY. After the Passero's moved to Long Island in the late 1950's, we were invited to celebrate this particular holiday with them and we did just that, ever since, up until the late 1990's, when they moved to Brick, NJ. This was a holiday every one of my children looked forward to. Not only is there going to be barbequed chicken (the special way Uncle Tony prepared it) but there are going to be a large variety of salads (only the way Auntie Rose made them) to select from. And if Uncle Tony felt the corn offered at the local farm stands was fresh enough, we would have the most delicious boiled corn you can imagine. That was only starters. After this scrumptious meal, as the sun began to set, Uncle Tony would start bringing out the fireworks. First, we would start with firecrackers. We had a safe zone established to ignite fireworks, in the back yard (we were very responsible and serious about safety). Everyone would sit on the patio (I mean all guests that wanted to participate in the firecrackers process - in other words spectators) adjacent to the firework zone but about 20 feet of lawn back, watching all the action and enjoying themselves immensely. Off would go the firecrackers, one after another, each with a big bang , with the sound getting louder as the night got darker and darker. Then, when it was good and dark, Uncle Tony would come out with the rockets. Now you're talking! That's the big stuff! Everyone was waiting for this! The anxiety level was at its highest peak while we prepared the launching site. We used the Passero, Clothes Line's metal pipe, just by moving it (it was a little lose anyway) to create the proper trajectory for the rockets. We wanted them to go straight up into the air and not fall spent on anyone's house, especially ours. We started to ignite them, one at a time. What a spectacle. After each one was bursting in the air, you could hear all the ooh's and aah's, as the colors gleamed and burned all the way down. It was so much fun! All of you enjoyed this part of the July Fourth activities more than any other part of the day. But it wasn't over yet. There is sparkler time coming. After all the rockets were launched into the air it was time for the sparklers, which Uncle Tony would bring out and distribute to anyone that wanted to set them off. He would have boxes and boxes of them. All of you would participate in this event. We would have buckets of water strategically placed on the lawn to extinguish the red hot stems after the sparklers burned out, for safety. Then we would ignite the first one and from that one burning sparkler all the others would light theirs. It was a scene that lives in my memory and is so vivid it cannot be forgotten. To see all those little faces smiling as they held the burning sparklers, has to warm any ones heart. They were so happy. They never wanted it to end. But the boxes of sparklers only held so many and would have to come to an end. And so did the day. It was always a joyous day for us. Thank you Uncle Tony and Auntie Rose, we will never forget those good times, you will always remain special in our hearts…

MY PART TIME JOB. To cover all the extra expenses that we were experiencing as a result of the expanding family, we decided that I needed additional income. I didn't want to leave my current work to find a higher paying job so I thought of searching for a part-time job. Uncle Julie always came to my rescue when I would mention a problem to him. When he heard of my dilemma, he suggested working as a night watchman at his concrete pipe factory. He was able to put in a few good words for me and got me a job as a night watchman, which helped our financial condition substantially. We were able to meet all our debts with on-time payments at last! Mom was very happy and so was I. Here was my work routine now; in the daytime I worked at Sylvania Corning Corporation as an inspector and at night I would travel to Westbury and do nighttime watchman duties for the Concrete Pipe Company. It was very interesting. At Sylvania I was learning quit a bit about Sonar Inspections. It was so fascinating learning about this marvelous new type of probing through all types of metals as if you were X-raying it, being able to see any fault that is present in the material being examined. This phenomenon has always amazed me and continues to do so. That's one of the reasons I have been a subscriber of Popular Science and Popular Mechanics for over 50 years (when I could afford the subscription, that is).

1957

S-BABY SUSAN'S FIRST BIRTHDAY.

Baby Susan's first birthday was celebrated on April 7, 1957.

Baby Susan began walking when she was 10 or 11 months old. She was so curious, she wanted to investigate everything. In fact her curiosity was so intense, she often got into trouble (You know, the childhood mishaps kind.) The amount of energy baby Susan would expend was unbelievable. We were living in Brentwood, LI, and we had purchased what at the time was a new type of baby chair, it was only about 30" off the ground, with four legs on wheels with the baby sitting in the middle of a large square. It was about 30" square, so there was a lot of room all around the baby, for toys, food, etc. The main benefit of this new invention was that it allowed the baby to attempt walking whenever it suited her. Her feet touched the floor when she stood up and when she was tired, all she had to do was sit down, all in the same chair. It appeared to be revolutionary at the time (see the photos that contain the image of this chair in the albums). I believe that chair was instrumental in helping her to develop into walking sooner than normal. Just a theory of mine (I'm afraid you're going to get a lot of theory's as you kids grew up.) For some reason, whenever a phenomenon presented itself concerning one or another of you, I would begin formulating a theory to explain the occurrence (at least in my mind). It is how I survived the countless mysteries that presented themselves as you children grew up. And of course a lot of prayer was mixed in there too. In retrospect, I believe prayer was the mainstay that kept me in balance. Often, if you ask me today, "Dad how did mom and you do it, taking care of five of us?" And the answer is, "It was done with the help of the Lord". We sincerely believe that. Without His help, we could not accomplish it alone. That is advice we would give anyone who asked. It was our life's philosophy, simple, astounding, real and always giving us hope! Thank you Lord for our wonderful children, the second of which was baby Susan!

It was your first birthday. Everyone was there, your grandmothers, your grandfathers, your aunts and uncles, cousins, friends and even neighbors. The house was full. You were in your new high chair, with your pretty birthday dress, wondering what the fuss was all about. Well, it was about you! We were celebrating the one full year of your growth, which Italians among others, consider very important and in their own way an excuse to celebrate. Aside from food and drink, we devoted much time to dialogue, telling stories and incidents that were often very funny and sometimes hilarious. Also, if you recall, the No Smoking sign was placed by the entrance door way, and every guest was asked not to smoke in the house while celebrating. I was very adamant about this subject, and everyone knew it by now.

Then the moment arrived, the birthday cake was being carried into the room by mom, with the single candle, lit and flickering, accompanied by the singing of Happy Birthday to You. It was wonderful. Those are beautiful memories. Thank you baby Susan for giving them to us...

MOM HAD A MISSCARRIAGE. In everyone's life some rain must fall. Baby Susan was almost three years old when this occurred. We would have had six children if this baby went full term. It was not meant to be. Mom was hospitalized when it happened. To my best recollection it was in the spring of 1958. It was very emotional for us. The doctor did not know why it happened. Soon, mom was well again. And life went on. Another year went by and we were blessed with another infant...

1959

C-OUR THIRD CHILD CHRISTINE IS BORN.

Christine Marie was our third child born to us. A beautiful blessing that made us forever grateful to the Lord. We were so happy when baby Christine arrived. We were living in Brentwood, LI at the time.

It was the month of November, in the year of 1959, on a Friday morning, mom was two or three weeks late (baby Christine was supposed to be born at the end of October) and mom said to me, as I was leaving for work, "I feel a little something, but you go to work, I'll let you know by telephone if anything develops". "OK", I said, "but make sure you let me know the minute you get uncomfortable". She replied, "Don't worry I will." Then I left, I was working for the Fairchild Engine Corporation , Farmingdale, at the time as an Inspector, about 30 minutes from home. When I arrived at work I told everyone that my Ann was expecting any minute now and that if any call was made to me, to let me know immediately. The day progressed, then around noon, mom called and said the pains were increasing and our neighbors, Freddy and Frieda volunteered to take me to the hospital (to keep from disturbing me at work) and I said, "No thanks, if you can wait till I arrive, I prefer taking you". She said she could wait, so I left immediately and got home in about 20 minutes (in record time)! There was mom holding her big tummy while proceeding to the car. I grabbed the little suitcase and rushed to the car too. At the hospital, in Bay Shore, Long Island, they put mom in a wheel chair and the registration process began. A very young girl was asking the questions. As the questions were being asked, the girl exclaimed, "Oh! Today is Friday, Friday the 13th." Mom immediately responded, "Why is that bad?" "Is that bad luck?" "Oh, no, that's "good luck" for you!" the attendant said, trying to recover from the faux pas. So, your birth changed the luck pattern of that day, as announced by this young girl, and it has been lucky for us ever since. Then the process continued. It was now in the afternoon. The attending doctor, Dr. Nadel had to be called, who personally felt the timing was not too convenient for him, because he had scheduled visits at the office in the afternoon that he had to cancel. Nonetheless he rushed to the hospital to attend to mom and brought our little treasure into the world. You were a beautiful birth according to mom. All I knew was that when the doctor came to me in the waiting room, I was so excited, and when he announced that I was the "Father of a healthy and beautiful Baby Girl" I couldn't contain myself with joy! I was a Father again…I was so happy! When I went in to see mom, I was beaming with happiness; I hugged her and kissed her in sheer delight. We now had baby Christine! We brought into this world not only another person but another soul too! (With the help of God!) I went to see you in the nursery as soon as I could. You were born at the Southside Hospital in Bay Shore. You were so beautiful, all bundled up in the crib. You seemed to be content with all that was happening. Mom and I were so very happy!

Actual date born…Friday, November 13, 1959….Christine Marie Petti…5:05 PM…

As soon as I arrived home from the hospital I got on the telephone to let my mother and father and all the relatives know about the good news, we now have another baby, baby Christine! Then I called your grandfather and grandmother who said they were so happy and were planning to come and see you as soon as they could arrange transportation (remember grandpa Passero did not own a car nor drive). But my father told me he would pick up my father-in-law and my mother-in-law when they were planning to visit. So it was all set. Over the weekend, all of them were at the hospital to visit mom and to gaze upon our darling baby Christine. They all said you were beautiful and of course all asked the eternal Italian question; "Is she healthy?"…A resounding "YES" was the answer! OK, now that we have that perpetual Italian inquiry out of the way, let us begin planning for the Baptism. I don't believe mom wanted to do the planning right now, it was too soon. First we had to choose a name.

C-THE NAME CHRISTINE. I guess you're wondering why we chose Christine for your name. You were born at that time near the Feast of Corpus Christus (Latin for Body of Christ), which is a moving feast but has been changed to Our Lord Jesus Christ the King, which originally had an old Latin title, when translated to an American name it becomes Christine! As you know, we had used all the female names of your grandparents for baby Lucille and baby Susan, the fact that you were born near this important holy feast day was destiny. To further understand why our mind set led us to this choice; it's important to consider our upbringing, where the naming of a child in Italian tradition is usually the names of grandparents or significant holy feast/ saints days on the Catholic Calendar (You must know many people named after Saints which is common Italian practice too.). It was a natural recourse for us at the time to follow this custom. We also loved the name and did not hesitate giving it to you to carry through life. Hope you like it too, CHRISTINE!

C-BABY CHRISTINE IS BAPTIZED. Now that a few weeks elapsed, we began the plans for your Baptism. We were living in Brentwood. Baptism in our culture is a very important event. First we had to select Godparents. Of all the candidates, only two stood out. It was the suggestion of my mother that we considered Sal and Ann Jacarusso, who although were not family members, he was the son of my caretakers as I was growing up. Remember the Jacarusso's from Chapter 3 – My Boyhood? They were also paisanos since their families came from the same town in Italy my parents came from. The son was married now and had children. He and his wife would make wonderful Godparents for baby Christine we thought. So we contacted them, since they were living in Brooklyn, NY, to see if they would like to do this. They were thrilled and definitely would want to do it. So a time was set. All the family members were notified and the day of your Baptism arrived. Everybody was there, my mother, my father, your grandfather Passero and your grandmother Passero, Uncle Tony and Auntie Rose, Auntie Mary and Uncle Julie and all their children. Baby Lucille and baby Susan stood marveling about all the fuss we made about you. The long white dress (Italian custom) was placed on you and you looked so beautiful. Sal and Ann Jacarusso arrived and soon you were off to church in St. Anne's Chapel. Mom stayed home to care for baby Lucille and baby Susan (this was an old custom too) and Sal and Ann took you to join the Church. I came along, primarily to record the event on film. I took many photos. You went through the pouring of the water just fine, not a whimper. I was expecting you to begin crying but you didn't, that meant to me that you liked water. And I believe you do, you seem to have an affinity for water in every aspect. Anyway, as soon as they brought you home, the festivities began. The soup was served to a lot of guests, followed by macaroni and gravy meat, then roasted chicken and roasted potatoes, followed by salad. Of course we all had Dad's Wine Punch followed by desserts of all kinds. My mother and your grandmother Passero brought Italian pastries that were out of this world (I'm gaining weight just writing about it). It was a wonderful celebration. Everyone enjoyed themselves. We felt bad that they had to travel so far to reach us, but the food and drink I believe compensated a little for the sacrifice. They were very happy becoming your Godparents. Unfortunately, because of certain forthcoming events in their life, it prevented us from developing a closer relationship. Therefore as you grew up, we saw less and less of them until we lost complete contact with them. Some of the occurrences that were reported to us about them were so devastating that it is difficult to explain (one of the main occurrences was losing a young daughter to cancer). So many negative life altering happenings made their way to their family that it is almost impossible to describe. I like to remember the times when they were with us, enjoying our baby Christine and all of the family, being happy and in a celebration mood. That's how I recall the Jacarussos. Everyone welcomed you into Christ's Church that day and we will never forget it…

C-NEWS IN 1959. The biggest news story was Alaska becoming the 49th State and the largest state in the U.S. On April 12, Russia's famed Bolshoi Ballet visits U.S. for only the fourth time in almost 200 years. In August another big story, Hawaii becomes the 50th State of the U. S. And Mattel Inc. introduces Barbie. Also, the Solomon R Guggenheim Museum, designed by Frank Lloyd Wright, opens in New York.

This is also the year Fidel Castro forced Fulgencio Batista to resign the presidency in January and took over the leadership of Cuba. He was a communist and hitched his wagon to the Soviet Union. In another area of the world, Communism and Democracy were centered in the personalities of Krushchev and Nixon (a presidential hopeful at the time), two indefatigable sparring partners in scenes described as the

Kitchen Debate (the details are very interesting if you want to know more July 23, 1959-NY Times).

Although many world wide events were unfolding, life continued at the Petti's in a normal and caring way. Now there were three children to love. And believe me that took all the time and effort we could muster. All other family activities also continued, as I will describe...

NEW YEAR'S EVE CELEBRATION. This holiday was also requested by Uncle Tony and Auntie Rose (as part of the Holiday assignment ritual in our family) to be celebrated at their home in Brentwood. This holiday routine was a little different from the others which were a one day activity only. This one was a two day affair. We would arrive on the Eve for a delicious dinner of Italian Antipasto (specially prepared by auntie Rose), Anchovies, fresh baked Italian bread, fried flounder filets and the plece de resistance, oven roasted whole Main Lobster (All you can eat!) Italian style with olive oil, garlic and parsley. Oh, was that good! Everyone at the table waited anxiously for the lobster to come out of the oven. I can see the delicate steam drifting into the air coming from the succulent white sweet flesh hiding inside the protective red tinged shell of that delicacy. It was so delicious! It made everyone alert and focused, I don't care what mood you were in! No fooling around now. This is the real thing. The lobster is coming, make some space on the table. Everyone was smiling at this point because the feast was now beginning.

After this gourmet meal, we all began preparing for the End of the Old Year and the beginning of the New Year. Balloons had to be filled up with air and hung, the Happy New Year's sign had to be pinned up, the confetti and the streamers had to be placed where everyone could reach them, the table had to be moved so the dancing could start. A lot of preparation had to be done. The Champagne had to be chilled and the Italian Pastries and the Black Italian Coffee had to be readied. The TV was on, with all our eyes glued to DICK CLARK, where the New Years Crystal Ball remained motionless until the right time approached. Then the count-down, 10,9,8,7,6,5,4,3,2,1 and HAPPY NEW YEAR!!! (Then the lighted ball at Times Square would come down) Everyone in the room begins kissing everyone, throwing confetti in the air, throwing streamers above each other, popping balloons and wishing everyone a "Happy New Year", after which I would hear them saying what a wonderful party this is!!! And it was; every one of those parties that we attended were wonderful. Thank you Auntie Rose and Uncle Tony! Then we went to bed at Uncle Tony's house…I don't know how they did it, but each of us would have a bed to sleep in on that New Years Day…

When we awoke, we would all get dressed and go to St. Anne's Church (the new one) and celebrate Mass on this first day of the year. It was a Holy Day of obligation; it was called the Feast of the Circumcision at that time, now it's changed to the Feast of Mary, Mother of God. When we returned to the house, Auntie Rose and Uncle Tony were busily preparing for a New Year's Day dinner. On this day, the food we would have was delicious, Noodle Soup, any leftover Antipasto (we loved Rosie's antipasto), Roasted Chicken, Peas and Bacon, Roasted Potatoes. It was wonderful! We all have so many precious memories from those past events and we feel privileged to have had them and given to us by our two loving aunt and uncle. This was the second day we were guests of your Auntie Rose and Uncle Tony. We would head home after dinner on that day for a well deserved rest.

Those memories are so embedded in my mind, that I can remember every single detail and I sincerely believe it was the love that was shared that welded it to my brain in this fashion. There is no other explanation for me. Thank you Uncle Tony and Auntie Rose! You helped us form a beautiful past that is so pleasant and joyful that we sometimes are overwhelmed by them when we think back. Thank you for giving us those wonderful moments to reflect on whenever there is an occasion. We are so grateful for the both of you being in our life. We wouldn't be the same without them. Thank you Auntie Rose and Uncle Tony again and again…

This is the way I remember Papa' Erminio...

1960

GRANDPA PASSERO DIES. Just before we moved to Williston Park, we lost our beloved Papa' Erminio. On January 30, 1960, Erminio Passero (your Grandfather) died of a blood clot. He had been operated on in the middle of January for unexplainable pains he was experiencing. During the operation they discovered massive cancer activity throughout his prostate and spine leaving them no alternative but to abandon the surgery at that point. He remained with us only a few days after the surgery. In fact it actually occurred while Auntie Rosie and I were visiting. He had gone without a shave or haircut for days and requested that I shave him and cut his hair. I was there all prepared to give him a shave with an electric shaver and then give him a haircut. We both entered the room where he lay, after Auntie Rosie greeted him, I bent down to greet him and all of a sudden I felt a tremor pulsate through his body, which left him motionless. I immediately ran outside the room calling for help. A nurse and a doctor came running and as soon as they saw him asked us to leave the room immediately and sounded a "code 3" alert. We stepped out of the room while countless attendants, some with equipment (looked to me like an EKG monitor), came rushing in. After about 15 minutes a doctor came to us in the hallway and told us that they could not save him, he had experienced an aneurism (a blood clot reaching the heart). We lost our beloved Papa'! We both burst into tears. We consoled each other. Meanwhile down the corridor I spotted Uncle Tony quickly approaching us. I unhesitatingly ran to him with arms outstretched announcing his death with these words, "We lost Papa'! I'm so sorry!" He was stunned; he had no idea of the gravity of the situation because it had progressed so rapidly from the time he had received his last repot. He couldn't believe it. He rushed to the room where a doctor intercepted him and said he could not go in right then but that it was hopeless, his father had died! He burst into tears. We began hugging each other for consolation. It was very emotional. We could not stop crying, he was such a wonderful man, we loved him so much, how could we lose him? He was an integral part of our life. He just retired from work. He was telling us of the things he wanted to do in his retirement. How could this happen? It's not fair! But then who knows the reasons God has for such an end. One wish Papa' would always tell us is that when his time came, he prayed the Lord would take him fast, he did not want to be a suffering burden to his family. This, the Lord granted him! He was so loved by all his children and their children. We will miss him. As far as we were concerned, there will be no other Erminio! Goodbye Papa', Rest In Peace, Amen…

C-BABY CHRISTINE'S FIRST BIRTHDAY. A year has gone by and we are preparing for your first birthday celebration. We were still living in Brentwood. The date was November 13, 1960. My father and mother made the drive from Brooklyn to celebrate your first birthday. Grandma Assunta was not able to attend because of her medical condition. All the other relatives that could make it arrived. I took movies of the grand occasion so the attendees could be viewed along with the main activity of the singing of Happy Birthday to You and the Blowing-out of the candle was all recorded there for posterity. You were so happy; you seemed to enjoy everyone being there, all focusing on you. Everyone enjoyed it and they got to see our new home for the first time, for most of them. They liked it. It was also an opportunity to ask the parents and the uncles for some advice, on how to modify the house for more comfort. Meanwhile baby Christine had birthday presents to open, and since she was walking, we had difficulty getting her to concentrate on one subject at a time. She was going everywhere. You were talking too. "I want that Daddy" you would be saying, with a pointing finger. You were a joy for your grandmother and grandfather. They couldn't stop giving you their undivided attention (unfortunately Grandma Assunta was in a hospital then and couldn't make it). But your aunts and uncles certainly made up for the missing grandparents. Of course we had the traditional five course meal before the cake celebration. Everyone enjoyed it. You certainly had more company now, with baby Lucille and baby Susan both at your side and enjoying the festivities almost as much as you. It was wonderful seeing the three of you there. It was a very thrilling time for mom and me, especially at gatherings of this nature. You know how much we enjoyed the family and this was another occasion when family would get together for celebrations. Happy Birthday baby Christine!!!

Photo of Mamma Assunta with Papa' Erminio

1961

GRANDMA ASSUNTA PASSERO DIES. We (mom and I) were going to visit grandma Assunta frequently because her condition was deteriorating. When the doctor reported his findings as the result of many tests, he told us he found a type of hardening of the arteries, which was very serious and could not be corrected with medication. We were sad. She was in the Central Islip Hospital and every time we visited, her condition seemed worse, to the point, where she did not recognize us anymore. It was very disheartening. We loved her so much. She was a wonderful mother and grandmother and now this is happening. But we would wipe our tears before visiting with her and tried our best to cheer her up. We didn't know what else to do. And then on April 15, 1961, (one year and three months from the death of Erminio) we received a call from Uncle Tony telling us that Grandma Assunta no longer was with us, she died in the early hours of the morning. We both began crying. She was so good. We are going to miss her so much. You children are not going to have the opportunity of knowing her. How sweet she was. How caring. Goodbye Momma, we will always love you. Rest in peace...

MOVED TO WILLISTON PARK. Moved to Williston Park, LI, and N.Y. On April 18, 1961.

We were able to, in time, purchase a home in Williston Park, on 27 Goodrich Street, intersecting Willis Avenue, in Long Island, NY, so that we could provide more space for the children and at the same time locate closer to my workplace. It was an interesting story on how we acquired that house. Here is what happened; mom and I made the decision to find a place that not only had more space for living, but would shorten my commute (from Brentwood to Hempstead where my office building was), which took over an hour and a half travel. Not that it was an exorbitant distance to drive, but it was the time that had to be devoted to driving that distance. That time could be better spent at home, helping with the children and other important chores. So we took a map of Long Island, measured an 8 mile radius (maximum limit we chose for practicality) around Hempstead and began our search for a new home. We scoured all the newspapers for a suitable location. It was January of 1960 when I visited this house (During lunchtime) for sale in Williston Park, just about five miles from Hempstead (a perfect location). The owner, an elderly gentleman, showed me around the house (Mom asked me to house hunt alone since she was so busy with three baby's.) and said it belonged to his mother and father and he in turn raised his family there and that it contained so many sentiments that it was very hard for him to let it go. I was very sympathetic and seemed to understand his feelings since I was experiencing similar feelings about our Brentwood home that we had to leave. He also told me I resembled a son of his that he lost in World War II. Here is the interesting part. The house had no improvements since they acquired it at the turn of the century, but the selling price was at a premium. We really could not afford it. But he had so much compassion for me (especially when he heard we had three children), that he brought the price down just so we could buy it! I could not believe it (At first I thought it was a ploy-but in fact turned out to be genuine)! He asked how much could I afford and he made that the price. We only paid $16,000.00 for the house. Another miracle from the Lord! Mr. Hoeneker (the owner) who had held-out for over a year said he wouldn't come down with the price for anyone, before he sold me the house. But he did it for us! His name was Conrad Hoenecker and we owe him our gratitude for such a generous gesture. God Bless him! We were able to buy that house and moved in April, 18, 1961. The house had an entrance into the Living room, then a Dinning room, a Kitchen with a breakfast nook (two wooden benches and a wooden table in the center) and a small Bathroom on the first floor. The entrance to the basement (if you went to the right) was from a side entrance to the house and to the Kitchen (if you went left up three stairs). The second floor had a full Bathroom at the head of the stairs with two Bedrooms, one very large and one small. Then there was the Attic, unfinished but large. I made a lot of changes to that house, so that we would be more comfortable in it. Besides improving the Kitchen, I removed a hallway partition on the second floor to privatize the entrance to the Attic which I finished as a three bedroom space for all the girls. The small bedroom on the second floor was used for baby Joseph when he was born. The major construction I performed was in the basement. It was a full

Basement (same dimension as the house) that I finished-off mostly for Lucille who celebrated her sixteenth birthday there with her friends. I also built a two foot high wall all around the outside of the house to hold the soil that was about 18 inches higher than the sidewalk. It was interesting work. To accomplish those tasks, I had to assume the role of a Plumber, an Electrician, a Carpenter, a Plasterer a Landscaper and a Mason. Thanks to Uncle Julie, he helped me perform as those tradesmen's tasks with excellent outcomes. Everybody (including the extended family) was amazed at the results, especially when mom would say, "Gus did this!" (With obvious pride.) You children were so happy with the new quarters. You now had enough space for all your things. It's interesting to note that I believe life was a little different in Williston Park; LI, because the population was much denser and resembled a quasi city atmosphere. From a rural environment to a suburban life experience, it was a big change for us all. But you kids took it in your stride and mom and I had to adapt. And so, our life in Williston Park begins.

The house was coincidently only about 9 miles from Westbury where Auntie Mary and Uncle Julie lived. We frequently visited them and of course they were always welcome to visit us, therefore a very strong bond developed with them. There were so many times we needed them and they selflessly responded with such loving care that that we were overwhelmed with heartfelt gratefulness. We loved them so much for their attention and caring. Thank you Auntie Mary and Uncle Julie! I don't know how we would have done it without you. You are both so precious in our memories. We will never forget you and the love you gave us…

L-LUCILLE WAS IN GRADE 1. On May, 8, 1961, Lucille was in Grade 1 at the Elementary School of St. Aidan in Williston Park, LI. She was 7 years old. There is a class photo that is larger and provides better viewing in the "School" Album, in the closet, where we store it. She was growing up beautifully. We were so proud of her. She loved school and did very well in class; she especially admired the Nuns that taught her. She was happy at school here in Williston Park.

From this point on, for purposes of brevity, I will not be reporting each year's Grade level of Lucille's school experience (or the others for that matter). I will only tell you about her and the others Graduations from Elementary School to High School and so on. Since Lucille attended every grade normally, I am asking you to assume she progressed well every year, reaching her final goal of graduation, at every level. Lucille was a good student. She made us proud of her educational development. Keep up the good work Lucille!

J-OUR FOURTH CHILD JOSEPH IS BORN.

Actual date born....December 9, 1961....Joseph Erminio Petti......... 7:24 AM.... We were living in Williston Park, LI, NY, at the time. I was working for The Meadowbrook National Bank. I was the Eastern Operations Department District Manager, a very big title, but all it meant was I had the responsibility of supervising 5 rather large Proof Operations (which were primarily Bookkeeping Operational functions of the bank). It was an exciting part of my career life, since this was the first time I was able to implement so many new ideas that I had on my mind and to my astonishment were all working well. Top management was very happy with the outcomes. And I was pleased too.

It was very cold weather out there. Mom was pregnant and in her ninth month. On the night of December 8, 1961, mom was starting to go into labor. Mom remembers it being late at night close to morning. We had to wake-up Lucille (Lucille was close to 8 years old) because Susan and Christine were asleep. We asked her to care for them while we prepared to go to the hospital. Lucille said, "Don't worry Dad, I'll watch them." "Thanks", I said, "You're a doll". Then mom and I, after getting her suitcase, left for the hospital. The labor intensified at the hospital (we were at Mineola Hospital) and baby Joseph was born, the next day, in the early morning. No difficulty, according to mom. "A very smooth birth", mom says. It happened in the early hours of the morning. Joseph Erminio was our fourth child. A handsome infant (even if I say so myself), that appeared to me to be gigantic in size. He weighed 9 pounds 13 ounces (almost 10 lbs!) and was over 22 inches long! When I arrived home and told you all about having a baby brother, you were so happy to hear the news. You wanted to see him so much that I had to call the hospital to find out if you could visit the Nursery (children were not allowed in hospitals at that time) to view the baby. They said it was OK. You all got dressed and I brought you all to see baby Joseph in his little transparent plastic baby crib. He was sleeping at the time. Then you wanted to see mom, which I arranged and you hugged her so tight and told her how much you missed her and it was only one day without her! Then we went home and you continued your activities.

J-THE NAME JOSEPH ERMINIO. We added his grandfather's name Erminio to the first name of Joseph because we felt it important to honor mom's dad especially at that time. When you give a parent's name to your offspring in Italian culture, great honor and respect is shown to that parent. Of course the selection of the name Joseph was a given, since that name had been chosen even before baby Lucille was born. I was so happy . I couldn't hold back the joy! Just think; I'm the father of another baby and a BOY this time! It was overwhelming…I couldn't believe it…A BABY BOY!!! Thank you Lord. What a Blessing!

And all this took place without me being there at the hospital. I was sent home as soon as I escorted mom into the hospital. In those days, they didn't allow the husband in the delivery room, like they do today. In fact they didn't even want any expectant father to wait in the waiting room, the way they depict the waiting scene in the movies of the day. I was nowhere in sight. I wasn't even there to hold mom's hand during those crucial moments. I think I miss that? I'm so glad they allow the husband to be present nowadays. But none of this took away from the happiness I felt. I couldn't wait to have my son and mom home!

I had to notify all the family members of this new joy! I had to find the telephone numbers so I can call them about the good news. Here they are right here in our telephone book, I have to call my mother and father, too bad Papa' Erminio and Mamma Assunta (they both had died) were not here, they would have been so happy. Then I have to call Auntie Mary and Uncle Julie along with Uncle Tony and Auntie Rose, then my sister and Uncle Vinny, everybody has to get called! Naturally, the first question they all asked, "Is the baby healthy?" "Yes" was my answer, "Oh, good" they replied. And the tradition goes on... Then they began asking about the statistics, and when they heard them they were all amazed at the height and weight and all commented, "That's large" "I know" I said. Baby Joseph was born at 7:24 AM weighed 9lbs 13oz (of course my mother immediately rounded it to ten pounds) and delivered by Dr. John Malfetano. That meant I was on the phone for a few hours. Now that everyone got the news, it was time to go visit my baby Joseph and mom at the hospital again

For the record, on December 9. 1961, at 7:24 AM in the morning, at Mineola Hospital (now called Winthrop Hospital), Mineola, LI, and our fourth bundle of joy "BABY JOSEPH" was born!

J-EVENTS OF 1961- In 1961 the Soviet Union and the U.S. sent men into space for the first time. On April 12 the Soviets got there first when 27 year old Yuri Gagarin orbited Earth for 89 minutes. On May 5, 1961, Alan B. Shepard Jr. became the first American in space but he did not orbit Earth nor was he aloft as long as Gagarin. The Soviets continued to lead the way in the next frontier, SPACE.

IBM introduces the Selectric Typewriter, an invention that pleases mom very much since all her experience was on the manual typewriters of the day, but this automatic machine would revolutionize the process of typing forever.

The racing car driver A.J. Foyt pushes his car to a speed of 139.13 miles per hour in the Indianapolis 500. This was a world record in the auto car racing field. The first electric toothbrush becomes available. The popular singer of the day, Patsy Cline releases I Fall to Pieces and becomes Number One Hit instantly. Walt Disney produces 101 Dalmatians, a movie that is still popular today. In the science of geology, studies of the seafloor support continental drift theory almost 60 years after Alfred Wegener proposed it.

Although many world wide events were unfolding, life continued at the Petti's in a normal and caring way. Now there were four children to love. And believe me that took all the time and effort we could muster. All other family activities also continued, as I will describe...

J-BABY JOSEPH IS BAPTIZED. Baby Joseph was baptized in St. Aidan's Church, in Williston Park, LI. Right on Willis Avenue, just four blocks from where we lived. It was very convenient to have your Church that close. Joann my sister, was married to Vincent Scrocco and became the next spiritual parents to be asked the question, "Would you be willing to be the Godparents for baby Joseph?". Of course they both said "Yes. They would be happy to be his Godparents!" In Italian they would be called, Comare and Compare, which is an honored and greatly respected title in Italian tradition. Later in years, as Joseph grew up, he would use that Italian title every time he would refer to them. I'm not sure why he was attracted to that verbiage, I suspect he either thought it was cool, or on the other hand, he felt and understood the great respect the titles conveyed.

We have the scene on video tape showing the carrying of baby Joseph from the house to the church (it should be in the The Petti's 1961 section of the VHS tape). The planning of this celebration started to become a challenging and enormous event. The families were getting larger. More family members had to be invited. More food was needed. More drink had to be procured. It was wonderful. Let's see, my mother and father was there. My Uncle Julio and Auntie Mary, including Irene and Marie. Our Uncle Tony and Auntie Rose, including all your cousins and the rest of the family that could make it were there It was a full house, all attending to witness this newborn child entering the Church. Those were wonderful times. And baby Joseph was enjoying all the attention.

Just a note here: There is no doubt in my mind that mom and I were both improving in our parenting skills. Here with our fourth child, things seemed to go smoother. There was no panic when we would be planning events concerning the children and the different pieces of the puzzles all went into place easily. It got to the point where we were actually enjoying, not only the planning stages, but also the execution phase of all the family get-togethers. It was marvelous!

I would have to say that by this time, the birth of a child to us was in fact similar to a repeat performance on the stage. We knew exactly what to do, when to do it and how to do it. The only thing missing after the performance was the applause. We missed that. All joking aside, the birth of our son was appreciation enough. We couldn't be happier. He was such a bundle of joy. He seemed to enjoy our company also, including all his sisters!

One activity was different from the other children that deserves mention. With baby Lucille, baby Susan and baby Christine, all were fed their milk in bottles as formulas, according to the medical advice given to us during those days. But mom had an objection this time. She asked the doctor if she could breast feed this baby, He said there is no objection but he says science recommends you give him the bottle instead But mom stood firm, she said, "Doctor I would prefer breast feeding my baby, after all that is natural isn't it?" He agreed and allowed her to do so, but not happily. Wow, what a relief for me! Remember I was the bottle washer…which meant not only washing them in soapy water, but rinsing, sterilizing, filling and storing them every time a bottle was used. It was a tough job, especially when an emergency came up. You know, when the bottles are running out and it's in the middle of the night, or I'm not home, out working. There were so many times during the bottle washing process when things got a little difficult to say the least. I was so happy to hear, this duty was suspended, this go-around. Unfortunately it didn't last long. I'm not sure if it was two or three weeks after baby Joseph arrived that the breast feeding had to stop. What happened was that baby Susan (she was around five years old at the time) apparently was playing with other children in a driveway down the street and she accidentally ran into a commercial van vehicle operating on the street. It happened to be owned by our corner Butcher Shop. The driver was mortified. He was actually parked, but baby Susan did not see it stopping at the driveway and in her aimless running, collided into the side of the van hurting herself minimally. Our neighbor down the street Mr.- McLoughlin, a retired NY police Captain, ran to the scene and picked her up, tending to her; even before mom learned of the accident (of course I was at work). As soon as mom was told of the accident by another neighbor, she ran right out into the cold air (it was December) without putting on a coat or covering herself up with a sweater or something, running to the aid of her daughter. Without her knowing it, the incident caused her breast milk to freeze. No ambulance was needed for baby Susan since her wounds were not serious. Mom returned home with baby Susan. It was a superficial wound but the Butcher Shop owner was so distraught he sent us not only his sincere apology but a very large ham too. We enjoyed the ham, as baby Susan's wounds healed. Meanwhile mom had to go to the doctor because of the intense pain she began experiencing in her breast. The doctor explained what happened, gave her medication and told her she couldn't continue breast feeding baby Joseph. That was the end of that. The bottle preparation now began. I was in charge. The bottles were sterilized, filled and placed in the refrigerator ready for baby Joseph. Mom was feeling better. Baby Susan was almost healed by now. All was well again, except mom was not able to go full term with her breast feeding desire. It didn't seem to bother baby Joseph, he was just as content with milk from a bottle as he was the other way.

1962

J-BABY JOSEPH'S FIRST BIRTHDAY. It was December 9, 1962. Birthdays were getting more frequent when baby Joseph's rolled around. We were able to prepare them more quickly and more easily. Of course my mother and father would come to celebrate this occasion, especially my father whose name baby Joseph bears. The remainder of the family would also be invited. Whoever could come arrived. We were always about fifteen to twenty people. Baby Joseph was all dressed up in a suit and tie. It was two weeks before Christmas so it was a little difficult to get all the relatives to come to the house. Most of them did attend though. They knew how important this special birthday was. We were in Williston Park at the time. I was employed by the Meadowbrook National Bank as a Manager of the Port Washington Proof operation. We thought at the time that baby Joseph was not developing (You know how parents can be mistaken.) like our other infants. In our crude analysis, at one year old, we thought he was not talking or walking as rapidly as the others. We had no choice but to compare his development with our other children, but when we brought him to the Pediatrician for his one year-old check-up, the doctor reassured us that his developmental pace among boys was normal and not to fret. The doctor explained that boys in general, were slower than girls in terms of talking and walking. You can imagine how concerned we were. But shortly after baby Joseph's first birthday, there were definite signs of improvement. I believe his first word spoken was "apple" (I wondered why not "Daddy" but apple is OK.) and then he said "Mommy", so I had to wait a little longer until he called my name.

Nevertheless, the birthday celebration went on without a hitch. Baby Joseph opened all his birthday presents (notice he got double presents in the month of December due to Christmas) then blew out the candle on his birthday cake, then had fun with all his cousins and other relatives playing with him. Also, there were his sisters to keep him occupied. He had plenty of company especially at his birthday. We all sang Happy Birthday To You and then he blew out the candles. He had a good time. He loved the cake. Happy birthday baby Joseph…

PETER SCROCCO BORN. This was my sister's first baby. He was born on April 27, 1963. Born at Mineola Hospital in New York, the event was announced to us by his proud father, Vinny, my brother-in-law. He was so happy telling us about the birth of his first son. We couldn't wait to see our first nephew. My sister was doing very well and very happy too. When we went to visit, my mother and father were happy to be called grandparents again. They were so proud of their daughter. Joann insisted that mom hold the baby, which she did without hesitation. We were Aunts and Uncles to this precious baby. We all celebrated! HAPPY BIRTHDAY PETER!

PART-TIME WORK-1963. In 1963 the economy of the country was heading for inflation and the costs of living were increasing at an alarming rate. Since I was employed by the Meadowbrook National Bank, salaries were sort of stagnant; they apparently were not in tune with the economics of the country at large. I had to do something. My solution had always been, if one needs more income, one has to add jobs, so I began searching for a part-time job. A friend at work knew of some openings at the Huntington Town House, a catering establishment for Weddings, Bar Mitzvah's, Seder's and all get-togethers of all types. They needed a Chapel Director for all the religious celebrations they would be conducting and with my Chaplain's Assistant experience I gained in the Air Force, I was a shoe-in for the job. My schedule was usually on Friday nights, Saturdays and Sundays. Affairs usually began at 7:00 PM on Fridays and 5:00 PM on the other days. It was an interesting job. I met a lot of Famous people there and although I'm sure they don't remember me, I certainly will never forget them. I met Bob Hope and Richard M. Nixon, and George Burns, to mention a few of the more popular ones. And all I said to them was; "Good Evening, Sir", not a memorable statement from me I'm afraid.

It was only a way of earning additional income to support the family, to help cope with the expenses, which were leaping in bounds. The extra work accomplished the intended purpose. We were able to keep food on the table, pay the mortgage, keep clothes on all of you and pay all the household bills. By the way, mom was our bookkeeper (by default) and she kept excellent accountability. We not only were able to care for all of you, but we were able to move forward also. An inimitable accomplishment, thanks to mom.

I worked part-time at the Huntington Townhouse till 1970. Before I resigned from there, management called me in and offered to promote me to Banquet Manager a position I had to decline for many reasons. But it made me feel good that I was appreciated

1964 World's Fair-Peace Through Understanding

1964

NEW YORK WORLD'S FAIR – 1964. This was a once in a lifetime event for our children! In February of 1964, in Flushing Meadows, Corona, N.Y., the second New York World's Fair 1964-1965, opened on the same acreage that was used for the 1939-1940 World's Fair. It was wonderful. The theme was different, but the spectacular array of exciting buildings was the same. In the 1939 World's Fair the theme of the architectural structure was a lofty Trylon and a gigantic Perisphere that represented The World of Tomorrow! But the theme of the 1964-1965 World's Fair was Peace Through Understanding, dedicated to Man's Achievement on a Shrinking Globe in an Expanding Universe. The Fair's architectural symbol that was constructed at the center of the quasi mile square perimeter was a 12 story high, pure stainless steel model of the earth called the Unisphere. It still stands today in Flushing Meadow Park where it was erected.

Even though my enthusiasm to visit the '64 Fair along with mom and the children was at an all time high, it was not meant to be. Unfortunately at the time I had experienced a ruptured disk in my spinal column that necessitated mandatory bed rest whenever I returned home from work. This was a special therapy that was recommended by my Godfather, Dr. Iamele and a friend of his Dr. Palma. It avoided surgery and therefore was my preferred choice of recovery from that condition. It meant that not only did I have to wear a steel cage type of support for my upper body while sitting at my desk at work, but that the minute I arrived home; I had to go to bed (where a strong bed-board was installed, under the mattress) and stay there until the next morning when it was time to go to work again. It was a very difficult routine. It required the discipline of Job! Of course this prevented me from accompanying the family on any type of tour or visit to any planned event. That included visits to the Fair. I didn't want the children to miss seeing the World's Fair so I coaxed mom into taking all of you, even though I knew how difficult it would be taking four children to such a populated place. When we mentioned this to Marie (Galano at the time) and Uncle Julio and Auntie Mary, Marie volunteered to join mom on the trip and help her with the children. Marie was so giving and the children loved her.

They went soon after they made plans. Lucille was 10 years old, Susan was 8, Christine was 6 and baby Joseph was 3 and in a stroller. Off you all went with mom and Marie. When you returned, you all had so many stories to tell me. I could tell that you really enjoyed the trip and that you were overwhelmed with the spectacles that you observed that day. I felt so bad that I could not attend and be with you. I had read so much about it; I followed all the activities in the newspaper. I was familiar with the controversy that Robert Moses (Fair Director) created as a result of his decisions. I almost knew every building there and was absolutely fascinated with certain ones that practically blew my mind away. For instance the IBM building was the most outstanding one in my mind. A gigantic egg shaped building; people would sit in a grandstand type of seating arrangement, and then be elevated up into the egg container to view a gigantic screen. On the screen and the accompanying audio, announced the beginning of the computer age. It showed how computers easily solved complex problems that amazed almost everyone attending those shows. The problem exhibited was how to select the seating arrangement of a 22 guest list dinner. For humans it was almost an impossible accomplishment. For the computer it only took two seconds! The most amazing part was when the picture mode goes into slow motion, showing how the computer made its decisions. You just sat there in amazement and were absolutely awed by the logic that was graphically displayed in front of your very eyes. That's unbelievable, you would be saying to yourself as you exited from your seat. The second most popular site was the Pepsi building where Disney designed puppets and audiotronic characters singing and dancing for the public's pleasure. Believe it or not, the Illinois building (which was not considered to be outstanding) was quit a popular attraction, with its life size Abraham Lincoln standing and sitting and talking to the audience in a very realistic and lifelike manner, it absolutely amazed everyone (Another Disney audiotronic creation). Let me not leave out the Ford contribution. They built a circular roadway that could accommodate their cars on tracks and allowed you to ride them around with audio accompaniment explaining all the features of their new product. It was very exciting and free... The 1964-1965 World's Fair tried to duplicate the 1939-1940 World's Fair in many ways, but was not that successful. For some reason, and the critics are at odds as to the cause, the Fair was not a hit with the World at that time. In the end, I understand New York City had to bail them out financially, as 1964 drew near. But I feel it was an exemplary effort and everyone involved with its development should be commended especially Mr. Moses… I'm glad you children were able to experience this happening. Thanks to your mom and Marie Galano (now Rossi) who made it possible. I'm indebted…

A Note: Shea Stadium was completed in 1964 also and made its grand opening at the same time the 1964-1965 World's Fair opened. It is the center piece for Queens and is the NY Mets Baseball Team's official home.

1965

C-CHRISTINE IN GRADE 1. There is a class photo, in the School Album, on our closet shelf, that shows Christine in her 1st Grade Class with all her school mates and her Teacher Mrs. Seidell. The photo is dated 2/4/65. When I look at these photos, many memories flash through my mind, that relate to our Christine. It is really an exciting feeling to see her when she was this small. I often wonder, how did people in the past recall such scenes, without the wonder of photography? It must have been very difficult to remember these moments in the life of their little ones. But we are blessed with the permanent record of her image, imprinted on paper, to refer to whenever we want. And I remember the most expressed comment, as soon as mom and all the relatives viewed the photo, "Oh, how beautiful she is!"…I agreed!

Now Christine is on a roll, after Grade 1 it's all downhill (my opinion of course). Christine like the other children did well in school. Each in their own way, they progressed from grade to grade without incidents. Everyone had different dreams and aspirations and they diligently grasped education in a positive way. We were blessed.

Since Grade 1 was one of the most significant markers in life's journey, I emphasized it by noting it here. After this, I will only mention graduations at every level only.

1966

M-OUR FIFTH CHILD MICHELE IS BORN. Our fifth child born to us was Michele Marie Petti. She was born on April 12, 1966 in the late morning. Her birth was so pleasant, according to mom, that we have difficulty describing all the details. To us, after four births, it becomes easier and easier to go through the process (That's what mom tells me.). Mom says "I don't remember anything about the birth, except that it went well with no problems" and I said, "That's great!" what more can anyone want, except for everything to go smoothly. I believe that's the best I can report on how it happened. Mom remembers beginning her labor during the night of April 11, 1966 and going on till early morning when I called Auntie Mary, to see if she could come over and be with the children while I took you to the Hospital. You were born shortly after mom arrived. There were no complications, you were a beautiful baby girl, and born at Mineola Hospital (it has a different name now). When you were born, I immediately made the calls to my mother and father, all your aunts and uncles, friends and all the other relatives. They were so happy. Of course they all asked the question, "Is she healthy?", to which I responded, "Yes", then they wanted to know your height and weight, which I told them. Baby Michele was born at 4:50 AM, weighed 8 lbs, 10 ozs. And was delivered by Dr. John Malfetano our family doctor. Now I had time to come and visit you and mom. There you were in the Nursery, all bundled up, content and sleeping (I guess it's a fatiguing task, being born). After visiting with you, I went to see mom. She was sitting up and was very alert. After kissing her and hugging her for her labored journey, I commented on how well she looked. She said, "Well, I believe this one was the easiest of all the births", I said "That's wonderful", then she asked how I found you in the Nursery and asked if I thought you were beautiful and I said, "Yes, she is beautiful", and added, "We have received another blessing from God!". She agreed. You were not only another daughter but were also another soul that we, with the help of the Almighty, brought into this world. You made us so happy...We loved you...

Actual date born...April 12, 1966......Michele Petti...At 4:50 AM ... at Mineola Hospital

M-CHOOSING A NAME FOR MICHELE. Michele was our fifth child. Your name was chosen from my Grandfather's name of Michele (Italian spelling) and coincidentally was also the name of my brother Michael (who died at 2 years old), so to honor both, we named you Michele. It was almost a natural choice, derived from our Italian cultural norms used in the naming process for our newborns which made it very easy. I know I'm repeating myself, but we were very fortunate with choosing names.

M-1966 NEWS EVENTS. These are only some of the important news items the year you were born. Of course there were many others. Peggy Fleming wins Olympic gold medal for U.S. in figure skating. In January, Indira Gandhi became prime minister of India. She was called Bharat Mata (Mother India) by her people. American forces launched their biggest attack against the Viet Cong in Vietnam and shelled Cambodia for the first time during the Vietnam War. Roman Catholics are allowed to eat meat on Fridays, except during Lent. Star Trek, Family Affair and Hollywood Squares debut on American TV. The chemical structure of DNA is discovered. The Beatles release the song Eleanor Rigby.

Although many world wide events were unfolding, life continued at the Petti's in a normal and caring way. Now there were five children to love. And believe me, that took all the time and effort we could muster. It was wonderful being a Father. All other family activities also continued, as I will describe...

M-BABY MICHELE IS BAPTIZED. Your Godmother and Godfather are Marie and Joseph Rossi who were to be married in October of this year, when you became a member of the Church. They were preparing their wedding at that time. They were our preferred choices for this honored responsibility at the time. They were so close to us and we loved them very much. They are your Comare and Compare, forever! They were so thrilled and honored when we asked them if they would be willing to be your Godparents. I have movies of them carrying you to the Church. You were baptized early in May of 1966. The weather was beautiful and you were in your white long dress, according to Italian custom. I don't remember you crying when the Priest poured the water over your head. You seemed to be happy, especially with all the attention you were getting. At home, there was my mother and father, Auntie Mary and Uncle Julio, Uncle Tony and Auntie Rose with all your cousins and other relatives. Everyone was celebrating. Its baby Michele's Baptism...Thanks be to God...

MARIE & JOE WED. On October 15, 1966, Marie Galano (daughter of Mary and Julio Galano) and Joe Rossi were married. Since this was the first niece of Ann to marry, this was one of our many special weddings. Everything had to be perfect, as mom would say. All the formal clothing had to be just right and all the arrangements had to come about flawlessly. You get the picture; every detail had to have the attention needed to bring the desired result to fruition. And so everything did go well (Thank God), in spite of all the anxiety. It was beautiful.

The wedding ceremony took place at St. Bridgid's Church in Westbury, NY, with the reception taking place at the Huntington Town House, Huntington, L.I., NY. It was a marvelous celebration of two people in love, that decided to spend the rest of their lives together and have children. For mom and me, that was an exemplary decision...All the Petti's were there, all the children except Michele (too little) attended. In church, the singing was beautiful, putting us into a peaceful mood. When you witnessed the beautiful dresses and all the men dressed in formal suits, the atmosphere of joy was present everywhere. There, in front of the church was Joe and the Best Man. The ushers were escorting the guests to their seats. It was time for the entrance of the Mother of the Bride...here she comes, resplendent, in her flowing dress, smiling down the aisle. Now the Bride's Maids. The music changes; Here Comes the Bride begins playing, everyone stands, here comes our

Marie (in a beautiful Wedding gown) and Uncle Julio, smiling and together walking toward the alter. It was beautiful. May God Bless you all! Congratulations Newly Weds"...

As in almost all Italian weddings, at the reception, there was a lot of hugging and kissing! I believe there was a smile on every face I viewed. Everyone was happy, eating and drinking; wishing the happy couple well into the future. Uncle Julio and Auntie Mary were so happy. It was their first child to marry and they couldn't contain themselves with joy. The happy couple (now the Rossi's) set-up home in Fresh Meadows, NY, for a few years. Everyone was happy for them. Buona Fortuna was said very often, in the greetings during the reception.

JOSEPH SCROCCO IS BORN. It was the second week of December and very cold outside when we got the telephone call from our brother-in law Vinny that my sister Joann had given birth to a second child who was a boy and whom they called Joseph after my father. Vinny was so happy while telling us about the birth and explained that my sister was doing fine. Then we talked to Joann and of course she was very happy too. Baby Joseph was born on December 13, 1966. We began making plans to go visit our new nephew as soon as Joann got home from the hospital. When we visited, we found a beautiful baby boy, seemingly content with everything going on around him. He didn't even flinch when mom held him. Mom said he was adorable. My mother and father were very proud of their new grandson. Now Peter has a brother. HAPPY BIRTHDAY JOSEPH!

1967

M-BABY MICHELE'S FIRST BIRTHDAY. Baby Michele's first birthday was celebrated with lots of company this time, including three sisters and a brother, on April 12, 1967. Lucille was 13 years old, Susan was 11 years old, Christine was 9 and Joseph was 6 years old. What a crowd! And this did not count your grandmother and grandfather, your aunts and uncles and all your cousins. The house was full. It was baby Michele's first birthday. It was time for celebration. It was time for music. It was time for family fun. You were so excited, seeing all these familiar faces, all bending down to kiss you and wishing you a happy birthday. It was wonderful when the family got together to experience the love that comes from each member. It is difficult to explain how this affects each person attending the activity. You were walking and talking so you were not left out. You were right in there enjoying everyone that was there, especially the time you spent with my mother and father (your grandmother and grandfather). It was a joy to watch the proceedings. It was now time to open the presents. Here comes the cake with the single candle lit and now the singing of Happy Birthday to You. You blew out the candle flame and the cake was cut and distributed. Everyone was having fun. Happy 1st Birthday baby Michele...Everyone loved you...

IRENE & BOB WED. On August 12, 1967, Irene Galano (daughter of Mary and Julio Galano) marries Robert Mascola at St. Bridgid's Church in Westbury, L.I., NY, and had their reception at the Woodbury Country Club, Woodbury, L.I., NY. We were so excited that day. It was the wedding of mom's first niece and that made it special...everyone would be there, smiling and happy. We would all be attending, except for Michele, she was too young. But Lucille was there, as was Susan and Christine and Joseph. All the Petti's were there, celebrating a wonderful begining of a new life together. The wedding at the church was extraordinary, the church was beautiful, the dresses were magnificent, the singing in the church was moving and joyous. Near the Altar was Bob, standing nervously with the Best Man next to him, waiting. Here comes an usher with the Groom's mother holding his arm and his father following, all dressed up. Next comes another usher down the isle, escorting the bride's mother, Mary how beautiful you looked! The other Bride's Maids slowly come down the isle holding their beautiful flowers, then the Maid of Honor. Now the organ plays Here Comes the Bride and down the isle walks Irene resplendent in dress (her Wedding gown was beautiful), led by her proud father Julio, who was smiling from ear to ear, as he passed the congregation. It was a very happy day for everyone! Thank you Irene and Bob for that beautiful wedding...we will never forget that event! God Bless You Both! Congratulations!

They made their home in Fresh Meadows, L.I., N.Y. till 1970.

1968

L-LUCILLEGRADUATESELEMENTARYSCHOOL. We were living in Williston Park, LI, NY when Lucille graduated Elementary School at St. Aidan. She was so excited. I believe the date was June 8, 1968. Boy! did we have a party! You were all dressed-up. Along with your grandmother and grandfather and all your relatives, an added surprise was your Uncle Lorenzo and Aunt Raffaella that were living here in America at the time. I believe we have some scenes of that get-together on film. You were 14 years old! My, how the years go by. One of the reasons mom and I continue to call you "kids" is for the simple reason that in our minds, you never grow up and therefore remain a child, figuratively that is. Although the years roll by, we persistently remember you as kids and can't get that out of our minds (this of course is also an apology for when we slip after calling you kids). You were so happy and couldn't wait to start High School. That is when you really blossomed. Both mom and I had to admit that you were growing up (our way of realizing that you were maturing). We were proud and we loved you so very much. It was wonderful witnessing this amazing development. These are the moments in life that you remember forever. Good fortune to you Lucille!

J-JOSEPH ENTERS 1ST GRADE. On February 8, 1968 we enrolled Joseph into our local religious school. We were living in Williston Park, on Goodrich Street. Joseph enters the first grade at St. Aidan's School. His Teacher was Sr. Alice and was very impressed with Joseph and must have detected the many talents he had, talents that mom and I were not aware of at the time (like his love of music). He progressed well and now we had four children in school at the same time. Joseph was a joy to our family and although at this age he was a little shy, he participated in all our activities with enthusiasm and sincerity. He was treasured by the whole family, especially by his sisters. We all loved him.

DAD EMPLOYED BY C&F. On April 22, 1968, I was hired by an Insurance company called Crum & Forster. It was a rather extreme departure from the banking business that I was in, but it was secure employment and a brand new occupation which I was very excited about. Crum & Forster was the 17th largest insurance company in the U.S. at the time. We insured people mostly for liability and property. The company needed System Analysts to ensure they were performing their tasks efficiently and profitably, that was my duty. This assignment also led me to personal computer work (which IBM was initially promoting at our site). Although I had extensive computer experience at the Bank, my experience was with "Main Frame" computing only. The personal computer was a new device that I had to learn along with the principles of insurance. Unfortunately the subject of insurance was not a popular discussion choice at the family table when I was growing up as a child, so my knowledge of it was rather sparse. It's interesting, that my parents who were brought up in Italy, a country where personal insurance was almost non-existent, there was never any need of discussing the subject. But it didn't take me long to learn and understand the rudiments of insurance and to quickly become an asset to my company. In fact, I became so interested in the subject of insurance, I was asked to teach certain parts of it in a few training classes held at our corporate building, when I was a system analyst. That phase didn't last long though, for after two years of system analyst work, I was asked by George Muriello (our Department Manager) to enter the Statistical Department of the corporation. I'll be honest with you; I didn't even know the definition of the word "statistical" at the time (as it relates to the field of insurance). It turns out, the statistical department, is an integral function of the Actuarial Department. Without the statistics that are developed by the statistical department, actuaries cannot perform their usual duties of determining the rates for insurance coverage's. This is the paramount function of any insurance company; establishing the rates. So, the duty accompanying this new department I was asked to enter, was very important to the actuarial department and very challenging to me. I went in with a lot of enthusiasm and energy. It was very exciting and I was ready to take on all those responsibilities. For record's sake, my employment at C&F would last for <u>25 years</u>, after which I would actually retire from this last occupation. Needles to say I loved the Crum & Forster Ins. Co. and I made many friends that have remained close to me, over the years. This company contributed substantially to my life and my hope is that my contribution to its endeavor has been just as rewarding. It will always be a treasure to me for many reasons. Thank you Crum & Forster, I am very grateful...

I have to tell you the story that led to my being hired...remember, the economic times in '68 were stressed and jobs were scarce. I was searching for a better paying job earnestly. One of the want ads referred to "System Analysts" which I felt I was qualified for, so I applied. To my pleasant surprise, I was called for an interview at the Crum & Forster building on William St. in New York City. At the meeting, my future supervisor, Bob Morgan and his superior, Mr.Sailing Hayward, Asst. Vice Pres. were present. During the interview, Mr. Hayward would be referring to the place of my birth a number of times which I thought was odd, but shrugged it off as a curious focus of interest (later I was to learn the real reason). The interview went well and I believe I was what they were looking for. Even though I wasn't hired on the spot, in a few days I was called and told that I had the job. It made me very happy and the family too!

At the working orientation, when I started my job, at one point Mr. Hayward approached me and told me he was born on a ship too. What a coincidence! His parents like mine, were asked to name the child after the ship, but he was born on the S.S. Queen Mary! We both started to laugh; he had a wonderful sense of humor. "They couldn't call me "Queen" or "Queenie" or "Mary" " and no derivative would work either, then the parents asked what the S.S. stood for and were told it stood for Sailing Ship, and that's how I got my first name "Sailing", the same way you got your first name of "Augustus", and that's what we have in common. So now I knew why he was so interested in my birth history during the prior interview. He was the only person I ever met that was born on a ship. It was interesting that our birth's occurred in such a similar way. We remained fond friends all during my career at C&F (and not because we were both born on a ship)... I will talk more about my job in later sections.

It should be noted that the location of my employment with C&F was in New York City; their headquarters was on William Street in downtown Manhattan. They owned a 36 story skyscraper and occupied four full floors of that building. So, I would go by train to work, mom would drive me to the Williston Park Railroad station in the morning and pick me up at night, usually with you kids romping in the car. I would then proceed to the Queens Central Station where I could transfer to the subway and continue on to the city. This type of transportation was used for only two years at which time C&F built a new headquarters (on some land they owned) in Basking Ridge, New Jersey. Not only would my mode of travel need to change, but the location of our home had to change to. We would have to consider relocating and that had to be considered in a very serious way because it not only affected me, but mom and all of you would be affected too. Just to give you an idea of the dilemma, Lucille was 16 years old and a sophomore in High School. Susan was 14 years old and had just graduated grammar school. Christine was 11 years old and in grammar school. Joseph was 9 years old and also in grammar school. Michele was four years old and at home. All of them were attending St. Aidan's School except Lucille who was at Maria Regina High School.

MARIE AND JOE MOVE. While Marie Rossi (Mom's niece) was visiting one day, she told us that she and Joe were moving to New Bern, N.C. (where they would remain for the next 10 years to 1978) due to his job. Joe was working for Grumman Aviation at the time and there was a Naval Air Station there where he was needed. Although it was not pleasant news (there was nothing we could do about it), we immediately realized it was to their advantage, so the parting was made easier. We would miss them. Their family would miss them. But you know, its times like this that we recall our own parent's decisions, to leave their homeland in Italy and travel long distances to search for new opportunities, to make a better life, somewhere else. So it was, on October 15, 1968, we said goodbye, with kisses and hugs and all good wishes, with promises to visit soon and then and they left. We wished them our best…Goodbye Marie and Joe…see 'ya soon… (Little did we know, it would be sooner than we thought-see next section)

1969

DEBORAH ANN ROSSI BORN. Marie and Joe were living in New Bern, North Carolina when baby Deborah was born. It was on June 22, 1969. We got the news immediately, as soon as Joe could get to a phone. We were so happy to hear the announcement! This is Marie's and Joe's first child! What a wonderful event... Although the news did not make the front page of the Times, in their hearts it was headline news for all the families, the Rossi's, the Galano's, the Mascola's, the Passero's and the Petti's. Now Auntie Mary is a grandmother and Uncle Julio is a grandfather. We all congratulated them. They were so happy! HAPPY BIRTHDAY BABY DEBORAH!!!

Just a short time later, we received a call from Irene informing us that she and Bob were going to drive to New Bern to be baby Debbie's Comara and Compare and would we be interested in accompanying them to attend the event. We immediately said "Yes", we would be honored to be present to witness such a wonderful moment. We learned from Irene that Auntie Mary and Uncle Julio would also be there, so it would also be a small family reunion. We also would be able to visit Marie and Joe's new home too. Our only problem was, who would take care of our children? We had five children and even though Lucille was 14 years old we could not place that heavy a responsibility on her. Our first thought was Aunt Jenny, who joyfully accepted the task (she was a treasure). All you kids loved her and we were blessed with her generosity and caring. So it was all set. We would be traveling with Irene and Bob to attend baby Debbie's Baptism in New Bern, North Carolina. It was a fun drive, even though it took about 8 (or maybe 7) hours as I recall. The new house was beautiful. We have a number of photos in the album showing the many phases of the celebration. Baby Debbie was very calm and took all this in, while we adults scurried around preparing and enjoying the christening.

1970

S-SUSAN'S 8TH GRADE GRADUATION. On February 4, 1970, Susan graduates from 8th Grade at St. Aidan's School in Williston

Park, L.I., NY. It was a wonderful graduation, all the students in their finest clothes, waiting to receive their certificates. All that excitement filled the air. Everyone was smiling. I was taking photos and taking movies of as much as I could. For some reason I thought I could capture all the excitement on film to be relived in the future somehow…an illusionary expectation. I soon learned, what you experience at the moment, can never be relived…only the memories last forever. But we all had fun. The families began arriving to congratulate her, the food was being served and the drinks were flying. Everyone was having a great time! The happiest one of course was SUSAN!

Now we had to give some thought to High School. Since we were planning to move to New Jersey, what schools are there in the Morris Plains location that a Junior can enter? Let's see, there is the Catholic High School, Baley Ellard and then there is the Public High School, Morristown High School. Which will it be? A tough decision…so we all pondered (Susan wanted mom and me to help with the decision). We talked about all the benefits of each school. Also, we talked about the disadvantages of each school, trying to come up with a good choice. You know, the same process every student and parent goes through at this point in life. After all the Pros and Cons were considered, the choice was made. It will be Morristown High School that Susan will attend. A good decision we thought.

WE MOVE TO MORRIS PLAINS, NJ. This was a monumental move for us. Little did we know that we would be spending the next 23 years there! We were moving from Williston Park, L.I., NY where we lived for almost 9 years and now we were going to New Jersey. The family had grown to seven members (including mom and me). Every change affected more of us now. It was July 1, 1970 that we actually arrived at the new house. Unfortunately the movers did not arrive till July 3 (the next day would be the 4th of July) with all our furniture and contents; when we moved to Morris Plains, NJ. This meant we couldn't move into the house for two nights. We had no beds or any furniture for that matter. We quickly checked into the Howard Johnson's motel for two days. We had a lot of fun for those two days, we went sightseeing and we went to the movies to see Airplane (that hilariously funny movie), we had a good time. We also were visited by the local newspaper,r that sent a reporter and photographer to write our story and take photos of us. We were in the newspaper the next day. It was an idea that was hatched by my company, to show how effortless it is to relocate when your company is behind you. The new house was at 33 Glenbrook Road and Keenan Place. It was on a corner and structured as a 2½ story colonial style house with a front porch. The garage was about 70 feet behind the main house, which was a little unusual, but that's because the property was 224 feet deep but only 75 feet wide (among other things as a result, I had to shovel 299 linear feet of snow off of the sidewalk. when it snowed-a formidable task).

On the same day we moved (7/3/70) we met our first neighbors Mr. & Mrs. Benoit who lived across the street. As soon as the moving truck parked and began unloading our furniture, Mrs. Benoit came over and introduced herself. She and her husband invited us to celebrate the 4th of July the next night at the Morris Plains Baseball field where we witnessed a spectacular fireworks display. I wonder if you remember that Lucille and Susan (you were 16 and Sue was 14 years old). It was a great deal more than we expected. What fantastic rockets, with colorful bursts of flame filling the sky, with luminous sparkles and of course the loud explosions. This was big time fireworks, almost as good as New York City performances. It was quit a welcome for us, it helped us become more at home with our new surroundings and having someone in the neighborhood to talk to on the first day of our arrival was especially comforting. They gave us a timely overview of the town and its people. The schools, the utilities, you know, town talk that really helped us learn about the local environment quickly. It was special and we thanked the Benoits for the kindness.

The next day we were all busy placing our furniture where we wanted it and the unpacking began. We asked Lucille, Susan and Christine to help both with the unpacking and the baby sitting for Joseph and Michele. During the day other neighbors came to visit and introduced themselves. Of course the Goginski's were there (Pat and John), then the Toy's and the Van Orden's and the Sokolowski's, eventually we got to meet all the neighbors, up and down Glenbrook Rd. and on Keenan Place, which was only one block long. It was interesting listening to all these new acquaintances with all their stories of the previous owners of our house and the many experiences that led up to our move there. The kids got a lot out of the conversations. In fact the subjects that were introduced those few days by our neighbors were the focus of our family conversations for many a meal at our table and for weeks to come. It was interesting to see the dynamics of community interaction, adding to our personal family values. Needles to say our geographical transfer to a new environment seemed to evolve seamlessly. We soon began feeling at home in this new house. It was larger than our home in Williston Park. It had a larger back yard, which the children enjoyed. One thing it didn't have was a Barbeque Grill, but I was already thinking of a solution. Since the Kitchen door led to the back of the house and there was a concrete platform at the foot of the stairs, I thought that it would be a perfect location for a barbeque appliance outside. Only this time it's going to be a natural gas fed grill, not charcoal and not Propane. I had already investigated the basement gas piping and determined that it would be easy to install. So I installed it. The kids loved it. Anytime they wanted to grill something, all they had to do is turn the valve and press the igniter. We used it a lot.

IRENE & BOB MOVE. We were pleased to hear that Irene and Bob purchased a home in Williston Park and were going to relocate soon. It was on August 21, 1970 that they moved. Irene was pregnant and expecting their first child. Although we were a little sad that we didn't live there anymore, nonetheless we were able to give them many tips about that location, that were very helpful. Also, this put them very close to the soon-to-be grandma and Grandpa Galano whom you recall lived in Westbury. We were told the move went well and they were anxiously waiting for the birth.

ANOTHER PART-TIME JOB. It wasn't long after we moved, that I found it necessary to find a part-time job. The date was October 21, 1970. Again I checked the local newspapers and there was a want ad that caught my attention. Although I had never performed the task that was advertised, I felt I could do it and it would be interesting, it was for a motel desk attendant. The motel was Howard Johnson and since we had our reception at a Howard Johnson in Queens, NY, I felt a little comfortable with the pending association. As it turns out, they liked my application and hired me on the spot. I didn't have much of a training period, in fact thinking back I didn't have any at all. They started me in the daytime at first and there was another attendant that I was standing next to and would watch her do her thing and of course learned that way. But before I knew it I was on the grave yard shift (12 midnight to 7AM) and all alone, working on Friday and Saturdays nights. This shift only lasted for about 2 years, luckily another employee left that was on the morning shift. I was given his time spot (now I worked from 8AM to 3PM) Saturdays and Sundays only. If you recall, it was located in Whippany on Route 10, between Route 202 and Route 287. Quite a short distance from the house. The work was pleasant and the clientele was civilized, so the job went very well, in fact I remained there over 6 years. They asked me if I wanted to become manager, I declined. My objective was to earn an additional income, not to take on the responsibilities that would be required of that position. So I accepted my six year award (Yes, they gave me an award for lasting that long and a dinner!) and left with many fond memories.

1971

ROBERT JAMES MASCOLA BORN. We received a call from Bob, whom had just returned from a business trip, on February 11, 1971, announcing the birth of baby Robert with such joy, he barely could contain himself. He sounded so happy. We congratulated them both. Irene was fine and baby Robert was fine and it was just a very happy time at the Mascola's. Of course our next call was to Auntie Mary and Uncle Julio to congratulate them on being a grandmother and grandfather again. They were so happy. They couldn't wait to have us come over and celebrate, which wasn't going to be long since we would be coming at Easter soon. When we got together at Easter Sunday, boy did we celebrate (two big events this time)! We were so happy for them! HAPPY BIRTHDAY ROBERT! AND GOD BLESS YOU!

DENISE MARIE ROSSI BORN. These were the years of the Galano's baby boom. On the 4th of July, 1971, baby Denise was born to Marie and Joe Rossi who were living in New Bern, NC. They were so happy. When Joe called to tell us, you could almost see the smile on his face as he was telling us about his second baby daughter. "Is she healthy", was our perpetual question and the answer was a resounding "Yes"! "Oh, that's all that counts" was our retort (all coming from antique ingrained Italian customs mindsets). "But she is also beautiful" added Joe..."Well, that's wonderful" we commented. And so it went, but the air was filled with joy and the moments are so memorable. HAPPY BIRTHDAY DENISE AND GOD BLESS YOU!

1972

M-MICHELE-GRADE 1. Baby Michele is 6 years old now and begins school in First Grade at St. Virgil's School in 1972. We have a photo of her in 1st Grade along with her teacher and the whole class. The date on the plaque displayed shows the date of February 3, 1972. You were very anxious to start and were very happy following your sisters and brother's path. You were so excited that first day, all dressed up and ready to start. When you got home you told us all about the experience and what happened to some of the other children that day. Some of the stories were very funny. It was a time in your life you would never forget. All your sisters wanted to know how it went and your brother too. Now all of you were attending school. It was a new phase for mom and me. What was mom going to do with all that time she needed to care for you, that will now be available for other things? It's going to be lonely and you will be missed, she told me. The important fact is that Michele is now going to school and we must support her in her new journey. So we did, and all went well.

C-CHRISTINE-GRADE 8 GRADUATION. This was an important day! It's Graduation Day! According to our records we have the date as February 14, 1972. Christine was growing up. You were 14 years old. It's hard for us to imagine! What we are remembering is holding you in our arms and seeing you start walking and talking. It seems just yesterday that you were an infant. Fourteen years is really not that long a period of time. It's very difficult for a mom and dad to realize that you have grown. Time went by so quickly. Here you are standing there in the living room to get your picture taken, so tall, so beautiful...yes, I'm going to cry... with happiness. No matter what our memories are, its happening and we are going to celebrate! All our relatives were invited. Although your Grandfather Erminio and Grandmother Assunta have passed away, Uncle Tony, Auntie Rose and all the cousins came. Of course your Grandmother Lucia and Grandfather Joseph were there. Your Aunt Joann, Uncle Vinny and baby Joseph and baby Peter came also. It was a big party, they were so happy for you. You received so many gifts, kisses and hugs...you know how emotional Italians get. You were the center of our attention. With the most sober thought in mind, that you were growing up. CONGRATULATIONS CHRISTINE-BUONA FORTUNA!

L-LUCILLE-HIGH SCHOOL GRADUATION.

Another Graduation! Lucille Ann Petti is graduating High School. Unbelievable! Just yesterday we saw her graduate grammar school. How time flies. Lucille you are 18 years old and Mom and I can't believe it. Where has the time gone? The date I have for this event is June 2, 1972 at Morristown High School. The relatives have been called. They are all going to be there. It's going to be a large celebration, after all this is our first child who is now a woman. Is the graduation gown ready? Is the graduation peaked hat ready? We were living in Morris Plains at the time. This time, not only will all your immediate relatives going to be at your party, but also your Uncle Lorenzo and Aunt Raffaella (Cousin Tomasso's parents) from Italy will be there. It's going to be a lot of fun. Auntie Mary and Uncle Julio will be there along with Uncle Tony and Auntie Rose with all your cousins. Everyone is going to be there! It's going to be a joyful celebration...

CONGRATULATIONS LUCILLE-YOU GRADUATED WITH GREAT EXPECTATIONS...

1973

L-LUCILLE-DRIVER'S LICENSE. Although you were 19 years old when you first received your driver's license, it was the right time for you. The other kids; forget about it; they all wanted their driver's license at 17 years old!!! But you waited. You had your reasons and we did not push you. And even though they taught Driver Ed In High School, you were not interested in that subject till now, so 'I' had to teach you how to drive. You were a very good student and paid attention to all the requirements associated with the driving skill. We used some back roads in Morris Plains for the training and you did very well. It wasn't long before you felt confident enough to apply for a driving test. You passed the first time around. I knew you would, after all who taught you! Well, now that you have a license to drive, what are you going to do about a car? It was an interesting question. OK, for starters you can use mom's car while you search for a car of your own. That didn't take long. The next week you found a good buy in the papers. We went out to look at it and bought it. I had to do some repairs (like tires, etc.), but it was safe enough to drive, so off you went. Oh, by the way, I was the mechanic that kept all the cars working. Whenever one of our automobiles broke down, I was called to repair them. It was the only way we could afford to maintain multi-vehicles in the family. We could not afford to send them to local mechanics for repair. But it worked. In most cases, I was able to repair anything that happened (even a burned-out engine; but that's another story). Lucille was happy with her newly acquired driver's license and wheels (as she put it)!

S-SUSAN-DRIVER'S LICENSE. Susan you were 17 years old when you applied for your Beginners Driver License. The year was 1973, the same time that Lucille got her first Driver's License. The license that Susan received had a number of restrictions, but it was a license to drive, and that's all she wanted to do. Susan took Drivers Ed In high school and was ready to drive when the testing took place. But I insisted that I add some of my experience to the skill, so a little reluctantly, she agreed to take some spins around town with me as the instructor before the test. Actually, she did very well and that's when I realized that others can teach driving as well as I can. I want to thank you Susan for humoring me. Now you're on your own. Congratulations, happy driving.

CRUM & FORSTER TILL RETIREMENT. If you recall, I started my employment with Crum & Forster Insurance Co. back in 1968. Can you believe me spending 25 years, trying to improve this company's standing among the greats. Actually, when I retired from Crum & Forster, it had moved up to No. 14 in the books (Remember, it was No. 17 when I started). I like to think that I helped it move up a bit. Whether I helped it or not is a mute point, what I did do was develop so many new programs, some of which I believe are still used today to keep it running smoothly. I'm proud of that. And while I was implementing all these new methods (Initially I was a Systems Analyst) I met so many wonderful people with aspirations of their own, that it was a pleasure to go into work each day and be with them. I also made many new friends on the personal side there at C&F. One of my first friends that I met in 1968 was Jack Kelly. He was sitting about three desks away from mine (this is how we designate location in the office) and we became friends immediately. Since we didn't have much time in the office to socialize, we would take the Lunch opportunity to exchange dialogue and learn more about each other. Jack was in the Knights of Columbus and held a high position there. As odd as it seems, it was Jack Kelly (Who was a proud Irishman) that introduced me to an Italian restaurant which I should have known but didn't. It was so famous I couldn't believe I never heard of it. The restaurant was located on Mott and Hester Street, Downtown, NY and was simply called Vincent's Restaurant. But this was no ordinary restaurant. First of all, at lunch time, every day, there was a one to two block waiting line, to get in. Within those walls, the quality of food that was served, nearly equals the food of the gods... Its out-of-this-world specialty of fame was Fried Shrimp. But this was no ordinary fried shrimp, Oh no...it is in my opinion (and the opinion of thousands of others, including Frank Sinatra) the most tender, most succulent, most crispy, tastiest shrimp you have ever eaten. But that's not all, it is accompanied with a spicy seafood tomato sauce that is literally manna from heaven (In fact it is so good they sell it now in jars at Food Markets under the

Brand Name: "Vincent's Tomato Sauce"). Now when I said spicy, I really mean spicy. In fact, as soon as the waiter takes your order and you are having shrimp or mussels, he must know the intensity of the spiciness you want. There is mild, medium and hot. Only order hot if you are superhuman! Jack Kelly ordered it once and asked me to taste it and I never forgot it! Boy was it hot!

In around 1971, another person joined our Methods Team. His name was Tim Gaffigan and believe it or not, he was taller than me. Up to this time, everyone had to look up to me to make eye contact, now I had to look up to him. All kidding aside, Tim and I hit it off immediately. It was absolutely refreshing finding an individual with all the same philosophies and attitudes about the world that I had. We became friends instantly. Tim's only problem with my likes and dislikes was food. We didn't gravitate to the same foods, but that was Ok because I was very flexible in that regard. I also liked meat and potatoes, so to speak, so there was no problem there. With time, Tim and I became the dynamic duo of performance improvements in terms of methods analysis and were assigned to a number of jobs together as a team and produced some very fine outcomes if I say so myself. We were receiving letters of praise from most of the offices we visited, where we helped them improve their operations impressively. We both got a promotion for our work which made us very happy. In our personal lives, we were able to visit each other at our homes and Tim met my wife Ann and I met his wife Helen and then meeting the children, who were then introduced to each other, and this is interesting, he had four sons and I had four daughters and one son. They got along fabulously. I couldn't believe it. They were out there playing with a football and my girls and son loved it. We got together quite often. We became fast friends. Thank you Tim and family for being our friends.

But the corporation was changing. It needed a Statistical Department. Crum & Forster hired a Statistical Analyst Manager and assigned him to me to review all of the company's structure and help him organize a new department. His name was George Muriello and we worked so well together that when he formed his department he asked me to join him and become a Statistical Analyst. I said yes even though I didn't know what the job entailed. Now 'he' taught me.... Everything I know about the insurance world of statistics I owe to him. There was only one regret I had joining George in his quest and that was having to leave Tim in the Methods Department. But that is life, it's constantly changing. It did not affect our friendship though. His close location in the office allowed me to at least greet him every day. So we continued our work and I soon became intensely involved with the creation of a new department. From two of us (George and I) the department grew to 33 employees. It did not happen overnight, it took years, but the department became a vital function of the Actuarial Department. In an Insurance company, the Actuarial Department is one of the most important operations of that business, obviously because it determines all the rates (or cost of product) used to sell its insurance policy's. So, I like to think we were number two in the level of importance in the company, but alas we were not, the second most important function in our company was Underwriting, then in the order of things was Claims, followed by Investments. I'm afraid we were fifth or sixth in importance, but we were important; there is no doubt about that. What's interesting is that George and I became very good friends also, even away from work. He met my wife Ann and I met his wife Vi and we had many good social times together. I believe in 1975, George hired a person called Steve Cernek who held a prior position in a State Statistical Bureau. These bureaus collected our statistical reports and monitored all of the insurance company's activities in the state. When Steve joined our Statistical Department, many things changed for the better. We became a closer cohesive team to begin with. Steve answered every question we had concerning statistics that we came up with from that moment on. I learned a lot from Steve and we became very good friends too. Both our wife's name was Ann, we laughed at that. We went everywhere together, George and Vi, Steve and Ann and the both of us. We enjoyed each others company tremendously. Most of the time we were talking about our children, you know, how they were progressing and all that accompanying information. It was good to have other parents dialoging about their difficulties and successes and learning about other approaches to the same subject. It helped a lot. Thank you George and family and Steve and family for being my friends.

The Crum and Forster Insurance Company was the most important endeavor of my life. Never had I devoted so much time and effort in any other enterprise in my life. I was a member of this organization for 25 years (Oops, I believe I said that before) and proud of it. It was where I was introduced to the Personal Computer in the 1970's and where I received my recognition for the innovative and inspiring work of my life. In the 1980's Crum & Forster merged into The Xerox Company and although our new owners were in a different field, the C&F remained relatively stable in the field of insurance. Actually it advanced a bit during that tenure. But in the 1990's, Xerox decided to change the name of C&F to Talegen, then began selling Crum and Forster sections to the highest bidder, piece by piece, so the whole company does not exist anymore. Good-bye Crum and Forster Insurance Company, I have many fond memories of you stored in my mind. Especially all the associates I worked with and then became friends with, like Richard (Mickey) Gray and Joe Lee, Mary Travers and Flo (Abhrams) Federico, Rosina Wiedman, Jean Immerso and last but not least Tony Pawlowicz , friends who have remained close even though distance and circumstance have made it difficult to be together as friends. These friendships I made in the company, so thank you C&F for all the opportunities you provided. It shall not be forgotten.

Jumping ahead a little to complete the C&F story, on July 10, 1993, I retired from the Crum and Forster Insurance Company. I was 63 years old. At that time the Headquarters was at Industrial Park in Morris Plains on Sylvan Way. It was a little strange for me going to this office, because I practically spent most of my time at the Basking Ridge Office. I had accrued over 25 years of service and was ready to relax a bit. The first thing they asked me was what did I want as a service gift? They showed me a pamphlet with many choices, but when I came to the page that pictured a Grandfather Clock, there was nothing more appealing to me than that. So I chose the Grandfather Clock (Which stands in my living room to this day). What made it so important to me is that no one, to my knowledge, in the Petti family, owns a Grandfather Clock. I'm the first! When you open the door to the clock, there is a plaque that reads; AUGUSTUS L. PETTI…25 YEARS SERVICE 1993. How one can put the meaning of twenty-five years of service in a few words borders on Shakespearian phrasing imagery. Every time I pull the clock weight up to wind it (Yes, it's mechanical), I read the inscription and I think back in a flash, of all the experiences I lived through during my service. Sometimes it's overwhelming...but they are all great memories. Thank you Crum & Forster!

FRANCES AND TOM WED. Of course we received our invitations a couple of months ago and we have been preparing for this special occasion and now it has arrived. The date is September 22, 1973. This is the day our niece Frances Sue Passero is going to marry Thomas Vincent Ackerly at St. Anne's Church, Brentwood, NY. The wedding was wonderful and the bride was beautiful, walking down the aisle to be married. It was a wonderful wedding ceremony with Uncle Tony giving the bride away and Auntie Rose in her radiant gown. The music during the wedding and the joyous day just made it a magical moment and there was more to come. A Reception at the Westbury Manor in Westbury, NY was expecting us right after the wedding to celebrate this joyful union. We enjoyed it very much. CONGRATULATIONS FRANCES AND TOM!

L-LUCILLE MARRIES SCOTTY. We were preparing for this wedding for a whole year and now it has arrived. Lucille Ann Petti is going to marry James (Scotty) Carnegie at St. Virgil's Church on October 14, 1973. They met in high school. The wedding went without a hitch. The reception was at The Manor, in Orange, NJ. Everyone enjoyed themselves. Now we have a married daughter. Things will certainly be different now.

IRENE & BOB MOVE. During a phone call that Irene had made to mom, she told her that they had sold their Williston Park, NY, home and are moving to Greenlawn, NY. This was a surprise for us because Irene was pregnant, but Irene explained the circumstances and we felt it would go well. We wished them good fortune. They actually moved to their new home on November 8, 1973.

1974

ANDREW PETER MASCOLA BORN. It was spring when Bob called us to announce the birth of baby Andrew. The date was April 17, 1974 and he was born in Greenlawn NY. Bob sounded very happy on the phone as he described the scene. Of course we had to ask the traditional question, "Is the baby healthy" and a clear "Yes" was answered by Bob. I don't know why we keep asking that same question all the time (traditionally, it probably was used so often in the past, when the good health of babies was not that prevalent). Bob also assured us that Irene was doing well too. We were very happy to hear the good news. We congratulated them. HAPPY BIRTHDAY ANDREW!

ANN STARTS NEW JOB. Although mom was working at Morristown Memorial Hospital, part-time, it was Mrs. Tukel (Susan's best friend, Nacy's mother) who suggested that mom enter the full-time work force, I agreed. Mrs. Tuckel knew of an opening at the Morris County Mosquito Commission and encouraged mom to apply for the position of Secretary that was available. An interview was set up and mom got the job. Little did mom know that it was also a career altering change. This job would last for the next 20 years! In time, mom became the Office Supervisor and a Notary Public to boot. It was exciting for mom. The work was very interesting and challenging, even though workers at the Commission were referred to as Squita-beaters, a nickname obviously referring to their task of exterminating mosquitoes in the County. After all someone has to do it! Thank you Mrs. Tukel, mom will never forget that kindness.

S-SUSAN GRADUATES HIGH SCHOOL. You could not believe how happy Susan was when she graduated High School. She was bubbling all over the place. She looked beautiful in her new graduation dress. Her cap and gown were lying on the bed, ready to be worn. She was graduating from Morristown High School, NJ. The date was June 4, 1974, she was 18 years old. She was so excited. We wanted to know how to locate her at the graduation, so we asked where she was sitting in the auditorium, so we could sit close-by. We took lots of photos. I believe we have photos of her in every important action she made all during the ceremony. We were so proud of her! It's our second daughter's graduation and she wanted to go to College. Isn't that wonderful! CONGRATULATIONS SUSAN! We Love You...

1975

J-JOSEPH GRADUATES 8TH GRADE. When we moved to Morris Plains, Joseph continued elementary school in St. Virgil's Catholic School where Christine and Michele were attending. In grade 5, Joseph transferred to public school. He continued at Borough School which was the elementary school in Morris Plains until his graduation. On February 8, 1975, Joseph graduated from Borough School. We had our customary celebration at home with all the relatives. His grandma and Grandpa Petti attended, along with his Uncle Tony and Auntie Rose along with all the cousins. His Aunt Joann and Uncle Vinny were there with Peter and Joseph, his cousins on the Petti side. There was a very large crowd gathering to congratulate our son. He told us that he wanted to continue at Morristown High School. But only stayed for two years then transferred to Vo-Tech and began his Trade studies. It was very clear to us that he wanted to work with his hands, so he would be perusing a different path than the girls. We were very proud of him. And so it went...

IRENE & BOB MOVE TO PITTSTOWN. On May 16, 1975, Irene and Bob, along with the two boys, moved to their new home in Pittstown, NJ. It was a beautiful home among the trees, in a rural area of our state, where they would remain to the present. Both Bobbie and Andrew were practically raised there. We visited them a number of times and you kids must remember the swimming pool that Bob and Irene provided for our swimming pleasure. It was great!

1976

C-CHRISTINE - DRIVER'S LICENSE. I'm almost sure it was the day after her birthday that Christine applied for her temporary driver's license. That would have been November 14, 1976, at 17 years of age. Only a parent knows how anticipated an event of this magnitude is for a growing daughter. Because Bayley Ellard did not have a class for Driver's Ed, Christine asked me to teach her how to drive. Although this took many weekends, it was fun. I don't know how many times we drove to the Modell Sports Store driving around the parking field and past the FMC Store's (Father, Mother, Child) parking area and through the Greystone Hospital grounds, but it became quit familiar in time. Near the end of your driving period, I explained that I felt it important to learn how to change a tire also. Of course you thought this strange (reasoning; what does this have to do with driving skills) and rightly so. But because I was a parent, I don't know why I kept imagining you on a road with a flat tire. I did not want you to be at the mercy of others. So we went through the drill, boy was it hard work. Getting the heavy tire out of the car was the hardest. Then handling the scissor jack was next. I was proud you were able to perform all those tasks well (even though you didn't need this information for the test). Your driving skills were great and I had nothing to add, except to say, "Never try to read another driver's mind and anticipate what they are going to do next - always be defensive when you drive". I'm not sure if you were even listening to me at the time, you were so focused on driving the car, that I believe I was relegated to background noise in that instance, but I'm happy to say, that inattention changed once you got your license. You were issued a license on the first testing. Mom and I were so proud of you. Your first car was a Chevrolet, Belvedere I believe. Now we had four cars in our driveway (it would have been five-but Lucille was living in Morristown). Congratulations Christine!

1977

THE TUTANKHAMUN EXHIBIT. I was waiting all year for this event! The first announcement of Egypt's plan to release certain objects found in the Tomb of Tutankhamun in 1922, by the English Egyptologist Howard Carter, overwhelmed me. Being an amateur Egyptologist myself I could not wait for this exhibit to arrive in New York City. Of course I secured tickets for the exhibition (way in advance) and was surprised to learn how many of my family members and friends wanted to be included. If my memory serves me right, we were about 14 people converging on this marvelous place, to actually see objects, with our own eyes, that were fabricated for a Pharaoh more than three thousand years before the birth of Christ. It was so exciting, just talking about it now gives me goose bumps. The location of the exhibit was the Metropolitan Museum of Art in New York City (80th St. and Fifth Ave.). Our visit was scheduled by the staff of the Museum (each touring party had to be assigned a day and a time to visit), as a means of keeping the masses from hogging the viewings. It worked out well, but it put intense pressure on the touring group. Try to synchronize the activities of 14 individuals to be in one place at one time could become a headache, but as I recall all went well except for the parking of the cars. I remember some of the drivers to our cars got to the ticket window just in time (that means they had to run to get there to make the deadline). But they did it and I was proud of them! They all knew how much this meant to me and were not about to disappoint me. After arriving, we immediately proceeded to the rooms that contained the exhibits. When we entered the first room, there standing about five feet off the ground, in a glass case, was the Golden Mask of Tutankhamun a sculpture in pure 3/8" gold, wrought by artisan hands in ancient times (being viewed by me-at this moment), it was perfect! What beauty! What detail! What luster! The praising descriptions go on and on. But its real value I believe lies in the shape of the metal. For there, rendered to last for eternity, is the likeness of a living Pharaoh, Tutankhamun (the "thrill" was all consuming for me at that moment). I will never forget the joy at seeing all the objects, that up now, I only read about in the many volumes of books I digested over the years. And now I am actually seeing them. It's too much! I was becoming weak with happiness. But I would make it through. I've been saving up the strength all year. I've got to make it. And I did. It will stay with me forever. Thank you Howard Carter for the grueling work you did to find it and preserve it. Your efforts did not go in vain. I must also thank Lord Carnavan for providing the finances needed to afford the greatest Egyptian find of all time (It is the 'only' Egyptian Tomb that contained over 5,000 articles). We also want to thank you Egypt for sharing your priceless treasure with us. We are truly grateful.

It was an experience that will remain with us forever…

There was so much more to describe about the exhibit that I probably could write another book explaining all the wonders that were before us. Because this was an exclusive showing, with some of the major findings in the tomb of the boy Pharaoh Tutankhamun and all of the objects were his personal belongings, which made it an extra special occasion. We must have spent over two hours marveling over the displays. I wasn't aware of this at the time, but it seems a bit of my enthusiasm spilled over to some of my son-in-laws who were in attendance (My daughters were all aware of my interest). I was told about this later and it pleased me a great deal. Obviously, they began to see the value of such objects, as I had a long time ago. There were 60 objects in that exhibit, including the three sarcophagi or coffins, one of them (The one they found his mummy in) was made out of ¼" plate, solid pure gold!

C-CHRISTINE GRADUATES HIGH SCHOOL. Christine was so excited about her graduation. She was preparing for the occasion days and days before time. The year was 1977. It was a beautiful ceremony. When we witnessed Christine, in cap and gown, walking on stage to receive her certificate, we couldn't help holding back the tears of joy. Unfortunately her grandmother and grandfather were on a three month sojourn in Italy, visiting all of the relatives both in Lucera and Celenza, and could not attend. But Joseph who was 16 years old and Michele at 11 years old were there and enjoyed the proceedings quit a lot. When we got home, we had a house full. Not only were all our relatives there, but we also had our neighbors who were our friends, there too. We had lots of food, drink and good cheer to help celebrate this wonderful accomplishment. Her numerous relatives showered her with many gifts. CONGRATULATIONS CHRISTINE!

ANN AND I TRAVEL TO ITALY. The year 1977 was a marvelous year! I didn't think I could experience anything more exhilarating than the "Exhibit of a Pharaoh", or the graduation of a daughter, but I was wrong! When the month of August rolled around, a phone call was made to us from my mother and father, who were spending three months in Italy, visiting all the relatives, asking us if we could go to be with the family for a week. It would be an all expenses paid trip. How could we have refused? What I didn't anticipate when we said "YES", was all the logistics necessary to even be able to leave the house! First and foremost were the children (who by the way, were growing up and did not appreciate me calling them "children"), where and how would they be cared for? Secondly, do we have the clothes for such a trip? Do we have luggage? What about Passports? We had a lot of catching up to do. Could we make it in time? Too many questions, maybe we should have said "no". This was the year I was told by the US government that I was not a citizen of this country. Let me explain, I went to apply for my passport, the Immigration Department informed me that they could not issue a passport to me because of my citizenship status. But, I said to them, "I served four years in the US Air Force during the Korean War, doesn't that count for something?" They opened up a book called, The "US Code", and pointed to Chapter 368 which states, "Any person born on a ship that is flying the flag of a foreign country is a citizen of that country.", which makes me an alien. Well, "What can I do now?" I asked the Immigration officer? He said you have to become a citizen (If you want an American Passport), before he can issue me a passport. Mom's application was okay, she was born in Brooklyn (Lucky her!). But I had to begin the Naturalization process, and in all fairness, it went extremely smooth. What helped was my father had become a citizen around 1935 and had his Naturalization Paper, so all they had to do was to include me as a son, which automatically makes me a citizen. But I had to take a test (which I aced -thanks to my schooling) and had to present myself in front of a Federal Judge, to swear my allegiance to the US. I'll never forget that moment, while I was reciting the Oath of Allegiance to the United States of America, tears came to my eyes, I became so emotional at that moment because I was promising to uphold all the truths of this Great Nation and swearing to give up my life, if need be, to protect it against all enemies wanting to destroy it. This is an oath that I believe every American should recite in front of a Federal Judge (One of my many dreams). Then maybe, American citizens, who were blessed by being born here, would appreciate what being a citizen of the United States of America really means. As you can see, I am very proud of being an American!

After becoming a citizen, I quickly received the passport I needed. We were ready. Now we can go to Italy. What excitement, after all, I had never visited my relatives over all this time (about 47 years), my uncle Michelino Petti would be there, and my two Aunt's, Zia Liccia and Zia Anna never saw me (This is on the Petti side) and then there were all my cousins. On the Bucco side, we had met my Uncle Lorenzo and my Aunt Raffaella who came to the US and lived here for about five years, but I hadn't met his children Tommaso and Lucietta and her children. Meeting my, never seen relatives, became a fever. Even mom was reminded that she had an aunt and cousins close to the town of Casserta in Italy, not a long distance from where we were going. So there were a lot of relatives we were going to meet; this was going to be great!

This was our plan for the wellbeing of the children. Susan was 21 years old and working at Acme Supermarket and engaged to Bill Lauter and could stay alone at the house. Christine was 18 years old and preparing for college and worked a part-time job somewhere in town during this summer and would be able to stay home comfortably. They were both adults. My sister Joann and my brother-in-law Vinny both agreed to take care of Joseph, who was really eager to stay with them since they had Peter and Joseph enjoying their school vacation at New Hyde Park, LI, NY. We are convinced, these three cousins bonded during that stay. When we spread the news among family members that we were looking for someone to take care of Michele, we never expected the results. Everyone wanted Michele, but Irene and Bob won out, their plea was the strongest and besides they had this great big pool that was going to waste (not really). Now that we had arranged for the children's safety and caring, we were ready to go.

Our Itinerary was pretty simple. We would leave JFK and land in Rome (the closest airport in Italy to our relatives). Since this would have been our first time in Rome, my parents suggested we remain there for three days, touring. They wanted us to see the Pope and the Vatican, so we stayed in an American-Italian Hotel near the Piazza Naverone. I had each day precisely planned (step by step). The first day we would visit the Vatican and try to arrange an audience with the Pope, but he was away in his vacation villa. We visited the Vatican on our own, which was a mistake (we should have taken a tour), because although what we saw was breathtakingly beautiful, at every object, we kept saying to ourselves; "I wonder what I'm looking at?" It was frustrating to say the least, but we got through it. In fact our ignorance actually worked to our advantage when it came to climbing up the steps in the Rotunda or Dome of the Church of St. Peter. If we knew how many steps and the constriction of space that must be negotiated to reach the top, we probably would never have attempted it. But we were happy we did it and my reaching the top was rewarded with the best photograph I ever took during that whole experience (It's also the Background screen on my PC Desktop view) It definitely had Post Card qualities. Take a look at it, it's in the 1977 Photo Album of our Italy Trip. The Album is on the shelf in the clothes closet near the front door. It's the first photo displayed and I'm sure you will agree that it is a fine shot, even though I am not a professional photographer. From the top of St. Peters we then went to the bottom of the Church. Let me explain, when we came down from the Dome, we needed to have lunch so I asked two kind Nuns if there was a restaurant close by. One of them smiled and said why don't you eat in the Church's Cafeteria downstairs. Mom and I were notably astonished to hear that suggestion, so I replied naively, "Is there a Cafeteria in the Church?", "Yes they said and it's wonderful." We instantly decided to go. They pointed to the stairway that went downstairs; we thanked them more than once and quickly began our descent. There to our amazement, below this magnificent church, is an extraordinary Americanish style cafeteria! We could not believe it. But there it was! We each took a tray and began our journey, pushing the tray along the rails and surveying all the wonderful food before us. Mom said to me, "Gus, why don't you go first to help me identify the different foods, so I know what to get". I said, "Sure, no problem" and began describing the various preparations being offered. Some of them even puzzled me; I had to ask the attendant what the item was, speaking in Italian. We got past that phase with flying colors, but when we got to an empty table, we realized we forgot the drinks, so I volunteered to get them. "I want a cola" said mom. I left and headed toward what appeared to me as the soda fountain. I took two paper cups and headed for the spouts, but before I could reach them a little boy, I guess 11 years old, jumped in front of me and reached the spout first and poured out one full container of the liquid. It didn't look like soda to me (no bubbles) so I asked the boy, what was it, speaking n Italian, "Che e questo" (What is that?) I inquired, he turns to me in surprise and says, "E vino, che ti credo?" (It's wine, what did you think it was?) I was flabbergasted! This is absolutely Un-American! Not only is wine not sold in our cafeterias, but it is against the law to sell it to a child in our Country. And here it is, in a free flowing spout, available to everyone, without limit! And in a Church to boot! There were so many incongruities striking my brain at one time, I believe I lost conciseness for a second, but as soon as I recovered, I senselessly said in Italian to the boy, "Va bene!" (Great!). What an experience! I have to tell mom immediately. So I quickly went to our table and told mom the story. She listened, chuckled at the outcome then asked, "Where are the drinks?" In my haste to describe the happening, I forgot to get the drinks, so I had to go back. But I will never forget that experience, which could have only happened in Italy. I still cant' believe it, a little boy, drinking unlimited wine in a church. It baffles the American mind! But that was Italy… We continued to the Vatican Gardens after lunch and finally to the Sistine Chapel where we viewed in awe the ceiling of Michelangelo, with all that splendor and overwhelming impact of artistic creativity. There is no art like it in the world! After visiting the Sistine Chapel, we went to the Vatican Museum where we saw so many magnificent objects that they are a blur in my memory, there were so many! What beauty, what craftsmanship, what treasures, what art, what uniqueness…it was all unbelievable! Jewels, gold, silver…We were very fortunate to have seen and experienced Vatican City and all its treasures. Thank you Lord for the gift…

On the second day, our Itinerary listed a walk, to as many famous Piazzas that could be reached by foot. So we started at the closest one, which was Piazza Naverone. In this Piazza are four fountains with statues carved by Bernini that represent the four seasons. They are magnificent, with the water shooting into the air and dropping on all the statuary as if to say, you are being refreshed repeatedly so you can display your imaginative engagement constantly. The artist was influenced at that time with depictions of Roman gods that for them were responsible for the seasons, therefore when you see those forms that make up the fountains; it may be puzzling and require some explanation. We also tried to get from place to place by utilizing the Italian Bus System. This was no easy feat. It seems, when you travel abroad, everything is different. Our first mistake was entering the bus at the front end (you must enter via the rear). The bus was over crowded; everyone was squeezed against one another. The next boo-boo I made was talking to the driver. Not seeing a device to collect money for the ride, I became desperate, I needed information. So I went over to the driver and said in Italian; "Where do we pay?" He did not answer me nor acknowledge my presence at all, but while he was driving he pointed to a large sign overhead that read, in very large letters, in Italian, "Do not speak to the driver at any time!" Oh, oh, I was in trouble. I went over to where mom was standing and began explaining the dilemma when a very young man stepped over to us and said in English, "I overheard you talking and you must pay for the fare in the rear of the bus.", "Thank you I said" and at the next stop, I ran from the front of the bus to the rear to pay for us both (Remember, the bus was so crowded I couldn't get through). When I got there, I was looking for a coin machine, but there wasn't any. I looked around and saw a man sitting in a bench seat with a wooden contraption on his lap. It was a money holder, with about five concave depressions containing coins. I approached him and said in Italian, "How much for the fare?" He said, "Five Lira's, per person". I immediately opened my wallet and looked inside. I only had a L.10,000 bill. I took it out and wanted to give it to him when he immediately put up his hand, in a stop gesture and said in Italian, "What do you expect me to do with that, I have no change for such a large bill?" I said embarrassingly, "That's all I have" At that moment he made an unmistakable gesture, that signified, "Go ahead" then said, "Va tine, passe franco" (Go ahead, you can go free). That was very nice of him. I thanked him and proceeded to tell mom the whole story. She also thought that was very nice of him. We were on our way to the Spanish Steps (Piazza di Spagna), another very popular tourist attraction. By this time of the year, the steps were decorated with beautiful yellow flowers, planted in the center; going all the way up to the Church it was quit a sight. At the bottom of the steps was a famous street (Via del Corso) that contained many shops for the travelers to wander through. We did not hesitate to take advantage of this opportunity and even though our budget was limited, we found things affordable and still enjoy to this day. This street leads you to another Piazza called the Piazza Venezia and then to the Piazzo del Popolo. And then on to the Piazza della Rotonda, where the Pantheon, that was built in 27 BC stands. After visiting the Pantheon we walked to the Piazza Navona again where Bernini's breathtaking sculptured fountains can be observed and appreciated in a more casual manner. They are magnificent! Then we went to the Piazza Colonna where the Trevi fountain awaits, the work of Niccolo Salvi and made famous in the movie, Three Coins in the Fountain. Now every visitor that visits Rome and wants to return to this spot, must throw three coins in the fountain. Mom and I tossed three Italian coins in the fountain and made a wish to return (it's only an old superstition-but its fun to do). When mom turned around and couldn't see what I was doing, I tossed an extra five coins in the fountain…in my mind that was a way to insure that we would return to Rome someday (And, believe it or not, in 2006, we did!). There are so many Piazzas' in Rome that I could go on and on. But at the end of the day, we ended up on a very famous street, Via Veneto, a tree lined, S shaped and very famous street of interest for visitors (Something like our Hollywood and Vine Streets), where we stopped at a sidewalk café and had an espresso and gelato and watched all the hurrying pedestrians go by, thoroughly enjoying that treat. It was exhilarating to say the least. It was getting dark so we headed for the hotel. We changed our clothing and reviewed our plans for dinner. On my Itinerary I listed a famous restaurant called Taverna Trilussa that was recommended in my tour guide. We hailed a taxi cab and gave him the restaurant's name, upon which he immediately responded, "It's closed for the whole month" We quickly learned that many merchants go on vacation during the month of August and close their businesses. We asked if he could suggest an open restaurant and without hesitation said I'll take you to a great restaurant that you will like very much and quickly sped away. The restaurant was called, Checchino and was a fine and elegant place. The restaurant even had a theatrical stage built into it. We didn't know it but we were in for a memorable evening. During our dinner, waiters and waitresses broke out in operatic song, singing some of the most famous arias in opera that we knew. I forgot to tell you that about one third of the clientele appeared to us to be Japanese tourists. They were all enjoying their meals, when one of the waiters went over to the microphone and announced a Japanese name and said that we were honored to have him here and he is from Japan. He is going to sing for us, "E lucevan le stelle" from Puccini's opera Tosca. This Japanese man stands up, in the middle of the restaurant and sings with an overwhelming powerful voice, in perfect Italian, one of the most beautiful renditions of the aria we have ever heard. He was a Tenor, with a voice that seemed five times larger than his body. Absolutely amazing! Mom and I will never forget that performance. It was one of our most surprising, emotional experiences that only happens once in a lifetime and without planning to boot. I must tell you about a funny thing that happened at that restaurant that night, when the waiter brought us the wine, mom wanted some ice with it and asked the waiter for some, the waiter looks at her and says, "Sorry Madame but we don't have any ice" Witnessing the disappointed look on mom's face after the announcement, he added, "but if you want, I can "scrape" the ice that forms on the pipes outside of the refrigerator for you". Upon which mom politely declined. When we left the restaurant, we burst into laughter at such a suggestion, Mom said, "Can you imagine that, he wanted to give me scrapped ice from the pipes" and laughed, then we both laughed hysterically. We had a wonderful time in Rome.

The next day and the last day of our stay in Rome, it rained heavy and according to my Itinerary we would be visiting the Villa d'Este, in the city of Tivoli, just 19 miles east of Rome. When I awoke, mom said to me, "Where are you going?" I said, "Getting dressed to visit the Villa d'Este." She said, "But it's raining cats and dogs, you can't be serious?" My reply was, "Ann, if we don't go now, in spite of the rain, I feel we will regret that decision for the rest of our lives". So she begrudgingly got up and began preparing for the trek. When we arrived at the Villa, the rain was coming down so hard, crashing to the ground with such force, it was creating a mist from the splashing water, and it was torrential. We were standing on the colonnade porch overlooking the beginning of the garden and all the sculptured fountains, we both looked at each other (as if to say, "are we crazy?"), smiled at each other, opened our umbrella and quickly descended the stairs out into the teeming rain and began admiring all that fabulous art! We are the only ones that descended the stairs, the other tourists stayed under the protection of the roof over the porch, but we went to every statue (And there are over a 1,000 of them!). It was an experience we will never forget and we both got soaking wet. All of our clothing was soaking wet. We were embarrassed to get on the tour bus to return to our hotel. We wet the seats, but we were happy. To this day, we congratulate each other for undergoing that little inconvenience and being courageous enough to witness such an outstanding artistic achievement. I'm sure we will never get that opportunity again. Here is what we saw. Historically the period was 1549, when Cardinal Ippolito d'Este asked Pirro Ligorio to construct a magnificent garden for him filled with stone carvings but functioning as fountains. Because there was a natural lake close by (Lago S. Giovanni) and about 300 feet above the level of the garden, with clay pipes, it was feasible. The flow of water would be perpetual; as long as the lake existed, water would be available for the fountains. Some of those fountains, depending on their structure, sent the water into the air, practically reaching 300 foot heights. It was spectacular! Over 1,000 fountains were constructed there by over 400 artisans, coming from all the known countries at the time. They were housed, fed and paid, while they labored to create this exclusive, one place in the world, work of art and function. It was breathtaking. Ask mom! It should be noted, that the Most Reverend Cardinal d'Este was independently wealthy in his own rights and did not use church money to finance this dream Villa. It is one of those very interesting facts in history that deserves more inquiry and research to understand. But there is no doubt that it is there and is available to the public for viewing at any time. What a gift!

OUR FIRST "HUGS" WITH FAMILY IN ITALY. Now it was time to visit our loved ones in Foggia. It took about five hours to reach the town of Foggia by train from Rome. Although our family lived in Lucera and Celenza Valfortore, this was the closest train station to those locations. And there, on the station platform, was ALL my family (the Petti's that is), my ants, my uncle, their children and all the In-Laws, including my mother and father. It was great seeing my parents again. You can not believe how emotional I got when I began hugging and kissing my Aunt Liccia (this was my first meeting with your Grandpa Petti's sister) and her husband Amedeo Pesce, and their children who were Gioachinno and Anna. Then there was Zia Anna with her husband Angelo and their children, Tonino, Rita and Pinna. Behind my aunt were standing my Uncle Gianbattiste and Raffaella, his wife and their children, Pierino and Michelino. The happy tears just flowed down my eyes as I embraced them and stood there in amazement, trying to bring reality to the picture, but the emotions just wouldn't allow it. Mom and I were so happy to meet them, I will never forget those moments! And then the dialogue! Oh, Mamma Mia, the dialogue! The dialogue was unending and all in Italian. We were asked first about our health, then about the travel, then about our kids, then about our impressions of Italy and on, and on, and on. Everyone was smiling…it was a very happy time! There were four "macchinas" (my relative's automobiles) waiting to carry our luggage and take us to Lucera, where most of them lived. Our Bucco family could not be there because of the distance, about another 30 miles away, but we will see them in a day or so. My mother and father were so happy we were able to visit and meet our family in Italy for the first time! It was the main purpose for the visit. Now we could actually see the dear ones my mother and father talked about as I grew up. I can put faces to the names they mentioned, while telling us stories of times gone by. It was so exciting; it's very hard to describe the many emotions that I was feeling at the time. But it was all good and it made me happy! Thank you mother, thank you father for this precious gift you decided to give us. We will never forget your generosity and your unselfish wish to have us travel, to be with our Italian Family. It is too precious for words…

After a few days in Lucera and many phone calls from the Buccos, who were asking when we were planning to come and see them, we were brought to Celenza to visit my Uncle Lorenzo and my Aunt Raffaella (whom we met in the U.S. where they lived for five years prior) but meet, for the first time, their children, Lucietta, Concetta and Tommaso. Lucietta was married to Tonino (nickname) and had two children of their own and so was Concetta, married to Francesco, with three children of their own. Tommaso was single. We were so happy to meet them. This is the town, up in the mountains that my mother and father were born in and grew up in. They knew this town very well. They took us on a tour almost immediately, to show us where they lived and where they stayed after they got married. I took photos of all the places. They were very proud of their beginnings and were very happy with their life as it unfolded. You could see it in their cheerful expressions, as they described all the places of importance in their lives. "There is my house", my mother would point and there is where your father's family Wine Tavern was (a house replaced it now) and there is where we first lived when we were married, pointing to a second story apartment location as we walked along the hilly and narrow streets. It was wonderful. Your mom and I got a big kick out of this. We stayed with them about three days at which time we were invited to have a 'Feast of Family Acquaintance Dinner' at a restaurant in another close town, so that we could all be together, before we part. It was at a nearby restaurant in another town, but in the mountains. The restaurant was called "La Fontanna dei Pisserelli", sometimes Italians are outrageously comical, it translates to "The fountain of little boys peeing" mainly because it had this very long, tank like stone fountain, with many spouts, all in a row, flowing water constantly. It was in my opinion, a childish feature of the restaurant, deserving some hilarious laughter and all sorts of comments, encouraging more laughter and so it went, until we were ushered into this large room and seated for a memorable dinner with all our relatives in Celenza, my uncles, my aunts, all their children and their children and so on.

Here are those who attended:

My Mother
My Father

Ann (My Wife)
Augusto (Me)

My Uncle Lorenzo Bucco (My mother's brother)
My Aunt Raffaella Bucco (and Thomas' mother)

Concetta (Bucco) Di Iorio (Thomas' sister)

Francesco Di Iorio (Concetta's husband)
Gianfranco Di Iorio (18 years old)
Carlo Di Iorio (16 years old)
Rosanna Di Iorio (9 years old)

Lucietta (Bucco) Carrozza (Thomas' sister)
Gaetano Carrozza (Lucietta's husband)
Maria Grazia Carrozza (15 years old)
Rosario Carrozza (9 years old)

Tommaso Bucco (Thomas)

Also in attendance was our paisano Michael Di Vitto (Our wedding photographer, remember!) and his wife, Ann Di Vitto who were visiting from the U.S. as we were What a coincidence and we all feasted together because it was not a supper, but a feast of food, drink and good times. We had so many laughs together, patting each other on the backs as Italians do and hugging every chance we could find. This was our bonding method, the process that brings us closer and the way that we accept one another. It was a great feast! We all enjoyed ourselves immensely. Thank you all!

After this memorable feast in Celenza Valfortore, we were driven back by car to Lucera to spend our remaining days there. The departure was a little sad when we left Celenza, (we had to say good-bye to all of them) but the happiness of meeting and being with the Bucco family and their descendants, for those few days more than helped replace those feelings of leaving loved ones. Then we left..."good-bye everyone", waiving to each one with tears in our eyes, the macchina moves away and we loose sight of them. What made this parting so sad and I guess all partings somewhat painful, are that you have no way of knowing if you will ever see them again. As destiny would have it, many of my relatives that were there on that day passed away before we were able to visit again in 2006, so we never saw them again. That's the main reality and the apparent sadness that seems to be in the back of your mind when you are saying goodbye.

Now that we have arrived in Lucera, we are hearing a lot of buzz but it is being kept from us. We hear our aunts and uncles discussing things, but as soon as we appear they become silent. So we know they are planning something that they want to surprise us with. "What could it be?" I questioned mom. She had no idea. Then on the day it was to occur, we both were asked to escort them to their places of business. We stopped first at Uncle Angelo's Department Store. He led us to the entrance door and pointed to a large sign that read in Italian,

Negozio Chiuso Per Celebrazione Di Anna e' Augusto	Translation =>	Store Closed To Celebrate Our Ann and Gus

When we read the sign, we both started to cry uncontrollably, my uncle patted me on the back and said, "Don't cry, this is a happy day!" "That's why I'm crying". I said, "We are so happy that you honor us this way" "That you would close your business for us is far more than we deserve" I said. He answered, saying, "Not so, we have great admiration for the two of you, and this is how we show it". "Thank you Uncle Angelo" we both responded. Then we got back into the car and sped off to another shop a few blocks away. We stopped and Uncle Angelo led us to another large store which had the commercial sign hanging that read, Tabacchi which means Tobacco Shop, but in the front windows, on display were shelves and shelves of jewelry, so I was a little puzzled (Uncle Amedeo explained it all to me later). But when my Uncle Amedeo pointed to the Store Closed sign, the crying started again. We couldn't believe that the two shops would close to celebrate our reunion. It wasn't over yet. We were again ushered to the car and driven to another street, the car stopped at a "Sports Shop" featuring hunting gear including shot guns and rifles for hunting. We were led to the door where another sign was hanging that read, "Negozio Chiuso per Festa di Anna e' Augusto". Ann and I could not hold back the tears, and this time with our dear Cousin Gioacchino at our side, who owns the shop, trying to console us at our joy for such a wonderful gesture. It was an unbelievable experience and it wasn't over yet. We then drove to another shop which had a commercial sign that read, "Vin di Petti" (Naturally I was proud to see our family name displayed); this was a beverage business that our Cousin Pierino owned. He also closed his business for us. We could not believe the admiration they had for us. Can you imagine four major businesses closed, resulting from our visit! I don't think we were contributing to the welfare of the Italian economy at that moment. But it was "Festa" time and feast and dance we will! The next place we were brought to was this gigantic restaurant up in the hills, in a nearby mountainous town. The whole restaurant was reserved for the Petti families and all the relatives. It was immense. The first thing that happened was the opening of cases of Spumante (Italian Champagne) and glasses were being filled with the bubbly stuff. When all the glasses were full, my Uncle Gianbattisto (my father's brother) made a wonderful toast expressing his joy that not only was he happy that his brother visited everyone in Italy but that his son was able to visit also. It was a very emotional toast; of course we couldn't hold back the happy tears that were running down our faces as we drank that 'heavenly' tasting Spumante. After my uncle's toast, not to be outdone, all my other uncles had to toast my mother and father and us. That took over an hour, I estimated. And the effects of the Spumante were beginning to bring more cheer into the affair. Everyone was there, for the record let me enumerate;

My Mother
My Father

Ann (Your Mom)
Augusto (Me)

My Aunt Liccia (Petti) Pesce (My father's sister)
My Uncle Amedeo Pesce (Her husband)

Anna Pesce (24) (Their daughter)
Gioacchino Pesce (22) (Their son)

My Aunt Anna (Petti) Lusuriello (My father's sister)
My Uncle Angelo Lusuriello (Her husband)

Tonino Lusuriello (28) (Their son)
Adele Lusuriello (27) (His wife)
Angelo (6) (Their son)
Annarita (9) (Their daughter)

Rita (Lusuriello) De Mare ((Their daughter)
Luigi De Mare (Her husband)
Giovanni (3) (Their son)
Rosella (1) (Their daughter)
Josepina Lusuriello (13) (Their daughter)

My Uncle Gianbattisto Petti (My father's brother)
My Aunt Raffaella Petti (His wife)

Michele Petti (Their son)
Antonietta Petti (His wife)
Gianluiggi (14) (Their son)
Lello (Raffaelo) (9) (Their son)

Pietro Petti (Their son)
Nunzia Petti (His wife)
Giovanni (10) (Their son)
Massimo (7) (Their son)

If my count is correct, we were about 29 family members, all happy, all enjoying each other's company and with all those children it was quit a joyful moment in time. Don't ask me why but when we sat down to dinner, for some reason I made notes of the food that was being served. Maybe I wanted to record it to keep the facts accurate some time in the future, when the subject would come up for discussion again, or because I thought it was so fabulous…I don't know the exact reason but I did, it was August 24, 1977, a Wednesday evening and here is what was served to us in large portions; Antipasto which was Honeydew melon sliced and wrapped in Prosciutto and Salami. Second course was Strochiatelli (hand-made, long pasta-made with unused guitar strings) served with red tomato sauce, very delicious. Third course was, Broiled

Lamb Chops with French Fried Potatoes (Yes they make them in Italy-a little American twist here). Fourth course was a Fresh Tomato Salad with Extra Virgin Olive Oil, Garlic and sliced Red Onion. Fifth course was Braciola (rolled thin steaks with wild mushroom stuffing) in Red Sauce. Sixth course was Pizza Margherita with sliced fresh Tomatoes and Provolone, shaved on top. Seventh course was a bowl of Fresh Fruit including Grapes and Chocolate covered Pears served separately. The eighth and final course was the one that got to us emotionally the most. Before they revealed this magnificent surprise, we were first brought Espresso with bottles of Ammereto being passed around, then the Champagne glasses were filled to the brim with Spumante, then everyone began singing their Italian rendition of "For He's a Jolly Good Fellow" or something like that and in comes Gioacchino carrying this great big aluminum box to our table and asked Ann and I to open it. We did, and inside was this beautiful sheet cake with the inscription, "WELCOME ANNA AND AUGUSTO" in perfect English! Ann and I burst into tears; we were so overcome by the magnanimous gesture that I believe we cried for over fifteen minutes. We could not stop. We did not expect that! We were overwhelmed. All of our family members patted us on the back and kept saying, "Don't cry", but we couldn't stop. It was so moving. Another reason we were so moved was that the cake was made American style and had two layers, one filled with chocolate custard and the other with vanilla custard, and frosted with whipped cream, absolutely delicious! We spent the rest of the dinner thanking each, one by one! Kissing them and hugging them, our joy was overwhelming. It was one of the most wonderful dinners spent with our relatives ever! And it wasn't over yet...downstairs in the Night Club section of the restaurant was a dance floor and a Disco playing station which we were invited to. As we were leaving the table, we could hear the loud music coming from that direction, and as we approached we could see the flashing lights of the mirrored globe moving around as we entered. Another surprise! My family made me proud! There is no end to their surprises and I've got to be honest with you, it certainly helped increase our enjoyment that evening. Now everyone was dancing and all my aunts wanted to dance with me (I guess because I was always shy). mom was dancing with all my uncles. It was great! The music was typically modern but soon changed to traditional. Now came the customary Tarantella, when everyone participates. We made a big circle and while dancing, my father was the first to enter the center of the circle, along with my mother, to do his fancy steps, then they come out of the circle and my Uncle Batisto and his wife goes to the middle with their steps, and couple by couple, all the relatives did their thing in the center. The dancing was so exciting, I remember that scene the most, I guess it's because I was witnessing my loved ones enjoying themselves so much and because of Ann and myself being there. Those moments I will never forget. Thank you Family! We love you so very much! You have always been there for us. We treasure your generosity and love for us. You are all priceless to us, never forget that! Thank you so much for that wonderful evening, it was absolutely marvelous! Ann and I felt we knew you for all the time we have been apart…a remarkable transformation took place while we visited with you. Thank you for being our family!

We talked about that evening for the remaining days until we departed to return home. When the time came, we began dialoging about transportation and I suggested we return to Rome via the railway. My mother and father said why inconvenience yourselves that way when we have a paisano in Lucere that can take you right to the airport in a limousine for a reasonable price. We quickly opted for that mode of transportation, especially after seeing that spacious Mercedes Benz limo. We can travel in style and comfort, who wouldn't choose that? That was our decision, we are going by Limo. It was settled. The really difficult part was saying good-bye to the whole family. No matter how sad this is, it had to be done. So we began. First my Aunt Liccia and Uncle Amedeo, then my Cousin Anna and Gioacchino…it was very hard saying good-bye to them. "Tanti baci e abbracci" (Many kisses and hugs), we said over and over again, showering them with all the kisses we could muster, and we hugged them so tight, and we asked them to stay well, with tears coming down our faces. We dreaded that day when we had to part from our loved ones, but we had no choice. Next, we said good-bye to my Uncle Batisto and Aunt Raffaella, then Michelino and Antonietta, along with the children Gianluiggi and Lello. We then said good-bye to Pierino and Nunzia and the children, Giovanni and Massimo. We then said good-bye to all the Lusuriello's, the Pesce's and the De Mare's. We all love you and we will miss you all.

God bless you, each and every one. Good-bye Family! We got on the plane, then returned home to the U.S. We were now missing not being home with our children very much.

As soon as we arrived home, we immediately gathered all our children for a joyous return to our normal routines. And boy! Did we have stories! We must have described our adventures over and over again to the point of exhaustion for the children, but as I recall, they were very forgiving and probably made believe they seemed interested. Thank you kids. Well, the important thing is that we are home now and the family is together again. Back to normal! So ended our trip to Italy in 1977 to meet and visit all our relatives for the first time.

1978

MARIE ROSSI GIVES BIRTH TO JOSEPH. The Rossi's celebrated another birth into the family, they ushered into the world a baby boy, Joseph on February 6, 1978. They were still living in New Bern, North Carolina at the time. They were so happy and wanted us all to come and visit. We wanted to go, but there was a problem we could not resolve and therefore missed this opportunity, but we sent our best wishes and were very excited and happy about the event. They understood and thanked us. HAPPY BIRTHDAY JOE!

FRANCES ACKERLY GIVES BIRTH TO KAREN. The date was July 3, 1978 when baby Karen Marie was born at the Riverside Hospital in Secaucus, NJ. I know Tom was very happy when he called to make the announcement. He told us Frances was OK and all was well, so we were all happy. After a month or so went by, Frances invited us to the Baptism for baby Karen. We immediately began planning for the Christening and were anxious to be together with family, to celebrate our new addition to life. HAPPY BIRTHDAY KAREN!

S-SUSAN AND BILL LAUTER WED. It's our second daughter that's getting married. The date was October 7, 1978 and the church was St. Virgil's. We can't believe it! It's so wonderful! We wanted them to have the most beautiful wedding. Many options were being considered. Susan and Billy (As we used to call him…with his consent) started to focus on the Columbian Club facility in Morris Plains, for the reception. Of course the wedding would take place at St. Virgil's RC Church where both of them were parishioners. In the nearly eight years we attended St. Virgil's Church, I was proud they were to be joined in matrimony there. It would be an understatement to say there was excitement in the air. Everyone was bustling and hustling. Some times situations got a little tense. But in the end all went well. Susan planned to have three bride's maids, three grooms, a maid-of-honor and a best man in the bridal party. Nacy Arnold and Mike Daley were the Maid-of-Honor and Best Man respectively. The bride's maids were Laura Lauter, Lauren Merritt and our own daughter, Christine Petti. The grooms were, Tim Lauter, Mike Arnold and Tim Scanlon. They had so many good times, laughing and having fun in all the activities that accompany the preparation of a wedding. They were good times. My mother and father were so excited. It was their granddaughter that was getting married, what joy! Of course mom and I were so happy to see you marry Bill, a wonderful man that we came to regard in a very loving way. I had to get a tuxedo and had to look my best, after all, I was going to give you away in front of all our loved ones. It was such a beautiful wedding. I believe Father Doody performed the ceremony. Everything went well. You looked beautiful. All the attendants were gorgeous. The flowers were stunning. The weather was a little unpredictable. Sunny skies dominated with some rain clouds here and there. I believe it was drizzling while we were attending the ceremony. Then after the wedding, as the newly married couple arrived at the open doors of the church, there in the sky appeared a vivid rainbow, seemingly ending in front of them. Absolutely astounding, with the colors of red, orange, yellow, green, blue and violet, stretched across the heavens, as if saying: "God Bless you two forever!" Even my mother, who was at their side by now, exclaimed in broken English, "Oh, looka da Watermelona cola inna da sky"…(probably meaning: Watermelon Color in the sky), inimitable words I dare say. It was a beautiful occurrence, and almost everyone witnessed it. This appeared as truly a blessing from God. We will never forget it.

Now on to the Wedding reception. When I got there, I couldn't believe how crowded it was. It seems everyone I knew was there and then some. I believe there were over 160 guests in attendance. There were the Lauters, Lenny and Pat, all dressed up and smiling. Their children were there and all of Susan's and Billy's friends. Our family was there, and not only our friends but also our neighbors and my work associates attended. Everybody was smiling and enjoying themselves. My mother especially liked it, because there were more guests than at the other wedding we had for Lucille. Now the music started, it was a great band, the music was special. Here came the bride's maids across the floor and their escorts, then the Maid of Honor and Best Man and now for the first time as man and wife, came the beautiful bride and her husband to the center of the ballroom floor, for their first dance together, as a married couple. It was a wonderful sight. It made us cry, but tears of joy this time. We all prayed God would be with them for the rest of their days. It was also time for celebration. My mother and father were having a good time. Mom and I had quite a few dances together and we were enjoying ourselves. All my friends came to me and told me how much they were enjoying themselves. Which was a good thing to hear. The family was having a great time too. Congratulations Susan and Billy!

J-JOSEPH – DRIVER'S LICENSE. You can't imagine how excited Joseph was when it was time for him to be tested as a driver of a car. It was a day after his 17th birthday and the world was changing for him. He had to pass the test. I had no doubt, but his apprehension caused all kinds of doubts so he was in a nervous state, to say the least. Anyway I drove him to the testing site, he and the Inspector got in the car and off they went. When they returned, even though Joseph didn't look so good, the Inspector told me on the side, he did well. Not only did Joseph get his license but he got his first car also. What a day that was! I believe it was an orange used Dodge Charger. That's all he needed, now he was off, disappearing into the horizon. Those were exciting days and even though we worried sick when he was out driving, we knew he had to mature and this was one of the steps.

This concludes Chapter 6, and was the time when I was a Father. All my children were born and grew up during this phase of our life. Although it lasted for a good 25 years, it appears to me to have gone by in the wink of an eye! It's funny how perception plays tricks on you like that. Also, like the title of husband the title of father also continues with me. All my children call me Dad. I probably will live with that title for a long time. But in the next chapter, you're going to witness another facet of me that sort of brings out another person. We shall see…

CHAPTER 7 ... GRANDFATHER

New persons mentioned in this Chapter

Jerry Our Son-In-Law .... Gerhard Angersbach
"Fred" Our Step-Grandson................................ Friedrich Angersbach
"Ralph" Our Step-Grandson .... Ralph Angersbach
"Sabine" Our Step-Granddaughter .... Sabine Angersbach
"Monique" Our Granddaughter ....Monique Dawn Cummings
"Eric" Our Grandson .... Eric Lauter
"Kimberly" Our Granddaughter............................... Kimberly Lauter
"Melissa" Our Granddaughter .... Melissa Lauter

1979

You will be reading about many events (especially becoming a grandfather to seven children) that occurred during these years. I feel blessed at being able to enjoy, not only their introduction into my life, but also their growing years. What a joy to see the little ones grow-up before your eyes. How they take their first steps. Hear them say their first words. It's almost as if mom and I were raising our own children again, which is actually a type of fantasy; it's only a moment of parental illusion and is not real. The reality is, that I now become a Grandfather, which is an entirely different role than those already experienced. What's very interesting is that as a grandfather the direct responsibility is gone but the happiness they bring is not. Mom and I were so happy when the grandchildren began to appear, and especially when Christine married Jerry, we lovingly chose to take into our family, our wonderful step-grandchildren. Here is what happened, starting with Lucille...

L-LUCILLE WEDS TIM. Lucille was working and living in Florida at the time. After meeting Tim Cummings, they decided to get married. Everything was happening so fast, it was not possible for us to attend the wedding, but aboard a boat and at sea, on a friend's 52' cruiser called "Crack of Dawn", by a Justice of the Peace, our Lucille married Tim Cummings on January 27, 1979. They were able to invite a Justice of the Peace on board to perform the marriage ceremony. Lucille told us she was very happy and sent us photos of the wedding. We were happy for them. CONGRATULATIONS LUCILLE AND TIMMY!

L-MONIQUE DAWN CUMMINGS BORN. At this point, they were living in Colorado. Lucille gave birth in Colorado Springs. The date was May 27, 1979. We got the call right away. As soon as Timmy was able to call, he told us about the wonderful birth of our granddaughter whom they named Monique. He also told us Lucille was doing well and was very happy. We were all happy too for them. When we called Susan and told Christine, they were very happy too. So were Joseph and Michele. Now they had a cousin. We soon received photos of baby Monique in the mail. She was sooooo beautiful. There was Lucille holding baby Monique. Your mom began crying for joy, as she was looking at the photos. We wanted to be there, but we couldn't arrange it. Now we were grandparents! I became a Grandfather for the first time. It was a strange new title and I was searching to find the meaning of being a grandfather. I heard other men state that title but could not grasp its true meaning until now. The feelings were slowly moving in. First I had to become accustomed to the name of grandfather. Then I had to acquire the emotions that come along with that name. And as time proceeds, the meaning of grandfather, increases in memories and experiences and that for me made it the wonderful part of the life it becomes. It is truly a wonderful word, Grandfather. Not only is it an extraordinary title that begins with the birth of a child, but it continues to include all the others that are introduced into our family. Now in my 77th year, I have 9 grandchildren (By adding baby Margaret and baby Marie). This is the first; I will tell you when the others are born. HAPPY BIRTHDAY BABY MONIQUE!

J-JOSEPH GRADUATES HIGH SCHOOL. You can not believe how happy Joseph was when he was told at Morristown High that he had passed all the tests and will be graduated! The date, as I recall was June 8, 1979. So many of his friends had dropped out of school and there were many a time when he would become anxious about this ever happening to him, but he did it and we were very proud of him. His grandmother and grandfather were so pleased; they gave him a very substantial gift. Our gift to him made him even happier (Now he could purchase that Citizen Band Radio system he wanted so desperately). We had a big family get together that day, including his Aunt Mary and Uncle Julio, his Uncle Tony and Aunt Rose along with his many cousins and their families. We had lots of food and a happy ceremony took place on that memorable occasion. I know Joseph was happy. He was beaming all over the place. His family was happy for him too. CONGRATULATIONS JOSEPH! Everyone wished him a great future...

MARIE AND JOE ROSSI MOVE TO CAL. Marie had called us earlier to tell us she was moving from New Bern, NC to California. They bought a home in Mission Viejo and were relocating due to Joe's new job assignment. They were happy to be moving to California. Now baby Debbie and baby Denise and baby Joseph could be out playing in the sun all the time. And Marie and Joe could play tennis to their hearts content (just kidding). But in terms of distance from us, we knew it would be hard for us and we were going to miss them, even though we weren't able to visit them in NC as often as we wanted, it was the matter of the distance that made us emotional, I think. Anyway, they were happy about the move and we were happy for them too, so we said our teary goodbye's over the phone and wished them well on their journey to the new land. On around October 15, 1979, when they arrived in California they called us and told us that it even exceeded their expectations. They couldn't believe how pleasantly different living there is and how friendly the people are. They were really enjoying it and we were happy for them. BUONA FORTUNA CARI!

1980

M-MICHELE GRADUATES 8TH GRADE . Michele was attending St. Virgil's School and had reached the eight grade and now graduating. The date, as I recall was February 10, 1980 and she was all dressed up in her graduation dress. Her grandmother and grandfather were there to celebrate her graduation, as were all the relatives and neighbors and friends. We had a great time, Michele cut the cake and everyone had some with coffee, wishing her well. Can you imagine that, our youngest child is graduating! My, how time flies. Michele enjoyed the party and was ready to enter High School. CONGRATULATIONS MICHELE!

ROBERT AND DIANE WED. Well, that big day has arrived for Robert and Diane. Yes, on October 11, 1980, Robert was married to Diane at St. Anne's Church in Brentwood, LI, NY. All our families were waiting for this event and now it's here. Everyone was looking forward to the wedding after Robert announced the plans (We the Petti's love weddings). Not only does it mean celebration, but it also is a time of reuniting as a family. The wedding was beautiful, with the bride and groom showing their joy with all their smiles. The bridal party looked stunning and it was good to see the groom's father and mother all dressed in formal clothes, a sight that is not that common in our every day routines. It was wonderful to attend this joyous time in their life and to be part of the celebration. The reception was held at The LaGrange in West Islip. Everyone had a wonderful time. CONGRATULATIONS ROBERT AND DIANE!

1982

S-ERIC LEONARD LAUTER BORN. This is the day our second grandchild is born. Baby Eric was born on May 12, 1982 at Morristown Memorial Hospital, Morristown, NJ. There was no doubt, when Bill called us, that he had joyous news, that he was extremely happy. Even though he went through the rigors of birth along with Susan, he seemed to be refreshed and excited as he was telling us about the event. We were so very happy for them. Susan was doing fine and she gave birth to a son whom they named Eric! That was marvelous… everyone was happy! We were congratulating the Lauters as they were congratulating us for becoming grandparents. Those were more happy times. HAPPY BIRTHDAY ERIC!

EVAN ROBERT PASSERO BORN. On August 1, 1982, our telephone was ringing off the hook and when we answered it, Robert was telling us that baby Evan was born. Boy was he happy! They were living in Mineola at the time and baby Evan was born at the Mineola Hospital, Mineola, NY. Diane was well and happy with baby Evan all bundled up, sleeping in the Nursery. Robert was so happy and so were we. HAPPY BIRTHDAY EVAN!

1983

M-MICHELE - DRIVER LICENSE. I still don't understand why my children get so excited about driving a car? Of course this could very well be a national phenomena but I can only speak about my experiences. Anyway, Michele was full of anxiety when she had to take the driver's test, but I knew from the beginning, especially since I was at her side during her learning phase, that she was going to pass. No doubt about it. And she did. The date was April 13, 1983. As soon as she got her driver's license, she was talking about a car. She had a lot to choose from since her brother Joseph was ready to buy a truck; he would give her his car. And Christine was ready to give up her car for another one, so Michele had a pleasant dilemma on her hands. Not only that, but Uncle Tony was looking to give her his car to. It's the kind of problem many a person would like to be confronted with. It seems, she preferred to take Uncle Tony's car and was happy with that decision. Now we had five children driving out there on the roads, can you imagine the state of mind we were in (You know, worrying about each one when they go out driving.). But as time goes by, the fear slowly dissipates and is replaced with confidence, which helps greatly with the concern. When they would all be visiting and were home at one time, there were 7 cars in our driveway! It looked a little odd to say the least, but they were my children and I was proud that they were all driving and all had earned their driver's licenses. Good job kids... CONGRATULATIONS MICHELE... HAPPY DRIVING!

1984

M-MICHELE GRADUATES HIGH SCHOOL. Michele attended Bayley Ellard High School like Christine. Her graduation day was June 10, 1984. Everyone was so excited. She chose to continue onto college and was accepted at Rutgers University of New Jersey. Her grandmother and grandfather were as happy for her, as we were. All the relatives were invited to the graduation celebration and all of them attended. After the cap and gown ceremony, we drove home, where a number of the relatives had assembled and were waiting to congratulate her. She was so happy. She was in her new clothes and enjoyed the celebration immensely. CONGRATULATIONS MICHELE!

C-CHRISTINE AND JERRY WED. Although we all called him Jerry, his birth name is Gerhard. When Christine announced her intention to marry him, it was a very pleasant surprise. Even though she was filled with anxiety and apprehension, the announcement made us very happy. And not only were we adding to the family another son-in-law, but we were also receiving three more grandchildren (of course they were not children in years-they were mostly grown up). They were lawfully our step-grandchildren, but because we Pettis preferred to skip formalities of this nature, we embraced them as our own grandchildren which they have always been. The important event of the day was the wedding which was June 16, 1984. They were married at the Knolls West Country Club in Parsippany, NJ where I walked Christine down the aisle, in the Chapel toward the Minister. Christine in her beautiful white silk wedding gown and veil and me in a white tuxedo jacket (it's the first time I wore a white formal jacket). And before us, walking in procession, the Maid of Honor Lisa Galdieri, then Michele and Ernie, followed by Susan and Kurt. Of course standing at the altar was Jerry and the Best Man Rick. It was a beautiful sunny day which made it special too. They were so happy when they took their vows and so was the entire congregation. The reception was extra special, with a wonderful cocktail hour and a great band lending pleasant music in the background as we drank our cordials and had some delicious warm hors d'oeuvres. Then everyone became silent, the sound of drum-rolls filled the air. Something was going to happen. Onto the dance floor appears two of Jerry's friends from Switzerland, Beatt and P.J., holding a gigantic bronze cow bell (It is usually worn by cows grazing in the mountains-but this was a symbolic bell). They began prancing around the dance floor, ringing the bell as they passed Chris and Jerry, and singing a traditional wedding song in their native language, German/ Swiss. They were wearing Leder Hozen too (Leather short pants with large colorful suspenders and Alpine hats with feathers). Then they presented the bell to Chris and Jerry, wishing them joy and happiness all through their life. Of course mom was crying for happiness and I was too. It was a joyous day for everyone…CONGRATULATIONS CHRISTINE AND JERRY!

COREY RYAN PASSERO BORN. On December 28, 1984, our telephone began ringing and when we answered it, Robert was telling us that baby Corey was born. Boy was he happy! Another son… They were living in Mineola at this time and baby Corey was also born at the Mineola Hospital, Mineola, NY. Diane was well and happy with baby Corey all bundled up sleeping in the Nursery. Robert was so happy and so were we. HAPPY BIRTHDAY BABY COREY!

TONY UNDERGOES SURGERY. This was a critical time. Your uncle Tony had elected to have the by-pass surgery performed which according to the Doctor's opinion was extremely difficult, with a 50/50 chance of success. Very low odds indeed, but Uncle Tony courageously chose to have it done. The scheduled date of December 28, 1984, was historically the same as the birth of his grandson Corey, which of course he could never have anticipated that happening. But fortunately, the operation went very well and Uncle Tony survived this medical procedure with flying colors. The operation took place at NYU Hospital in New York City and we all commended the surgeons and praised their work. Now begins the recuperation which although was lengthy, the important thing was that the operation accomplished all the necessary repairs. Well done Doctors! I know Uncle Tony thanked them many times. Get well soon Tony, we are praying for you.

1986

S-KIMBERLY ANN LAUTER BORN. It's interesting, during a conversation with Mom, Susan (who was pregnant) was given specific instructions by her mother to not have the baby on Easter Sunday, because we were hosting that holiday and there would be too many visitors attending to handle both occasions. But do you think Susan listened to her mother? Noooo. Here it is Easter Sunday, March 30, 1986 and guess who was rushed to Morristown Memorial hospital to have a baby? You guessed it, Susan, who delivered a beautiful bundle of joy, baby Kimberly! Nice going Susan, but you didn't listen to your mother... Yet, after visiting her and seeing baby Kimberly, we couldn't fault her at all! Baby Kimberly was so beautiful and lying there quietly sleeping in the nursery, wrapped in her little blanket. Susan was doing well and everybody was happy especially Billy, but what a crowd came visiting at the hospital! All our guests insisted on going, we were about 14 people. It looked like a mob was converging on the hospital. You certainly had a very large audience when you were born baby Kimberly. It was spectacular. What an entrance! HAPPY BIRTHDAY BABY KIMBERLY!

ALLISON MARIE PASSERO BORN. It was October 3, 1986 at the Mineola Hospital when baby Allison was born. Robert called us to give us the good news. We were so happy for them. Although we were living in Morris Plains, NJ, we went to visit Diane and Robert and baby Allison as soon as we could. When we arrived, your mom wanted to hold baby Allison all the time, she was so beautiful. I believe I held her too. It's so wonderful when a new born is present among the family. It's hard to describe the joy that a family member experiences. Thank you baby Allison for that joy. HAPPY BIRTHDAY BABY ALLISON!

OUR TRIP TO SWITZERLAND. This was a trip to dream world! It was not expected and was conjured up by Jerry and Christine. Although it was being planned for the Angersbach children (Fred, Sabine, Ralph, Paul and Heidi) to provide an opportunity to ski in the Alps, asking us to tag along was sprung on us as the Christmas holiday got closer. At first we said "no", but they insisted and explained that we would be able to visit with Michele who was studying at the University of Tours in France, so we finally gave in for that reason. When I describe the itinerary you will see why we said no at first. The departing date would be December 26, 1986 (The day after Christmas!) Can you imagine that? We have never planed a trip to start the day after Christmas! And don't' forget it was winter! What about the snow and ice that could fall at any time. Who would even consider having to leave a cozy fireplace at home, the day after Christmas, to travel? But when we contemplated meeting Michele and hugging her and seeing her happy face, we could not refuse the offer. Oh, I forgot to tell you that our son Joseph was invited too. That meant we were going to have three of our children skiing all at one time in the Swiss Alps! That would be great! How could we say no? So we began the process of packing our suitcases and getting ready for this dream trip. Our flight would leave JFK at 8:30PM to Luxemburg and then on to Switzerland by bus. It sounded fantastic and we were all excited. Our first stop was in Iceland, at Reykjavik Airport for refueling. That was an eerie experience. We landed close to 10:00 AM, but we landed with all the runway lights on, since it was pitch black outside. When we left the plane, there were spot lights all over the pathways helping us to see the steps so we could get inside the warm airport quarters. While inside, I asked an attendant who (Thank God) spoke English, why it was so dark outside (A really dumb question in Iceland!), she said that we were at the apex of winter in Iceland and that they were only able to enjoy 1 hour of sun at around 1 O'clock and that was it for sunlight that day. I couldn't believe it. Although I remember studying the phenomenon of winter darkness in the Arctic in school, I never imagined experiencing it. But here we were, in total darkness, close to noontime in Iceland! What an experience…

Needles to say, we surprised Michele in a big way when we went to meet her at the railroad station, when she came to visit. She was led to believe that only Christine and Jerry, along with their kids would be there. She did not know mom and I, with Joseph, would be there too. At the train station, mom, Joseph and I hid behind the station door, inside. When she got off the train, Christine was there with Jerry and as they were saying hello, we jumped out into view. You cannot believe her surprise! She was so happy to see us! Of course she began crying for the happiness in her heart. That was a very memorable encounter... We will never forget it. Thank you Jerry and Christine for that trip...it is etched deep in our memories.

1987

PETER SCROCCO AND DEBBIE WED. We had received the invitation sometime at the end of June, 1987, and were excited about the forthcoming wedding of my Nephew Peter to Debbie. My sister and her husband Vinny were busily preparing for this wonderful event. Then on August 14, 1987, the wedding took place at St. Patrick's Church in Smithtown, LI, NY. We all gathered to witness the beautiful wedding. My sister was stunning in her gown, as was my brother-in-law Vinny in his tuxedo. And of course the bride was so beautiful in her wedding dress along with the groom Peter who was in his tuxedo. Then, down the aisle, followed the complete bridal party in their attractive formal wear. It was a very sunny day, the church was brightly reflecting all the rays of the sun and the music was beautiful. It was a beautiful wedding. Everyone was happy. CONGRATULATIONS PETER AND DEBBIE!

1988

MY FATHER DIES. The year was 1988 and my father JOSEPH PETTI reached the age of 82 years (he was born April 22, 1906), but he was frail and suffering from advanced diabetes, he had fallen and fractured his thigh bone and recovering, but the diabetes with all its accompanying effects was his worse obstacle. He was being treated for many medical conditions at the time. But he was a fighter and was surviving until a blockage in his esophagus occurred that could not be corrected. On September 17, 1988, he expired... When my sister called me at home to tell me that he was critical, mom and I rushed to his side at the hospital but arrived too late, he had died. Looking at him; still and motionless, my first thought was to ask God to mercifully take him to heaven and then the second thought was a mental interpretation of Shakespeare's famous lines that Mark Anthony utters when he first sees the lifeless body of Julius Caesar, which now I was applying to my father; "Oh my caring father, are all thy accomplishments and life endeavors shrunk to this low measure?". It was so sad to see him go…I loved him so much… My family members suggested that he purposely waited until the day after my birthday (9/16) to "take his last bow"! It was a noble thought, but I knew in my heart that it was his destiny. He was dearly loved… He will be dearly missed… He was my strength and my inspiration…it is so difficult to lose a FATHER… It cannot be described how a son feels at that moment… Although I was hurting a great deal, my mother needed me to be strong and consoling at this trying moment in time, including my sister and of course you're mom also needed me at this time. Mom was very close to my Papa'. My father loved you're mom so very much (and the feeling was mutual), he would not only confide in her, but also express his innermost visions and expectations, of all the future events he saw in his dreams, to her. He was so at ease with her. Mom felt the loss a great deal also. All the grandchildren mourned him tremendously. It was a very sad moment for all of us when we buried him, we loved him so. Goodbye to our loving earthly Father, Grandfather and Great-Grandfather Joseph Petti… God bless you… We will miss you…You will always remain in my heart…REQUIESCANT EUM IN PACE…REST IN PEACE PAPA'…AMEN…

I AM DIAGNOSED WITH DIABETES. One of the annual requirements of my company at Crum and Forster was to go through a medical check-up via a comprehensive blood test. They did need three vials of blood to do the exam, but it was worth it, to know you were in good shape. Only this time it didn't turn out so good. They discovered that my blood sugar was very high. Since the test is not conclusive, I was asked to visit my primary care doctor for further examination. He scheduled me for a Glucose Tolerance Test quickly. At the test site, it was discovered that I had Diabetes without a doubt. The date was October 11, 1988. I was hoping this day would never come, but it did. My doctor put me on oral medication to begin to control the condition. I was also introduced to the Blood Glucose testing instrument, along with skin piercing Lances and Testing Strips, which combined, allows you to read the level of glucose (sugar) concentration in your blood stream at any time. My father had diabetes in his fifties and I got it in my fifties. Talk about genetic transmission duplicity. Because of the family history of the Petti's, as my father would describe, almost every member of the Pettis had diabetes, my great-grandmother (D'Amico) Petti, my grandmother (Cioccia) Petti, and my grandfather Petti and both my aunts and one uncle on the Petti side. Reviewing this history made me realize that apparently it was just a matter of time that the condition would show up with me. Looking back, I believe I could have helped myself avoid the early onset somewhat, by controlling the "eating of sweets" during my early years. Unfortunately one cannot go back in time to correct poor diet behavior, so I must pay the penalty now. Needles to say, I was not shocked or surprised at the diagnosis but I was apprehensive, for even though I assisted my father with his glucose testing and injecting him with Insulin, I really was not experiencing the condition myself, so it was an out-of-body experience, whereas now it is an in-body actuality. I want to explain how the prophetic announcement that I had diabetes struck me, it was as if a condemnation was decreed like a prison sentencing, and I conjured up in my mind an image of a Judge instead of a doctor, pointing his finger at me and saying in a Courtroom, "I sentence you to life imprisonment with diabetes". That's how the medical findings hit me at the time. I was really depressed when I got home to give the news to mom and the family. Although you were all very supportive and helped me emerge from my temporary depression, the reality of the condition still bothers me today. But I learned how to live with it. My struggle is daily; in fact it occurs approximately three times a day. Whenever its meal time, the fact that I am diabetic always comes into play. I have to dialogue with myself, "Let's see, I can't eat that and I can only eat a little of this and that is a definite no, no". It is constant and it is minimally depressing, but it must be done to survive when one has diabetes. Therefore I will go on strongly. Thanks to my father's example, I have the strength to live with this disease. Thank you Papa'!

1989

C-CHRISTINE AND JERRY MOVE TO BRICK. Up to now, the Angersbach's were living in Wall Township. For a while, a new home was being built in Brick Township where they planned to move. The new home was finished and ready to receive its occupants. It was a beautifully planned house and was situated on the shore of a calm inlet, with an enclosed pool and many amenities. It was time to move and the date was, if my memory serves me right, approximately January 16, 1989. It was cold outside but the house was cozy and warm inside. It all went well. They were happy in their new home, even the kids were happy which you could see it in their smiles. It appears the new location is going to work out just fine. I knew they were going to be happy there. CONGRATULATIONS ON THE NEW HOME ANGERSBACHS!

1990

I ATTEND THE "PASSION PLAY" IN GERMANY.

This was one of the most exciting times of my life, thanks to Jerry my son-in-law and Christine my daughter. There is so much history attached to this experience, it will be difficult to describe accurately, but I will try. The Passion Play I'm referring to is a world famous phenomenon that occurs in Germany, in the town of Oberammergau every 10 years. An earth moving experience (my opinion) forms there, that is so spectacular it seems to overshadow any event being planned or executed in the world. And this has been happening since medieval times.

It began happening, I'm told, after the "black plague" struck Europe and people were dying by the thousands. In desperation, the town of Oberammergau got together and prayed in unison for help from Above, to spare their lives during this crisis. The Heavens must have heard their plea for mercy and apparently were spared the fate fallen to others. Four years after the apparent end of the crisis, the city was in utter jubilation for being spared that terrible fate. In thanksgiving, they all agreed to perform some act of community penance as an offering to their Great God. They wanted to remember His Blessing, to the end of time. In their history, it was proposed that the whole community participate in a pageant to depict the 14 Stations of the Cross and the Resurrection. Only residents or family members of residents of Oberammergau could participate in the production of this extravaganza. The evolutionary performances became known as The Passion Play, a world wide offering, that takes years to organize and is only performed every ten years, plus on some other special occasions. The year 1990 was one of those "special" times (it was not a ten year interval) when they would present another production for the world to experience. Here is where my son-in-law Jerry comes in. He and the other members of the family were wondering what gift I would want for my up and coming 60th birthday. Knowing that in 1990, Oberammergau was offering a special performance of The Passion Play, he reminded everyone (my kids) that I always wanted to see the Passion Play because I considered it one of life's great achievements. They all agreed and decided to give me that for my sixtieth birthday. Can you imagine that! The tickets were acquired and presented to me at my 59th Birthday, so I could prepare for this fantastic trip the next year. I was overwhelmed! I couldn't believe it. I was walking on air from that moment. One usually never expects a dream to come true. But this one did! I didn't know how to thank them all, but when they saw the joy on my face, when I returned from Germany, it seemed to be thanks enough… I was going to see The Passion Play!!! On September 16, 1990 I was sitting in the Oberammergau Theatre, waiting for the performance to begin. When the play began, I couldn't' believe the spectacle on that stage. I could not have even imagined what was to happen, along with camels, horses and sheep, there were armies of Roman soldiers and country people all on the stage. It is hard to explain and there is Jesus, being condemned and put to death on a cross, in front of thousands watching the scenes. I will never forget it! Thank you everyone, you were too kind. It was a birthday I will never, ever forget, either!

1991

J-JOSEPH AND DENISE WED. Our Joseph is getting married! Even though our three older daughters were all married, it was hard to imagine our Joseph getting married. He was such an avid outdoorsman, it was our impression he would spend his life in the woods or something like that. Of course that was fantasy; the real Joe followed the path of us all. When he got engaged to Denise, we were so happy for them. Then they announced their wedding date and the marital plans began. On September 21, 1991, at 10:30 in the morning, Joseph Erminio Petti married Denise Laura Sansevere at St. Virgil's Church in Morris Plains. It was a beautiful wedding. Everyone was there, except my father who had passed away, but my mother was there and all our loved ones, including all of our friends. There was only one hitch that week, before the wedding, and that was one of Denise's Bride's Maids cancelled and needed to be replaced. Thank God for the generous volunteering of Sabine Angersbach to take her place at the last minute. That was really a Godsend... Thank you Sabine, it took a lot of courage to assume all that stuff the last minute. You saved the day! I know Denise and Joe were very grateful. The wedding took place on a very sunny day and the Bride and Groom were very stunning together as they took their vows. The reception followed and everyone had a good time especially me (and of course all the others). CONGRATULATIONS JOSEPH AND DENISE!

1992

S-MELISSA ROSE LAUTER BORN. Susan's pregnancy culminated with the birth of baby Melissa on May 11, 1992 at Dover General Hospital, Dover, NJ. Bill called us as soon as he could. "It's another girl!" he exclaimed. The mother is doing well and we have a beautiful baby girl to add to the Lauter family, isn't that wonderful he said to us. Yes, we are so happy for you and we are happy to have another granddaughter too! " we replied. Susan told us how beautiful you were. We came to see you immediately and your mom was right, you were so beautiful there in your blanket. Then we talked to Kim and Eric to find out what they were experiencing at this event and discovered they were happy too. These were wonderful times. Happiness just permeated everywhere. HAPPY BIRTHDAY MELISSA!

A CRITICAL DIAGNOSIS FOR ME. For some reason, this particular morning was different for me. When I woke up I was seeing double. The date was December 14, 1992. As I was walking, all the objects in my view were double images. I tried blinking, or readjusting my eyes by squinting but the double vision did not change. I called Dr. Nigerian immediately (my primary care physician) and he told me to come right over to the office and took me in on an emergency basis. After the examination, with no prior complaint and in good health, according to the last visit, he was puzzled as to the cause and what the diagnosis might be. He uttered a number of possibilities, but none seemed to fit the symptoms as well as he would like. He suggested seeing an Ophthalmologist first to see if the vision distortion could be corrected, but his suspicions ran deeper. So he prescribed an MRI to see if something else may be going on there behind the eyes. Luckily, the Ophthalmologist was able to correct my vision problem with prescription eyeglasses and I was able to see clearly again. Then I went for the MRI, which was an experience in itself. It was the first MRI I had taken. The technology was in its infancy. When they put me in this very narrow tube that fit my head only, the area was so tight, I thought my face was going to be pushed against its sides. It was a very scary feeling. Then the noise began, evidently a large metal disk was circulating my head (of course out of sight), then at a precise moment, it either crashed against another piece of metal, or it sounded like some kind of crash of another sort, but a loud crash nonetheless. The banging sound was deafening. Then a voice through a speaker above my head said, "Don't be alarmed by the sound, its part of the process and everything is alright". Not too reassuring when you're hearing that very loud sound. But I tolerated it, for my own good. The MRI was a success and the results were on their way to Dr. Nigerian. We went home. That evening around six o'clock, Dr. Nigerian called us and told me that he has some bad news and some good news. The bad news is that I have a tumor in my brain, but the good news is that it is benign. "THANK GOD, THE TUMOR IS BENIGN!!! The tumor (which was approximately three centimeters in diameter-about the size of a golf ball) was situated behind my left eye and was wrapped around the optic nerve. What devastating news! I couldn't believe it! And of course, because of the inimitable feeling of 'Why me?' I was beside myself. But I immediately recovered from that self-pity mood I got myself into and began facing the actual meaning of the diagnosis. I asked Dr. Nigerian what was my next step, to which he responded, it must be removed, it's pressing on your optic nerve and will only get larger, causing more trauma. My next question was what type of doctor should I seek to perform this procedure and he immediately replied, a Neurosurgeon of course. Our quest began. Many recommendations surfaced and we visited one in New Jersey, a doctor who was renowned. Then we were told about this doctor at NYU in New York City and after visiting with him, I knew beyond the shadow of a doubt, that he was the one. His name is Dr. Benjamin (whom I ask God to bless every day of my life) and he accepted my case. The operation was scheduled for February 11, 1993. This was after a postponement due to a much more serious case that he had to operate on as an emergency; who was a professor in an Iowa University. This patient's life was saved by Dr. Benjamin, who removed a massive tumor from his brain. Now it was time for my operation. I'm not going to go into all the details, but it was a little frightening for me. Without the help of the Lord, and all of my families and friend's prayers, I don't think I would have had the strength to see it through. Thank you Lord. Thank you Family. Thank you Friends. What is important is that Dr. Benjamin removed the benign tumor from my brain successfully and restored me back to health, of course with the help of Dr. Seltzer whom I will never forget either. Dr. Seltzer was my Endocrinologist who controlled my insulin levels during the whole process. But I'm sure he was also my guardian angel in the hospital. One day, while visiting me, he detected that I was suffering from an embolism to the lungs (a blood clot that was life threatening) and immediately took control, ordering all the necessary remedial requirements to revive me. Blessings to Dr. Seltzer. I owe them both my life! Obviously I recovered, even though it took about seven months. But I am Ok now. THANK YOU DOCTORS AND NURSES AND ALL OF THE NYU HOSPITAL FACILITIES!

Christmas 1992 with whole family together. (L-R) Susan, Michele, Lucille, Joseph, Christine – Mom and Me in front.

1993

RETIRED FROM CRUM & FORSTER. On September 10, 1993, while recovering from my brain surgery, I retired from the Crum & Forster Insurance Company (also called Talegen, Inc.). Even though I could have retired in 1992, I decided to postpone it until mom was ready to retire, which was in 1993. When I went to the administrative office to retire, all of the staff was very cordial and helped me through the tedious process without a hitch. I was a C&F employee for 25 years! I couldn't believe it. Everyone was congratulating me as I walked by their desks. I enjoyed being employed by this great company and now the company was responding in like manner. I want to thank you Crum & Forster for allowing me to make my contribution to your endeavors and thank you for your kindness at this difficult parting. It was especially difficult saying goodbye to George Muriello and Joe Lee, Mickey Gray and Steve Cernek, who had already retired and the rest of the staff including Mary Travers. The company awarded me a Grandfather Clock (which I treasure) for the 25 years of service. Never was I beside myself as this one time…I shall never forget them. God bless them all.

MOM RETIRES TOO. On October 28, 1993, a Thursday, mom went to work for her last day at the Morris County Mosquito Commission, located in Morris Plains, NJ. Although she was excited, she was also a little anxious about having to say good-bye to so many associates and friends. She was an employee at this Commission for about 20 years. This she accomplished with many days of hard work and absolute dependability. When she returned home from this experience, she recounted the many good-byes she had to make and the many people she came to hold in high esteem. It was very difficult for her I know. And this was not the end; a big party was planned for her the next day, October 29, 1993, a Friday (which I was invited to attend also). Her actual retirement date was December 1, 1993, but because she accrued so many vacation days and sick days, she accumulated a whole month of off time, before her actual retirement date. It was a wonderful retirement party and farewell gathering. Everyone was there, including the prior Superintendent, Mr. Kuschke (the one who hired mom originally). Now we were both retired.

No more going to work for the both of us…Yea!

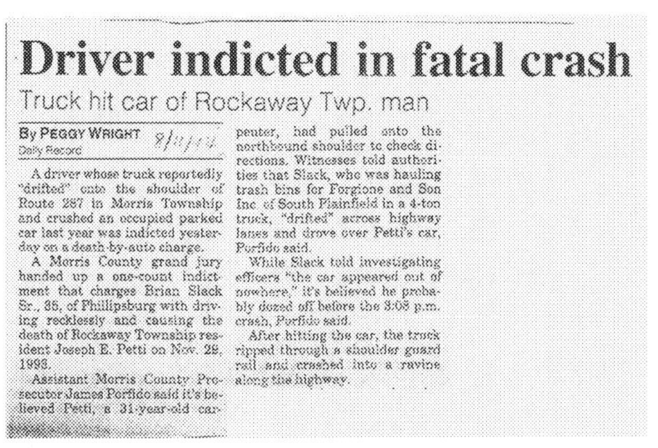

Driver indicted in fatal crash

Truck hit car of Rockaway Twp. man

By PEGGY WRIGHT
Daily Record

A driver whose truck reportedly "drifted" onto the shoulder of Route 287 in Morris Township and crushed an occupied parked car last year was indicted yesterday on a death-by-auto charge.

A Morris County grand jury handed up a one-count indictment that charges Brian Slack Sr., 35, of Phillipsburg with driving recklessly and causing the death of Rockaway Township resident Joseph E. Petti on Nov. 28, 1993.

Assistant Morris County Prosecutor James Porfido said it's believed Petti, a 31-year-old carpenter, had pulled onto the northbound shoulder to check directions. Witnesses told authorities that Slack, who was hauling trash bins for Forgione and Son Inc of South Plainfield in a 4-ton truck, "drifted" across highway lanes and drove over Petti's car, Porfido said.

While Slack told investigating officers "the car appeared out of nowhere," it's believed he probably dozed off before the 3:08 p.m. crash, Porfido said.

After hitting the car, the truck ripped through a shoulder guard rail and crashed into a ravine along the highway.

Newspaper Article Describing Joseph's Accident

J-OUR SON JOSEPH DIES. This will be the most difficult section in the book to write for me. I will be writing with tear filled eyes all the way. It was a loss that mom and I never expected. We could not believe our ears when we were told of the accident. This is what the Policeman said to us; "Yesterday, Monday, November 29, 1993, your son Joseph was on Route 287, at about 3:00 PM, parked in the safety lane (we do not know why), when a large multi-wheeled Container Truck (4-ton) struck him from behind, going over the top of his car and crushing your son Joseph to death, instantly." He also explained that the victim driver (our son) had no identification on his person; he was wearing sweats with no pockets, so they had difficulty identifying him. In the glove compartment was my Automobile Registration (we had loaned him our car) but the age of the owner did not match that of the driver, the authorities were still puzzled. Then they found a letter on the passenger seat from his Carpenter's Union and called them, which allowed them to begin unraveling the identity of the driver. This is the reason for the delay in notifying us also. After I described the car, a Chevrolet Cavalier, which I had loaned him and after describing our Chevrolet, it matched the color and model, and was the one in the accident. The only additional identity requirement was an actual physical facial viewing by a family member. The Policeman realizing that at this moment mom and I were in such excruciating trauma, bereaving our son's loss of life, he asked if someone else in the family could accomplish this task. We did not have an answer for him right then, but after informing all our children, we told him we would contact him shortly with an answer. After hearing the terrible news, Christine, with an extremely charitable desire to save us from having to do this, offered to go and identify Joseph (knowing that mom and I could not do it). Jerry and Christine went to the Morgue and performed that kindness for us. Yes, it was Joseph... He was dead, lying there, motionless and barely recognizable. We were so sorry Christine had to experience this, but the law requires it. No one should have to do that, but unfortunately it is a necessary requirement. Thank you Christine, we wish we could have spared you from having to experience such an emotional situation. We love you and we will never forget the courage you showed when times were difficult for us. For the remainder of that Friday, no one could console us. We cried the whole day, and the next, until it was time to make the funeral arrangements. At the funeral home, the crying started again. I don't know how we got through it. We prayed for strength from the Lord and he granted it. We do not know why the Lord wanted Joseph with Him at that time in his life A slight consolation for us was that Joseph was in a better place now, away from this mortal world and eternally serene. But the pain of loss was so intense; there were times when it became unmanageable. Those were desperate moments. With the help of Jesus, we got through them slowly. Our family was so supportive when we needed them.

At Joseph's wake, there was literally a multitude of mourners. At one time, there were so many attendees; they lined the street before the entrance of the funeral home. I can't remember how many young people came up to mom and me and told us how much they admired Joseph for his caring ways. How many friends he would lend money to, and how many others he would perform a kindness, that they said no one else would do. This was a dimension of Joseph we knew nothing about until now. All the relatives, bereaving our loving Joseph, was too much to take, but we knew that he would want us to go on. At the funeral, my mother along with Denise and the Sansevere family cried uncontrollably during the ceremony along with us. Joseph received a military honor of being covered with the American flag (he was a veteran) on his coffin, because he received an honorable discharge from the Army after serving his tour. We have that flag in a case in his honor. He was buried in East Hanover, New Jersey, Gate of Heaven Cemetery, in Section 25. It is our family grave site and can hold four coffins in the ground, with the Petti name engraved on the tombstone. All the carvings on the stone were applied by Denise and us. We both wanted the birds standing guard to be Hawks. Denise chose the quotation which pleased us too. We can tell Joseph's grave site is visited often by his friends and other family members, by the number of rocks we find placed on top of the tombstone, when we visit. It is very warming when we see the pebbles. God Bless them all for caring, his family, his friends, all his loved ones... The loss of our son Joseph has been the most painful trauma ever experienced in our life. We dearly miss him. We are so sorry for his wife Denise. We cannot imagine the pain our daughters have experienced as a result of this tragedy. Our whole family, till this day, continues to bereave his death. It will always be with us, the sadness, the loss, the memories, the fact that our son is not with us anymore. It's almost unbearable, but with the Lords help we go on…REST IN PEACE JOSEPH, WE WILL ALWAYS LOVE YOU…

CHRISTMAS OF 1993. This Christmas will never be forgotten. All of the events that had taken place for us during this year were overwhelming. Every situation we encountered, my Brain Surgery, selling our home in Morris Plains, buying a new home in Brick, my retirement, mom's retirement, losing our son Joseph…all life altering situations, that in many instances happen over time (but usually at different times) and to experience all of them in one year, made it a year of unbearable changes for us. This of course affected our Christmas to the degree where we cancelled all of our traditional preparations and customs (we could not bring ourselves to celebrate normally) so that we could mourn our loss and decide what adjustments were needed. It also gave us time to review our life with many sober thoughts. We were trying to set paths that would help us on our was, this was our primary concern. We did not want these personal burdens to affect our relationships with our remaining children. Devoting most of our time in prayer took up the rest of the time. It was a very different Christmas than those we were accustomed to. It was quiet. It was sorrowful. It was hard for us to bear. But with God's help we made it through. The only thing we did on Christmas Eve, at midnight; was we carried the Infant Jesus to his cradle and prayed. WE PRAYED FOR JOSEPH MOSTLY…

1994

C-SABINE GRADUATES COLLEGE. Although we were aware Sabine was graduating in June of this year, with everything going on, it appeared to come upon us so quickly. Nonetheless, in preparation for this wonderful event, we wanted to make it special for Sabine. We decided to give her a very special gift for her once in a lifetime achievement. We wrapped it up nicely and carried it with us to her school in Pennsylvania. We traveled with Jerry and Chris to attend this important event. The date was June 11, 1994. After morning

Mass, the school distributed their diplomas. Sabine was so proud and smiling, while going to and from the podium where she received her treasured Bachelor of Arts in Medicine diploma. We applauded so hard and loud…hope she heard us celebrating with her. She said later that she did indeed hear us and couldn't mistake our joyous outcry! We took photos. Then we went to lunch in town where everyone gave her a gift. When she opened ours, we could see the tears coming down her face. She couldn't believe it! We had a STAR in our celestial universe named after her…Sabine! It was officially named and certified by the International Astrological Society, along with its exact location, among the other stars in our universe. She was so happy with that gift, and we were very happy presenting her with it. Now when she looks up into the heavens, she knows there is a star up there that is called Sabine after her. And we all know there is her star up there too. May your star be shinning on you all of your days. Bless you Sabine and CONGRATULATIONS ON YOUR COLLEGE GRADUATION!

1996

JOSEPH SCROCCO AND CINDY WED. My youngest nephew Joseph marries Cindy on July 19, 1996 at St. Aidan's Church. It brought back many memories for Lucille, Susan, Christine and Michele, when they came to attend the wedding. St. Aidan's was our Church when we lived in Williston Park and coincidentally was Cindy's parish too. My sister's son Joseph was very happy and Cindy was beautiful in her wedding dress. Their reception was at the Westbury Manor, which mom and I attended along with our children. It was a wonderful reception where we celebrated the beginning of a new life. We gave them so many kisses and hugs…well why not, they had to last their whole life through.

CONGRATULATIONS JOSEPH AND CINDY!

1997

MY MOTHER LUCIA DIES. She was 88 years old and had begun her 89th year when she succumbed to all the body failures she was enduring. Even though her most debilitating condition was deteriorating quickly (leg venal weakness) and without resolve, which then affected her heart detrimentally. Unfortunately I had come down with acute Bronchitis at that time and was bedridden and could not go visit her. So mom and Christine went to visit and were the last ones in my family to see her alive. When my sister Joann called to tell me she was in critical condition. I got myself out of bed and mom and I rushed to see her. I did not reach her in time, although my sister told the doctor that I was on my way, they had her under oxygen where I found her, but she couldn't speak nor did she recognize me. Since there was nothing we could do, we returned to Joanne's home and while we were having dinner, the call came announcing her death, her heart had failed. My sister and I went, along with all the others, to the hospital to say our last goodbyes and left. It was a very tearful parting. The date was February 19, 1997. Since I was the Power of Attorney I began the funeral proceedings, but with Joann at my side. After the wake, the funeral was held at St. John's Cemetery, Brooklyn, NY and she was laid to rest next to Papa' Joseph. Now there were three Pettis buried there, my brother Michael my father Joseph and now my mother Lucia. GOD BLESS YOU MAMMA...YOUR LOVE AND CARING WILL NEVER BE FORGOTTEN! REST IN PEACE...

1998

DENISE AND KIRK MARRY. Although our invitation to the wedding arrived last year, the excitement began in January of this year. Denise is the daughter of Marie and Joe Rossi, who also have two other children, Debbie and Joey. Everyone wanted to attend this affair but in the end it was left to those who were retired from work that could make it. To travel to California was a hard decision, what with the eight hours of air travel and then the land travel, it seemed overwhelming, but the event called for tough people and the Petti's and Passero's are those kinds. So Uncle Tony and Auntie Rose along with mom and me began packing our suitcases. No matter what, we had to attend this joyful union of two happy lovers. While we were talking to Marie on the phone, describing our plans with her, we could hear the joy in her voice about the upcoming wedding and we declared our happiness for them too... She and Joe were so happy to hear we would be joining them at this wonderful moment in life. We arrived a couple of days ahead of time and were present for the beautiful wedding of Denise and Kirk, on February 7, 1998. The bridal party was glowing with happiness in the church. After seating the mother of the bride, Marie, the procession began. Here comes Debbie, the Maid of Honor, and two more Brides Maids, now the Bride and her Dad, Joe. The music was beautiful. The Priest begins the readings. They take their vows and they are Husband and Wife. Everyone is applauding. It's such a happy time! Uncle Julio was beaming with joy. And even though Auntie Mary couldn't make it, when we went to visit her, she was so happy when we were describing the wedding to her. The next day we were invited to a brunch at the Country Club, with all our family and Kirk's family. It was a sunny glorious day. Everyone enjoyed themselves and were well fed. Thank you Marie and Joe, you helped make our visit so pleasant. And...CONGRATULATIONS TO DENISE AND KIRK...MAY YOUR LIFE TOGETHER BE FULL OF JOY!!!

SIDE TRIP TO LAS VEGAS: Since we were close to Las Vegas (According to my calculations.) and wanted to tour it, we decided to drive there after the wedding. Uncle Tony, Auntie Rose, mom and me drove there in our rented car. We stayed at the MGM Grand Hotel / Casino. We took an automobile, passing tour, of all the other famous buildings, some under construction, like the Bellagio and the Venezia, but we saw the Monte Carlo, the Excalibur, Luxor (Pyramid and Sphinx), the Tropicana, Caesars Palace, the Mirage, Treasure Island, Circus Circus and the Stratoshphere Tower, where we went to have lunch in a rotating restaurant, very high above the City of Las Vegas. It was glorious! We had a good time and returned home from Las Vegas to Newark. It was wonderful. We did not win! (Yes, we did play some games.)

OUR TRIP TO BERMUDA. I'm not sure if we traveled to the Island of Bermuda off the coast of South Carolina in 1998 (or close to that year), but the experience was unforgettable! This was a trip planned by our wonderful brother-in-law Jerry and our wonderful daughter Christine. What was extra special about this particular adventure was that it would include our grandchildren Sabine and Ralph. On that trip were Ernie and Lillian too. Our excitement was increasing every day that we came closer to the departure date. Mom was all packed and so was I. We received expert advice from our hosts and that made a big difference. We were ready. Visiting this Island was so fascinating. Although we were familiar with driving in opposite lanes for automobiles and traffic, it was a little strange to witness this difference in an English speaking country. We learned that Bermuda was occupied by Great Britain from early days, and even though they had abdicated rule, continued to influence the government and all its social customs and traditions. The Police looked liked English Bobbies. A lot of the men wore Bermuda Shorts. In other words, it was almost like visiting England in the summer but only a few miles from South Carolina! It was neat. And, oh, I forgot the English accent. The natives spoke with an English accent. Rather quaint, wouldn't you say, ol' chap?

A number of firsts happened to mom and me in Bermuda. One morning, we were all at the breakfast table, mom, Chris, Jerry, Ernie and Lillian and me. We were reading the breakfast menu and I commented to Jerry about the fact that Fish was listed there. Trying to be funny, I said, "Who ever heard of fish for breakfast". Nobody laughed; instead many looked at me in dismay. Jerry immediately responded, "Why? Haven't you ever had fish for breakfast?", "No" I answered. "Well, you should at least try it, you may be surprised" Jerry replied and instinctively ordered a portion of Maui Maui (?) for me. Before I could object, he said, "Don't worry, if you don't like it, I will have it" That seemed like a fair deal, so I just said, "Thanks Jerry". When the fish arrived, it actually looked good! I tasted a small piece, and to my amazement, it was delicious! Not only did I eat it all, but I had fish every morning after that! Now, every time I pick up a breakfast menu, I search for fish. Isn't that interesting? Thanks again, Jerry.

After touring the Island on a PINK bus (that color happens to be the Island's custom because of the "pink sand" phenomenon that occurs along its shores), we saw so many scooters, and mom and I wanted to rent one. Along with Chris and Jerry, we went to a scooter rental store and inquired about renting one. There were single seat and double seat. The attendant suggested testing one first. So me and mom mounted a double seated vehicle, and scooted away down this testing path behind the store. Everything was going well until I spotted a rut ahead. I would have gone around it except that the rut was completely across the roadway. I had no choice but to go through it. I yelled to mom, "Brace yourself, the road is going to get bumpy" She had just said, "OK" when the front wheel of the scooter hit the rut and instead of bouncing through, the whole scooter with mom and me came crashing down on the ground, forcing me to land on my face with mom on my back, pressing me into the ground. My knees were also forced into the ground and received the heaviest injuries. My face was all scrapped, but mom, thank God, was protected by my body and was not injured. Obviously I was her shield, so she was OK. Meanwhile, Chris and Jerry who were standing at the storefront waiting to rent their scooter witnessed the whole scene and began running to where we were lying in the dirt. They helped pick up mom and me and began describing my injuries. By now the pain was setting in, so I knew what part of my body sustained the damage. It was kind of embarrassing, but it was an unfortunate accident that could not be avoided. I survived, but not without bandages. It was an unforgettable experience that I have proof of (just view the photos we took). The remainder of the visit was marvelous. The sun was nice and hot. We visited the famous Pink Sand beach. We did the paddle boats and did some surface snorkeling and I played a lot of handball with Ralph during that stay. Mom and I also enjoyed Tea and Crumpets at 3PM every afternoon (the hotel would ring a bell at 3PM announcing the serving of tea-an English custom). It became a habit with us, and a pleasant one. Ralph could not believe that I would quit playing handball with him to go for tea and crumpets. We had a lot of fun. It was a beautiful experience. Thank you Jerry and Chris. We will never forget it.

S-SUSAN DIAGNOSED WITH BREAST CANCER.

You must have realized as you were reading this book, not all of the stories are happy ones. This was one of the most critical incidents of our lives when on December 4, 1998, Susan was diagnosed with breast cancer, with the only resolve as a choice, a mastectomy. That was very devastating news for our daughter, to say the least. Susan was beside herself. The whole family couldn't believe it. The news eventually traveled to the different family homes and the prayers began coming in. It was an overwhelming wave of concern and all of it reaching out to her, not only by the immediate family and friends, but by many members of the community too. Everyone was praying. You could actually hear it in their voices, when they were talking about Susan, how much they cared and began hoping for the best. Then on December 15, 1998, Susan was operated on at Morristown Memorial Hospital, by a group of Doctors who were Specialists in this type of surgery. Till this day, I insist that Our Lord and Savior spared her life, and these doctors and assistants were God's instruments, that helped perform that miracle! Thank you Lord. And our everlasting gratitude and praise to those wonderful Doctors and staff members who actually performed the wonder. When Susan arrived home, mom and I immediately went to her aid and practically moved-in to handle the day to day transactions so she could rest and recover peacefully. Then in January of 1999, she began Chemo-Therapy. We would usually be there from Mondays to Fridays, because Bill was traveling for his work during the week, but he would be home on the weekends. As I recall, we did this for about two to three months or longer. The Chemo-Therapy lasted till June and was substantially debilitating. Her energy level would be down and although she wanted to do things, the physical strength she tried to muster just wasn't there. We prayed for her. She slowly began to get stronger. Her treatments were over and she was able to resume many tasks she wasn't able to accomplish before. She was recovering. . It's times like these when family love and affection is most needed. We gave it generously. We all were there for her, helping her recover and eventually she was able to resume her normal functioning. We were all praying that your recovery would be forever…

1999

M-MICHELE AND BILL WED. Yes, our youngest daughter is getting married! I'm still imagining Michele as a little baby and here she is announcing their plan to get married. How quickly they grow up. It was wonderful news. Mom and I were very excited, watching

Michele make all the plans. As she was explaining the location and some of the details, mom and I sort of relived the moments when our other children were planning their weddings. It was a type of de ja vue, but it made us very happy that she was marrying such a wonderful man that we had met about a year ago, Bill Lee. Her wedding ceremony would be at the Woodcliff Lake Hilton in Woodcliff Lake, NJ where her reception would follow. It was a very nice place, the flowers were everywhere and the guests were beginning to arrive in large numbers. It was almost time to begin. The day was June 12, 1999, the organ was playing and everyone was seated. The wedding ceremonies went very well. The Minister wished them a long life of happiness, as we all did. Now the reception and the cocktail hour started. It was one of the most memorable experiences I've had and many of the guests were commenting about the same thing. It was truly a beautiful wedding. Everyone had a wonderful time.

CONGRATULATIONS MICHELE AND BILL!

2000

M-MICHELE GIVES BIRTH. It was January 30, 2000 when Michele and Bill were blessed with their first child and my granddaughter Margaret. Baby Margaret was born in the early morning at St. Joseph's Hospital, Milford, NH. They were living in New Hampshire then and when Bill called to tell us of her birth, it had snowed when baby Margaret was born, but they were both warm and cozy and Michele was doing well. They were very happy and so were we. We had another granddaughter…isn't that wonderful! HAPPY BIRTHDAY MARGARET!

A GRANDFATHER'S NOTE. This is the last event occurring in my life with the title as a Grandfather. In the next chapter, I assume another role, that of a Great-Grandfather which also concludes the book. My book ends in the year 2007, when I have reached the age of 77. Of course there will probably be subsequent sequels in my life, than those events I already stated and I may write about them later on if I am given the motivation, who knows? Maybe I will publish a supplement to this book in the future, especially when and if I become a Great-Great-Grandfather (That's Two "Greats" if you noticed). If that is my destiny, then I will write about it and publish it for all of you to read and I promise every one of you, that has a copy of this book, will receive a copy of the addition. And now to the next phase of my life...

CHAPTER 8 ... GREAT-GRANDFATHER

New persons mentioned in this Chapter

Dylan Our First Great-Grandchild..................................Dylan Torres
Evan Our Second Great-Grandchild.................................. Evan Torres
Marie our Granddaughter ....Marie Lee

2001

BEING A GREAT-GRANDFATHER. This is a different kind of happiness! It is impossible describing the emotions that I felt when I became a great-grandfather. Although it is not a life title that is directly earned, it nonetheless could not have occurred without my presence. All I had to do was be there when our beautiful great-grandchildren were born. And presto I am a great-grandfather. Very easy… and I was so very happy being there to witness these wonderful events. I wouldn't have missed it for the world. How happy our granddaughter Sabine was when Dylan and Evan were born. I will never forget that. It's interesting, even though technically Sabine is our step-granddaughter and her children are our step-great-grandchildren, we (Ann and I) do not use the prefix 'step' when referring to them. We have grown so close over the years that the connotation seems to limit our love, which is actually boundless. Therefore, you will not see me use the word 'step' except when necessary in an explanatory note. This is only one of the many licenses an author has while writing a book... so you'll give me that one won't you…

All I know is that the feeling of being a great-grandfather is great! I wouldn't trade it for any other feeling in the world. When I am with my great-grandchildren, I am in a separate place, full of happiness, peacefulness, joyfulness and most of all a loving world that fulfills all ones needs. What a pleasure it is being with the children, they go about pointing and explaining their favorite toys to me while playing with them and they go from subject to subject at lightning speed, it's hard to keep up with them. It's all fun. I think I'm smiling all the time when I'm with them. There isn't much in this world that can do that for me these days.

That's it…that's it, it's just a joy! That's the main feeling of being a great-grandfather. Here is how it all happened…

C-DYLAN TORRES BORN. This event, caused me to be a great-grandfather, another turning point in my life. Our first great-grandchild was born on September 12, 2001.

HAPPY BIRTHDAY DYLAN!

2002

M-MARIE LEE BORN. Another grandchild is born. Our daughter Michele gave birth to a beautiful baby, Marie, born on November 11, 2002 at the St. Joseph Hospital in New Hampshire. When Bill called us to tell us about baby Marie being born, he was so happy making that announcement and we were happy for them all. Now Margaret would have a little sister and I have another granddaughter. Life is wonderful when you add all the pluses. Mom and I couldn't wait to see her. Bill told us Michele was doing fine and she was happy too. Everything went well. We immediately made plans to visit our new granddaughter in New Hampshire. HAPPY BIRTHDAY MARIE!

2003

OUR 50TH WEDDING ANNIVERSARY. We were looking forward to this day for quite a while now. As the time approached, a number of celebration suggestions were made but the one we liked the most was having a renewing of our wedding vows in church and then having a celebration reception for our family and friends. So that's what we planned and that's what we did. We sent formal invitations to all our family and friends. Our Bishop Smith was celebrating a Mass in Trenton which we were invited to attend. At that Mass, mom and I renewed our marriage vows and when we returned, all our children were home to greet us. The next day we had a 50th Anniversary reception at the Waterview Pavilion in Belmar, NJ where the family and everyone cheered us. Mom and I gave every couple a gift (a favor), comprised of a stainless steel salad set, with gold trim, boxed and wrapped in gold paper & ribbon. Just a small memento to those we love that have brought us much joy and happiness and have helped us to reach this milestone. After dinner, our children presented us with a beautifully framed Blessing from Pope John Paul II. It meant so much to us! (We have such loving children…) because when we first married we received as a gift, a Blessing from Pope Pius XII that we treasure and had hanging up in our bedroom, for all these years. We were married on May 2, 1953 so we set our 50th Anniversary date for that same day, May 2, 2003. Not only did we have a big hall to celebrate together, as we did fifty years ago, but we even had a DJ for dancing. Everyone had a wonderful time. Mom and I were so happy. All our children except Joseph were there (we missed Joseph). They made us very happy; we love them very much, to see how wonderfully they grew up and were there to celebrate with us. Thank you Lord for all your everlasting blessings. You brought us joy that night that cannot be described. When the cake was brought out with the 50 lit candles, everyone sang HAPPY 50TH ANNIVERSARY TO YOU!

THANK YOU ALL!

C-EVAN TORRES BORN. Baby Evan was born on September 19, 2003. It's interesting that they would both be born in September and only seven days apart from each other. HAPPY BIRTHDAY EVAN!!!

2004

MY DIABETES CHANGES. According to my doctor, during my quarterly visit, he said according to the tests he conducted, the oral medication prescribed for my diabetes was not bringing my blood sugar (glucose) down low enough. He told me that it was now necessary to put me on Insulin. With Insulin I would be able to control my glucose level better which would in turn improve my health significantly. It was no surprise to me. My father had been on Insulin for around 20 years and I was well versed with the procedure and I knew all about the necessary equipment that is used to administer Insulin. All I felt was sort of a repeat of past health situations that were necessary for my father and now were needed for me. It's hard to explain; (This is the mental image I envisioned), to me it was kind of like a Judge sitting in a large chair, sentencing me for life, to spend the rest of my days injecting myself with Insulin, until death. What I mean is that I felt it was like a Life Sentence. Nothing can be more absolute. This happened on June 23, 2004. It was a day that will go down in my memory as more than significant...

2005

M-MICHELE, BILL & FAMILY MOVE TO NC. In January of 2005, the Lee family moved from Milford, New Hampshire to Cary, North Carolina. Since Bill was transferred to the North Carolina office of his company CISCO, both Michele and Bill felt they needed to move closer to his work place. They found a beautiful house in Cary and moved at this time to this warmer climate. I mentioned to Bill that one of the benefits to this move, is that no snow blower would be necessary where they were moving to. I'm sure Bill thought of that himself, I just had to emphasize it though. We both laughed and agreed.

2007

ANTONIO PASSERO DIES. My brother-in-law and long time friend passed away in April of this year. It was on April 28, 2007 that Rexie (as I called him) died while we were all at his bedside here in Brick, NJ. The doctors had told us that it wouldn't be long before he would leave us. All we could do was pray. Then it was announced to us as we were standing there, that he had no pulse. We couldn't help but cry. And crying we did, even while we were saying good-bye to him, lying in bed. The tears just came out and they couldn't be controlled. We will miss you Rexie, I uttered to him, while bending over to kiss him. Rest in peace Rexie. Rexie was the first member of the Passero family I met while courting your mom. Mom and I were talking, as teenagers and standing near the doorway of the entrance to her apartment house, when down the street comes walking your Uncle Tony. As soon as he gets within close proximity of me, he extended his hand and we shook hands for the first time, while mom introduced him. She said to me "This is my brother Rexie" and he has remained Rexie to me throughout the years. My memories of him go way back. And in the last few years, after moving close to us, we were able to rekindle our family values and our friendship, getting even closer, with many gatherings of love and happiness. I will never forget you Rexie. May God bless you in your new journey. REST IN PEACE…REXIE

KING TUTANKHAMUN'S EXHIBIT IN PA. This exhibit was experienced on August 11, 2007. In my opinion, I believe this will be the last time an exhibit of this nature and magnitude will be conducted in the United States again concerning King Tut. Remember, in Chapter 6, in the year 1977, the Pettis went to see the first exhibit of its kind of the Boy Pharaoh. That is when the nation of Egypt decided to allow a significant number of priceless artifacts found in the tomb of King Tutankhamun, to be sent to American Museums for our viewing. Just to be able to see a necklace worn by an Egyptian king over 3,000 years ago is an amazing experience, but there were 59 more objects in that exhibit that were mind boggling also. At that exhibit, which was the greatest ever, we were able to see the Golden Mask of Tutankhamun, a 3/8 inch thick, hand hammered, and solid gold mask of the Boy King, beautifully polished and untouched for all those years! It was breathtaking! We were also able to feel and touch his outer sarcophagus, the wooden one (the mummy of King Tut was in three coffins) which was unexplainably thrilling. There were so many objects there, I lost count. But that was an extraordinary exhibit and although this new one was touted in many periodicals as spectacular, it was not the same. But it didn't deter or disappoint me or any of the other family members and friends that came to see those priceless pieces either. This exhibit reached Pennsylvania in 2007, exactly 30 years after the first one. The exhibit was on display at the Franklin Institute Science Museum in Philadelphia, Penn. The whole family had to travel there on the day of our scheduled visit which was August 11, 2007. Usually, when a group this large, attempts to simultaneously leave and arrive at a destination and on time, the odds of a success are slim. But I was amazed at how punctual everyone was and how cooperative each member was toward the desired accomplishment of arriving on time and without incidents. It absolutely floored me (it made me think there is hope). I was pleasantly surprised. It was a great day. All the family members and friends were there and we were ready to experience a one time event that will practically change our lives. You're probably saying how an exhibit could change one's life? Here are some ways…first, you are viewing objects that were fabricated over 3,000 years ago… second, you can see with your own eyes the art and beauty of their creators (the jewelry, unguent jars, statues, carvings) that were never meant to be seen by anyone! (These objects were meant to travel with the King to the Nether World of the Dead). And this next thought haunts me all the time, when the Egyptians buried a King, their religion dictated that he would live forever in that world of the dead, but as a result of the discovery of his tomb, he now lives among us too. This added dimension to his eternity just magnifies his importance to us and becomes, in my opinion, a life altering experience. I hope you all agree.

After the exhibit, which ended around dinner time, we all decided to go to a place close by to eat. We went to a TGIF that was near the Museum. We enjoyed each other that day tremendously. Mom and I will never forget it. Just having the family and friends together like that, can only be measured in terms of joy. It was wonderful! Thank you Family, thank you Friends…we enjoyed your company so much and THANK YOU KING TUTANKHAMUN!

CHRISTMAS OF 2007. It was around the second week in December when mom began getting intense pain in her neck and was experiencing dizziness especially when she moved her head back. She didn't know why and neither did I. She called Doctor Pedicine who asked her to come right over for an examination to determine the cause.

I accompanied her since she couldn't drive and as soon as he verified the symptoms ordered her to go to the Hospital Emergency Room for X-Rays and further evaluation. Luckily we were in Pt. Pleasant and that facility is just across the street. After she got her X-Rays, it was determined that she was suffering from inflammation of the upper vertebrae arthritis (neck area) and needed steroid injections to reduce the swelling and help it to calm down. She required three injections which could only be applied after being anesthetized. This had to be hospital procedure. So the appointments were made and the applications began. Because this process would take some time, the children were concerned that we would attempt to begin preparing the Christmas traditional foods we usually prepare. Our daughter Christine said she would make the Anginette cookies so we don't have to bother with it. Then our daughter Susan said she would make the Lasagna and would be inviting the family to her home so we wouldn't have to do that. Also our daughter Lucille prepared the "Seven Fish" dinner for Christmas Eve. This freed us of all the customary preparations we addressed every Christmas and gave us the time we needed. Now we couldn't do it, but our daughters pitched in and saved the day. Their results were so exceptional; mom and I decided to send each one a "Certificate of Accomplishment" in diploma format by mail for making our holiday so joyful and not abandoning our traditions (Mostly for humor, but with a message). We love you all, including our daughter Michele in North Carolina. We had a wonderful Christmas. Not only was this the last Christmas I would be writing about (December 25, 2007), but it was also a time of "handing down" the recipes and customs of our ancestors to our children. It was bitter-sweet, but in the end inevitable. Thank you children for being so loving and readily accepting the baton as we passed it on to you. We now know you will do it justice...

On Christmas Eve, after a wonderful dinner served by Lucille, mom and I went home to contemplate all these things that were happening and stood in awe for experiencing all those wonderful moments. At midnight, as is our custom, mom and I began singing "O Bambino" while I brought Baby Jesus; in procession, to the crib...it was beautiful. We cried with happiness and we kissed, wishing each other a very Merry Christmas, with thoughts of all our children... "MERRY CHRISTMAS TO YOU ALL"

LAST DAY OF 2007. This is the last day of 2007, at which time I decided to end the book. My intention has always been to record and describe all of the important events that I experienced for seventy-seven years. Since the Lord granted me this goal, I chose to leave these recordings for my children to have as a reference for future inquiries. Of course, in reality, it would be impossible to have included every happening that entered my life, so if I have omitted an occurrence that is important to you, please know that I am sorry, I did my best. Here is what happened on December 31, 2007, and the end of the book in terms of events....

Mom and I woke up around 7:30 AM and were getting dressed when the phone rang. It was Auntie Rose and she sounded like she was in distress. "What's the matter?" mom asked. "Something happened to my hip while getting out of bed and I can't move." Auntie Rose said. "Marie is beside me but is not able to help." (Marie was the 24 hr. Health Care person assisting her). "I just called my daughter Frances and she said to call you and 911 for assistance." "We will be right over; don't move until we get there." mom responded. After filling me in on what was happening, we both rushed to help her. As soon as we arrived and she explained what happened, it was apparent her hip had dislocated again. We immediately called 911. In four minutes an Ambulance arrived with three attendees. The woman Emergency care person talked to Auntie Rose as soon as she entered the bed room. Coincidentally, she diagnosed the condition the same as we did, a dislocated hip. She had to be brought to the hospital. Then they began preparing her for the trip. Because the gurney would not fit into the hallway, she had to be brought out in the wheel chair to the living room and then onto the gurney. Once in the Ambulance, she was quickly brought to the hospital and we followed them. After hours of waiting, we were told that the doctor in Newark that performed the last hip operation gave permission to the doctors here to relocate the hip at the Brick Hospital location, which they did and Auntie Rose was now in recovery and was OK. It was around three o'clock in the afternoon when we were able to get home, since there wasn't anything else we could do. Frances was with Auntie Rose by now.

When we got home, we began reviewing our pending activities. Let's see, what's on the calendar for today? The only notation we have is

New Years Eve Party at Club House-7:00 PM. "Oh, that's right" mom exclaimed after I read the writing from the calendar, "We forgot about that, with all the goings-on". Since we had time to prepare for, it we decided to attend. So we put on our formal clothes and went to the Club House. We sat with Paul Monello, Ellen and Ed McNamara, Jean and Vinny Gramuglia and Susan and Frank Termini, at a table all set up with Champagne and noise-makers, including New Year hats. The food was cafeteria style but very good. We had a DJ, who announced that he was retiring and this would be his last gig. So we danced the evening away, me and mom. Then the big screen was rolled down at the front of the auditorium where they projected the TV station broadcasting the New York City celebration of the lowering of the New Years Crystal Ball (But no Dick Clark…we missed him). Now the count-down started, ten, nine, eight, seven, six, five, four, three, two, one…Happy New Year!, everyone began screaming, noise-makers sounding, horns blowing, people hugging and kissing, you know, the typical New Year, greeting scene. We all joined in. Mom and I looked at each other and mom said, "Do you realize this is our 55th year of marriage", I acknowledged with a "Yes" and we kissed, wishing each other a happy and joyous new year. It's moments like these that cause us to reflect on our lives and our most prominent thoughts are our children. We thank God for all our children and our family… I had the champagne bottle open and was pouring it out into everyone's glasses, we all drank with a toast, "Hoping the new year will bring happiness and joy to all"… HAPPY NEW YEAR EVERYONE!

It was twelve midnight…concluding the year of two thousand seven.

This was the last RECORDED event of my life, occurring at the end of my seventy-seventh year.

THE END @ 77

Note:
The next two chapters are devoted to our family roots (Chapter 9) and a sort of philosophical wrap-up of my life's perceptions acquired during seventy-seven years of observations (Chapter 10).

CHAPTER 9 - LA FAMIGLIA (THE FAMILY)

REALATIVES! RELATIVES! As I was growing up, I don't know how many times I would ask my mother and father; "Who is this person, is he/she a relative of ours?" And they would reply in astonishment, "Why this is your Uncle Lorenzo, on your mother's side!" Was I supposed to know that? I was having enough trouble keeping tract of my four grandparents and their names, no less uncles and aunts and cousins too! Not that I didn't love them all, especially at holidays when I would sometimes get to see them, but to remember each one of them, takes quit an effort. So, to help decipher your families and have a reference of their relationships to you, here are some simple charts of The Family...

FAMILY TREE

MOM'S SIDE

YOUR...

GREAT-GRANDFATHER	GREAT-GRANDMOTHER	GREAT-GRANDFATHER	GREAT-GRANDMOTHER
ANTONIO PASSERO	MARIA PASSERO	ADAMO TESTA	ANNA TESTA

GRANDFATHER	GRANDMOTHER
ERMINIO PASSERO	ASSUNTA (TESTA) PASSERO

PASSERO CHILDREN

AUNT	UNCLE	MOTHER
MARY (PASSERO) GALANO	ANTONIO PASSERO	ANNA (PASSERO) PETTI

SPOUSES

UNCLE	AUNT	FATHER
JULIUS GALANO	ROSE (DEPERINO) PASSERO	AUGUSTUS L. PETTI

C H I L D R E N

FIRST COUSINS	FIRST COUSINS
IRENE (GALANO) MASCOLA	ANTHONY PASSERO
	FRANCES (PASSERO) ACKERLY
MARIE (GALANO) ROSSI	ROBERT PASSERO

OUR CHILDREN

LUCILLE A. PETTI
SUSAN C. LAUTER
CHRISTINE M. ANGERSBACH
JOSEPH E. PETTI
MICHELE M. LEE

FAMILY TREE

DAD'S SIDE

YOUR…

GREAT-GRANDFATHER AND GREAT-GRANDMOTHER		GREAT-GRANDFATHER AND GREAT-GRANDMOTHE	
MICHELE PETTI	MARIA GIUSEPPE PETTI	TOMMASO BUCCO	CONCETTA BUCCO

GRANDFATHER	GRANDMOTHER
GIUSEPPE (JOSEPH) PETTI	LUCIA MARIA (BUCCO) PETTI

PETTI CHILDREN

FATHER	AUNT
AUGUSTUS LOUIS PETTI	JOSEPINNA ANNA (PETTI) SCROCCO

SPOUSES

MOTHER	UNCLE
ANNA THERESA (PASSERO) PETTI	VINCENZZO (VINNY) SCROCCO

CHILDREN

(SEE "MOM'S SIDE" WHERE YOU ARE LISTED)

<u>FIRST COUSINS</u>

PETER SCROCCO JOSEPH SCROCCO

EXTENDED FAMILY. From this point, you should be able to piece the puzzle together, meaning you should be able to match all the other members of the family using these basic charts. I hope this display of the initial family tree helps. You can imagine how large an actual chart of all the spouses and offspring children would have been if put together. And to be honest, I don't think I could do it!

One obvious omission on Dad's Side chart was the brothers and sisters of Grandpa Petti (Who are my Aunts and Uncle but your Great-Aunts and Great-Uncle too.) I didn't have space to include them above, so here they are.

FAMILY TREE

DAD'S SIDE

(INCLUSION)

GRANDPA PETTI'S BROTHER AND SISTERS

GREAT-UNCLE GIANBATISTE PETTI DECEASED	GREAT-AUNT LICCIA (PETTI) PESCE DECEASED
GREAT-AUNT ANNA (PETTI) LUSURIELLO	GREAT-AUNT JOSEPINNA PETTI (Youngest) WAS KILLED IN A BOMB-RAID IN 1943

OMISSION-GRANDMA ASSUNTA. I had to omit all the brothers and sisters of your Grandma Assunta (Testa) Passero but not because of space constriction, but because those records have unfortunately been lost. According to your mother, grandma Assunta had seven brothers and sisters in Italy. Only one brother immigrated to the USA and that was Uncle Adam. The other six remained there on the Italian continent. Mom tells me that two of Grandma Assunta's brothers died, one in an accident and the other of a heart attack, both as young men. Unfortunately we don't have any of this information in a written form or documented in any way. Sorry. Wish we had this information in writing. It would have been nice to be able to pass it on in a more positive way. This is another reason I was so motivated to write it down in this book. Now you have the information that I was able to contribute and can reference it any time a relative type of question comes up (play on words). I can't imagine how many times you will be picking up this book to check on a fact of the family just to get it right. And that is great! Just what I wanted to happen...

It should be noted that your Grandfather Erminio Passero was an only child. So additional charts are not necessary for his lineage.

It might be interesting to view the offspring's of the Aunts and Uncles on Dad's Side of the family. I was able to include them on Mom's Side, but I didn't have enough space on Dad's Side, so here they are:

FAMILY TREE

DAD'S SIDE

(INCLUSION-MOST LIVE IN ITALY)

GRANDPA PETTI'S BROTHER AND SISTERS

YOUR...

GREAT-UNCLE
GIOVANNI BATISTE PETTI

GREAT-AUNT
LICCIA (PETTI) PESCE

SPOUSES

GREAT-AUNT
ANTIONETTE PETTI

GREAT-UNCLE
AMADEO PESCE

(All above deceased)

CHILDREN

COUSIN

PIETRO PETTI

MICHELE PETTI

COUSIN

GIOACCHINO PESCE

ANNA (PESCE) DE MARE

ALSO

GREAT-AUNT
ANNA (PETTI) LUSURIELLO

GREAT-AUNT
JOSEPINNA PETTI
DECEASED
1945

SPOUSE
ANGELO LUSURIELLO
(DECEASED)

CHILDREN-continued from above

COUSINS

MARGARITA (LUSURIELLO) DE MARE – (RITA)

JOSEPINNA (LUSURIELLO) BARBERO - (PINNA)

TONINO LUSURIELLO - (whereabouts unknown)

PRESENT FAMILY STATUS: Here are the names of family members and some information about them that exists today as of circa 2007. I have tried to group them in a logical configuration which of course would require many alterations as time and conditions change. At least it is a starting point. Hope one of you continues to make all the changes that are taking place to keep it up-to-date. It also should provide a singular reference source for all our family tree information to date.

FAMILY TREE

IN U. S. A.

PETTI......OUR CHILDREN

LUCILLE PETTI, SINGLE MOM, ONE CHILD, HAS A HOME IN BRICK, NEW JERSEY

SUSAN LAUTER, MARRIED TO BILL, THREE CHILDREN, HAS A HOME IN BUDD LAKE, NEW JERSEY

CHRISTINE ANGERSBACH, MARRIED TO GERHARD, THREE CHILDREN, HAS A HOME IN BRICK, NEW JERSEY

JOSEPH PETTI, DIED, LAID TO REST AT "GATE OF HEAVEN" CEMETERY, HANOVER, NEW JERSEY (WAS MARRIED TO DENISE SANSEVERE))

MICHELE LEE, MARRIED TO BILL, TWO CHILDREN, HAS A HOME IN CARY, NORTH CAROLINA

SCROCCO...AUNT JOANN AND UNCLE VINNY'S CHILDREN

PETER – MARRIED TO DEBBIE, THREE CHILDREN, HAS A HOME IN SHOREHAM, LONG ISLAND, NEW YORK

JOSEPH – MARRIED TO CINDY, THREE CHILDREN, HAS A HOME IN LAS VEGAS, NEVADA

GALANO....

AUNT MARY (WHO IS NOW 95 YEARS OLD) MARIED TO UNCLE JULIO (DECEASED) LIVES IN MISSION VIEJO, CA.

IRENE, MARRIED TO BOB MASCOLA, TWO CHILDREN, HAS A HOME IN PITTSTOWN, NEW JERSEY

MARIE, MARRIED TO JOE ROSSI, THREE CHILDREN, HAS A HOME IN MISSION VIEJO, CALIFORNIA

PASSERO.......

UNCLE TONY (DECEASED) . AUNT ROSE LIVES IN CINCINATTI, OHIO

FRANCES, MARRIED TO TOM ACKERLY, THREE CHILDREN, HAS A HOME IN GLEN RIDGE, NEW JERSEY

ANTHONY, MARRIED TO CHRIS, ONE SON (DECEASED), HAS A HOME IN CARTHAGE, NORTH CAROLINA

ROBERT, MARRIED TO DIANE, THREE CHILDREN, HAS A HOME IN CINCINATTI, OHIO

NEXT GENERATIONS

<u>FAMILY TREE</u>

<u>CONTINUED</u>

PETTI FAMILY IN U.S.A.

<u>PETTI</u>…LUCILLE'S CHILD

MONIQUE (CUMMINGS) – MARRIED TO GREG PAPA ON SEPTEMBER 8, 2007, HAVE A HOME IN PT. PLEASANT, NEW JERSEY

<u>LAUTER</u>…SUSAN AND BILL'S CHILDREN

ERIC – EMPLOYED AND LIVES IN NEW JERSEY

KIMBERLY - ATTENDS UNIVERSITY OF NEW HAMPSHIRE

MELISSA – ATTENDS HIGH SCHOOL

<u>ANGERSBACH</u>…CHRISTINE AND JERRY'S CHILDREN

FRED – EMPLOYED AND HAS A HOME IN BRICK

RALPH – SELF EMPLOYED AND HAS A HOME IN MANASQUAN

SABINE – SINGLE MOM, TWO CHILDREN, HAS A HOME IN BRICK

LEE…MICHELE AND BILL'S CHILDREN

MARGARET – IN SECOND GRADE – IS 8 YEARS OLD

MARIE – IS FOUR YEARS OLD

ACKERLY…FRANCES AND TOM'S CHILDREN

KAREN – MARRIED TO JAMES EVAN, ONE CHILD, HAVE A HOME IN VIRGINIA

LISA – PRACTICES LAW AND LIVES IN NEW JERSEY

TRACEY – EMPLOYED AND LIVING IN RALEIGH, NORTH CAROLINA

PASSERO…ROBERT AND DIANE'S CHILDREN

EVAN - MARRIED TO SARAH, HAVE A HOME IN CINCINATTI

CORY - GRADUATED FROM OHIO STATE U – LIVES IN COLUMBUS OHIO

ALLISON - ATTENDING COLLEGE

PASSERO…ANTHONY AND CHRIS CHILDREN

MICHAEL- MARRIED TO EMMILY, TWO CHILDREN, HAVE A HOME IN CARTHAGE, NC (MICHAEL WAS KILLED IN IRAQ-ROAD BOMB)

MASCOLA...IRENE AND BOB'S CHILDREN

BOBBY – MARRIED TO JENNIFER, TWO CHILDREN, HAVE A HOME IN OAKLAND, CALIFORNIA

ANDREW – EMPLOYED - CURRENTLY LIVING IN ENGLAND (1 YR) OTHER-WISE IN NEW YORK CITY

ROSSI...MARIE AND JOE'S CHILDREN

DEBBIE – MARRIED TO GREG FAULDS, ONE CHILD, LIVE IN RANCHO SANTA MARGARITA, CALIFORNIA

DENISE – MARRIED TO KIRK KENTON, TWO CHILDREN, HAVE A HOME IN DUBLIN, CALIFORNIA

JOSEPH - EMPLOYED, LIVES IN MISSION VIEJO

PETTI FAMILY IN ITALY

PESCE...ZIA LICIA AND ZIO AMADEO (BOTH DECEASED)

CHILDREN

GIOACCHINO – MARIED TO RITA, SELF EMPLOYED, LIVE IN LUCERA

ANNA – MARRIED TO MICHAEL DE MARE, TWO CHILDREN, LIVE IN LUCERA

LUSURIELLO...ZIA ANNA AND ZIO ANGELO (UNCLE DECEASED), LIVES IN LUCERA

CHILDREN

RITA – MARRIED TO GINO DE MARE (MICHAELS' BROTHER), THREE CHILDREN, LIVES IN LUCERA

PINA – MARRIED TO RAFFAELO BARBERO, TWO CHILDREN, LIVE IN LUCERA

TONINO – ABANDONED FAMILY – STATUS UNKNOWN

PETTI...ZIO GIOVANNI BATISTE AND ZIA ANTOINETTE'S (BOTH DECEASED)

CHILDREN

MICHELINO – MARRIED TO ANTOINETTE, TWO CHILDREN (ONE DECEASED), LIVES IN CASSERTA

PIERINO – MARRIED TO NUNZIA, TWO CHILDREN, LIVE IN LUCERA

BUCCO FAMILY IN ITALY AND U.S.A.

BUCCO...ZIO LORENZO (UNCLE DECEASED) AND ZIA RAFFAELA (WHO IS NOW 96 YEARS OLD)

CHILDREN

LUCIETTA – MARRIED TO GAETANO CARROZZA, TWO CHILDREN, LIVES IN CELENZA VALFORTORE - ITALY

CONCETTA – MARRIED TO FRANCESCO DI IORIO (BOTH DECEASED), THREE CHILDREN, LIVED IN CELENZA VALFORTORE - ITALY

TOMMASO – MARRIED TO ROSINA, THREE CHILDREN, LIVES IN PHILADELPHIA, PENNSYLVANIA, U.S.A. (TOMMASO DECEASED)

CHAPTER 10 ....
LIFE SUMMARY AT AGE 77

WHERE DO I BEGIN. What I intended to accomplish in this Chapter was to attempt a 'life encompassing' reflection at my present age of seventy-seven (77). Although my life is not over, I feel that I have put enough years behind me to achieve this goal. Well anyway here goes...

Because I divided my life into the growing years and the human titles that accompany them, I now have a new respect for those periods of growth. Even as an infant, when my development was just beginning, in retrospect, I am able to see things through my parent's eyes and it paints a very different and poignant picture. What sacrifices they made! It boggles the mind... I myself have not been put through even one tenth of their torture and misery, plodding through life. Yet, they survived! It could not have occurred without the help of the Lord! I'm convinced of that.

(The following is a greatly admired statement that I ran across in my readings and have kept among my private papers, but would like to share with you now) Author Unknown

"There is no doubt in my mind, that despite our status in life as self-conscious, sentient beings equipped with brains that can reason impressively and be wonderfully inventive, we live a finite lifespan bounded by the physical limitations of heredity and the dictates of personal circumstance.

Much as we may choose to ignore it, and that too may be an adaptation for survival, the plain fact is that all life carries not only the risk but the sure eventuality of death.

In contrast to the observable limits of the material life, the lived and experienced life of the soul reaches into another plane altogether. Here, love supplants survival of the fittest as the basic mode of existence and to attain the fullest potential means emptying rather than enlarging the self.

Perhaps this is why God does indeed seem to be close to the poor and the brokenhearted rather than the self-sufficient and the strong. There is something paradoxically promising about being empty, broken, and not full of self or any created thing that opens a space for the spiritual life and a place in the heart for the uncreated God.

Being fragile, wounded or an outcast can also shrink the sense of self so that others become worthy of consideration. Weakness invites reliance on God, and others. Often the beginning of faith is found at that point where human powerlessness and God's compassion meet through the kindness of other people.

Babies are the ultimate example of the power of weakness. Completely needy, their trustful receptivity draws us to care for them. Curiosity and openness enables small children to learn at a faster rate than at virtually any other time in their lives. Empty of knowledge, human babies absorb prodigious amounts of information including languages, the mechanics of physical mobility and the complexities of social interactions.

It is interesting to note that babies learn all of these things so critical to their survival during a time when it looks as if they're not doing very much at all. Seemingly random, ordinary daily occurrences are the catalyst for this vital learning and growth.

It all seems perfectly designed and yet it's not without very obvious risks. Why would God have left so much to chance where babies are concerned? Countless studies offer suggestions as to why human beings are so apt to take care of children but since we're not compelled by sheer instinct we do have the ability to opt out of doing what's right. We have the freedom to choose poorly, even in regard to our own children but perhaps that's exactly the point.

The world that God has created for us is based upon love and free will. He has already taken the greatest risk and has paid the price for loving us. There are no limits to God's love that has no boundaries at all. Love is always worth the risk"........... My note: This is my philosophy also...

IMPORTANCE OF PRAYER. In my life, prayer has occupied a very compelling inclination. Since I was 9 or 10 years old, when I told my mother and father that I wanted to become a Priest when I grew up (my childish dream), the desire to communicate with God was unrelenting. After reading The Imitation of Christ by Thomas A. Kempis, I felt initiated into the Hall of Christ and wanted nothing else but to lay at His feet forever. But as this autobiography of mine reveals, that was not the life He planned for me. And although I was not inducted into the religious life per say, when you read my pages, in many of the chapters, I was very close to the clergy, performing the work of the Lord. For that I am grateful. Thank you Lord for those opportunities.

That is why I found prayer to be constantly at my side. There were times when I recited the daily 'Office' (the prayer every Priest recites daily). It was such a consolation and helped me withstand the many bludgeonings of the day. I also turned to the Rosary whenever I needed extra help, and it always came. Thank you Blessed Mother for interceding for me the many times I needed our Lord at my side.

THE ROSARY. I have always had a long standing personal fidelity to my prayer favorite, the Rosary. The Rosary for me has always been a way to bring to mind the life and Gospel of Christ in companionship with Him, and our Blessed Mother Mary.

If you are not aware, the origin of the Rosary dates back to St. Dominic de Guzman in the 12th and 13th centuries. It was said that the Virgin Mary instructed him to promote the Rosary to combat the devastating Albigensian heresy that preached a destructive theology of two gods – a good god and an evil god.

Now, mom and I often turn to the Rosary when a special petition is needed in the family. We pray it together, sometimes in the living room but often in the car while driving to Susan and Bill's home (we would be reciting it to Christine and Jerry's home, along with Lucille's home, but the distance is too short to complete the payer, so we can't). Nonetheless it has helped us a lot.

As for how the name Rosary came about, it comes from the Latin word 'rosarius' meaning a garland or bouquet of roses And as you recite the Rosary, it is said, each Hail Mary becomes a rose bud that our Blessed Mother weaves into a garland which she places upon her own head.

Since I traveled to so many distant and exotic lands, I was given the opportunity of reciting the Rosary in many languages. My mother was the first asking me to accompany her in Italian. Then, while studying Spanish in school, a friend of mine brought in a copy of the Rosary in Spanish, which I recited. Another friend of mine in high school who was of German extraction brought in a copy of the Rosary in German which I recited along with him (and remember I was in public school-but religion is everywhere). When I visited Hawaii at Sunday Mass, in the pew was the Rosary printed in Hawaiian (which I attempted quietly to recite), I'm sure our Blessed Mother understood me! Then on Guam where the language is Chamoro I often recited the Rosary along with throngs of Guamanian natives, in their own language (which is a type of Polynesian/Spanish mixture) and spoken in some sort of sing-song fashion that they emanated. It all reminded me of the passage in Scripture that speaks of "Praising God in many tongues"…I certainly did that many times.

HOW TO SAY THE ROSARY. For those of you that want to, or need to pray the Rosary, here are the basics. In the 1990's, Pope John Paul II added a part to the Rosary that focuses on "God the Light" which brought into view another aspect of our spirituality. I don't have those instructions, but they can be found at any Catholic Shop if you are interested in pursuing this special devotion.

The Rosary-One of the many offerings of the beads.

PRAY THE ROSARY

The Apostles' Creed is said on the Crucifix; the Our Father is said on each of the Large Beads; the Hail Mary on each of the Small Beads; the Glory be to the Father after the three Hail Mary's at the beginning of the Rosary, and after each group of Small Beads.

When reciting the Rosary, it is important that the Mysteries of the Rosary be vocally announced when two or more devoted persons are praying. For private recitation, it suffices if the mysteries are accompanied by meditation in silence.

PRAYER BEFORE THE ROSARY

Queen of the Holy Rosary, you have deigned to come to Fatima to reveal to the three shepherd children the treasures of grace hidden in the Rosary. Inspire my heart with a sincere love of this devotion, in order that by meditating on the Mysteries of our Redemption which are recalled in it, I may be enriched with its fruits and obtain peace for the world, the conversion of sinners, and of rogue groups, and the favor which I ask of you in this Rosary. (Here mention your request.) I ask it for the greater glory of God, for your own honor, and for the good of souls, especially for my own. Amen.

The Mysteries are divided into days of the week, as follows:

The Joyful Mysteries

(Said on Mondays, Thursdays, the Sundays of Advent, and Sundays from Epiphany until Lent)

1. The Annunciation (Humility)
2. The Visitation (Fraternal charity)
3. The Nativity (Love of God)
4. The Presentation (Spirit of sacrifice)
5. Finding in the Temple (Zeal)

The Sorrowful Mysteries

(Said on Tuesdays, Fridays throughout the year; and daily from Ash Wednesday until Easter Sunday)

1. Agony in the Garden (True repentance)
2. Scourging at the Pillar (Mortification)
3. Crowning with Thorns (Moral courage)
4. Carrying of the Cross (Patience)
5. The Crucifixion (Final Perseverance)

The Glorious Mysteries

(Said on Wednesdays, Saturdays, and the Sundays from Easter until Advent)

1. The Resurrection (Faith)
2. The Ascension (Hope)
3. The Descent of the Holy Spirit (Zeal)
4. The Assumption (Happy death)
5. The Coronation of B.V.M (Love for Mary)

Prayer after the Rosary

O God, who's only-begotten Son, by His life, death and resurrection, has purchased for us the rewards of eternal life; grant, we beseech Thee, that, meditating upon these mysteries of the Most Holy Rosary of the

Blessed Virgin Mary, we may imitate what they contain and obtain what they promise, through the same Christ our Lord. Amen.

May the divine assistance remain always with us. Amen

And may the souls of the faithful departed, through the mercy of God, rest in peace. Amen.

THE PRAYERS OF THE ROSARY

The Our Father

Our Father who art in heaven, hallowed by Thy name; Thy kingdom come; Thy will be done on earth as it is in heaven. Give us this day our daily bread; and forgive us our trespasses as we forgive those who trespass against us; and lead us not into temptation, but deliver us from evil. Amen.

The Hail Mary

Hail Mary, full of grace! The Lord is with you; blessed are you among women, and blessed is the fruit of your womb, Jesus. Holy Mary, Mother of God, pray for us sinners now and at the hour of our death. Amen.

Glory be to the Father

Glory be to the Father, and to the Son, and to the Holy Spirit. As it was in the beginning, is now, and ever shall be, world without end. Amen.

The Apostles' Creed

I believe in God, the Father Almighty, Creator of heaven and earth; and in Jesus Christ, His only Son, our Lord; who was conceived by the Holy Spirit, born of the Virgin Mary, suffered under Pontius Pilate, was crucified, died and was buried. He descended into hell; the third day He arose again from the dead; He ascended into heaven, and sits at the right hand of God, the Father Almighty; from thence He shall come to judge the living and the dead. I believe in the Holy Spirit, the Holy Catholic Church, the communion of saints, the forgiveness of sins, the resurrection of the body, and life everlasting. Amen.

Although "The Hail! Holy Queen" prayer is not a required part of the Holy Rosary, it is usually said at the conclusion of the recitation as an everlasting "tribute" to our Queen in Heaven:

The Hail! Holy Queen

Hail! Holy Queen, Mother of Mercy, our life, our sweetness and our hope. To you do we cry, poor banished children of Eve. To you do we send up our sighs, mourning and weeping in this valley of tears. Turn then, O most gracious advocate, your eyes of mercy toward us; and after this our exile, show unto us the blessed fruit of your womb, Jesus. O clement! O loving! O sweet Virgin Mary!
Pray for us, O holy Mother of God, that we may be made worthy of the promises of Christ.

This concludes the prayers accompanying the Rosary, I only inserted them here as a handy place to contain them, where they will be as close to you as a library shelf, at any time. Hope I'm right.

SOME REFLECTIONS. Looking back, after describing my life to the present, I am awed by the Grace of God that made it all possible! I don't know of any other way of explaining it. I know for a fact that there were many events in my life that could not be accomplished without the assistance of my Lord. That is one of the wonderful lessons I learned in life, that I was never alone spiritually, that my Lord accompanied me every step of the way. I guess being human, our senses often times confuse us into thinking we are alone, for the simple reason that He is invisible. But through the grace of faith He appears!!! Praise to you Jesus. Praise to God in the Highest!

If I can give my children one single priceless treasure it would be the GIFT OF FAITH!!! And this I do bequeath you, in the name of the Father, and the Son, and the Holy Spirit. Amen.

As far as my earthly life is concerned, I point my eyes to the heavens and say, Lord I have done my best, I have followed your commandments, and I have tried to please you in every action of my being. I await the moment I will be with you eternally. Please protect my loved ones, my beloved Ann, my Lucille, my Susan, my Christine, my Joseph and my Michele" If you Lord grant this request, I will be forever grateful…

EARTHLY ACCOMPLISHMENTS. In reflecting on the unusual and earth shattering occurrences of the past years, circa 1930 – 2007, I can't help but feel some sort of thankfulness for having witnessed such events. I'm referring to the worldly inventions in the development of electronics, in every field, such as the Radio, VCR, TV, PC, MP3, BLUE RAY, etc. I'm sure I haven't even scratched the surface of the subject. I'm convinced; electronics has literally changed the way we humans live now.

Then there are the medical discoveries achieved during my life, which never cease to amaze me. Who ever thought such devastating illnesses such as Polio could ever be cured. Amazing! And thanks to Dr. Jonas K. Salk's polio vaccine (1955), it was.

Up until the 1940's, the only thing we knew about space travel was in a cartoon strip called Buck Rogers! Then in 1957, the Soviet Union sent the world's first satellite into space called the Sputnik and the space race began. Now we all think of space travel as common events, in fact I read the other day that a private company is taking reservations for a trip into space, viewing the earth from hundreds of thousands of miles away. Can you imagine that? I recall as I was reading, it all sounded very exciting, until they mentioned the price, the ticket costs about three million dollars for the trip, my interest just dissipated at that announcement! I think I will enjoy that traveler's account, when he/ she returns to earth and writes about it, to satisfy my curiosity!

The world is changing so fast. Not only are the changes mind boggling but the speed with which the technology changes is amazing too. To give you an example, about three years ago I purchased a brand new, up-to-date PC from Dell. The main specifications were an Intel, Celeron CPU type processor, 240 GHz speed, 512 MB of Ram capacity, with an 80 GB Hard Disk, 15" Flat Panel Widescreen, CD & DVD R-W Drive and Microsoft Windows XP. This week (that's less than 3 years) I received a brochure from Dell offering; (Hold on to your Hat), an equivalent PC (in price) that has the following: Intel Core 2 Duo Processor, <u>2 GB</u> Dual Channel Ram, <u>320</u> GB Hard Drive, <u>20"</u> Widescreen Flat Panel, <u>2x</u> Blu-ray Disc Drive R-W High-Quality HD Video and Microsoft Vista Home Premium Software! I mean, 320 GB Hard Disk! That's incredible! It would take me 6 lifetimes to fill that disk with data! Oh, well, there really isn't anything we can do now, except to accept it. It reminds me of the new TV Channels that have reached 200 in number and are increasing. How can any human watch 200 channels, no less remember what's on what channel at any given time. It boggles the mind!

Then there is the development of aircraft, from the single engine propeller driven airplane in the 40"s, to the jet engine and now rocket engines that send aircraft into space. By utilizing all the principles of physics and incorporating all the modern technology into the designs of future airplanes, all types are emerging, with unbelievable capabilities, that again, boggles the mind.

And now the development of nano science is surfacing, which I predict will revolutionize our world as we know it. Through this process, scientists will probably succeed at miniaturizing every conceivable device ever invented, to a size that will defy detection. Can you imagine carrying a cell phone on your necklace, as one of the beads? Or being able to view HDTV on your sun glasses? Having your laptop PC on your wrist, replacing a watch (and giving you the time to boot)? These are some of my predictions. It's absolutely amazing! That's all I can say...Have Fun!

LIFE GOALS. Or "Things to do while you're alive", can be a subject of intense interest for each one of us, for a multitude of reasons. Everyone has fantasized at one time or another about what she/he wants to accomplish in the short life span given to us. Although I never devised a list of this nature to follow early in life, recently I read a Credit Card advertisement that listed some intriguing places and things to do while you are alive. I took the list and slightly altered it to fit into my desires and wants as goals, as if I were to write this in my younger years. To my amazement I found that I have already accomplished almost all of them, save those that are still in progress. It was a great deal of fun. Here is the revised list 'a la Petti' with all those things done marked accordingly. In fact, if you read my past chapters very carefully, you would have spotted the exact places where I described these events. For example, (I'm choosing this moment in time because it's easy to remember) in Chapter 4 – Man/Soldier, I cited the many times my friends and I were part of the crowds cheering the Matadors fighting bulls in Juarez, Mexico. Hope you remember. While you're reviewing my list, have a little fun of your own and come up with a list that would express your life goals and things to do while you're alive. You are still young and can use it as a guide. It will be fun and it might be revealing too!

THINGS TO DO WHILE YOU'RE ALIVE
OR
LIFE GOALS

CHAPTER LOCATION OR STATUS

[x] WALK ON THE APIAN WAY .... Chapter 4
[x] GET TICKETS TO THE NEW YORK METROPOLITAN OPERA..... Chapter 7
[x] FLY TO ICELAND .... Chapter 7
[ ] MASTER ITALIAN BAKING........ Searching for a school Online
[x] MARRY A WONDERFUL GIRL .... Chapter 5
[x] HUNT FOR PALM HEARTS ON A PACIFIC ISLAND .... Chapter 4
[x] PAY THE TOLL FOR THE CAR BEHIND YOU .... Chapter 8
[x] SEE THE 'PHANTOM OF THE OPERA' ON STAGE........ Chapter 7
[x] CRUSH GRAPES FOR WINE .... Chapter 3
[x] SIFT PURE WHITE SAND FOR TREASURES........ Chapter 4
[x] GO CAMPING IN PENNSYLVANIA .... Chapter 6
[x] VIEW SNOW COVERED ROOFTOPS FROM A SWISS CHALET ...... Chapter 7
[x] SPEND MANY CHRISTMAS EVE'S WITH FAMILY .... Chapter 6
[x] TAKE A SWIM AT WAIKIKI BEACH........ Chapter 4
[x] PRAY IN A MOUNTAIN TOP STONE CHURCH .... Chapter 4
[x] TEST DRIVE A SCOOTER IN BERMUDA........ Chapter 7
[x] VISIT AN EMPEROR'S ISLAND........ Chapter 8
[x] SEE THE 'PASSION PLAY' IN OBERAMMERGAU .... Chapter 7
[x] GROW A MUSTACHE........ Chapter 4
[x] SAIL BENEATH THE GOLDEN GATE BRIDGE........ Chapter 4
[x] NAME A STAR .... Chapter 6
[ ] GET A DEGREE IN THE STUDY OF FUNGI...Searching for a school Online
[x] SPEND A WEEKEND IN LAS VEGAS........ Chapter 4
[x] RAISE FIVE CHILDREN TO ADULTHOOD .... Chapter 6
[x] EXPERIENCE THE MAGIC OF ROME AT NIGHT .... Chapter 6
[x] BECOME A MEMBER OF THE GOLDEN DRAGON CLUB........ Chapter 4
[x] YELL "OLE!" AT A BULLFIGHT .... Chapter 4
[x] WRITE A BOOK ABOUT MY LIFE.........Completed 12/31 of 2007

This was a lot of "fun" for me...hope it provides you with the same.

WHAT DID I SEE. In my life, that is. It's like looking back at all those years, months, days, hours and minutes. What did I see? One very significant chunk of my life was the days I spent with my mother and father. I can't come up with the number, but there were so many countless times that I remember the closeness, the caring, the loving that was poured on me by my parents, that I still feel today. It is without a doubt, the most securing and warm feeling that permeates both my mind and my heart. My mother and father were my life until I reached the age of twenty three, when I was married. They stood by me in times of glory and in times of peril. They created the safe passage for me to pass. Life for me was very exciting. My father was not only a master craftsman in metal but had these aspirations of becoming a world renowned inventor. My mother was not only a skilled seamstress but reveled in the preparation and cooking of food.

Memories of my father always warm me. I remember when he became fascinated with alternating current AC electricity. We were living in a seven story apartment house. There must have been about 30 families living in that building. It was around Christmas time. My father had bought me an advanced Christmas gift, a set of Lionel railroad trains with tracks. After he set them up, he needed an extension to plug the transformer into. I've got to tell you, that up to this point, he only had experience with direct current (DC), the electric power system of automobiles. He knew nothing of alternating current (AC). He cut a piece of wire from an old appliance. He cut a plug from another old appliance and went to the store to buy some electrical tape. When he got home, he attached the plug to the wire, tapped them and slipped the plug into the wall outlet. A gigantic spark flared at the site.! A loud sizzling sound simultaneously filled the air, then all the lights went out in the apartment. Before I could say anything, my father covered my mouth with his hand and made the SSSSHH sound. It was very dark. My mother was out shopping. Then all of a sudden, we started hearing the banging sound on the steam pipes (it was a communication method of alerting the building superintendent of a problem). That sound made us realize the electricity was out for the whole building. What a blowout I thought! When my father does something, he does it in a big way! It meant the superintendent had to go into the inner depths of the basement, find the main fuse that probably had burnt-out and replace it. This took a few minutes. Actually it took over half an hour. Of course my father had removed the badly burnt extension out of the wall outlet, so when the new fuse was installed in the main terminal box in the basement, all the lights went on again. The superintendent then began searching the building in an effort to determine the cause. We did not answer his knockings on the door (to make believe no one was home in that apartment). My father was a very proud man, he couldn't admit to such a blunder. "We'll just let it go, there's no harm", he told me. "OK', I replied. And we continued. He quickly learned the technological differences for wiring techniques within the two electrical systems. He never made that mistake again. Life was exciting with my father. One very valuable attribute of his being, is that he had no fear. Nothing was impossible (because he was never afraid of entering the unknown). He was always asking Why?, about everything. And he had to find the answer, no matter how long or how much effort it takes. What admirable qualities! I'm sure some of his philosophies have been passed on to me.

My father was also a person that wanted to have every new gadget that was being sold over the counter. I just told you about the Lionel Train, it had just come out. Also, when I was seven or eight years old (1937), he insisted on having a movie camera and a projector. This is why I have movies of myself at that age. Of course, we had a car by 1935 and all the years subsequent. We had several radios. A large standup RCA radio in the living room and other little shelf type radios in the kitchen and in my room. Although telephones were available, we did not need them because our family and friends were so close, we never needed it. Then there were telephone toll booths on practically every street for important long distance communications. We always had the other newest appliances whenever they became available. We had an electric toaster as soon as they were invented and sold. Incidentally, we soon discovered that an electric toaster was primarily designed for what we call American Bread and therefore was not able to toast Italian Bread (To our likeness) unless you sliced it paper thin (which none of us liked), so we had the electric toaster, but practically never used it (we always had Italian bread). This may sound odd, but the only modern day invention available to the public that we did not rush to the store to buy was a Television Set. For some reason, one theory is, because I wasn't home, (I was in the Air Force, overseas) when the first TV's became the rage, that my mother and father did not succumb to buying it. What is interesting is that In fact, this is one of the gadgets that were purchased by the Passero's (I found out later) and was enjoyed by them long before the Petti's became viewers of TV. My father lived to age 82 and has been missed since. He died on September 17, 1988.

My mother has always been a wonder to me. Her ability and endurance have always amazed me. Even though she reached the age of 88, and at that age, she still stood at our kitchen table helping to prepare Christmas Eve and Christmas day meals. Even your mom commented on how wonderful she was, when she witnessed the extraordinary amount of effort my mother made during those moments, which only helped validate my knowledge of her durability, all driven by love. She loved us all so much, she poured out every ounce of energy for our wellbeing (this was her inimitable way of caring for us). How commendable! How honorable! How devoted she was to us all! Everyone in her space knew how much she loved us. She passed away in February of 1997. We will never forget her… I love you Mamma!

PASSING OBSERVATIONS. This one fact, I am certain of. I owe most of my delicate earthly existence to my parents, and in many instances, I could never fully appreciate their sacrifices on my behalf. I know that parents don't have to pass mental/health tests to procreate, and parents with difficult personalities, come in many flavors as emotionally challenged suitors. I've read of the different types of parents that exist in the world. Some are helicopter parents, always hovering , anxious and over protective; some neglect their children's needs out of selfishness or mild depression; others seethe with anger, unhappiness or jealousy, lashing out at their offspring-physically or verbally-on a regular basis. What's interesting is that such parent's can many times come across to outsiders as involved and loving, so children receive little independent confirmation that something is wrong with the way they're being treated. This is really sad and breaks my heart whenever I encounter such a relationship.

I am so grateful to God for providing me with my loving parents. They taught me right from wrong, what is good and what is bad, how to approach unknowns and how to overcome fears, how to strive for goals and how to succeed. They gave me everything! I was so well prepared when I met my 'Soul Mate' (Mom) that life from that point, could only take off like an airplane that is defying gravity, entering the open sky, through the clouds, picking up a few new passengers (our five children) and then to it's final destination (figuratively, landing now at age 77).

I cannot help but feel, that without my Almighty God at my side, none of my accomplishments would have been possible. My paramount accomplishments are, in my estimation, the management of my childhood, boyhood, manhood, becoming a husband, a father, becoming a grandfather and now a great-grandfather. All these life forces were granted to me by my parents and God. I cannot deny this.

"Our life is a gift from God…What we do with it is our gift to God". (I spotted this saying on Lucille's refrigerator-thank you Lucille.) Most of these elegant quotations encourage much thought and resolve. I always loved to read these sayings and then take something away with me. Christine, Susan and Michele also all have inspirational plaques on their walls, which say to me that they must have inherited something from mom and me.

ANOTHER OBSERVATION. Navigating in this modern world of endless choices has been a dizzying challenge. Hopefully it will not bring out the worst in us. Let me explain. We are the first generation in history to decide not only where to live and what profession to enter (fundamental choices that now feel like a birthright) but whether to spend all that money for a 32, 42 or 52 inch flat-screen, LCD or LED TV.

From breakfast cereal to birth control, we are assailed with options at every moment in our day-choice that's often marketed as dire necessity. Our big decisions are also subject to spin: Colleges vie for applicants; doctors are poised to help us choose not just the time of conception but the profile and pedigree of our progeny. Entire industries - travel agents (sorry Jerry), interior decorators, and portfolio managers- are devoted to the navigation of a selection-saturated world.

Our ancestors would be overwhelmed by this array of options. Our brains still are. That's because we evolved in a world where choice was limited by chronic shortages of food, absence of transportation other than one's own two feet and few reliable sources of information. In a world without menus, speed dating, or iPods, you ate, found a mate and enjoyed a moment of music or went without. Often, the choice was between something or nothing. In such a world, our ancestors could afford to simplify decision-making to always get the best.

Striving to maximize each opportunity makes sense when your choices are obvious and few. Since we have through the ages developed our instinct to such a high degree for hoarding and now find ourselves no longer needing to hoard, we are going batty. Our minds went through a period of scarcity then, today, by contrast, we are overwhelmed by having to cope with plenty. Just try going into R.H. Macy's and buying one item in two minutes.

Choices often bring on anxiety because we compare what we have with what we could and should have. Our ancestors could not become alarmed over what they could not envision having in the first place, just as most people today don't imagine having jets or deeded islands because they're so far outside a normal frame of reference.

When scarcity forced choice, there was no reason to blame yourself for a poor outcome. But if you choose poorly today, you feel you have no one but yourself to blame, because the decision was yours alone. Such circumstances generate pressure to make the right choice. Think of this, if, after you have seen 25 properties at the same price in your neighborhood, it's tough to feel you've spent your money wisely after making your decision.

Today, we are told, that the availability of too many options leaves us inherently unsatisfied, no matter what decision we make and how great its outcome. We focus on the unrealized possibilities, simply because we can. We are always worried about making the right decision. When the benefits of a decision are not immediately obvious, the result is worry and paralysis-buyer's remorse.

Here is the remedy. We know that today, most choices are frivolous and rarely jeopardize our existence, though this fact doesn't stop us from fretting. And we overestimate the importance of big choices all the more. We are equipped with amazing cognitive abilities, but the capacity to foresee how we'll really feel about a decision is not one of them. That's why it's critical to avoid thinking we can tailor a fulfilling life from an unlimited number of options. Limiting choice doesn't just curb anxiety, it actually creates happiness. When you accept limitation or make a commitment you feel fulfilled. The aim of a fulfilling decision is for good enough rather than the best. That means consciously renouncing perfectionism and letting go of regrets. Choice can be great if we refuse to obsess about all the alternatives. In spite of our emotional makeup, options can be our allies. Not agonizing about a choice is a choice itself.

This is what I learned in these modern times and this is what I practice. I learned to fight emotional paralysis-buyer's remorse by seeing that even making the wrong choice is often better than making no choice at all. It is better to blunder my way through life than to avoid making a decision.

(Some of the above thoughts borrowed from an article in the Sep.2006 "Monitor")

SOME LAST THOUGHTS. A main reflection of mom and myself. We did not start LIFE with a plan. We had no goal, except to live life as God-Worshiping people. I must admit, after all, that mom and I are examples that life can be lived under the frame-work of God's Plan (not ours) by following His Commandments and Teachings. During the course of revealing my life's history, the main theme was that I was ordinary…not a genius, not a notable celebrity, not a great scientist; you get the picture. My life had nothing to do with pride. All of my experiences were ordinary, nothing outstanding and yet, when put together as I have in this book, it resembles an amazing undertaking, that I seemingly achieved so much, for so many…a truly marvelous impression! But that's really the story of every person on this planet! If each and everyone's experience were told, theirs would be undoubtedly extraordinary tales! Which makes each and everyone of you "special"…never forget that?

My story is now finished. Thank you for listening. Thank you for understanding. Thank you for being there. God Bless You All !

FINAL THOUGHTS. All throughout this book, not only did I try to describe my life as I lived it, but also to show that if it weren't for the joy of Marriage and the ensuing eventuality of Fatherhood, life to me would have been meaningless! This is only my view in relation to my life and does not represent a philosophy for all mankind. Each must find their own way. The only lifelong advice I can give is Always Have God at Your Side, to do that, all you need do is Call Him!

Whenever I reflect back on our life together, Ann and myself, I always come up with the same conclusion, that we were truly blessed. The Lord our God blessed us in every conceivable way, He shed His Grace on us every day of our life together, even when He chose to take our son Joseph to eternity. Our loss was terribly painful, to the point where it became unbearable, we prayed for enlightenment and then it came; one day we looked at each other and said; "You know, Joseph is really better off in the presence of our Lord forever, rather than here on this temporal earth - Thank you Lord for delivering him from here." And our life continued...we had closure...Praise to You Lord!

ADIOS ! ! ! In conclusion, we are two loving parents who follow God's commands and teachings, To Love Our God above all things and to Love One Another as we love ourselves... We loved each other...We loved our Children...We loved our Parents... We loved our Relatives... We loved our Paisanos...We loved our Friends...We loved every Person we came in contact with...We loved our Country... Without Love we couldn't live! Thank you Lord for this Blessing...we are forever grateful...Amen...

The End

Completed December 31, 2007

INDEX

INDEX...CONT'D.

Person Code	Page